9 .N4 W38 1998
Craig

REPRESENTING

REPRESENTING

hip hop culture and the production of black cinema

S. CRAIG WATKINS

THE UNIVERSITY OF CHICAGO PRESS / CHICAGO AND LONDON

S. Craig Watkins is assistant professor of Sociology, African American Studies, and Radio-Television-Film at the University of Texas at Austin.

The University of Chicago Press, Chicago 60637
The University of Chicago Press, Ltd., London
© 1998 by S. Craig Watkins
All rights reserved. Published 1998
Printed in the United States of America

07 06 05 04 03 02 01 00 99 98   1 2 3 4 5

ISBN: 0-226-87488-5 (cloth)

Library of Congress Cataloging-in-Publication Data

Watkins, S. Craig (Samuel Craig)
    Representing : Hip hop culture and the production of Black cinema
/ S. Craig Watkins.
        p.   cm.
    Includes bibliographical references and index.
    ISBN 0-226-87488-5 (cloth : alk. paper).
    1. Afro-Americans in motion pictures.   2. Afro-American motion
picture producers and directors.   3. Hip-hop.   I. Title.
PN1995.9.N4W38   1998
791.43′652396073—dc21   97-43151
                                                              CIP

⊗ The paper used in this publication meets the minimum requirements of the
American National Standard for Information Sciences—Permanence of Paper
for Printed Library Materials, ANSI Z39.48-1992.

To my mother and the memory of my father.
Words cannot express how your love, strength, and
sacrifices continue to sustain me.

With the warmest of gratitude to young African
Americans, whose creativity and resilience inspired
this book.

Contents

contents

Preface

Black youth are not the passive victims of history but are instead actively involved in its making. In the chapters that unfold, I consider some of the creative ways in which black youth intervene in the social world around them. And while my aim is to develop a better appreciation for the cultural politics of black youth, I also understand that their innovations do not take shape outside the compelling currents of history. So in addition to discussing the vitality of black youth popular cultures, it is important to map the social and historical terrain upon which their practices take shape.

To the extent that it is even possible to discern elements of ideological struggle in the popular expressive cultures created by black youth, we must understand the social and historical specificity of these formations. If the cultural practices of black youth represent distinct forms of resistance, an immediate question emerges: What are black youth opposing? To be sure, the expressive cultures of black youth are not produced in a vacuum but rather in relation to social, economic, and political conditions from which new forms of social antagonism and political struggle become possible. One way of understanding the counterideological possibilities of black youth popular cultures is to discuss them in relation to other socially circulating discourses. Moreover, by examining how racially inflected themes, ideas, and representations are socially produced and strategically fashioned to strengthen the making of competing political voices, we can begin to understand the intonations that give black youth popular cultures their distinctive resonance.

The cultural practices of black youth are very much related to the discourses about race, youth, gender, and societal change that circulate throughout the orbit of public discourses. And while this book focuses on the continually evolving symbolic practices played out on the terrain of popular media culture, it also acknowledges that cultural and representational politics are played out in other locations. The insurgent presidential campaign of Patrick Buchanan in 1992 is a convincing example.

Buchanan's campaign was buoyed by a calculated effort to exploit a growing conservative mood shift in the United States. During his speech at the 1992 Republican Party National Convention, Buchanan revealed what many believe is the underbelly of Republican Party politics: a calculated exploitation of racial and cultural fault lines to achieve an electoral advantage. During that convention, Republicans made the mistake of "appearing" to be xenophobic toward virtually any kind of difference imaginable—difference in family type, sexuality, gender, and race. In truth, Buchanan declared on a more public stage what the architects of the conservative movement had been practicing for several decades: a fierce and oftentimes hostile struggle to define the nation's identity, values, and body politic, or in the apocalyptic words of Buchanan, "a cultural war for the soul of America."

Toward the end of his speech, Buchanan shifted to a racially coded and derisive cadence when he discussed, "the bloody riot in Los Angeles, the worst in [American] history." He praised the bravery of two young soldiers from the National Guard, which had been called in to restore order. According to Buchanan, the young soldiers "had come into Los Angeles on the second day, and they walked up a dark street, where the mob had looted and burned every building but one, a convalescent home for the aged. The mob was heading in, to ransack and loot the apartments of the terrified old men and women. When the troops arrived, M-16s at the ready, the mob threatened and cursed, but the mob retreated. It had met the one thing that could stop it: force, rooted in justice, backed by courage." Buchanan's speech would evoke even more sinister imagery and further explains why the Republican Party was so desperate to keep him offstage and repair its image during the 1996 convention in San Diego. He continued, "Here were nineteen-year-old boys ready to lay down their lives to stop a mob from molesting old people they did not even know. And as they took back the streets of LA, block by block, so we must take back our cities, and take back our culture, and take back our country."

Buchanan's fiery discourse was drenched with metaphoric language and age-old tropes that represent black Americans in the most perverse fashion. What is most remarkable about the speech was its ability to enliven the allegedly threatening specter of blackness without mentioning race or African Americans. The forcefulness of the speech was driven by popular commonsense ideologies about race. More important, the language and imagery evoked were also designed to exploit the perception that black American youth were the cause of the nation's social, economic, and moral afflictions. The symbolic structure of the narrative—images of young black marauders looting, burning, and molesting—derived much of its currency from distilled representations of blacks as social problems, sexual predators, and potential pollutants of white purity, privilege, and nationhood. In fact, the images of blackness evoked in Buchanan's speech were strikingly similar to the racist fantasies played out in D. W. Griffith's 1915 film *Birth of a Nation.*

His oration that night illuminates with frightening clarity one of the main claims of this book: discourses about and representations of black youth facilitate the making of a social and political climate that has become increasingly hostile toward them. Buchanan's claim that the deployment of force was necessary to take back our cities and our country was, of course, premised on the widespread assumption that, because black youth lacked discipline and respect for authority, they constitute a serious threat to the nation. The ominous tone of the speech dramatizes the manner in which black youth are implicated in some of the more prominent social and political episodes that define the culture wars at century's end.

And yet, to suggest that black youth are simply the passive victims of the culture wars would certainly overlook the strategic ways in which they maneuver to stage their own struggles in this theater of social and political action. Buchanan's assault is in many ways a reaction to the increasingly complex ways in which black youth articulate their growing discontent with social and economic marginalization. To be sure, black youth have become skillful and active participants in the culture wars of the late twentieth century. Both the everyday practices and media representational politics practiced by black youth suggest that they are constantly devising new strategies that enable them to forge their own spaces from which to wage their own versions of today's culture wars. Moreover, black youth recognize both the importance of gaining access to the resources and technologies of representation and the need to engage the discourses that seek to police them. This book explores how black youth carve out a distinctive niche in the rapidly evolving struggles to shape the nation's values, identity, commonsense ideologies, and popular mediascape. It is also an attempt to illuminate the politics and pleasures associated with the production of black youth popular culture and why media—music, video, cinema, and literature—have become such an important site in the everyday lives and struggles of black American youth.

Acknowledgments

Anyone who has ever worked on a book that demands extensive thought and research understands the occasional feeling of isolation that writing brings about. It can also be very refreshing to look back and realize that new relationships were created and old relationships enlivened during the book-making journey. My experience is no exception. At the risk of leaving out many who deserve recognition, I would like to express my sincerest gratitude to a few people who made this particular book possible.

The framework for the book was established while I was a graduate student at the University of Michigan. Although he was not a member of the Michigan faculty when I arrived, Aldon Morris demonstrated confidence in my ability to make substantive intellectual contributions. In addition, Donald Deskins was a bedrock of support during my years of Ph.D. work. Mark Chesler, Jimmie Reeves, Andrea Press, and Janet Hart served graciously on my dissertation committee and provided the intellectual nourishment that led to the development of my doctoral thesis and the eventual flowering of this book.

A number of friends have kept me both humored and grounded during the completion of this book. While there is an endless list of dividuals I wish I could thank, I want especially to thank Raina Price-Webster, Kelley Faykus, John Beale, David Harris, Bernard Shaw, and Julia Simon for both respecting and appreciating the time and effort devoted to this book. I would also like to thank Jill Louis, Randy Bowman, and Malcolm Peter Louis Bowman for their unswerving fidelity. Thank you, Debbie Rogow and Howard Winant. You are a constant reminder of what is so good about this world.

Supportive colleagues are crucial to the book-writing process. I have benefited immensely from several outstanding colleagues: Magali Sarfatti-Larson, Kevin Delaney, Sherri Grasmuck, Annette Lareau, Ronnie Steinberg, William Yancey, Ronald Angel, John Butler, Cynthia Buckley, Christopher Ellison, Omer Galle, William Kelley, Mark Warr, Anne Kane, Lisa Sánchez González, Ted Gordon, Kamala Visweswaran, John Downing, Janet Staiger, Horace Newcombe, Susan Gonzalez-Baker, Gigi and Frank Durham, Donald Heider, Paula Poindexter, and George Sylvie. Another vital fountain of energy was provided by Raphael Allen, Eddie Glaude, Paul Jefferson, Wahneema Lubiano, Lucius Outlaw, Fasaha Traylor, and Howie.

I owe a special debt to Robin D. G. Kelley, who continues to be a constant source of inspiration to those who benefit from his energy, enthusiasm, and goodheartedness. Also, Michele Lamont and Christine Williams volunteered to read early parts of the manuscript despite their own rigorous schedules. I am also extremely appreciative of the hard work and meticulous care that Doug Mitchell, Matt Howard, Carol Saller, Susan Cohan, and the entire staff from the University of Chicago Press exercised while guiding this book through its multiple stages. The anonymous readers provided keen insight and commentary that greatly informed my writing. Words cannot adequately express the profound influence of Jimmie Reeves, Herman Gray, and George Lipsitz on this book. Each read multiple drafts of the manuscript, shared insights that compelled me to rethink and nuance many of my original arguments, and taught me long-lasting lessons about intellectual generosity.

Family members contribute in many ways too, often providing emotional support and encouragement. Thank you all. I owe special thanks to Dorothy Lewis, Myrtle Robinson, the Wynns, Lenice Watkins, Karen and Larry Munson, Sherry Watkins, Jeffrey Watkins, Carolyn Castaldi, Kenneth Hall, and Gloria Hall. James Wilson, Jr., has been a source of enrichment, good times, and growth. Finally, Angela Hall Watkins has closely shared the moments of discovery that fueled the completion of this book. Our many conversations, mutual respect, and warm affection ultimately provided the sustenance that enabled us to see this project to a rewarding end while beginning a promising future. Thank you.

Introduction

Black Youth at Century's End

It is difficult to think or write cogently about the popular cultures of black youth without considering the material world young African Americans inhabit. The post–civil rights generation of African American youth inherited a world defined by sharp contradictions. It was generally assumed that the generation would be the chief beneficiaries of the civil rights struggle for racial justice and equality. But for many black youth, a less optimistic experience has become the reality instead. A look at the most recently available census data reveals that black youth are the most likely of all Americans to live in poor households and neighborhoods, to be jobless, to be victims of homicide or AIDS, or to spend at least part of their lives in prison.[1] Moreover, this particular generation of black youth lives in a period in which the political climate has become increasingly hostile to the goals and modest achievements of the civil rights struggle. The political ground has shifted greatly as conservative movements have aroused public anger and anxiety against "big government," welfare, and youth social and economic dislocation. And as Buchanan's speech, discussed in the preface, suggests, the rising tide of social conservatism has also developed tenacious racial characteristics. Black youth seemingly have been in the eye of a public storm against crime, drugs, and the alleged erosion of traditional values. As a result, new punitive technologies and legislation have been initiated in order to exercise greater control over black youth.

And yet, at the same moment black youth have become the targets of a fiercely determined social and political backlash, they have also flowered as a source of entertainment and pleasure. Black youth live in a cultural environment upon which the growth and cross-fertilization of the various popular culture industries—film, television, music, sports, and advertising—have enabled new regimes of cultural production, performance, and representation to emerge. It is in fact a great irony that at the same time black youth are so prominently figured in the nation's war on drugs, the largest prison industrial complex buildup in history, and tightening welfare restrictions, they are equally prominent in the marketing of $100 athletic shoes, the corporatization of collegiate athletics, and the breaking of new trends to a robust youth consumer economy. Today, black youth perform a meaningful role in shaping the contours of the popular cultural universe in which we all live. In fact, many of the best-known culture industries appropriate expressive elements from a vast creative community of black cultural producers in order to maintain their commercial viability.

How do black youth struggle to make sense of these contradictions? In other words, how do they grapple with a social, economic, and political world that, on the one hand, is becoming increasingly hostile toward them yet, on the other, has developed a voracious appetite for the cultural products and performances created by black youth? Despite shifts in the postindustrial economy and the collapsing of a viable urban infrastructure, black youth still manage to cultivate the skills and ingenuity that enable them to find a prominent niche in a flourishing popular media economy. For many black youth, the sphere of popular culture has become a crucial location for expressing their ideas and viewpoints about the contradictory world in which they live. Black youth have mobilized creatively around a rapidly evolving communications media landscape, thus developing their own cultural practices and strategies that facilitate the making of conditions from which they are able to pattern popular cultural styles, commodities, and production.

This book explores the ways in which popular culture dramatizes the constantly shifting formations of race relations. In the following pages, I try to illuminate some of the salient features that organize the complex relationship between black youth, the popular industrial image-making landscape, and a rapidly evolving cultural marketplace. It is difficult to discern a substantive relationship between black youth and the popular culture industries prior to the 1950s. Due to a lack of discretionary income on the part of black youths and their families, and racial exclusionary practices on the part of the culture industries, young African Americans have not participated as long as their white counterparts in the youth consumer economy.[2] But the racial and class dimensions of the youth marketplace began to experience dramatic changes in the 1950s. It was also during the fifties and sixties when the relationship between black youth and the popular culture industry began to take shape in earnest, corresponding with rising black incomes, the wider distribution of television, the transformation of black-appeal radio, and the creation of an elaborate "star system" made possible by promotional vehicles like Motown, *Soul Train,* and black teen magazines. These and other pop culture formations heightened the culture industry's awareness of the black youth consumer market.[3] Due to the regulatory social norms of segregation, black youth did not enjoy wide-open access to movie theaters, ballparks, and public amusement sites.[4] As a result, the symbolic practices of black youth did not easily make their way into the cultural mainstream before the 1950s. But the steady flow of black migrations to the industrial cities of the nation, the social production of rock 'n' roll, and the juvenilization of the popular music industry began to circulate the popular styles of black youth with more ferocity than ever before.[5] So even though residential segregation persisted, important transformations in the cultural landscape enabled black youth to begin penetrating the popular cultural mainstream, albeit in ways that were still tenaciously policed.

But the sphere of popular media culture, and especially its relationship to youth subcultures, is inherently unstable. In fact, the most reliable aspect of popular culture is its steady gravitation toward new and seemingly different trends. Consequently, one of the most difficult aspects of studying popular culture is keeping pace with its voracious appetite for change. At the precise moment one attempts to make sense of distinct trends and formations, emergent forms displace previous ones. Therefore, it is necessary to specify and historically situate the formation and production of distinct cultural practices, styles, and objects that attain some measure of popularity. Popular culture is generally popular because its users are able to derive pleasure from its content. Additionally, it is popular because it draws from and resonates with people's lived experiences. But because public moods, sensibilities, and desires are constantly changing, popular culture forms and trends must also change.

Studying the forms and conditions of black popular culture is indeed a difficult enterprise. As definitions of blackness change, the symbolic practices of black cultural producers change, too. Racialized ideologies and practices do not stand still. On the contrary, these formations are unstable and hardly, if ever, impervious to external forces. Black popular culture illuminates the volatility of racialized discourses and the fact that they are constantly being formed and reformed. Of course, the packaging and commodification of "blackness" are not unique to any one period of American history. Race has been an enduring feature in the American popular culture imagination. Echoes of the perniciously controlling racial ideologies that pervaded the original forms of mass popular culture in the United States can still be sensed. Minstrelsy, vaudeville, and even the origins of radio and film speak in particular ways to the enduring presence of "race" in the American popular imagination.[6] But as the material conditions and lived experiences of race are subject to change, so, too, are the ways in which race is imagined, represented, and performed.

In the pages that follow, I address a particular period in the popular cultural history of the United States: the last two decades of the twentieth century. During this period, historically situated cultural politics pivot around race in inventive ways, thus enlarging the scope and terrain of racial politics. During the middle 1980s, many black youth began proudly wearing a T-shirt boasting the inscription "Black by Popular Demand." The shirt was simultaneously a statement of style and a distinctive articulation of racial and generational identity. It was no coincidence that these shirts and other forms of black youth expressive culture became popular during a period of intense political retrenchment—that is, as social and political conservatism was becoming more deliberate in its attack against a changing racial order created in part by black political struggle.

For black youth, the sphere of popular culture emerged as a preferred location to cultivate alternative notions of their racial, gender, and generational identities in the face of an ascending conservative hegemony that was making its own set of distinctive claims about black youth. To be sure, the popular cultures of black youth made it possible to galvanize new movements and inventive ways of resisting the dominant ideas and representations that stigmatize them. Today, like generations before them, black youth struggle to combat their social, economic, and political subordination. But unlike previous generations of black youth, the vast communications media landscape has become a site for conducting their collective struggles. The expansive frontier of communications media is marked by unprecedented perils and possibilities. For example, a dominant trend is the megamergers that enable already formidable and massive media corporations to achieve even greater size and controlling interests across the communications mediascape. But this new media landscape also creates possibilities for the emergence of new forms and regimes of cultural production. The strategic maneuverings of black youth around the emergent mediascape represent efforts to exploit the fissures produced within the new media and information economy.

I began this project interested primarily in the filmmaking practices of African Americans. However, as you shall discover in the story that unfolds, my discussion extends beyond this particular field of cultural production as I consider questions related to the lived experiences of black youth and the political dimensions of popular culture more generally. Indeed, it is difficult to write about black filmmaking without also considering the specific social and historical processes that forged the space for its production and the spirit for its imagination and vigor. I started with the premise that the representation of the social world is an inherently political act, and believe that even more so now. Therefore, this book is an attempt to elucidate how popular expressive cultures are intensely political insofar as they animate larger societal antagonisms.

The characteristics of popular American culture continue to evolve with the introduction and innovative uses of new technologies and shifting social, economic, and political currents. Indeed, the production of film, television, and music develops its own particular dimensions of struggle regarding not only how society will be represented but also who will represent it. During the late twentieth century, the expressive cultures of African American youth have achieved greater currency and popularity than ever before. But what accounts for the increasing popularity of black youth cultural productions? How do transformations in the various culture industries and the cultural marketplace produce spaces for the creative skills of black youth? How do changes in discourses about blackness influence the production and reception of black youth cultural practices? Moreover, how does the commodification of blackness correspond with historically distinct social, economic, and political formations? These are some of the questions that drive my discussion of black youth, popular media culture, and politics.

This Is How We Represent: Black Youth and the Production of Black Cinema

I think we are now seeing more direct access by young black film makers directly to the industry in a way that was much more policed and much less easy at an earlier stage. I think it has to do with, among other things, the centrality of questions of race and ethnicity. . . . But I think it also has to do with a certain creative confidence in that younger generation, which is at the moment very full of ideas and wanting to represent themselves rather than be represented by somebody else. That has pushed the industry to give

> *black people, young people, slightly more visibility than*
> *perhaps they had at an earlier stage.*
>   STUART HALL[7]

Throughout the 1990s, young African American image makers have made repeated references to the importance of representing; hence, the title of this book. The recognition by black youth that representational practices are an important and necessary mode of politics and pleasure is a response to a world saturated with various forms of communications media. For black youth, representing the world and how they experience it has evolved into a complex set of cultural practices, styles, and innovations. In addition, representing their world has become a source of empowerment and an avenue of upward mobility for some.

The idea for this book grew out of an internship I performed with the Black Filmmaker Foundation in New York City during the summer of 1991. That same year, a number of films directed by African Americans were scheduled for release. During informal discussions with filmmakers, I began to notice that they understood that something was unique and exciting about the cultural landscape. They fully recognized their historically specific role as new participants on the cultural stage and moved assertively to take advantage of emergent opportunities. Because the arena of popular film is such a prestigious site of cultural production, some of the more prominent African American filmmakers have been able to amass symbolic capital, which gives them the opportunity to pattern popular discourses about the social world. In addition, many of the filmmakers openly acknowledged the ideological role of the media and were also cognizant of the symbolic power it endows. Take, for example, the boastful claim of John Singleton: "[W]e all have opinions but I have a voice."[8] Singleton, paradoxically, both understands and misunderstands his arrival on the cultural stage. Yes, it is true that the commercial success of Singleton's film *Boyz N the Hood* granted him enormous popular appeal and increased access to the highly public and visible medium of popular film. Singleton's voice, however, was not of his own making. That is to say, his prominent appearance on the stage of popular film culture was historically situated and a result of factors he did not completely dictate.

The period that frames my analysis of black filmmaking—1986–1993—was not selected at random. This is the period when black youth began to mobilize around the resources of the popular media in ways that are simultaneously visible, complex, problematic, and commercially viable. Furthermore, this particular formation of black youth cultural production takes shape within the context of profound social, economic, and technological transformations that reorganized the possibilities for collective and symbolic action, especially from the social margins of society.

While the book emphasizes the production of black cinema, it does not pretend to be an exhaustive analysis or history. In fact, I omit a number of feature-length films directed by African Americans during this period. For example, the intriguing world of black independent cinema—a field that deserves its own analysis and historical treatment—is never fully examined. As a result, I do not explore the important contributions made to black cinema by filmmakers like Charles Burnett (*To Sleep with Anger,* 1990) and Julie Dash (*Daughters of the Dust,* 1991). In addition, the emergent body of popular film narratives produced and created by black women is also underexamined. Even the sphere of popular feature releases is limited. For example, teen pictures like *House Party* and *Livin' Large* are also excluded from this study. The omission of these and other films does not imply that they are not worthy of analysis. The films excluded from this study add important dimensions to a fuller comprehension of black American cinema. Similar to the films that I discuss, the films omitted provide important clues about the production logic that governs the commercial film industry's conceptualization of black cinema and its perceived market potential. Moreover, the landscape of black cinema illustrates just how varied black cultural discourse is.

The diverse inventory of black cinema suggests that African American filmmaking is a multilayered form of expression that ruptures its own racialized connotations. Despite the fact that black filmmakers are often viewed as a monolith, their approaches to filmmaking are actually made up of an expansive repertoire of styles and techniques, genres, audiences, and (non)commercial strategies. In many ways, the term *black filmmakers* implies that there is little differentiation in the creative labor of black filmmaking. But in reality, differences proliferate both within and across the body of films written, produced, and directed by African Americans. Since it does not operate in a uniform fashion, I do not attempt to discuss the multiple features, styles, and genres that truly define the world of black filmmaking. Rather, in this study, I have selected two specific sites of black cinematic production and discuss them with some degree of historical specificity and analytical rigor. The first field addresses the popular ascendancy of a particular filmmaker: Spike Lee; the second addresses the popular ascendancy of a particular genre: the ghetto action film cycle.

I selected these two areas of black filmmaking for three main reasons. First, Spike Lee's strategic use of cinema and the ghetto action film cycle foreground some of the more contentious issues that shape black American life in the late twentieth century. Second, films like *Do the Right Thing* and *Menace II Society* were generally successful at the box office because they benefited from moderately wide distribution. An additional benefit of wider distribution is the greater likelihood that a particular filmic discourse will circulate more broadly throughout the cultural landscape, thus enlarging the filmmaker's prestige and his or her ability to pattern popular culture. Finally, although these films fit under the broad umbrella of black cinema, they represent different spheres of creativity and production and also illuminate the diverse and complex character of African American cultural discourse.

Any analysis of black commercial film during this period that excludes Spike Lee makes an obvious and serious omission. Indeed, Lee's personal success in the commercial arena, his participation in the popularization of black expressive culture, and his presence in a burgeoning black culture industry raise fascinating questions about the constantly evolving relationship between African Americans and the industrial image-making landscape. Still, even though Lee is a central figure in the commercial revitalization of black cinema, he is not *the* dominant figure. By shifting my analytical gaze toward the ghetto action film cycle, I try to make clear some of the distinct nuances that color black filmmaking practices in varying forms. This wave of films circulates among a host of other representations and discourses that compete to render the transformations of postindustrial ghetto life more comprehensible.

Design

The book is organized into three parts. Part 1 seeks to explain how black youth cultural practices do not emerge out of a vacuum but rather emerge in relation to historically specific conditions in which new forms of political agency are made possible. Chapter 1 explores how the architects of social conservatism mobilized in part around racially coded themes in order to imbue their ideologies with renewed vigor and cause.

More precisely, I consider how the articulation of ideologically charged themes—like personal responsibility, the war on drugs, and "family values"—was inflected by social and political antagonisms that pivot around changing conceptions of blackness.

In chapter 2, I argue that a complex series of crisis discourses has been constructed as a way to make sense of the social, economic, and political transformations that shape late twentieth-century America. Moreover, I contemplate some of the ways in which the urban ghetto, the "underclass" debate, and black youth in particular are prominently figured in these period-defining crises. Further, I argue that black youth are fiercely implicated in the widespread contention that society has drifted from the virtues of personal responsibility and traditional values. What's more, I consider how black youth maneuver to contest material deprivation, social stigma, and the general upsurge of racial conservatism. In particular, I argue that black youth have transformed their marginal status into cultural practices that enliven their capacity to engage competing discourses about black life. In this instance, the evolution of hip hop has become an especially important reservoir of youth production and agency that stimulates the creative confidence of black youth. I also consider how hip hop, in addition to reshaping the popular music cultures of youth, influences black filmmaking in the postindustrial United States.

In chapter 3, I shift to a general discussion of the commercial film industry. More precisely, I argue that the reemergence of black cinema as a commercially viable product is not accountable on its own terms but rather in relation to developments that transform the production logic and industrial image-making processes of the film industry. Since the 1950s, the film industry has undergone several changes, responding to population shifts (especially suburbanization), changing patterns of consumption, and an ever-expanding landscape of popular cultural commodities and services from which to choose. More recently, the trend toward market segmentation, technological innovations like cable television and the videocassette recorder, and the maturation of the independent film movement continue to reshape the logic governing the production of popular film. These and other changes force the industry to adopt more flexible modes of production in order to maintain a competitive edge in a fiercely competitive cultural marketplace besieged by a profusion of media products and services. A central question this chapter asks is, How do these and other shifts within the film industry create spaces for the production of black cinema? In addition to changes within the industry, the production of black cinema has been stimulated by other factors: emergent youth cultural practices, popular music trends, low production costs, and the rise of independent film distributors. More specifically, I contend that the growth in the production of black cinema during this period was a response by the film industry to a changing cultural landscape invigorated, in part, by the expressive cultures of black youth.

In part 2, I turn to a detailed discussion of the popular ascendancy of Spike Lee. Although Lee did not create the conditions that produced the space, resources, and energy for the commodification of black cinema, he did respond creatively and decisively to the emergent conditions discussed in part 1. Lee's breakthrough success in 1986 played a pivotal role in the industry's renewed interest in black cinema. Chapter 4 discusses Lee's transition from a filmmaker operating on the periphery of the commercial film industry to a filmmaker operating inside the most powerful corridors of film production. Further, I look at specific film industry practices and production strategies that routinized the production, packaging, marketing, and dissemination of films directed by Lee. I look, too, at how the filmmaker struggled with budgetary constraints, conflicts over creative license, and censorship (both from studio executives and from specific segments of the African American community) to establish a distinct niche in American popular film culture. Despite his initial commercial success, Lee's relationship with Hollywood can be characterized as ambivalent. I address some of the critical factors that sustain this ambivalence—mainly the fact that Lee and industry executives maintain conflicting concepts regarding the thematic and aesthetic possibilities and potential audience appeal of black cinema.

Any serious consideration of Lee's relevance to American popular culture must certainly address his ideologically charged deployment of the popular film apparatus. That is the aim of chapter 5. The filmmaker established himself as a formidable player on the field of popular culture by skillfully appropriating the resources and the arena of popular film as a prelude to engaging the rise of conservative discourses about the experience of race in the United States. Lee's cultural and representational politics have been the subject of intense academic and popular debate. What are some of the ascendant thematic ideas and representational strategies that inform Lee's explicit politicization of popular film? I also view Lee's directorial style and signature as a specific form of ideological production. The stylized motifs that mark his films represent a distinct formation of cinematic authorship.

Although Lee stands out as a central figure in the revitalization of black commercial cinema, it is difficult to maintain, however, that he dominated the production of black cinema. In fact, the most frequently produced genre during the post-1986 resurgence of black cinema—the ghetto action film cycle—is not directly associated with Lee. The narrative thrust of this particular trend in filmmaking revolved around the precarious relationship between young black males and the postindustrial ghetto. The focus of part 3, then, shifts to a discussion of the popularization of films like *Boyz N the Hood* and *Menace II Society.* My analysis of this film cycle is balanced by a consideration of two crucial factors: first, the historical context for production, dissemination, and reception of these films; and second, the thematic ideas and representations that give these films a distinctive resonance. The first set of factors tells us something about *how* the repetitious production of this cycle occurred. The second set of factors seeks to understand the ideological strategies, representational politics, and filmmaking techniques that structure this field of popular film discourse. In chapter 6, for example, I maintain that the film industry's exploitation of the genre was a swift response to new market opportunities made possible by the currents of social and cultural change. I look at how a growing market for rap music, film cost/profit projections, and multimedia cross-promotional strategies stimulated the repetitious production of the genre. Moreover, in this chapter, I argue that the genre's appeal was partially attributable to the precarious rise of urban ghetto imagery in American culture.

Chapter 7 considers a different set of factors by closely examining the filmmaking techniques and strategies that mark the genre's distinctive ideological configurations. The narrative politics of the genre foregrounds important questions about the lived experiences of young black males and the postindustrial ghetto. Moreover, this particular formation of black filmmaking takes shape within a complicated cultural landscape from which the construction and representation of postindustrial ghetto life circulate in and across various spheres of discourse. To be sure, the ghetto action film cycle circulates not only among other films but within a broad universe of print media, news narratives, rap music and video, television programs, popular fiction, and even political discourse. I explore some of the dominant thematic ideas of the cycle. In addition, I consider to what extent filmmakers working within the genre create representations that challenge popular tropes, discourses, and representations of postindustrial ghetto life.

The study of popular culture is a burgeoning enterprise. More specifically, how racial, gender, and class formations penetrate popular culture continues to generate numerous Ph.D. dissertations and social histories. One distinct and elaborate focus of exploration is the study of the context and content of black popular culture forms. If the increase in the number of books, conferences, and college course offerings is any indication, interest in this subject area is surging, thus demanding even more rigor and analytical nuance. The flourishing of black American cultural studies fills a crucial void in our understanding of the complex relationship between race, (popular) culture, and politics. Let me indicate, briefly, some of the ways in which I hope this book contributes to a fuller appreciation of black popular culture.

First, I locate the cultural productions of black American youth within the shifting context of more flexible regimes of industrial image making that characterize late twentieth-century capitalism. I consider how transformation of the culture industry facilitates the making of conditions that challenge long-established hierarchies in the production of media and other widely disseminated symbolic materials. More specifically, I consider how shifts in the production of popular media entertainment culture generate the conditions and the possibilities for the commodification of black youth expressive cultures.

Second, the story that unfolds in the following chapters also draws from cinema studies when necessary in order to discuss filmmaking, a particular mode of cultural production, as actively involved in the production of ideology. I consider the nuances of film technique while maintaining my premise that black filmmaking is a historically specific practice that takes shape within a specific period of image making and on a historically situated terrain of racial discourse. Film studies has grown into an elaborately defined academic discipline through emphasis on cinema as narrative, apparatus, and ideology.[9] Indeed, serious film criticism regarding the work of filmmakers like D. W. Griffith, John Ford, and Alfred Hitchcock is customary. And yet, despite its growing prominence in both the academic and popular press, the work of African American filmmakers is seldom rigorously studied beyond the limiting confines of the "positive versus negative" image debate. Like other black cinema scholars referenced throughout, I apply the salient conceptual issues in film criticism to black filmmaking practices.

Third, while parts 2 and 3 of the book discuss the production of black cinema, the analytical gaze of the book is much broader. More precisely, I contend that the discourses performed in black popular film specifically, and black popular culture more generally, engage an enlarged theater of racial discourse and politics. I aim to illuminate the relationship between black cultural producers, the social and political milieus that inform their discourses, the culture industries in which they work, and the audiences for which they perform. In order to better understand the changing demeanor of black youth culture and politics, it is also crucial to understand the changing demeanor of the social and political world young African Americans negotiate.

Ultimately, I am concerned with describing how the popular cultures of black youth operate as a complicated site of ideological struggle, commodity production, and pleasure. This book, then, takes black youth cultural practices seriously. It is my hope that the pages that follow do justice to what is indeed a remarkable chapter in American culture and history. Despite the blighted circumstances that surround them, black youth develop incredibly optimistic worldviews and aspirations that belie the widespread notions that typically construct them as dangerous and deviant. And yet my goal is not to rhapsodize about the popular cultures of black youth but simply to give them their analytic due. After viewing, reading, and listening to the various repertoires of black youth popular culture, it strikes me as extraordinary that a generation cast off by politicians and most of the general public exerts such a forceful influence on the contours of a popular mediascape that is becoming more global in scope. In the process of "representing" themselves, their communities, and the world they inhabit, black youth reveal much about their own struggles and, indeed, the struggles of our nation.

PART ONE

1

Social Conservatism and the Culture Wars

No social or political force can hope to create a new type of society or raise the masses to a new level of civilization without first becoming the leading cultural force and in that way providing the organizing nucleus of a wide-ranging set of new conceptions. Ideology has its own modality, its own ways of working and its own forms of struggle.

STUART HALL[1]

The field of electoral politics is increasingly influenced by cultural producers—advertising agents, media consultants, Hollywood producers—who understand that the manipulation of images, symbols, and language is crucial to shaping a political identity and building a constituency. Electoral politics have long relied on packaging political ideas and candidates for voter consumption. Thus, it should come as no great surprise that, as the technologies of mass communication have become more advanced, efforts to package candidates and their ideologies have become more intense. The elaborate formation and mobilization of social conservatism in American politics is an excellent illustration. In this chapter, I consider the symbolic organization of social conservatism and, more precisely, the racial contours of this social and political movement. Conservatives regenerated their cause and transformed American politics primarily by waging a deliberate campaign whose core themes often hinged on the strategic manipulation of cultural and racial symbols. The architects of social conservatism understood the essence of the Stuart Hall commentary quoted at the beginning of this chapter: that before becoming a political force able to decisively build a more conservative social and political world, it was essential to become a cultural force.

But black youth also understand the significance of becoming a cultural force. And yet, as I shall discuss in the chapters that follow, the cultural and representational politics practiced by black youth operate

largely on the terrain of popular American media culture, a site not always understood as political. Late twentieth-century politics and culture are marked by a vigorous conservative political imagination that
has dramatically reconfigured the contours of racial discourse in the
United States. The shifting tide of the American political landscape has
made it both possible and necessary to create new and more innovative
forms of ideological struggle. For example, the creative ways in which
black youth have mobilized around the various popular media cultures
represent a distinct formation of cultural and political struggle. Questions of culture, representation, and ideology are not secondary to economic matters. On the contrary, the constantly shifting and vigorous
fields of culture, representation, and ideology are material forces insofar
as they perform a powerful role in the reproduction of society.

A central theme in this book is that, as the cultural landscape has
changed profoundly during the latter part of the twentieth century, the
formation of racial discourse changes, too. Discourses about race are inherently unstable, constantly shifting in relation to social, economic,
and political currents that make possible new ways of imagining and
experiencing the social world. Racial discourses develop characteristics
that are historically particular rather than fixed and unchanging. In this
chapter, I consider how the evolution of social conservatism has struggled to make sense of the transformations that mark the late twentieth
century in terms that are decisively racial. The invigoration of social
conservatism did not occur overnight. In fact, the broadening of the
conservative base and the popularization of its populist ideologies have
been carefully and strategically crafted over the course of three decades.

"It's the Economy, Stupid!": Economic Transformation and the Production of Social Conservatism

*As the economic vise tightens, despair turns to anger. But
partly because we have so little concept of class resentment
and conflict in America, this anger isn't directed so much at
those above as at those below. And when whites at or near
the bottom of the ladder look down in this nation, they
generally see blacks and other minorities.*

LILLIAN RUBIN [2]

Terms like the *New Right* and *Reaganism* are familiar parts of the late twentieth-century political vocabulary. One of the challenges confronting any analysis of the recent surge in conservatism is to make sense of these political formations, not as all-powerful forces that drive contemporary American society in irreversible directions but rather as a set of political strategies actively mobilizing against alternative political formations that struggle to occupy and dominate the same space. First, conservatism is not a monolithic political movement. Instead, it is made up of an uneasy consolidation of disparate political voices laboring to assert decisive leadership over a nation that is in the midst of great social, economic, cultural, and demographic change. It is, then, crucial to recognize that the ideological strategies that mark the late twentieth-century landscape take shape within the context of broad historical transformations. As Stuart Hall and Martin Jacques argue, a definitive quality of the late twentieth-century landscape "is that the world has changed, not just incrementally, but qualitatively," and that advanced capitalist societies are "increasingly characterized by diversity, differentiation and fragmentation, rather than homogeneity, standardization and the economies and organizations of scale which characterized modern mass society."[3]

One of the dominant aspects of change in late twentieth-century capitalist societies is the transition from an industrial to a postindustrial economy. In economic terms, the central feature of this shift is the emergence of flexible accumulation, displacing former, more rigid regimes of organizing and accumulating capital. But the postindustrial moment is also marked by social and cultural transitions. In this chapter, I concentrate primarily on the cultural politics that correspond with this transitional period and, more specifically, the ideological strategies deployed by conservative strategists and cultural workers to exercise decisive leadership over how this period of great flux is both experienced and understood. While conservatism is a core feature of the 1990s political and economic landscape, it is necessary to discuss, first, the formation of the New Right coalition that developed into a formidable, if not always harmonious, political body in the 1970s. Before discussing this formation, it is important to digress briefly and outline the transition from industrialism to postindustrialism in a more detailed fashion. It is this transition, to be sure, that is inextricably linked to the structuring of the social and historical context from which conservative popular ideologies and beliefs began to flourish.

The economic reorganization of capitalism since the end of World War II is widely recognized as a dominant form of change in the postwar new world order.[4] And while it is true that these economic shifts are paramount to understanding the second half of the twentieth century, this period is also marked by the independent formation of new social, political, and cultural antagonisms that correspond with and facilitate how advanced capitalist countries organize and accumulate capital. David Harvey outlines the salient features of this transition and the social, political, economic, and cultural milieu accompanying these structural changes.[5] The breakup of turn-of-the-century modes of capitalist reproduction ushers in a period of unprecedented change and uncertainty.

Industrialization is associated with the evolution of mass production and the organization of mass society. The industrial economic order was characterized by rigidity in the organization and accumulation of capital. This system of mass production relied heavily on the organization of economies of scale; a fixed labor market that standardizes jobs, tasks, and long-term labor agreements; growth in the blue-collar sector; and successful labor unions and collective-bargaining power. During this regime of capitalism, the bulk of productivity and industry growth was located within the national boundaries of the United States. This also made possible the creation of large industrial regions and cities that were bolstered by manufacturing jobs and robust economies.

This particular regime of capitalism hinged on a burgeoning postwar consumer culture. In fact, it was shortly after the conclusion of World War II that American families experienced unprecedented rises in their personal standard of living. With the aid of several federal government programs and policy initiatives, in addition to a robust postwar economy, middle-income households and home ownership sharply increased.[6] The era of industrialism, as Harvey suggests, has to be seen less as a mere system of mass production and more as a total way of life.[7]

This total way of life reached its most lively expression in the years immediately following the end of World War II. Ironically, it is this era of growing the middle class that is often cited as the model for American success, when in reality it appears to have been a unique period that has never been equaled before or since. The zenith of the industrial boom began showing signs of erosion by the late 1960s and early 1970s. It was during this period, according to Harvey, that the inability of the industrial economic regime to contain the inherent contradictions of capitalism became more and more apparent. By 1973, a combination of social, economic, and political crises converged to compromise postwar economic growth.[8] In addition, the rigid production modes of industrial capitalism came under increasing pressure, both internationally and domestically. The ability to remain competitive in the forward march toward the global economy meant turning to more flexible systems of capital organization and accumulation. Whereas rigidity was the basic organizing principle driving the industrial economy, flexible accumulation emerged as the basic organizing principle driving the postindustrial economy.[9]

Faced with a domestic economy that was unable to maintain the growth and prosperity of the postwar boom years, the U.S. corporate community was forced to develop new strategies, techniques, and practices in order to keep pace with the changing global economic landscape, which was also producing intense international competition for worldwide economic supremacy. The decades of the 1970s, 1980s, and 1990s, then, have been a period of rapid economic restructuring. The surge toward economic reorganization also accelerated deindustrialization, defined by Bluestone and Harrison as "the widespread, systematic disinvestment in the nation's basic productive capacity."[10] The trend toward corporate downsizing has also intensified the experiences of middleclass economic uncertainty and anxiety.[11] Moreover, the postindustrial regime is characterized by the movement and dispersion of capital and industry across many sectors and regions. With ever-increasing ferocity, the strong manufacturing base that had once laid the foundation for the erection of great industrial cities like Detroit, Chicago, and Cleveland became a relic of the past under the priorities of the new system as meaningful employment opportunities have virtually vanished. Deindustrialization ushered in the steady erosion of the industrial base economy in favor of a flourishing service, administrative, and information-driven economy. These economic transformations devastated the infrastructure of cities that were once robust centers of production and economic growth. The economic livelihood of urban communities rested almost entirely on a model of capitalist reproduction that by the 1960s was showing signs of withering as a result of massive restructuring. As a result of systematic neglect and institutional racism, these changes have led to the erasure of well-paying jobs, income, and tax base, which has generated acute fiscal and social problems in many inner-city communities. More recently, the work of historian Thomas Sugrue provides strong evidence that the devastation of urban communities began well before public recognition of capital flight and declining employment opportunities became commonplace fixtures in discussions about the black urban poor.[12]

It is important, however, not to read the transition to postindustrialization in rigid terms that reduce social, political, and cultural developments to an overdetermining economic base. Thus, we should keep in mind that social and cultural antagonisms develop their own specific motifs that must be carefully considered. What's more, not everyone was included in the benefits of the postwar boom. Built into this period of economic expansion were social and political hierarchies driven by racial, class, and gender privileges. For example, the industrial economy was preeminently a patriarchal order that privileged the male semiskilled and skilled worker over the female worker.[13] The postwar boom produced serious gender divisions between capital and labor. One of the distinctive features of the postindustrial economy is the feminization of the labor force, which radically reshapes the gender contours of work. Moreover, these changes transform established norms as women begin to spend more time in the paid labor force and less time in the domestic sphere.[14]

The postwar boom was also shaped by rigid racial boundaries that relegated black labor to low-wage sector employment and exclusion from significant participation in labor unions.[15] The postwar boom expanded the industrial-based economy and even produced fissures for the development of a black labor market. To be sure, the black migrations reshaped the landscape of America's largest industrial cities due primarily to push and pull factors that established a supplementary black labor force that was used to discipline radical white workers or simply exploit what was certainly perceived as a new source of cheap labor. And while the wartime economy created a greater demand for black wage labor, in general, the industrial economy formed a dual labor market that privileged white workers over black workers.[16] Thus, as Mark Stern points out, contrary to popular belief, there was no "golden age" of African American ghetto life.[17]

In addition to changing the racial geography of the nation, the great influx of blacks accelerated the progression of white flight, which laid the foundation for what social scientists Douglas Massey and Nancy Denton describe as "American Apartheid."[18] As a result, the postwar era was dramatically shaped by the construction of rigidly enforced patterns of racial and residential segregation. The geographical dispersion of blacks also broadened racial conflict beyond the South. In many ways, then, the story of the black urban poor is also the story of late twentieth-century America. Concomitant with the urbanization of African Americans was the massive restructuring of urban economies and, more important, the systematic relocation and erosion of industry from urban communities, which produced concentrated pockets of joblessness and social disorganization for the most vulnerable segments of inner-city communities.[19]

The immense racial inequalities that began to take shape by the mid–twentieth century established the conditions and the context for the emergence of new social movements. While the economic inequalities of the industrial period and its eventual demise are in fact implicated in the social and political antagonisms that began to erupt in the 1950s, social and cultural fissures also created frequent episodes of societal discord that operated independently from the economic sphere.[20] Central to the social movements of the fifties and sixties were the historical agents that confronted racial inequality. In response to the civil rights movement, barriers of de jure segregation were removed; blacks were provided with constitutional protection against disenfranchisement; and legislation was passed making all forms of racial discrimination unconstitutional. Moreover, black urban rebellions focused attention on the inequities and perilous conditions of American ghettos, and as a result, modestly effective social welfare programs were implemented to quell the rebellious energies festering in poor black communities. In addition, controversial federal policies born from this period were also directly linked to African American demands for racial equality — most notably, school busing for desegregation and affirmative action.

The economic transformations of the postindustrial economy interacted, then, with social, cultural, and political fissures to aggravate the crisis tendencies of the 1960s and 1970s. Many American families experienced tremendous inflationary pressures and labor market restructuring that drove wages and household income downward. Furthermore, stagnant job growth made it difficult for newcomers entering the labor force to locate meaningful employment. Whereas the years immediately following the end of World War II were marked by prosperity and expanding opportunity for upward mobility, the emergence of the new global economy has generated an intensely different national mood, as many middle-income and lower-middle-income families are experiencing downward mobility instead. Thus, as capitalism enters a historically distinct phase marked by globalization, information technologies, and seemingly boundless market opportunities, a lack of job security and slow-rising wages generate immense social and economic pressures on many American families.[21]

Moreover, the economic woes of postindustrialism severely compromised the fiscal capacity of the state to continue expanding the entitlement programs created to support the economically disadvantaged, a group that was often defined racially after the 1960s.[22] And while this economic climate produces high levels of anxiety and uncertainty about the future prospects for economic mobility, it also nurtures a more contemptuous attitude toward the federal entitlement programs created to curb urban blight and provide the poor with health care and adequate housing as well as other social services. The expansion of redistributive programs in the 1960s and 1970s came under increasing scrutiny as competition for education, skills training, and jobs became more intense. Michael Omi and Howard Winant contend that these programs became vulnerable to the harsh economic times and eventually were cited as a causative factor in the economic insecurities that began to surface in the 1970s. And because African Americans were associated as primary beneficiaries of the welfare state, space emerged for the cultivation of ideological strategies that transformed the political landscape by exploiting the volatility of race.[23]

Dominant groups struggle vigorously to maintain control over the same ideological and political landscapes for which subordinate populations struggle. The ideological strategies and practices articulated from the political right develop patterns that are shaped, in part, by the cultural strategies and practices asserted from the social and political left. Ironically, as the transformational movements of the 1960s and 1970s dramatically reshaped the political landscape, they also produced space and energy for the cultivation of countermovements that sought to curtail — and in many cases, erase — many of the political concessions the movements were able to achieve. The combination of social movements challenging the long-standing norms and practices of white privilege with a broadening number of whites experiencing downward mobility created a hypercontentious environment that incubated space for the mobilization of a new populist idiom premised on the production of racially inflected themes that sought to reconfigure the terrain of commonsense knowledge.

White Racial Formation

Because they are ignorant of even the recent history of the possessive investment in whiteness . . . Americans produce largely cultural explanations for structural problems. The increased possessive investment in whiteness generated by dis-investment in America's cities, factories, and schools since the 1970s disguises the general problem posed to our society by de-industrialization, economic restructuring, and neoconservative attacks on the welfare state as racial problems. *It fuels a discourse that demonizes people of color for being victimized by these changes, while hiding the privileges of whiteness by attributing them to family values, fatherhood, and foresight—rather than favoritism.*

GEORGE LIPSITZ [24]

A number of different factors converged to reinvigorate conservatism in the United States. Still, it is difficult to overestimate the role race has played in transforming conservative politics and ideology and the larger American political scene. In fact, the rise of a strategically articulated social conservatism has redefined the terrain of electoral politics and enabled a revived Republican Party to erode the long-standing electoral advantages of the Democratic Party.[25] It was during the 1960s when the Democratic Party was viewed as generally supportive of and committed to enforcing the new civil rights legislation that the racialization of the two major political parties began to take on sharply defined characteristics.[26] For better or worse, the Democratic Party was perceived as the party of racial "minorities," while the Republican Party was perceived as the party of whites.[27] Moreover, conservative activists monitored the political landscape of the middle to late 1960s and correctly gauged the evolving mood of white resistance to the assertions of civil rights groups. Detecting a swelling tide of white resentment, conservative politicos began crafting a series of strategies that adroitly countered claims calling for the redistribution of social and economic resources across racial lines. Conservative strategists recognized that a carefully orchestrated effort would be necessary to challenge some of the bolder claims of the civil rights movement. They were also cognizant of the fact that, in order for any countermovement to be successful, it was essential to fashion a discourse that maneuvered scrupulously around the nation's racial fault lines without appearing to be indignant toward the most basic claims for racial equality.

The formation of social conservatism vividly illustrates Raymond Williams's observation that dominant classes do not just passively retain their authority. In fact, hierarchical relations must continually be defended and recreated. The ideological field—defined here as that terrain where ideas, signs, representations, and other symbolic materials circulate and inform public discourses about the social world—functions as a battleground for the clash between competing political players and their views of the world. Dominant ideologies are never total; thus, they must constantly work to negotiate competing formations. The elaborate construction of the New Right in the 1970s is an exemplary illustration of how hegemonic boundaries must be vehemently guarded. Fearing that the balance of power had shifted toward "racial minorities" and "special-interest" groups, the New Right began to cultivate a countermovement. In the process, this new conservative bloc would appropriate a range of racially charged symbols and organize them in such a way as to bolster hegemonic ideas and belief systems about the social world.

A close examination of post–civil rights era conservatism reveals that the historical origins of this project date back to the 1950s.[28] The most distinguishing feature of social conservatism has been the transition from the "cold war" to the "culture wars." The turmoil over the Vietnam War; civil rights for blacks, women, and gays and lesbians; and abortion became the new spheres of political struggle from which new political actors and movements were created. As these issues began to percolate with greater fervor, they also became entangled with questions about cultural identity and difference.[29] It was not until the mid-1970s, however, when the conservative movement established a network of innovative strategies and techniques—new methods of fund-raising, organization, populist themes, tracking poll data, focus groups, mastery of electronic media images—to expand its constituency that it established itself as a formidable force on a variety of social, economic, and political fronts. Faced with the persistence of liberal-based social policies, the growth of federal authority over state and local rights, political action from the social and political margins, and changing social attitudes, sexual mores, and familial patterns, conservatives began to aggressively redirect their efforts toward shifting the gravity of the body politic toward the right of center. The foundation of the movement consists of three groups: the *New Right,* which is the political arm; the *religious right,* which provides the moral sustenance; and the *neoconservative wing,* which generates the ideas and the intellectual framework that inform conservative ideology and social policy.[30]

Inspired by the insurgent voice of the "angry white male," the New Right is best characterized as the political rearmament of the conservative movement. Driven by the belief that liberalism was eroding the basic tenets of American democracy, the New Right has been buttressed by grassroots organizing and the exploitation of wedge issues that work primarily to polarize the American electorate. In many ways, the growth and currency of the conservative movement are a product of the changing technological landscape of electoral politics. For example, the creation of computer networks and bulletin boards, direct-mail campaigns, and electronic media have dramatically changed the game of politics, allowing strategists to wage war on two different, but necessary fronts: what political analysts refer to as the "ground war" and the "air war."

The ascension of the conservative movement, for instance, was made possible by ground-war strategies that utilized direct-mail fundraising strategies in order to provide the recruitment and financial base for political organization.[31] The direct-mail campaign is crucial to the New Right in at least three distinct ways: first, it raises millions of dollars to support and promote the candidates it considers the most conservative; second, it builds crucial networks nationwide that allow the Republican Party to target and expand its constituency by broadly disseminating literature that plays on the fears and passions of voters concerned about issues like crime and abortion; third, and most important, it greatly expands the demographic profile of the conservative movement by targeting segments of the national electorate that historically have been members of a broad Democratic Party coalition, most notably, lower-middle- and working-class white Americans.[32] The air war serves a different purpose. The production of campaign "spots" has fully incorporated media and advertising consultants who work mainly to manipulate electronically mediated cultural images and symbols. All politicians have become more skillful in their use of electronic media. In fact, while I highlight how conservative (and usually Republican) candidates mobilized electronically mediated imagery to strengthen their cause, no politician has been more successful in recent years in mastering this aspect of politics than Bill Clinton.

Conservatives have been especially proficient at using the electronic media to animate their populist themes and practice their particular style of cultural politics. But whereas Ronald Reagan's "morning in America" media campaign evoked optimistic images of small-town and Middle

America, the television ad campaigns of conservative candidates since then have been much more derisive in tone. For example, much has been written about George Bush's campaign and the "Willie Horton" strategy. But other air-war campaigns conducted on behalf of prominent politicians like Jesse Helms (North Carolina) and Phil Gramm (Texas) frame issues like affirmative action in "blacks versus whites" terms that openly pander to racist sensibilities. More recently, Bob Dole ran a series of ads that featured grimly lit images of "Mexican marauders" charging across the border to paint the United States as a nation under siege by alien forces.

A second key dimension in the ascension of the conservative movement is the religious right. The interlocking themes of religious doctrine, morality, nation, and culture are dominant throughout the movement and are most clearly articulated by the Christian Coalition.[33] Elsewhere, Cornel West has argued that it is the moral disciplining of Christian fundamentalism that distinguishes the conservative lean in American political culture from other strands emerging throughout the industrialized world.[34] Fearful that liberal attitudes toward abortion, sex, feminism, and gay and lesbian rights represented a "clear and present danger" to the moral fiber of American society and threatened to undermine one of the nation's most sacred institutions—the nuclear family—the religious right developed new strategies and techniques to enhance its cause and exert more political influence, most notably broadcasting.[35] Television evangelists began to use the broadcast power of electronic media to disseminate their conservative politics, which fashioned a connection between the Bible, rigidly defined notions of Americanness, and support for social policies that sought greater authority over such private spheres as familial organization, reproductive rights, and sexuality. The religious right drives the political and moral justification for the need to restore "traditional values" and the marriage-based (heterosexual) family as the basis for defeating liberalism and generating a national spirit of cultural renewal.

A third influential voice, neoconservatives, supplies the ideological sustenance that helps nourish the movement and its policy initiatives. Moreover, neoconservatism has benefited greatly from the generous underwriting of corporate sponsors that supply capital for the growing number of think tanks that cultivate conservative ideas and policy.[36] And while neoconservatives do not constitute a monolithic body, they do share core beliefs about the nature of society and postindustrial change. For example, neoconservatives adhere to the culture-of-poverty perspective. This position basically maintains that the primary caus-ative agents of urban poverty are the values, belief systems, and behav-iors of the poor. It is further argued that inferior values and behavior are intergenerationally transmitted, thus reproducing both the cycle and the conditions of impoverishment. Another common theme in the ideological arsenal of neoconservatism is the mantra of "big govern-ment." According to the logic of neoconservatives, the expansion of fed-eral government bureaucracy has worsened social problems rather than functioning as an ameliorative instrument. The welfare state is the most often cited example of the failed experiments of big government.[37]

Moreover, Lawrence Grossberg contends that conservative groups seek control not simply of the apparatuses of the state but of the spheres of everyday life and popular culture, too. In addition to their efforts to shape the contours of social policy, conservatives struggle to exercise greater control over the popular culture landscape. Conservatives view the popular mediascape as a bastion of permissiveness and nihilism that erodes public civility and antagonizes traditional American values by promoting violence, sexual promiscuity, and familial disintegration. Their widespread discontent with the popular culture industry has led to new forms of censorship and social control—for example, the new com-munications legislation that specifically targets the Internet for polic-ing, the deployment of the V-chip technology to filter out programming regarded as unsuitable for family viewing, and the call for the television industry to toughen its efforts to both regulate content and develop a ratings system. These and other efforts labor to exercise greater control over the production, distribution, and consumption of popular media culture.[38] It is precisely because popular culture occasionally articulates viewpoints that conflict with conservative values that it has now be-come a location of intense political struggle.

Social conservatism, more generally, has been deployed as a means of exercising some degree of control over the social, economic, and political instability that marks the late twentieth century. But it is not a cohesive or uniform social movement. Nevertheless, this particular movement is composed of a symphony of voices that cohere around the central belief that the liberal takeover of American social, political, and cultural life is ruinous to the nation's democratic principles.[39] So-cial conservatives deploy their rhetorical devices, vast resources, and political imagination to create sharp and decisive symbolic boundaries that construct an image of society under siege from a number of sub-versive forces—feminists, gays and lesbians, liberals, racial "minorities," and labor unions—waging war on traditional American values, beliefs, and identity structures. As sociologist Michele Lamont reminds us, "boundary work is an intrinsic part of the process of constituting the self; they [boundaries] emerge when we try to define who we are: we constantly draw inferences concerning similarities to, and differences from, others, indirectly producing typification systems."[40]

Historian Michael Rogin posits that, historically, a kind of boundary-defining tradition has always loomed near the center of American social and political life in the form of political demonology, or what he calls countersubversive politics.[41] The countersubversive imagination, according to Rogin, splits the world in two, creating notional enemies often in "us-against-them" terms. Elsewhere, political communication historian Kathleen Hall Jamieson contends that there is a clear sense of political advantage in the strategy of demarcating "us" against "them." Further, she writes, "votes are gathered by promising to use power to prevent a threatening group from taking control. Unsurprisingly, political discourse routinely reinforces the public belief that one group or another is menacing."[42] The idiom of political demonology works to define certain individuals, groups, and practices as alien, if not dangerous to the preservation of the social order. The countersubversive is especially suspicious of efforts that contest long-standing symbolic boundaries and political hierarchies. Further, Rogin contends that countersubversives enforce divisions in order to maintain social and political boundaries. Ironically, it is the existence of the social and political margins that allows dominant classes to erect and safeguard the boundaries necessary to placate their political desires and interests. In fact, without the presence of political foes, countersubversives would be limited in their ability to define themselves in terms that legitimate their claims. While the practice of political demonology is traceable throughout American history, Rogin carefully points out that it is not a uniquely American phenomenon.

Inevitably, countersubversive ideologies arouse social anxiety for political expediency, often masking its primary goal, which is to secure the structural hierarchies that govern the unequal distribution of power and social resources. One enduring feature of this tradition has been the construction of racially charged symbolic boundaries that work to define blacks, Latinos, and immigrants as political enemies. The formation of the conservative right coalition in the 1970s, then, signaled yet another episode in American history when race was deployed as a powerful and effective theme in the mobilization of countersubversive politics.

The architects of social conservatism relied on a broad spectrum of emotions—anger, discontent, resentment, and fear—to invigorate a particular style of racial backlash politics. Backlash politics are inherently reactionary. Indeed, backlash politics are invigorated by a reactionary response to a changing social world and are initiated primarily by those groups of individuals experiencing a decline in a felt sense of importance, influence, and power.[43] The central thrust of social conservatism in fact hinged on issues that lead to the mobilization of whites, males, and traditionalists disturbed and frustrated by the perceived threat of alien penetration into the mainstream of American social and political life.

According to Ronald Walters, the proponents of social conservatism asserted a number of social, moral, and political themes as a "basis for restoring a pre-1960s social structure as the substance of Americanness."[44] Moreover, this selective reliance upon a mythological, Middle American collective past to define Americanness laid bare significantly defined racial, gender, and class antagonisms. For example, because African Americans were actively involved in social movements of the 1960s, the group has been targeted as a chief subversive element in the changes that seek to alter long-standing social, economic, and political hierarchies. More important, opposition to redistributive programs like school busing and affirmative action was used to galvanize support from many lower-middle- and working-class white Americans. This broadened the appeal of social conservatism, which was fully incorporated by Republican Party strategists who recognized and seized the opportunity to cultivate a new political alliance that emphasized populist themes as a way of resisting what were, in reality, only minor modifications in the race hierarchy.

The flowering of late twentieth-century conservative politics is rooted in a strategic and reactionary response to historically specific factors, most notably: a weakening domestic economy; white middle-class economic insecurity; and finally, the fracturing of the social and political order by movements that originated from the social and political margins. The architects of social conservatism transformed the ideological landscape by first disorganizing and then reorganizing the cultural discourses that defined the meanings of politically charged symbols like race, nation, and the family. Further, conservatives understood that the social, economic, and political spheres could be transformed, in part, by waging a systematic yet carefully coded culture war.[45] Consequently, the authors of the movement abandoned biological notions of superiority/

inferiority as a way of legitimating racial hierarchies and instead fashioned a coded political discourse that cloaked intolerant ideas and beliefs in democratic ideals and principles.[46] To be sure, the strategists who keep the movement mobile and vibrant exploited societal cultural fault lines to strengthen their political claims and position. Cultural critic Lawrence Grossberg argues that, in this case, culture leads politics.[47]

And while the formation of social conservatism and its subsequent fashioning of an imagined Middle America began, in earnest, to take shape in the 1960s, the movement lacked a mobilizing center that embodied its values, principles, and popular ideologies in such a way as to supply it with the appeal, vigor, authorization, and legitimacy necessary to assert social, economic, and political leadership over civil society. Even as late as the 1970s, it had not yet achieved substantive leadership in shaping the broader contours of public discourse. Enter Reaganism.

Reaganism: Popularizing Conservatism

Despite glib allusions to the "revolution" he was making,
Reagan was actually reconciling the different strands of
conservative populism. . . . George Wallace, Richard Nixon,
and the Christian Right had minted their own versions. . . .
But Reagan cleansed them of all but a modicum of
resentment and bitterness, making an ideology that had
once sounded extreme appear to be the bedrock of common
sense and consensual values.

MICHAEL KAZIN [48]

The significance of Reaganism extends far beyond the political biography and charismatic appeal associated with Ronald Reagan, the political figure. For as Thomas and Mary Edsall warn, "to see Ronald Reagan as the cause of an ascendant conservatism minimizes the significance and consequence of large-scale social and economic transformations—developments beyond the power of any single political player to determine."[49] In many ways, the term *Reaganism* identifies a definitive moment in the making of new forms and sites of social, economic, political, and cultural antagonisms in American society. While Reagan is a popular icon of the conservative movement, *Reaganism* embodies a broader set of conditions that dwarf any single figure.

First, Reaganism is not so much a dominant movement as it is a strategic reaction to the shifting currents of its times. A broad community of historians urges a reconsideration of what the experience of Reaganism means.[50] One historian defines Reaganism as a "return to old-fashioned Republicanism—large tax cuts for the rich, less government help for the poor, weaker enforcement of civil rights, fewer controls on industry, less protection for the environment, and emotional rhetoric on the virtues of hard work, family, religion, individualism, and patriotism."[51] It is the latter component of Reaganism—its most prominent symbolic features—that drives the focus of this section: more specifically, the language, ideas, and representations organized to package and disseminate this particular brand of conservatism.

One of the most prominent features of the Reaganite imagination resembles what Hall refers to as a form of "regressive modernization."[52] While certainly shaped by the postindustrial landscape, Reaganism also managed to shape the social, economic, and political terrain in which it maneuvered. Moreover, it is equally instructive to begin thinking about Reaganism as a strategic political movement composed of a complex body of ideas, values, and popular ideologies that were related to the social and political struggles that mark the 1960s and 1970s as periods of intense political antagonism. Jimmie Reeves and Richard Campbell maintain that the chief demon of the Reaganite imagination was not a person, a political party, or even a special-interest group but rather the turbulent decade of the 1960s.[53]

In a real sense, the strategic movement of Reaganism onto the political landscape was an attempt to reassert authority over a nation in great flux. Reaganism developed what one historian has called a "populist persuasion."[54] Like most populist appeals, then, Reaganism thrived on its ability to produce a vocabulary of protest and resistance that contested competing political projects promoting a different view of society. Reaganism positioned itself around a scenario of crisis, fissures, and conflicts that it proposed to manage, heal, and resolve.[55] To the extent that this particular movement in conservatism developed a populist demeanor, its main strength was the ability to skillfully incorporate many of the ideological themes articulated by the New Right, religious right, and neoconservatives in order to polarize the body politic to the right and, consequently, impose a new regime of social, political, and moral discipline over a society undergoing substantive change.

Issues related to cultural and racial difference emerged as fertile terrain for the ideological investments of Reaganism. The symbolic power of the movement centered on its ability to effectively invoke metaphoric language as a device for constructing a series of "us-against-them" confrontations that enabled it to redefine and reframe divisive social issues in a new conservative logic.[56] This ascendant rise in social conservatism would understand many of the alleged crises and social dislocations of the 1970s and 1980s racially, often in very polarizing terms.

The *racial formation* process proposed by Michael Omi and Howard Winant is particularly instructive and illumines the central role race can and often does play in shaping the social and political landscape of a given historical moment. Omi and Winant write: "The meaning of race is defined and contested throughout society, in both collective action and personal practice. In the process, racial categories themselves are formed, transformed, destroyed, and re-formed. We use the term racial formation to refer to the process by which social, economic, and political forces determine the content and importance of racial categories, and by which they are in turn shaped by racial meanings. Crucial to this formulation is the treatment of race as a central axis of social relations which cannot be subsumed under or reduced to some broader category or conception."[57] Reaganism managed the formulation of a new vocabulary of terms, myths, and cultural representations that struggled to recreate the meaning of race. Moreover, and as I discuss in greater detail in chapter 2, the contours of racial discourse also developed significantly defined gender and class features that facilitated the criminalization of African American youth and the poor inner-city communities that housed them.

This conservative vision of American society stood heavily on the mythic shoulders of rebirth, a political strategy that sharpened its appeal and molded its ideological disposition.[58] How did race, a historical source of societal conflict, figure in the rebirth rhetoric of Reaganism? Furthermore, how did Reaganism propose to heal the racial fissures of its era?

The Law-and-Order Spectacle: Reaganism and the War on Drugs

The call for law and order echoes throughout American political history. Law-and-order themes generally demand respect for authority, adherence to the legal apparatuses of the state, and strict compliance with core values, norms, and mores. In many ways, the law-and-order intonation is a call for the maintenance of a stable, integrated national community. The cry for law and order, however, is somewhat misleading because underlining this appeal for social integration is a strong desire to educate and discipline society in a position of subordination to official locations of authority. Law and order, then, is also about the maintenance of a social system that produces political and economic hierarchies. Exuberant calls for law and order generally signal the emergence of a crisis that directly confronts the legitimacy of state authority and fractures the social order.

During the middle 1960s, the law-and-order discourse developed its shape within the context of immense social and political ferment. Amid the rapid changes made possible by the social movements of the 1960s and 1970s, "law and order" symbolized resistance to changes in race relations, youth counterculture, family life and gender, and open defiance of authority as well as crime.[59] The sharpening of social conflict compels the state to rely increasingly on its coercive resources in order to maintain social integration. This reliance on the coercive technologies of the state signals the breakdown of ideological hegemony; that is, the failure of the dominant economic and political elite to shape consensus in a way that legitimates its authority over the subordinate classes. During those moments when popular ideologies are fractured, the dominant classes must struggle to reassert their legitimacy in order to move consensus in a preferred direction. It is here that issues of crime and popular morality serve as useful symbolic devices for recuperating a fractured ideological field. More precisely, as Hall writes:

> [T]he themes of crime and social delinquency, articulated through the discourses of popular morality, touch the direct experience, the anxieties and uncertainties of ordinary people. This has led to a dovetailing of the "cry for discipline" from below into the call for an enforced restoration of social order and authority "from above." This articulation forms the bridge, between the real material sources of popular discontent, and their representation, through specific ideological forces and campaigns, as the general need for a "disciplined society." It has as its principal effect, the awakening of popular support for a restoration of order through imposition: the basis of a populist "law-and-order" campaign. This, in turn, has given a wide legitimacy to the

tilt of the balance within the operations of the state towards the "coercive" pole, whilst preserving its popular
legitimacy.[60]

Themes of crime and social anarchy emerged as prominent targets
for the countersubversive strategies articulated by the architects of social conservatism. Black urban uprisings and militant gestures suggested
to many conservative ideologues that black protest demands were spiraling out of control and represented a genuine and subversive threat to
national security. It was during this period that the contemporary outlines of the law-and-order discourse began to develop their current, racialized connotations.[61] The appeal for law and order began to create a
new logic that demonized black militancy, re-presenting it as social anarchy, deviance, and hooliganism.[62]

Law-and-order themes played a significant role in the reconfiguration of the political landscape because they forged new territory for the
elaboration of socially conservative racial politics.[63] One of the first political players to understand this in recent years was the former governor
of Alabama and would-be president George Wallace. Well before the
"war on drugs" or Willie Hortonesque campaign spots, Wallace understood that law-and-order appeals could be given a racial spin that impassioned the antiblack sentiments of whites. In fact, Wallace's imprint
on social conservatism cannot be overestimated. Although a Democrat,
his use of populist themes as a vehicle for attacking the changes made
possible by the civil rights movement informed and anticipated conservative Republican Party electioneering strategies. As one historian of the
South writes, "George Wallace was not the first postwar political figure
to call for a return to 'traditional' American values. But the Alabama
governor—more than any other political leader of his generation—was
the alchemist of the new social conservatism as he compounded racial
fear, anticommunism, cultural nostalgia, and traditional right-wing economics into a movement that laid the foundation for the conservative
counterrevolution that reshaped American politics in the 1970s and
1980s."[64]

The political efficacy of law-and-order appeals facilitated a fundamental shift in the criminal justice system toward a greater emphasis on
get-tough laws, or what is euphemistically called "tough-love" in the
1990s political lexicon. The operations of law enforcement and political
discourse have been tilted toward more coercive responses to social in-

stability but in ways that legitimate the aggressive turn. Diana Gordon describes this new "justice juggernaut" as a move from "soft" rehabilitative approaches to "hard" disciplinary approaches that propose more punitive measures of social control.[65] According to Angela Davis, this decisive shift in the criminal justice system has been enhanced by an increasing fear and criminalization of African Americans and the subsequent building of what she calls the "punishment industry."[66]

Under Reaganism, the racial configurations of law-and-order politics developed an elaborate and sophisticated motif: the war on drugs. This law-and-order spectacle emphasized images of inner-city villainy—gang violence, crack cocaine, delinquency, and moral degeneracy—as a major urban pathology that required a militarized, get-tough posture. This dramatic play on law and order sharpened the racial dimensions of the discourse and clearly embodied the hostile relationship between social conservatism and America's inner cities—especially, poor, black, and Latino youth. The Reaganite coalition reinvigorated law and order as a primary basis for constructing itself and inner-city foes in such a way as to exploit popular morality and valorize conservative ideologies that moved to roll back many of the modest programs developed to curb inner-city blight.

Like all socially constructed notions of deviance, the war on drugs is shaped by specific social and historical relations and is best understood within the context of examining the role that social, political, and economic systems play in producing criminality. This approach to examining deviance shifts the focus of inquiry from the individual being labeled to the institutions doing the labeling.[67] Definitions of crime, and the ideas shaping the criminal justice system, according to this view, are articulated to sustain and reproduce dominant social relations. This shift in focus attempts to relocate the problem of the political economy of crack cocaine within a broader context that transcends the "Just say no" moral urgings championed by social conservatives.[68]

Reaganism's hyperbolic dramatization of the drug crisis often relied on metaphoric language to infuse popular ideologies about urban dislocation with images of urban criminality and moral degeneracy that created a sense of national crisis and moral outrage. The criminalization of black youth and inner-city communities was necessary to legitimate the crisis. Legitimation is the process by which the state secures consent from society by giving the illusion that it is acting in the common interest of society.[69] Despite claims of "making the streets safe for law-abiding citizens," political initiatives like the war on drugs actually create greater societal discord and drive crime rates upward because lawmakers have broadened the definition of what is considered criminal.

Generally speaking, definitions of criminality construct behavior most threatening to society in extremely narrow terms, often focusing on the dramatic and horrific acts associated with street crime. Images of crime are mediated by historically specific circumstances. Popular representations of crime portray the typical criminal as young, male, black, and poor. As a result, young African American males are figured as the "enemy within."[70] This interpretation gives criminality a specific character that belies the broader realities of behavior that threaten society. This narrow definition of threatening behavior fails to criminalize occupational hazardous conditions, improper medical services, and environmental infractions committed by corporate regimes that may, in fact, be more dangerous than the street crimes etched in the public mind. Further, Jeffrey Reiman contends that the merger of the "criminal classes" and the "lower classes" into the "dangerous classes" stigmatizes the socially and economically dislocated.[71] Law-and-order appeals bind the nation together at the same time they divide and polarize society along lines of race and class. The merger of the criminal, lower, and dangerous classes promotes the commonsense notion that the most pernicious threats to a harmonious society come from the bottom of the social and economic hierarchy. In this sense, then, the war on drugs deflects the anxiety and discontent of ordinary Americans and their resentment away from the corporate and political elite and against the poor.

The Failure to Thrive: Welfare Mothers and the Politics of Traditional Values

Reaganism's configuration of blackness is also articulated in very specific gender and class terms. For instance, poor black women are figured quite differently than poor black men, thus developing tenacious gendered connotations that function as a complicated form of social control. While the war on drugs principally images young black men as criminals, the representation of young black women takes shape along a different pole: the anti–big-government, political backlash against the welfare state. The conservative assault against the welfare state is, in essence, an assault on the values, moral codes, and behavior of the poor. This particular dimension of social conservatism harnesses to its political strategy commonsense notions about family, gender, culture, and nation. As a result, black families—and black women, specifically—are figured as chiefly responsible for the deteriorating conditions of inner-city communities.

A crucial element in the conservative response to the shifting social currents of the postindustrial landscape is the politicization of "traditional values." The insertion of family, values, and morality into the center of political discourse represents a nostalgia trap that invokes an imaginary past in order to mobilize resistance to the social changes in American family life.[72] Moreover, like most ideological strategies, the traditional values discourse attempts to locate the political interests of its advocates outside of the realm of partisan or ideological debate, thus aligning itself with the sphere of commonsense, down-to-earth logic that is universally true and therefore beyond argumentation. As a result, the rhetoric of traditional values does not so much combat alternative ideas but rather locates them outside the boundaries of what constitutes legitimate discourse. The insistence on invoking the past as a golden era of civility and decency is an attempt to make what are, in reality, intensely political claims on what constitutes Americanness seem natural and therefore nonideological. As Eagleton reminds us, *naturalization* "is part of the dehistoricizing thrust of ideology, [with] its tacit denial that ideas and beliefs are specific to a particular time, place, and social group."[73]

Embedded in the traditional values theme are particularly intense gender, racial, and homophobic antagonisms.[74] Examining the crucial role of values in the popular ascendancy of Republican Party conservatism, Edsall and Edsall define this element as a "belief in hard work, in the nuclear family, in self-reliance, in personal restraint, in thrift, foresight, and self-denial; belief in doctrines of individual responsibility, in obedience to the law, in delayed gratification, in respect for authority, and in more repressive (or less self-expressive) sexual morality."[75] The ideological thrust of this discourse represents the interlocking political interests of the religious right with the Reaganite project of renewal that interprets modern changes in the family as culturally inferior, deviant, and erosive of traditional norms and values.

The nuclear family is crucial to the construction of commonsense ideologies about nation and identity. As Errol Lawrence argues, the family "is portrayed as the crucial site for the reproduction of those correct social mores, attitudes and behaviours that are thought to be essential to maintaining a 'civilized society.'"[76] The heterosexual marriage-based household is portrayed as the only reasonable pattern of familial organization.[77] Further, as the guardian of conventional morality and the purveyor of traditional values, women perform a central role in the nuclear family idea. Because women are such a central element in the private spheres of domesticity, black women become especially vulnerable to the commonsense appeals and countersubversive aims of the traditional values logic.

The social construction of the welfare mother serves a number of conservative agendas. This specific representation of black motherhood simultaneously condemns the excesses of liberalism and the devastating social and economic impact of impoverished cultures while energizing a systematic attack against the welfare state.[78] As Patricia Hill Collins observes, the controlling image of the welfare mother appears to be tied to black women's increasing dependence on the post–World War II welfare state.[79] The welfare mother is repeatedly represented as the antithesis of traditional values. The welfare mother is characterized as a "social transgressor" who is outside the moral boundaries of respectability and traditional definitions of motherhood. Reaganism would explain the rapidly depreciating conditions of urban ghettos and the increasingly poverty-stricken status of children as the result of cultural deficiencies endemic to ghetto life, thus exempting society, racism, and profound structural and economic transformations from any responsibility.

As Collins writes, "the welfare mother is portrayed as being content to sit around and collect welfare, shunning work and passing on her bad values to her offspring."[80] The welfare mother does not exhibit a strong work ethic, nor is she self-reliant. In addition, charges of welfare fraud lead to images and myths welfare queens. Further, Collins contends that because she is often portrayed as unwed, the welfare mother violates a major Eurocentric masculinist thought: she is a woman alone. This deviation from the "nuclear family" model is also constructed as a pathological pattern in black culture. Also, because of the high rates of teenage pregnancy and unwed births, the welfare mother is stigmatized as sexually promiscuous, irresponsible, and unable to exercise personal restraint. This controlling image of the welfare mother obscures the role that racism, sexism, and economic dislocation play in the disintegration of poor, inner-city familial life.

Moreover, the mythical construction of the welfare mother is illustrative of the recent political currency and broad dissemination of a revitalized *culture-of-poverty* viewpoint into the center of contemporary political discourse that sharpens the attack on the welfare state. According to the culture-of-poverty thesis, the poor are poor primarily because of inferior values and cultural practices.[81] The crisis of inner cities, it is argued, is the direct result of a deviant lifestyle and culture that are passed on intergenerationally, thus failing to equip poverty-stricken children with the proper values and behavioral models—a strong work ethic, delayed gratification, thrift, and sexual restraint—that promote social and economic mobility. The social Darwinistic features of this explanation of poverty are not difficult to discern.[82] This critique of urban social and economic blight represents a distinct shift from biological notions of racial inferiority to a logic that focuses on black culture in order to explain social and economic inequality. The institution that is identified as the chief culprit in the accelerated decline of the urban poor is the black family.[83] And because women are construed as the guardians of conventional morality and the purveyors of traditional values, the welfare mother is essentially the main source of failure.[84]

But a second culprit in the attack against the welfare state has also emerged: the welfare state itself, or more specifically, the failed experiments of "big government." This theme in conservative political ideology is designed, in part, to "soften" the attack on the welfare state and blunt charges that conservatives are, in effect, mean-spirited and guilty of class warfare against the poor. So rather than attack welfare recipients, conservatives target much of their disdain toward the welfare state itself. Government, conservatives posit, is the primary cause of poverty because it encourages illegitimacy, familial disintegration, and the cultivation of values that trap the poor in a vicious cycle of poverty. Moreover, conservatives argue that by dismantling the welfare state, they are, in fact, aiding the poor by breaking their dependency on government and encouraging the poor to take more assertive aim at the ever-elusive "American dream."

Proponents of the culture of poverty invert cause and effect. Rather than explaining crime, drug addiction, female-headed families, and welfare dependency as a way of life due, at least in part, to social structural constraints and diminishing economic opportunities, the formulation is unequivocally turned on its head: social structural constraints and diminishing economic opportunities are the result of deviant values and cultural practices. The poor, then, are poor because they deserve to be poor or at least because they lack the proper values necessary to make democracy work for them.

41

Remaking Whiteness

[T]he politics of white identity is undergoing a profound
political crisis. . . . White privilege . . . has been called into
question in the post–civil rights period. Far from being
destroyed, however, the white "politics of difference" is now
being trumpeted as an ideology of victimization. The
situation would be farcical if it weren't so dangerous,
reflecting venerable white anxieties and fortifying the drift
to the right which, now as in the past, is highly conducive
to race-baiting.

HOWARD WINANT [85]

Central to the rising political resonance of the conservative movement was the exploitation of racially charged wedge issues as a strategy to turn white middle-class anxiety into political advantage. The cultural and racial politics of social conservatism vividly illustrate how identities are shaped within the context of historically specific circumstances. Kobena Mercer reminds us that social and political identities "are not found but made; that they are not just there, waiting to be discovered in the vocabulary of Nature, but they have to be culturally and politically constructed through political antagonism and cultural struggle."[86] Further, he adds, "different actors appropriate and articulate different meanings out of the same system of signs"; hence, identities are never static but "constantly subject to antagonistic efforts of articulation as different subjects seek to hegemonize discourses which support their versions of each signified."[87] Racially inflected signs work as specific sites of ideological struggle and are open to multiple definitions.

To be sure, social conservatives expressed a discourse that accented specific kinds of claims on the meaning of blackness. Conservative claims on blackness played a prominent role in reshaping the cultural and political landscape by creating new regimes of representation and forms of discourse that reorganized commonsense ideologies about race. Political rhetoric that invokes images of the "welfare queen" or routinely draws attention to the social dislocations of poor urban communities is an example of how blackness gets imaged and reproduced. Moreover, at the same time that conservative strategists endeavored to develop new commonsense notions about blackness, their reconstruction of "whiteness" was equally inventive if not always as easily discernible.

In addition to understanding how blackness is socially constructed, it is important to bring attention to the ways in which "whiteness" is also socially constructed, performed, and rearticulated. Implicit in popular discourses about blackness are claims that reproduce and struggle to sustain whiteness as the norm and dominant center of American life. Take, for example, the term *Middle America,* which circulates as though it were both race-neutral and ideologically neutral. Jonathan Reider contends that during the 1960s, when conservative ideologues and politicians began to enlist an audience responsive to many of their backlash themes, a new cultural identity was fashioned: Middle America.[88] According to Reider, Middle America did not exist as a popular term before the 1960s. The construction of this new political identity enabled conservatives to reposition themselves politically by maneuvering around serious class divisions within the larger white community in order to build an unlikely electoral alliance between members of the corporate elite and lower-middle- and working-class Americans. In reality, the growing of this new constituency was defined in sharply racialized terms. To be sure, George Wallace's appeal to "law-abiding citizens" and "ordinary Americans," Richard Nixon's gestures toward the "silent majority," and what journalists and historians later termed "Reagan Democrats" are all illustrations of how whiteness is both constructed and mobilized to carry out specific political interests.

Whereas the social and political movements of the sixties and seventies labored to rupture hegemonic definitions of blackness, these movements also sought to produce alternative definitions and connotations of whiteness as a location of power and institutional advantage. The shifting theater of racial politics suggested that the practices that sustained white privilege were not outside the remapping of political battle lines. The shifting theater of racial politics also made it clear that the material advantages of whiteness could not be taken for granted and would have to be fought for and actively reproduced.

This particular episode in the history of white racial formation did not represent the first time white hegemony would have to be struggled for. However, this moment represents a distinct shift in how whiteness was coded and constructed as a particular location of experience and identity. White privilege is powerful precisely because it is a complex body of practices that often go unmarked and unnamed.[89] As a result, these practices are naturalized and firmly established in the institutional life of American society.

One feature that enhances the efficacy of social conservatism is its capacity to politicize race without necessarily making explicit references to race. In fact, a new vocabulary for referencing whiteness has been elaborately fashioned over the last three decades. For example, the discourses pivoting around terms like *traditional values, reverse discrimination, Middle America,* and *family values* seek to develop an idiom that speaks to the often unspoken site of white privilege, power, and hierarchy. White racial discourse is organized and expressed in ways that conceal racial, gender, and class tensions. And yet, like all regimes of dominance, white racial hegemony must also be struggled for and, when necessary, modified. The racial and cultural maneuvers practiced by the leaders of social conservatism suggest that they understand that, in order to reproduce whiteness as a site of power and privilege, especially in the face of open and direct challenge, it is necessary to build alternative terms charged with new connotations.

But the sphere of electoral politics is not the only location where new conceptions of white cultural politics have been mobilized. The populist themes, ideas, and rhetorical strategies that define social conservatism enable and are enabled by new forms of white popular expressive culture. Grossberg reminds us that popular culture is an important location of study not simply because it has become a leading stage for ideological struggle but also because it plays an active role in the material milieus in which people live.[90] How does white popular culture correspond with the material worlds and lived experiences of whites?

Plain Folks: Producing Country Music, Reproducing Whiteness

Just as rock-and-roll foreshadowed many of the changes in gender and race relations that followed in the 1960s, country music today—with its suburban, middle-aged themes of family and renewal—may be the clearest reflection of many of the anxieties and aspirations that have just begun to bubble to the surface in American political life. . . . Ultimately the music . . . is one of the most vivid examples of America's reigning backlash against its own culturally liberal past. Hints of this trend have popped up elsewhere in American life—in the antiviolence campaign against Hollywood, in the movement against

violent rock and rap music lyrics and in the agitated white
suburban voice embodied by Newt Gingrich.
BRUCE FEILER[91]

Country is soul music for white people.
PAUL SHAFFER[92]

Whereas much has been written about the Reaganite entertainment of the 1980s, especially the action-adventure films that valorized the superiority of "white guys," three other spheres of popular cultural production have surfaced as specific sites in which historically distinct formations of white cultural politics are expressed, lived, and reproduced: country music, talk radio, and the Internet.[93] While country music has a longer history, the invigoration of talk radio and the proliferation of Web sites and computer chat rooms are made possible by the rapid transformation of information technologies.[94] However, I want to focus this discussion of how whiteness gets reproduced and popularized by looking at the boom in country music production and consumption. Similar to other popular cultural formations in the United States, the phenomenal growth of the country music scene is partially structured by the deep racial divisions that define late twentieth-century American culture.

The claim that country music has become white America's popular music of choice is convincing when you look at recent trends. With the introduction of the SoundScan computerized tracking method, the broad appeal of country music was made more evident. Because this particular method tracks activity in suburban shopping malls, the patterns of white music consumption are especially illuminated.[95] Between the 1980s and early 1990s, no popular music genre grew more impressively than country music. Whereas country music consumption made up about 7 to 10 percent of the market share in 1985, it had grown to about 18 percent by 1992. In 1985, country music was roughly a $440 million industry. In 1995, the industry generated over $2 billion annually.[96] The Gaylord Entertainment Company alone — owner of the Grand Ole Opry, Country Music Television, and The Nashville Network — generates $700 million in annual revenues. Just before the boom in 1985, ten new country albums went gold (sales of 500,000 units), while seven went platinum (over 1 million units sold). In 1993, fifteen albums went gold, and twenty-six reached platinum sales. And as journalist Peter Applebome asserts, the real "King of Pop" is Garth Brooks, not Michael

45

Jackson. In a seven-year period, Brooks sold 60 million albums, placing him second only behind the Beatles in total records sold in the United States.[97]

The country music boom is also evident in expanded radio airplay. By 1993, country radio formats had become the highest-rated program in fifty-five of the nation's top one hundred cities. The largest country radio station in the world is not in Texas or Nashville but in New York, where over 1 million tune in each day to WYNY. Country music is far and away the most widely distributed radio format. Since 1980, the number of country radio formats has increased from 1,534 to roughly 2,500 nationwide.

According to one study, country is the top radio format among some of the most important aggregates of consumers: college graduates, adults employed full-time, home owners, and high-income earners. The demographic spread of country is equally remarkable. While the majority of country listeners still reside in the South (47 percent), other parts of the country have increasingly tuned in: 26 percent of country listeners now live in the Midwest, 17 percent in the West, and 10 percent in the Northeast.[98]

A Nashville-based entertainment and music research specialist has identified three different markets that make up the orbit of country music consumption in the United States: traditionalists, transition thirties, and country converts. These markets are variously structured by class, age, gender, and the subgenre trends that demarcate different taste patterns in the consumption of country. It is the "country converts" segment that has catapulted country to new and unprecedented heights. It is also the fastest-growing segment and marks the noteworthy shift of white youth and baby boomers to the country genre. One market analyst defines this segment as "typically in the mid-20s up to the late-40s and predominantly in the 30s. This is the market that has expanded the country music industry to the northern and western corridors."[99] More generally, market research reveals that the enduring stereotype of the backward, rural, and poor aficionado of country music has been replaced by the face of today's typical consumer of country music, who is likely to live in the suburbs, earn an individual income of nearly $40,000, and be college-educated.

Several factors are offered to explain the meteoric rise of country music. One claim is that corporate takeover has dramatically altered the image and style of country music production. Indeed, many critics of the country music boom believe that the genre is undergoing an identity crisis, moving further and further away from its origins as a new generation of industry executives packages and markets country to a wider suburban audience. But the corporatization of the country music industry is certainly the norm rather than the exception in trends that typify the culture industry more generally. A second claim highlights the impact of cable television on the genre. To be sure, the creation of The Nashville Network and Country Music Television (CMT) has necessarily led to a significant image makeover of country. The use of music videos as marketing devices has made image management an important strategy in the production of most popular music forms. Today, country performers are younger and more telegenic than ever before. CMT, for example, is poised to influence country music style similar to the way MTV influenced pop and rock music styles.

While changes in the production, distribution, and marketing are clearly important in the popular ascendancy of country, the complex ways in which race penetrates and shapes popular cultural formations cannot be overlooked. Part of the popularization of country is related to the emergent mood shifts and sensibilities that underscore the suburbanization of American life. Since the mid–twentieth century, no development has had as profound an effect on American culture as what authors Douglas Massey and Nancy Denton describe as the formation of "American Apartheid." The authors contend that American society has become more racially segregated than ever before, thus producing vastly different lived experiences and everyday milieus for white and black Americans.

The suburban/urban racial chasm that distinguishes American communities, churches, schools, and electoral politics is vividly evident on the popular culture field. To be sure, whites and blacks not only live in segregated neighborhoods but also reside in segregated popular culture worlds. How different are the popular cultural milieus of blacks and whites? One report found that, of the top twenty television programs viewed in black and white households, only three appeared on the same list.[100] Moreover, the popular music genres and radio formats are also segregated along racial lines. Pop and rock music genres are generally marketed to whites, whereas rhythm and blues is traditionally marketed to blacks.

Popular culture, Lawrence Grossberg reminds us, is a place where individuals make emotional investments. The popular culture sphere, he writes, "is always more than ideological; it provides sites of relaxation, privacy, pleasure, enjoyment, feeling good, fun, passion, and emotion."[101] Furthermore, the pleasure we experience is socially and historically situated. Clearly, the heightened investment in country music is a complicated formation that cannot be reduced to one uniform "feeling" or sensibility. Nonetheless, the popular ascendancy of country animates how whiteness is socially constructed, popularized, and performed. The "feelings" many whites generate toward blacks and Latinos get focused and expressed in the dynamic interplay between politics, everyday life, and popular culture.

In his exploration of why the country has "gone country," journalist Bruce Feiler suggests that the genre has become the sound track for urban escapism and white flight.[102] Feiler maintains that country music is a direct beneficiary of suburbanization and the disaffection many whites feel toward urban communities. In addition, Feiler claims that just as rap music has become the voice of young black urban America, country music has become the voice of white suburban baby boomers. While it is true that popular cultural formations are certainly more enigmatic than Feiler implies, the claim is not entirely wrongheaded. Thus, some of the features of a rising white racial backlash are obliquely expressed in country's rising popularity.

The ascendancy of country music is not disconnected from the shifts in popular American media culture that increase the visibility and commercial vitality of black youth expressive cultures. In fact, country music executives acknowledge that part of their success hinges on the continued backlash against the popular cultures of black youth. In a *Time* magazine cover story on the country phenomenon, one industry executive was quoted as saying, "[T]hank God for rap. Every morning when they play that stuff, people come running to us."[103] Also, several pop and country radio stations run self-promotion ads that proudly boast "No rap!" The sentiments expressed by the record executive and the efforts of some radio stations (including some black-appeal formats) to repudiate black youth expressive culture demonstrate how racial antagonisms work on the terrain of popular culture. The appeal of both country and rap to their respective primary audiences is a manifestation of society's deepening racial chasm. The fact that country is produced and performed mostly by whites certainly differentiates it from a popular genre like rap, which is produced and performed mostly by blacks. And if popular culture is a site where pleasure, everyday life, and politics merge in unanticipated ways, we can read the revival of country music as a historically specific variation on a familiar but constantly evolving theme: the social production of whiteness as a source of pleasure.

Finally, Applebome reasons that country's evolution as the popular music choice of white America parallels and reflects the southernization of American life.[104] Applebome believes that American values, politics, and culture are increasingly being patterned by southern sensibilities, interests, and attitudes. It is not surprising that, in their efforts to appeal to middle- and lower-middle-class whites as "plain folks," Presidents Nixon, Reagan, and Bush all made it a point to associate with popular icons of country music. The popularity of country is not so much a reflection of the genre's moving toward the mainstream—although many of the younger performers blend pop and rock sensibilities with country—as it is a reflection of the center of American life's gravitating more decisively toward some of the themes and inclinations that have long defined the values of the South and the "whitening" of the country genre.[105]

Still, even though conservatives struggled to pattern popular ideologies about black Americans, the culture wars they declared were never completely successful. The struggle to consolidate hegemonic claims on blackness was continually resisted, limited, and altered by image makers determined to assert their own claims. Indeed, as Gray argues, "the new right's use of race and blackness as a marker of internal threats to social stability, cultural morality, and economic prosperity did not go uncontested. Indeed, African Americans produced an explosion of cultural, political, and social debate that sought to establish black claims, control, and affirmation of blackness[,] that contested conservative claims, repositioned traditional ones, and imagined new ones."[106] So even as black youth are prominently figured in popular discourses about crime, welfare, and the erosion of traditional values, they still struggle diligently to produce and circulate their own representations of social change. Ironically, the passionate struggle of conservatives to fashion commonsense ideologies about blackness and a rapidly changing world is enlivened by the symbolic practices of black youth that take place in the burgeoning world of communications media and popular cultural production.

2 Black Youth and the Ironies of Capitalism

[I]n the struggles of urban youths for survival and pleasure inside of capitalism, capitalism has become their greatest friend and greatest foe. It has the capacity to create spaces for their entrepreneurial imaginations and their "symbolic work," to turn something of a profit for some, for them to hone their skills and imagine getting paid. At the same time, it is also responsible for a shrinking labor market, the militarization of urban space, and the circulation of the very representations of race that generate terror in all of us at the sight of young black men and yet compels most of America to want to wear their shoes.

ROBIN D. G. KELLEY [1]

Although African American filmmaking is the primary locus of inquiry, the scope of my analysis is considerably broader. It is difficult to understand the significance of filmmakers like Spike Lee and the Hughes brothers in American cinema without situating their arrival on the cultural stage in relation to the social transformations that reorganize the material and symbolic worlds inhabited by black youth. The creative labor of African American filmmakers takes place upon a complicated sphere from which the production of blackness, a historically situated racial signifier, proliferates across many sites.[2] But before discussing African American filmmaking practices specifically, it is important to consider the historical formations and decisive shifts that transform the social landscapes, everyday experiences, and cultural productions of black youth more generally.

According to sociologist David Brain, cultural production is the "collective production of skills and practices which enable social actors to make sense of their lives, articulate an identity, and resist with creative energy the apparent dictates of structural conditions they nonetheless reproduce."[3] The cultivation of skills that allow them to participate in a rapidly expanding and global communications media culture enables black youth to produce a broad range of cultural products. The most arresting features of black youth popular cultural productions represent distinct forms of agency, struggle, and social critique. But the vigorous commodification of African American cultural productions also develops complicated features, as I will discuss in the following chapters.

The study of popular media culture generally oscillates between two opposing poles: containment or resistance. Whereas the former maintains that the ideas, values, and representations that shape popular media discourses are determined by the dominant classes, the latter argues, alternatively, that popular cultures have the capacity to subvert dominant ideologies and regimes of representation.[4] Yet popular media culture is remarkably more complex than the containment/resistance binary opposition implies. Similar to the social world from which it is produced, popular media cultures are marked by instability and change. It is, in fact, one of the main locations where the struggle for ideological hegemony is waged. But as Stuart Hall explains, this "struggle for [ideological dominance] is never about pure victory or pure domination[;] it is always about shifting the balance of power in relations of culture."[5] From this view, then, popular media culture is perhaps best understood as a perpetual theater of struggle in which the forces of containment and resistance remain in a constant state of negotiation, never completely negating each other's presence or vigor.

While the different spheres of commercial media culture—television, film, music, video, and the Internet—function as sources of pleasure and entertainment, they also perform a pivotal role in patterning the cultural and ideological landscape. The popular media productions created by black youth represent a distinct sphere of cultural production. Any serious consideration of black cultural productions must examine the relationship between several interlocking factors: the specific culture industries within which these productions are organized; the changing landscape of communications media technologies; emergent mood shifts and sensibilities that lead to the creation of new collective identities; and finally, the unsettled social world within which black youth cultural practices take shape. Sociologist Herman Gray argues that commercial media culture is an essential location to think and theorize about African American culture, representation, and politics.

Gray reminds us that "commercial culture serves as both a *resource* and a *site* in which blackness as a cultural sign is produced, circulated, and enacted."[6]

Commercial forms of popular culture are a rapidly growing field of study. Scholars and social historians are beginning to understand it as a plentiful and remarkably revealing reservoir of practices and formations that are inextricably linked to the changing contours of American life: urbanization/suburbanization, technological innovation, and shifting conceptions of racial, gender, class, and sexual identities. Commercial forms of popular media culture, for example, are central to how we (re)produce and experience socially constructed formations like race.

More precisely, my aim is to more fully explain the increasingly complex ways in which young African Americans have mobilized around a changing racial and popular media landscape. Moreover, it is a story about how the pulsing gestures, performances, and representations practiced by black youth are structured, in large part, by the profound ways in which they experience the changing contours of American life. The focus on the production of black youth cultural styles and popular movements also recognizes that a notable feature of the late twentieth century, as Stuart Hall and Martin Jacques write, "is the proliferation of sites of antagonism and resistance, and the appearance of new [actors], new social movements, new collective identities—an enlarged sphere for the operation of politics, and new constituencies for change."[7]

This book pivots around a particular site of antagonism and resistance—the sphere of popular media culture—and more precisely, the ferment and creative energy that drive the cultural innovations of African American youth and their strategic participation on this terrain. The buoyant surge in black youth popular cultural production raises important questions about the evolving disposition of cultural and representational politics in a media-saturated universe. Early critics of "mass culture" demonstrated concern that popular media culture was controlled by and for the dominant classes. But this view fails to consider how popular media culture functions as a site of intense ideological struggle. Quite simply, can the commercial media, long regarded by many critical theorists as the modern-day "opium of the masses," function as a location of counterideological struggle? Similar to other institutional milieus, commercial media also develop specific antagonisms. So as new subjects gain access to the most prominent sites of media and representation, the possibilities for new collective identities, social movements, and distinct modes of struggle are also established.

To contend that cultural innovation and production among black youth have flourished and achieved a discernible niche in the arena of popular media culture is certainly a tenable position. This is not to imply that African American youth have only recently begun to cultivate spaces for producing cultural objects and expressing themselves but rather that the symbolic practices created by the post–civil rights generation have achieved greater visibility and resonance in the global popular culture economy. But before discussing some of the specific attributes of black youth agency, I would like to consider an initial question first: Why have cultural innovation and production among black youth exploded or, as they might boast, "blown up"? Even more to the point, how has the social, political, and historical terrain on which black youth cultural productions do their work enabled them to intervene in the remaking of society in ways that are more visible, invigorating, and problematic?

The New World Order: Black Youth and the Racialization of Crisis

Oh you know what else they trying to do, make a curfew especially for me and you. The traces of the new world order, time is gettin' shorter if we don't get prepared people its gone be a slaughter. My mind won't allow me to not be curious. My folks don't understand, so they don't take it serious. But every now and then, I wonder if that gate was put up to keep crime out, or our ass in?

GOODIE MOB [8]

A cursory glance at the cultural landscape—music, video, film, television, advertising, and sports—reveals that the expressive cultures created by African Americans play a lively role in patterning the racial and gender identities of youth as well as the general popular culture scene. The precarious relationship between youth subcultures, media technology, and commercial culture has been the subject of numerous inquiries.[9] Still, despite the fact that we can speak broadly of youth cultural practices, it is essential to appreciate the historical specificities that enable distinct formations of youth culture to take shape. Historian Robin D. G. Kelley reminds us that, "unlike more mature adults, young people are in the process of discovering the world as they negotiate it.

They are creating new cultures, strategies of resistance, identities, sexualities, and in the process generating a wider range of problems for authorities whose job it is to keep them in check."[10]

Admittedly, it is difficult to pinpoint with precision when and why a distinctive mood shift or transition in youth cultural production originates. However, it is possible to identify those factors that work, more or less, to establish the circumstances from which youth popular culture formations emerge. Certainly, any discussion of late twentieth-century black youth cultural practices that does not consider the social context that situates their agency would be severely impaired.

So why have cultural innovation and production among black youth exploded? One approach might look solely at the innovators of the new symbolic practices that lead to the creation of new popular culture products. This can be called the genius view of cultural innovation because it presupposes that certain periods of cultural production are the result of talented individuals.[11] However, a more discerning approach would seek to understand the historical particularities that produce the resources and opportunities that unleash and enable the creative energies of cultural producers. Moreover, this view understands that the creative labor of cultural producers does not take place in a vacuum. Innovators of new symbolic practices and cultural products do their work in relation to other cultural producers and within specific social historical contexts. Like all historical actors, then, black youth operate within the context of structural and historical constraints not of their own making.

Consequently, any serious interrogation of the symbolic efficacy of black youth cultural practices must understand their social, economic, and political milieu. Sociologist Ann Swidler states that "unsettled times"—that is, periods of great disorder and transition: population shifts; wars; social, economic, or moral crisis—tend to create moments of fierce struggle, instability, and social action.[12] New ideas, social movements, and ideological strategies are mobilized to make sense of societal flux and instability. In the process, the ideas, belief systems, and symbolic terrain of a given period become more fragile and increasingly vulnerable to competing ideological worldviews. Similarly, dominant cultures produce "emergent" social formations that cultivate alternative/oppositional practices and ideologies that modify hegemonic practices and cultural discourses.[13]

To be sure, the presumed "dominant ideologies" of any given period do not always penetrate and shape the consciousness, ideas, and practices of aggrieved populations.[14] In fact, dominant economic and polit-

ical classes do not consistently fashion consensus in ways that legitimate their authority. This view of culture and society seems especially
plausible when thinking about the United States in the late twentieth
century, a period of tremendous political agitation and social discord.

As I discussed in chapter 1, the ideological and political formations
of the postindustrial United States are marked by profound social, economic, and cultural transition. Moreover, this period of transition has
established the conditions for the construction of different crisis scenarios, both real and imagined. In the process, crisis-tinted discourses are
mobilized to make sense of and effectively manage the flux and uncertainty that abound. Even in cases where crises may in fact be real, they
are typically *made* intelligible and, as a result, are defined, shaped, interpreted, and explained. For instance, a complex assemblage of crisis discourses revolves around the postindustrial ghetto. The ghetto has become an intensely charged symbol, particularly as it patterns discourses
about crime and personal safety, welfare, familial organization, and the
disintegration of American society.

African American (and Latino) youths are prominently figured in
the crisis scenarios that stage some of the more contentious social and
political episodes of the late twentieth century. Some researchers contend that increases in violent crimes, teen pregnancy, female-headed
households, and welfare dependency can be *partially* explained by the
sheer growth in the number of young people, particularly black and
Latino, residing in many cities across the United States.[15] Moreover,
the concentration of black and Latino youth in postindustrial cities
corresponds with structural changes in the postindustrial economy,
especially the movement of industry and meaningful employment opportunities away from the communities in which they are most likely
to live.[16]

One of the peculiar developments of postwar economic transformations is what economist Juliet Schor describes as an increase in work
hours for some segments of the population and the overproduction of
idleness for others.[17] Schor argues that, as the U.S. economy and the labor market continue to undergo substantive reorganization, they are increasingly unable to provide work for some segments of the population.
One of the persistent tensions in the postindustrial economy is the
widespread erosion of meaningful employment opportunities for poor,
inner-city youth. As the labor-force participation of black youth hovers
around chronically low levels, both their real and perceived prospects
for upward mobility become more grim. Indeed, a tenacious set of fac-

tors restricts the social and economic mobility of poor youth: inadequate schools, lower levels of educational attainment, low self-esteem and personal confidence, discriminatory hiring practices, and racially inflected tensions on the job site.[18]

As the face of urban poverty in the United States continues to evolve, one of the distinguishing features is the growing number of youth who now live in poverty-stricken households, a trend not replicated across other industrialized nations.[19] Cultural critic Mike Davis writes: "[C]orrelated to the economic peripheralization of working-class blacks has been the dramatic *juvenation of poverty* amongst all inner-city ethnic groups."[20] By the end of the 1980s, roughly 20 percent of America's youth were poor. And while youth and single-parent mothers represent a disproportionate share of the poor, the probability of being a poor child is not equal across racial/ethnic groups. In fact, research consistently indicates that African American children are significantly more likely to grow up in impoverished households and neighborhoods than their white counterparts.[21] By the end of the eighties, an astonishing 44 percent of African American youth were living in poverty. In contrast, 38 percent of Latino and 11 percent of white youth lived in similar conditions.

The incorporation of African American youth into a broad complex of crisis scenarios develops specific social and political dimensions. Black youth tend to be concentrated in poor communities that have been the primary targets of the post-1960s conservative social and political backlash packaged in numerous movements: antigovernment, antitaxes, antiwelfare, and anticrime. The drive to correct the perceived excesses of "big government" has ignited a broad-based movement of disinvestment in inner-city job training, social, education, and crime-prevention programs. Ghetto youth are prominent icons in the seemingly indefatigable efforts of an emboldened conservatism committed to the enforcement of "traditional values," law and order, and personal responsibility. But the association of black youth with social instability is indelibly marked by the production and popular dissemination of the "underclass" label.

The making of the "underclass" label is congruous with the general rise of social-issue conservatism in post-1960s American political culture. Social-issue conservatism is the explicitly focused debate about values, morality, behavior, two-parent households, and respect for authority. While cultural issues have historically shaped American politics, they have been elevated from a peripheral to a central role.[22] One journalist goes so far as to argue that whereas politicians and political consultants operate from the assumption that economic issues drive electoral politics, "values matter most."[23] However, the author's focus on issues like crime, welfare, and affirmative action suggests that perhaps "race matters most." The "values matter most" contention is at best disingenuous, but it nevertheless illustrates how conservatives have attempted to elevate what are increasingly racialized themes above concerns about the inherent nature and instabilities of capitalism as the central dilemma in American social and political life.

Contemporary discourses about African Americans are increasingly patterned by sensational representations of the black "underclass." Sociologist Herbert Gans maps the evolution of the "underclass" label and its absorption into mainstream social and political discourse. Despite the newness of the label, it plays a definitive role in shaping popular discourses about race, poverty, and social change in general. According to Gans, the term has passed through three descriptive stages: economic, racial, and finally behavioral.[24] By the 1970s, he argues, descriptions of the term turned decisively behavioral as news journalists began to devote substantial time and coverage to the proliferation of social dislocations in poor ghetto communities.[25] The emphasis on the alleged deviance of the poor refashions "culture-of-poverty" explanations of poverty and strengthens the notion that misbehavior is the primary culprit in the reproduction of poor ghetto communities.[26]

The "underclass" is customarily portrayed as one of the most distressing social problems facing the United States. Stephen Hilgartner and Charles Bosk have proposed what they call the public arenas model for understanding the rise of social problems.[27] According to the model, social problems are collectively defined, selected, framed, and disseminated within a dynamic arena of public discourse. In this arena, a broad population of potential problems compete against each other for attention and notoriety. Given the vast number of potential social problems, only a few are able to capture the attention of the public and major institutions. As a result, social problems are necessarily stratified: problems considered the most urgent occupy the top of the "social problems ladder," while those achieving little or no public cognizance are typically positioned near the bottom.

Furthermore, Hilgartner and Bosk contend that the career of a social problem variegates over time and hinges on its ability to capture the attention of the institutions that have the power and resources to effectively define the problem for broad public consumption. These institutions, in effect, *make* the social problem and render it intelligible to the broader public. The carrying institutions include, for example, the cinema, made-for-television movies, news media organizations, book publishing, and political parties. These are the major institutions that select, define, and disseminate social problems to the public. Because of the vast population of potential problems, creators of social problems must package them in dramatic terms. Once a social problem achieves prominence in one arena, it may then begin to saturate other arenas. When multiple carrying institutions devote substantial attention to a particular problem, it develops a "celebrity" status. Moreover, the problem begins to dominate public, and especially media, discourse.

Visualizing the Underclass, Representing Danger

> *Today's dangerous classes included segments of the diverse communities of racial and ethnic minorities; young people who exhibit some degree of independence from their elders' direction and values. . . . The likelihood that the identified group creates danger—crime, urban decay, challenge to authority—is an article of faith, as both the public and the policymakers point to high levels of urban disorder, family dissolution, and unwed motherhood. . . . What is needed to construct them as enemies is a bridge between group identity and an experience of social threat—a neighborhood mugging . . . or the dramatic depiction of a murder on the nightly news—that is familiar to many people.*
>
> DIANA GORDON [28]

It only takes a quick glance at legislative and electoral politics, the news media, public opinion polls, or popular entertainment culture to recognize that the "underclass," and poor youth especially, has attained the dubious distinction of being a celebrity social problem. The absorption of the "underclass" label into mainstream vocabulary corresponds with the social and economic transformations that configure postindustrial life. And even though the label circulates as if it were ideologically neutral, representations of the "underclass" are sharply coded in both racial and gender terms. Moreover, historian Michael Katz maintains that the label implies that the problem of late twentieth-century urban poverty is profoundly novel in character and kind, and unprecedented in scope.[29]

Take, for example, the proliferation of news media discourses that play a leading role in framing public perceptions of postindustrial ghetto life. Perhaps even more than social scientists or politicians, the news media industry has played a crucial role in coloring the public discourses that render the "underclass" seemingly more intelligible. The television news industry is a distinct sphere of commercial media and discourse production. Unlike most of television entertainment, it is nonfictional—in other words, real. But the news media is a peculiar blend of fact and artifice. Thus, while news media journalists deal with real-world phenomena, they do so in a way that is always selective and interpretive.[30]

News discourse is one of the primary means by which a society comes to know itself. In their analysis of television news, Richard Campbell and Jimmie Reeves contend that it is "a spectacle of surveillance that displays a range of cultural performances—all of which articulate visions of order by representing legitimate authority, reproducing common-sense, and visualizing deviance."[31] The news media are also an important site of racial discourse. In fact, part of the evolving role of the news media industry has been to determine what is most newsworthy about race, construct images and definitions of race, and pattern the range of potential connotations the idea of race produces. For example, television news discourse typically constructs African Americans as conflict-generating and problematic.[32] And though it would be faulty to conclude that the news media are the primary agent in the racial fissures that percolate throughout the late twentieth century, the way in which television news frames race certainly occupies a crucial position on the embattled terrain of racial conflict.

The news media serve several functions at once.[33] A primary purpose is to provide their mass audience with information and descriptions of events that take place in the world. However, another less obvious function is the news media's role as a mechanism of social control. The news media, to be sure, can be viewed as a central component of the social control processes that define and produce meaning about what constitutes difference and deviance. In this particular role, as explained by Ericson, Baranek, and Chan, the news media are a kind of "deviance-defining elite" that play a key role in constituting visions of order, stability, and change and in influencing the control practices that accord with these visions.[34] News media organizations specialize in visualizing—and accordingly, defining—deviant behavior for their audience. In the process, the news media also reproduce commonsense notions of civility, social order, and community consensus. Moreover, the focus on deviance develops an entertainment angle that appeases the commercial interests of news media organizations. Cognizant of its role in commercial television entertainment and the competition for ratings, the television news industry relies heavily on dramatic, sensational, and titillating images in order to attract and hold a wide viewing audience.[35]

The preponderance of television news stories highlighting black youth, violence, and the arrival of crack cocaine in the middle 1980s stands out as a dramatic orchestration of a "moral panic" and demonstrates how news media organizations aid in shaping the way social problems are selected, defined, packaged, and disseminated to the public.[36] Campbell and Reeves maintain that the news media's construction of the cocaine crisis in the 1980s embodied the racial, gender, and class tensions that shaped the most celebrated crisis scenarios of the period.[37] The authors argue that, with the emergence of crack cocaine, the news media developed a "siege" narrative that replaced earlier news stories regarding cocaine use. This rewriting of the cocaine narrative shifted from *class*-coded themes focusing on recreational drug use and therapy to *race*-coded themes focusing on violence, criminality, and punishment. Using production techniques like clandestine footage, the news media began to serve as a surveillance device, built largely on visual clichés that portrayed the burgeoning crack cocaine economy in hypervillainous terms.[38] The authors persuasively claim that this particular rewriting of the cocaine narrative fit the demonology of racial conservatism, stigmatized poor inner-city youth, and played a central role in legitimating, for example, the "hard" disciplinary ethos of social control initiatives like the war on drugs.[39]

A main set of organizing themes in the "underclass" discourse is the alleged social pathologies of ghetto youth. To be sure, the connection of black youth with illegal drugs, gangs, and violence performs a distinct role in shaping how many of the crisis scenarios of the period were understood. More crucially, inner-city youth arouse public anxiety and precipitate what Diana Gordon describes as "the return of the dangerous classes."[40] Members of the dangerous classes, she argues, are believed to pose a threat to the personal safety of law-abiding citizens and, if unchecked, to the social, economic, and moral order of the larger society. Accordingly, black and Latino youth are prominently figured in the widely shared notion that inner cities—and by association, their racially coded populations—constitute a fiscal and moral strain on national resources. Subsequently, some of the salient crisis scenarios coloring the postindustrial United States have been redefined. In the process, meanings about race, class, gender, and youth undergo substantial revisions.

In many ways, the "underclass" is as much a cultural construction as it is a sociological reality. At stake, of course, is how the widespread impoverishment of black youth is comprehended. To be sure, before any society can create new laws and mobilize punitive measures for the express purpose of controlling those portrayed as dangerous, it must conduct a sufficient amount of ideological work in order to legitimate the use of coercion. In essence, the general public must be made to feel vulnerable, to feel that the stability of the moral and social order is threatened, thus necessitating dramatic acts to preserve social order. Representing ghetto youth as dangerous is not simply a symbolic exercise; it has serious implications for social policy and also influences the social control mechanisms put in place to restore a sense of order. Indeed, initiatives like the war on drugs, school dress codes, and evening curfews achieve their popular status precisely because of the work that crisis discourses perform in the criminalization of black youth.[41] The perceived dangerousness of the urban poor legitimates the deployment of the coercive technologies of the state and the adoption of elaborate crime management operations.

It is within this social context that the cultural productions of black youth amass energy and ever-increasing ingenuity. The transformations of urban ghetto life situate different formations of racial discourse and enable them to take shape. One aim of black youth popular culture is to redefine the crisis scenarios that prominently figure young African Americans. The symbolic practices of black youth develop distinct styles, moods, and imaginative contours that engage a broad spectrum of cultural producers—journalists, politicians, scholars—about African American life. The explosive surge in popular cultural productions by black youth prompts a reconsideration of how unsettled times reinvigorate not only social control discourses but resistive discourses, too. This is not to suggest that social and economic dislocations are *the* determinate causes of black youth cultural productions. Instead, I am suggesting that the ways in which black youth experience a rapidly changing society and how they practice cultural politics to express these experiences correspond.

Paradoxically, the intensification of racial and economic polarization in the United States produces space for the emergence of cultural practices that derive much of their symbolic efficacy from locations of marginality. The popularization of black youth expressive cultures is an excellent case in point. Despite high rates of poverty, joblessness, and criminal arrests, black youth occupy a dynamic role in the shaping of the popular cultural landscape. Many of the major culture industries—sports, television, advertising, music, cinema—incorporate the innovative styles and expressive cultures of black youth in order to appeal to their respective markets and revitalize their own commercial viability. Ironically, social isolation and economic marginalization contribute to the energy and imaginative capacities that enable black youth to participate effectively in the ever-expanding universe of popular media culture. In the process, black youth have accumulated significant amounts of symbolic capital.[42]

So despite the currency of conservative discourses, black youth have mobilized their own discourses, critiques, and representations of the crisis-colored scenarios in which they are prominently figured. More important, young African Americans are acutely aware of the social world in which they live and the vast structural inequalities that impose severe restrictions on their economic mobility. All members of society exercise some measure of agency—that is, capacity to exert some degree of power over the social arrangements and institutions that situate their lives. Faced with the increasing trend toward structurally enforced idleness and state-sanctioned coercion, black youth have fought diligently to create spaces of leisure, pleasure, and opposition from the social structures and institutional arrangements that influence their life chances.

How do black youth maneuver to contest and destabilize the growing tide of racial conservatism? Ironically, at the same moment that black youth have become especially vulnerable to shifts in the postindustrial economy and the political landscape, they, too, have gained unprecedented access to the technologies of communications media. What has emerged in the process is the structuring of a historically distinct terrain upon which the varying repertoires of black youth cultural production dramatically reorganize the scope and possibilities of social and political struggle from the margins. Indeed, the popular cultures of black youth reveal that they experience, interpret, and make sense of the world in ways that are both historically specific and highly performative.

The Making of the Hip Hop Nation: The Social Transformation of Black Youth Culture

It was not long before similarly marginalized black and Hispanic communities in other cities picked up on the tenor and energy in New York hip hop. Within a decade, Los Angeles County (especially Compton), Oakland, Detroit, Chicago, Houston, Atlanta, Miami, Newark, and Trenton, Roxbury, and Philadelphia, have developed local hip hop scenes that link various regional postindustrial urban experiences of alienation, unemployment, police harassment, social, and economic isolation to their local and specific experience via hip hop's language, style, and attitude. . . . In every region, hip hop articulates a sense of entitlement and takes pleasure in aggressive insubordination.

TRICIA ROSE[43]

Despite the widespread popularity of black youth expressive culture and the vast amount of critical attention it currently receives, our understanding of the historical processes that situate its varied articulations remains underdeveloped. The relationship between African American youth and communications media technology is also underexamined. The histories of black youth and their relationship to commercial media culture, to be sure, remain largely unwritten. Black youth continue to create new cultural practices and products that penetrate and reconfigure the production and distribution strategies that govern the culture industry. Moreover, the collective mobilization around popular media technologies by black youth raises intriguing questions about their participation in a vast and rapidly expanding communications media and information economy.

Sociologist Claude Fischer explains that the study of technology and society is commonly informed by technological determinism.[44] According to Fischer, the determinism model views a technology as an autonomous or external "force" that "impacts" social life. The main assumption from this view is that technology dictates changes that are far-reaching and fundamental in scope. Further, it is assumed that a technology produces homogeneous consequences for the larger society. In other words, the impact of a technology on members of society is believed to be uniform.

63

Critics of technological determinism maintain that while technology can and often does lead to change, the process is socially rather than technologically determined. Moreover, Fischer argues, the determinism view fails to appreciate how specific technologies are adopted by particular members of society and used in ways that accommodate specific intentions and priorities. Fischer writes: "[O]nce we have understood the genesis of a technology, its development and promotion, we can begin looking at consequences. Here we should ask: Who adopted the device? With what intention? How did they use it? What role did it play in their lives? How did using it alter their lives?"[45] According to Fischer, the value of this position is that it emphasizes the agency and intentionality of those who use technology. Fischer adds, "[P]eople are neither 'impacted' by an external force, nor are they the unconscious pawns of a cultural Geist. Instead of being manipulated, they manipulate."[46]

Technological determinism typically informs how the relationship between black youth and popular media culture is comprehended. For example, it is commonly argued that communications media exercise unrelenting power in shaping the worldviews, behavior, and lived experiences of black youth.[47] There are at least two immediate problems with this position. First, it does not adequately specify how media technology has entered and altered the social lives of black youth. Second, and perhaps more important, it does not address how black youth manipulate media technology and, in the process, reshape the sphere of popular media culture.

Take as an example the study of black youth by historian Carl Nightingale.[48] Nightingale contends that analysts of the black urban poor fail to understand the ways in which black youth are connected to the larger mainstream culture. Whereas theories about economic, spatial, and cultural alienation emphasize the exclusion of black youth from the mainstream, Nightingale seeks to understand the problematic ways in which mainstream culture penetrates the lived experiences of black youth.[49] Furthermore, he directs his critical gaze toward popular media culture and its "impact" on the racial, gender, and economic identities of black youth. The exploration of the relationship between black youth and the commercial media is certainly an important site of study. But the framing of his inquiry presumes technological determinance. It is taken for granted that the practices of black youth are rigidly conditioned by the media and corporate strategies of consumer socialization. However, it is equally important to consider how black youth influence the culture industry, the cultural marketplace, and consumer trends. In other words, it is important to understand that youth are not simply passive victims of commercial media culture but are actively involved in its making.

The emergence of hip hop culture illustrates black youth agency. In many ways, hip hop represents a particular species of social movement. The movement is made possible by new social and economic arrangements, technological innovations, and the global dissemination of U.S. popular media cultures. Sociologists broadly define social movements as collective efforts to produce social change.[50] Any attempt to discuss hip hop as a movement demands careful delineation because it is variously preoccupied with style, performance, opposition, leisure, consumption, representation, and entrepreneurship. First, this particular movement takes place on the field of popular culture, a site not immediately discerned as political, or capable of producing social change. Second, hip hop is invigorated by the creative labor of a constituency not ordinarily regarded as interested in effecting social change: youth. Third, like social movements in general, hip hop enables its participants to imagine themselves as part of a larger community; thus, it produces a sense of collective identity and agency. To be sure, this particular movement constitutes a distinct mode of intervention in the social world.

Communications media have become an especially important location for both individual and collective agency. Many black youth believe that the sphere of popular media culture is an especially important space in which to articulate many of their frustrations and grievances with their disproportionate membership in the growing ranks of the underemployed/unemployed, impoverished, and incarcerated. Ironically, and as Kelley points out, capitalism has been both a foe and a friend of black youth. Within the interstices of late twentieth-century capitalism, black youth have fought to create productive spaces to counter the dominant discourses deployed to both demonize and discipline them. The hip hop movement has developed into a fertile reservoir of youth cultural production. In fact, numerous expressive cultures have been created in the process: graffiti art, break dancing, and most notably, rap music. The origins of hip hop are difficult to record precisely.[51] And while my focus is on African American youth, hip hop has never been an exclusively "black thing." Many of the creative elements of hip hop developed in correspondence with the postwar migrations and subsequent shifting racial geography of New York City. The interaction between Latino, Afro-Caribbean, and African American expressive cultures established the conditions for the development of alternative modes of youth expression.[52]

The evolution and transformation of hip hop are patterned by class, generational, and gender cleavages. These three markers of differentiation within the African American community make crucial imprints on black popular culture. According to cultural critic Todd Boyd, the most recent generational shifts in black popular culture came into view with the passing of what he refers to as the ideology of the race man, animated best by Bill Cosby.[53] This particular period of black cultural production, Boyd contends, reflected the views and aspirations of a generation concerned with civil rights, assimilation, and the production of what are often alluded to as respectable or "positive" images of black Americans. Further, Boyd maintains that a new black popular culture sensibility—the new black aesthetic (NBA)—supplanted the race man ideology sometime during the middle to late 1980s. This particular generation of black cultural producers—he uses Spike Lee and Wynton Marsalis as illustrations—came of age after the protests of the 1960s and represented the first creative community of African Americans to benefit from the resources and networks made available because of greater access to higher education. This generation practiced a black American version of bourgeois nationalism that emphasized the infiltration of mainstream institutions. These two periods or regimes of cultural politics were informed by a middle-class sensibility that distinguishes them from the most recent generational shift in black popular culture—a shift that is related to the ascendancy of hip hop as a leading signifier of black culture.

Whereas the first two periods are shaped by middle-class priorities and notions of assimilation and respectability (the Cosby era) and new conceptions of black-style politics and upward mobility (the new black aesthetic), the succeeding shift identified by Boyd is governed by a hard-core ghetto sensibility that represents a radical break. This particular generation eschews both the comportment of social acceptability and the racial chic of neo–black nationalist politics. More specifically, Boyd argues that the emergence of hard-core ghetto iconography altered the orbit of black popular culture and is representative of working-class definitions of blackness that contest bourgeois-inflected definitions. While the transitions and breaks that distinguish one period from the other are never total, Boyd's analysis does help to further elucidate class differentiation within the African American community and its implications for a varied terrain of cultural politics and production.

The issue of gender is equally important. While it is true that hip hop is shaped by narratives that emphasize male hegemony, pleasure, and desire, it is important to emphasize that female cultural practices also inflect this particular movement. In her analysis of black youth culture, Tricia Rose maintains that most academic and popular discourses tend to marginalize the presence and contributions of women to hip hop. The presence of females has been integral if not always adequately recognized. Although the commercial media landscape is overwhelmingly dominated by men, women continue to forge new territories for their active involvement and pleasure. The hip hop scene is no different. Indeed, as many female authors point out, women have long struggled to gain access to and control over the resources and sites that animate the production of hip hop culture.[54]

If hip hop is preeminently a generational discourse, it is also a historically specific formation that articulates with the shifting contours of the late twentieth century. The dominant themes expressed in hip hop develop their creative shape in relation to a social world in which new forms and sites of political antagonism proliferate. Romanticized descriptions of hip hop portray its emergence as an explicit reaction against the racially conservative policies of the Reagan presidency. However, the seeds of this movement were planted much earlier. The elaboration of hip hop preceded the Reagan years; in fact, the movement began to blossom in the mid- to late 1970s.[55] The creators of hip hop devoted immense energy to carving out spaces of pleasure and recreation in the face of an eroding urban infrastructure devastated by a diminishing tax base, decaying public schools and parks, drugs, and political retreat from the redistributive policies born from the civil rights era.[56] Hip hop began in public parks, on street corners, in subway terminals, and in apartment basements. It soon moved to community centers, dance clubs, radio airwaves, and later the visual media—music video, television, and cinema—thus accentuating what analysts claim is one of the central themes in the movement: the struggle over public space, who occupies it, and how its resources are put to use.

Yet it is the subsequent role of technology and the commodification of hip hop, more than anything else, that continues to drive and animate provocative debates about the relationship between youth, cultural production, and commercial media culture. Does the intrusion of technology and commodification—most notably, the mass production, distribution, and merchandising of rap music—conspire to dull the oppositional edges of hip hop? Moreover, is the participation of black youth in the popular cultural economy a legitimate expression of opposition? These questions, of course, rekindle debates about the capacity of commercial culture to contain oppositional cultural practices. But rather than view technology and commercial culture as resources that prohibit creative action, I would like to invert this idea and consider an alternative proposition instead: How do technology and commercial culture enable new repertoires of black youth agency and cultural production?

The use of technology to produce media cultural products was viewed by the early critics of commercial culture as an indication that mass production would enforce standardization and stifle creativity.[57] But technological innovations in the production of popular music, for example, facilitate the opposite effect: creativity has flourished, and new musical styles and genres continue to thrive.[58] Yet technology only provides the possibility for new practices to take shape; individuals adopt a technology and use it in creative ways that lead to new cultural formations. In the case of rap music production, digital technology, sampling machines, multitrack recording devices, and video forge new creative frontiers for "fresh" innovations and formations of youth culture.[59] The innovation of rap music production suggests that technology does not manipulate individuals but rather that individuals adopt and manipulate technology to accommodate their intentions.

Furthermore, the intersection of hip hop and technology vividly illustrates what Michael Schudson calls the integrative effects of mass-mediated culture on modern societies.[60] The electronic dissemination of hip hop has proved to be powerfully integrative. By that, I mean it has established the conditions for mobilizing a youth culture that is rapidly becoming global in scope as it connects youth from disparate conditions and places. For example, it would be impossible to make reference to the "hip hop nation" without the broadcasting capabilities of media technology. One of the most impressive attributes of the electronic media is their capacity to connect people and organize collective identities despite physical distance.[61] The communications media enable new forms of access to and association among communities that transcend geographical boundaries. The growth and spread of hip hop culture are an illustrative example.

While its origins in the United States are typically traced back to the urban polyglot of postindustrial New York City, the hip hop movement has expanded far beyond the local youth cultures of its social and geographical base. The electronic dissemination of hip hop multiplies its constituency, complicates its articulations, and serves as the primary circuit through which youth have been able to produce an expanding sphere of influence within the rapidly evolving global media village. To be sure, the hip hop nation is an "imagined community."[62] But as Schudson points out, all communities are fictive in the sense that "personal identification with any grouping of people beyond those one encounters face to face in daily life depends on an imagined leap."[63] So while black youth in New York City, Mexican American youth in East Los Angeles, and black youth in Brixton, London, do not literally know each other, the various media technologies—music, video, film, print, and cyberspace—allow them to communicate, interact, and create new collective identities. In addition, it is the increasing prowess of media technology through which youth have been able to mobilize competing discourses about the varied social, economic, and political currents that continue to alter their lives. Hip hop, then, develops both local and global particularities that build a broad terrain for youth production and discourse.[64]

Whereas early critics of "mass" media culture viewed technology as stifling creativity and encouraging passivity, they were even less optimistic about the effects of commodification on culture. The diffusion of hip hop throughout the different spheres of commercial culture is commonly viewed as undermining the authenticity of this youth practice. For example, it is common to see the sartorial styles made popular in hip hop merchandised and packaged in suburban shopping malls. The contention, however, that commercial culture subverts the intentions and resistive qualities of hip hop is, at best, misguided. Tricia Rose insists that this critique obscures the fact that many of the original participants in hip hop (i.e., break dancers, rappers, disc jockeys) were in fact concerned with monetary compensation for their creative labor. Further, she makes the crucial point that "the contexts for creation in hip hop were never fully outside or in opposition to commodities, they involved struggles over public spaces and access to commodified materials, equipments, and products of economic viability."[65] Still, it must be acknowledged that, as the popularity and profits of hip hop soared, the rap industry has changed substantially. The major shift, according to Rose, is not that hip hop suddenly became commercial but rather that "control over the scope and direction of the profit making process"[66] has shifted from local black and Latino entrepreneurs to the major media and entertainment industries.

The corporatization of hip hop is undeniable. Since its popularization in the early 1980s, the profits of hip hop–related products have increased exponentially. As a result, the linkage of corporate strategies and marketing techniques with the expressive cultures of black youth undeniably alters the trajectory of hip hop. But the corporatization of hip hop reflects a more general trend toward the global spread of consumer culture made possible by new media technologies, marketing techniques, distribution patterns, and a wider conception of consumer markets as well as potential profits. It is indeed difficult to imagine any aspect of cultural life that has not been influenced by corporate culture.[67] In the case of hip hop, then, what has taken place is the joining of an urban street and youth aesthetic with the technological resources and distribution muscle of corporate organizations.

But the corporatization of hip hop seems only to enliven rather than to stifle the struggle to control its commercial vigor. Similar to other subcultural practices, hip hop creates its own symbolic universe and commodities. Furthermore, hip hop has made more explicit the political nature of popular culture. When emergent cultural practices disrupt the social equilibrium, they usually provoke the dominant culture to take some kind of action as a means of maintaining order.[68] Dick Hebdige argues that the process of recuperation typically comes in the form of co-optation and commodification or labeling. I would like to discuss the former.

The commodification of rap produces paradoxical results. For instance, recognition by the music industry—the Grammy and American Music Awards—validates its place as an "official" genre of popular music and therefore stimulates production. But commodification also domesticates and defuses rap of some of its subversive energy. Once distributed on a mass scale, rap is packaged and made more palatable, rendered at once a consumable good and profitable merchandise. But is commodification simply a form of containment? In other words, does the packaging of hip hop erode its oppositional possibilities? While it is true that the transformation of hip hop into a vast assortment of commodities alters its course, it is presumptuous to view commodification as the utter erasure of black youth agency and cultural politics. For as Hebdige points out:

> [T]he relationship between the spectacular subculture
> and the various industries which service and exploit it
> is notoriously ambiguous. After all, such a subculture
> is concerned first and foremost with consumption. . . .

> It communicates through commodities even if the
> meanings attached to those commodities are purpose-
> fully distorted or overthrown. It is therefore difficult in
> this case to maintain any absolute distinction between
> commercial exploitation on the one hand and crea-
> tivity/originality on the other, even though these cate-
> gories are emphatically opposed in the value systems
> of most subcultures.[69]

It would be a mistake to assume that black youth have been idle in, or even resistant to, efforts to merchandise hip hop. For as historian Robin D. G. Kelley reminds us, black youth meticulously hone their expressive cultures and forms of play and leisure into income-generating practices.[70] Few today understand the exuberant and sometimes subtle ways in which black youth maneuver to exploit a cultural marketplace that generates a seemingly endless flow of commodities produced to satisfy changing consumer desires and tastes. One of the most striking ironies of late twentieth-century capitalism is the simultaneous structural and economic displacement of black youth along with the emergence of a voracious appetite for the cultural performances and products created by them. In the process, some black youth have been able to translate their creative labor into social and economic mobility as they carve out small entrepreneurial enclaves while still practicing, in their unique way, "small acts" of opposition.

Dipannita Basu sharply illuminates this point in her observation of Los Angeles's hip hop community.[71] Basu asserts that participation in commercial culture by black youth is *not* a sign of surrender to the re-cuperative powers of capitalism but is instead a crucial element in their attempt to counter some of its most crippling effects. In fact, many youth do not view association with the popular culture industry as a form of "selling out." In her discussion of the burgeoning rap industry in Los Angeles, Basu writes: "[R]ap music has given a substantial number of black youth a world view, a political philosophy, a language, and life-styles that have in turn become the articulating principles for economic activity, from creativity to business, from music to films, magazines, clothing, and a whole host of auxiliary positions."[72]

Admittedly, it is difficult to imagine that striving for and achieving economic success in a capitalist society are oppositional. Such practices are typically viewed as complying with rather than subverting the dominant priorities of capital accumulation. But as Basu claims, black

71

youth do not see a contradiction in their efforts to "get paid" and simultaneously contest the institutional practices that severely limit their prospects for social and economic mobility. No action or gesture is inherently oppositional. Social context determines the extent to which practices develop oppositional characteristics. The potential economic benefits and prestige associated with rap music production are viewed as a direct challenge to a social and economic structure that is becoming increasingly impenetrable for a number of black youth. From the perspectives of black youth, then, the production of popular commodities and economic success belie the widespread belief that they are criminal-minded and lack industriousness, intelligence, and a commitment to work.[73] So even though black youth turn their symbolic practices and creative skills into work that reproduces the master ideal of capital accumulation (a principle that historically works to their disadvantage), it is work that enables some to escape the serial employment and menial labor widely regarded as humiliating, stigmatizing, and oppressive.[74]

Angela McRobbie has described youth subcultures as practices that are both productive and empowering. According to McRobbie, the styles and commodities created by youth do more than just publicize subcultures. These practices also provide opportunity for cultivating skills that can be utilized to provide access to substantive employment or even self-employment. She writes: "[T]his involvement can be an empowering experience, particularly for young people with no access to the skills and qualifications acquired as a matter of course by those other young people destined for university and for the professions. Subcultures are often ways of creating job opportunities as more traditional careers disappear. In this undocumented, unrecorded and largely 'hidden economy' sector, subcultures stand at one end of the culture industry spectrum and the glamorous world of the star system and the entertainment business at the other."[75] To the degree that hip hop has produced an alternative economy that provides the resources and opportunities for black youth to exert their own creative energies and also realize their entrepreneurial ambitions, it can be viewed as a formation that enlivens rather than subverts the ability of youth to more effectively negotiate social and economic deprivation.

Consequently, rather than challenge the legitimacy of capitalism, black youth confront a more immediate problem—how to turn the contradictory contours of capitalism to their advantage. The strategic movement of black youth into commercial culture does not intend to destroy a flourishing information and entertainment economy. On the contrary, their skillful interventions drive the production and commodification of cultural products. Still, while it is true that they do not seek to subvert the notion of capital accumulation, black youth do seek to play a more substantial role in the rapidly expanding frontier of communications media and information technology. Describing this distinctive generational ethos, journalist Kevin Powell writes: "[T]he hip hop nation is no different than any other segment of this society in its desire to live the American dream. Hip hop, for better or for worse, has been this generation's most prominent means for making good on the long promises of the civil rights movement."[76] Black youth maneuver to exploit those emergent spaces that are opening up in the new information economy. And in the process of struggling for that space, black youth continue to shape the popular cultural world in which we all live.

It should also be noted that while some hip hop purists claim that commodification erodes the subversive demeanor and style of hip hop, the youth culture did not develop explicitly political expressions until after the road to commercial success had been paved. In truth, the earliest rap recordings were mostly first-person narratives that boasted about the acquisition of status-conferring objects: jewelry, designer clothing, and women. And though narratives that portrayed women as sources of heterosexual male pleasure were certainly political, they did not embody the counterideological themes that would later be labeled "message rap."[77] The production of message rap developed as the rap genre was becoming commercial. Indeed, the arrival of rap groups like Public Enemy in the late 1980s signaled a decisive turn in the politicization of rap lyrics. Thus, it is quite possible to argue that by enlarging the creative terrain of rap production, commodification, ironically, forged open spaces that now include styles and performances that nourish rather than impoverish resistive discourses.

Yet we must also bear in mind that black youth are operating on historical terrain clearly not of their own making. Moreover, the sphere of popular media culture is only one of numerous sites where the struggle for hegemony is waged. Additionally, the transformative powers of each site differ. For example, the symbolic efficacy of holding a political office (Newt Gingrich) versus occupying a niche in the arena of popular music production (Ice Cube) differs in kind and extent. Therefore, it must be acknowledged that the potency of black youth intervention on the field of popular culture has serious limitations for effecting social change. Still, it must also be noted that oppositional practices come in different guises and are governed by different intentions. Black youth are acutely aware of the social world they inhabit and that current structural arrangements produce limited opportunities for their generation. This particular formation of black youth culture is, then, a strategic attempt to make use of the fissures produced by social, economic, and technological change.

So while it is true that hip hop did not originate as an explicit critique of the rising tide of racial conservatism, its growth, evolution, and multiple deployments illustrate how the cultural politics, moods, energies, and lived experiences of everyday life provide black youth with the resources and imaginative capacities to respond creatively to material and symbolic domination. The evolution of hip hop teaches us, as cultural critic Michael Dyson writes, "that history is made in unexpected ways, by unexpected people with unexpected results."[78] As youth continue to recreate hip hop, they also continue to penetrate and shape the popular media cultures, which are becoming global in scope. In fact, hip hop has generated a broad range of cultural products that enlarge its creative community and sphere of influence. The diffusion of hip hop throughout mainstream culture has led to the creation of new independent record labels, magazines, television programs, and advertising campaigns.[79] More important, the success and spread of hip hop culture have forged open productive spaces for young cultural producers beyond the field of popular music. In the following chapters, I consider a distinct sphere of cultural production that has been significantly altered by hip hop: black American filmmaking.

Like their contemporaries in the production of rap music, black filmmakers attempt to exercise similar modes of agency and intervention in the intensely mobile world of information technology. Whereas the producers of rap attempt to manipulate the new technologies and distribution systems that govern popular music production, filmmakers, in like fashion, attempt to manipulate the new technologies and distribution systems that govern popular film production. But because commercial film is a more expensive arena of production, breaking through industry barriers is a far more formidable task. Besides, the commercial film industry is extremely insular, and practices of nepotism and cronyism are customary. The producers of commercial film tend to constitute a closed inner circle whose members are constantly recycled within the industry. Commercial film is a profession that requires specialized training, large sums of capital, and expensive equipment. Discussing the costs involved in film production, Robert Withers writes: "Perhaps only architecture can begin to rival it in the amount of capital required for production, and in the potential demand for laborers. The high cost of filmmaking has always placed limitations on the kind of work filmmakers could do, and the financial risk involved has consistently affected the relationship between producers and audiences. . . . Because of its high cost, film production is generally controlled or influenced by those powers in a society that command financial resources and determine how products are distributed." [80]

It is perhaps the high cost of film production that, historically, has limited the effective participation of African American filmmakers. However, for a select group of African American filmmakers, the transformation of the popular cultural landscape and the popularization of black youth expressive cultures changed the prospects for their own filmmaking careers.

Also, the production of black cinema is driven by the constant search for new consumer markets and expressive cultures to exploit. Historically conditioned opportunities in the production of popular film create productive spaces for the post–civil rights generation of African Americans that did not exist for previous generations. This is not to suggest that African Americans have never participated in the production of film but rather that the combination of a new film industry landscape, a changing cultural marketplace, and a more vibrant black culture industry establishes a creative environment in which the film narratives created by African American filmmakers attain greater commercial value. These particular arrangements work to give a small group of African American filmmakers a precarious niche along the production hierarchy of commercial film. [81]

The creation of popular cultural movements like hip hop suggests that black youth struggle to mobilize their own meanings about and representations of societal change. George Lipsitz argues that the emergence of new cultural producers and popular movements is made possible by the very economic shifts that also produce historically distinct forms of social and economic inequality: flexible accumulation. [82] It is crucial to point out, however, that the new formations in capitalism and the global spread of communications media do not intentionally produce new popular movements or expressive cultures. Rather, the new economic regimes, media technologies, and popular culture economy provide the resources and opportunities that make it possible for new symbolic practices to be created by historically situated cultural producers. The immediate challenge, then, is to further examine how the new mediascape enables black youth to creatively intervene in the making of the larger popular cultural universe.

3 Black Cinema and the Changing Landscape of Industrial Image Making

They claim that we are products from hell, but the Black is back, and it's bound to sell!

PUBLIC ENEMY[1]

The expression above by rap's most influential group in the late 1980s il-luminates the dramatic shifts that characterize the relationship between African American youth, the popular culture industry, and American society. The "Black is back" claim suggests that blackness, a socially ar-ticulated identity, has returned from a redefined status. The expression, much like the overall fervor of black youth popular cultures, is dialogi-cally related to the controlling discourses that seek to both discipline and demonize black youth. Additionally, the assertion "it's bound to sell" implies not only that black has returned but that it is also popular, dynamic, and marketable! Public Enemy's boastful declaration points, in numerous ways, to the changing universe of industrial image making and, more distinctly, to the shifts that establish historically specific conditions for the commodification of media products, performances, and services generated from the creative community of black American youth.

To be sure, any rigorous examination of the media products created by African Americans must locate these practices within the shifting context of more flexible regimes of cultural production. Moreover, this requires developing an appreciation for how shifts in the production of film specifically and the culture industry more generally create spaces for black cinema. The "mass culture" and "mass society" approaches to studying popular media culture fail to aptly describe the late twentieth-century mediascape. Rather than viewing the film, television, and music-recording industries as uniform enterprises, it is necessary to understand how each develops specific organizational characteristics and different creative environments for the individuals working within the respec-tive industries.[2] For example, the film industry has a production history and creative context that are quite distinct from those of the popular music industry. In many ways, the survival of the film industry has depended greatly upon its ability to reinvigorate theatrical film-going in the face of stiff competition from other forms of recreation and entertainment; adapt to and, when possible, integrate new technologies and information/media services into its production and marketing design; and control the escalating costs of film production.

though advanced capitalist societies like the United States are currently undergoing vast economic reorganization—capital flight, deindustrialization, and corporate downsizing—that generate acute middle-class anxieties and downward mobility, other aspects of the global economy are marked by unprecedented growth and prosperity. Indeed, one undisputed growth industry in the U.S. economy over the last two decades is the sphere of communications media technology. The widespread adoption of new information technologies—fiber optics, personal computing/Internet, satellite communication—invigorates the transition to a service and information-oriented economy. And in the process, new modes of cultural production and innovation, and new delivery systems, create a vast new world of possibilities in the production, distribution, and consumption of media commodities. As a result, the business of entertainment continues to grow and evolve in ways that are seldom anticipated by media analysts or executives. In fact, due to the continued development of new information technologies and multimedia services, the landscape of popular media entertainment is in a state of virtually constant evolution.

But ironic fissures also correspond with the profound changes made possible by the growth of the communications media and information economy. Take, for example, the globalization of communications media. On the one hand, globalization intensifies the concentration of media ownership and consequently makes corporate control over the production and distribution of discourse and information seemingly stronger. Indeed, the trend toward megamergers and acquisitions creates enormous multimedia conglomerates able to exercise tremendous influence across the various media technologies.[3] But the global expansion of media also complicates the production of cultural discourses, harnessing oppositional currents that struggle to work within the structures of corporate hegemony. The globalization of popular media cultures, then, does not simply create the opportunity for economic and political elites to exploit new markets or disseminate more widely a "ruling ideology"; it also facilitates new forms of expression and creative intervention from the social and political margins.

So rather than view the growth of communications media technology as only invigorating dominant discourses, it is important to understand how the ever-expanding universe of communications media creates spaces for the invigoration of resistive discourses, too. While questions of greater media concentration are indeed important, they should not, however, obscure questions related to access. In advanced capitalist societies, those who manage media resources or function as content providers typically do not own the organizations that supply the capital and distribution muscle for the various media products. This fact, to be sure, is one of the primary developments in modern capitalist societies that continues to confound, for example, claims like the ruling class/ruling ideology proposition. The production of black cinema is a good example.

Starting with the success of Spike Lee's *She's Gotta Have It* in 1986, black American–directed cinema reemerged as a popular commodity in spite of Hollywood's exclusionary filmmaking culture. One of the tendencies of the popular media industry is to exploit popular movements once they become both identifiable and amenable to merchandising. After years of neglect, African American filmmakers suddenly became "players" within the industry. For black filmmakers, the opportunity to collaborate with Hollywood studios was a welcome change because it guaranteed access to financing and moderately wide distribution deals. In 1991, the substantial increase in the number of feature-length theatrical releases in which African Americans worked as either director, writer, or producer was touted as a major breakthrough in the commercial film industry.[4] In spite of all the celebration, the substantial increase was in reality a blip on the larger filmmaking landscape. During the period 1986–91, the film industry released an average of 443 films per year. In fact, the number of theatrical releases directed by African Americans in 1991 represented roughly 5 percent of the film industry's total output that year.

The production of black films must be examined within the context of a moviemaking industry that is constantly shifting its production strategies in order to remain viable. In this chapter, I closely consider important shifts in the production of popular film. How has the shift from the studio era (a period in which distributors of film were devoted exclusively to film production) to the era of corporate and conglomerate ownership (a period in which film distribution is one of many commercial services performed) altered the organizational context of popular film production? Similar to other culture industries, the film industry has adopted more specialized production techniques. Diana Crane argues that, prior to the 1960s, the number of organizations disseminating media product on a mass scale was relatively small.[5] Cultural production in this context was characterized by standardization, rigidity, and limited competition. In addition, production strategies were predicated on social and cultural homogeneity—more precisely, targeting a "mass" and mostly undifferentiated audience. Crane contends that, as the number of organizations disseminating cultural products on a mass scale increases, this also creates opportunities for greater content and product differentiation. In more recent decades, the context for the production of popular media products has been characterized by differentiation, flexibility, and intense competition. In today's cultural marketplace, production strategies are predicated on social and cultural difference, which results in the targeting of specialized audiences.

Furthermore, the expansion of the popular media culture industry and consumer culture creates openings for new entrepreneurs and innovators of cultural products to flourish. Mike Featherstone maintains that structural changes in the culture industries have "necessarily led to some declassification and demonopolization of the power of the defenders of the long established symbolic hierarchies in artistic, intellectual, and academic institutions."[6] And so while social conservatives continue to villainize the media industry and selective members of its creative community, their attempt to regulate the production, dissemination, and consumption of popular media culture is severely limited by the new cultural practices fashioned to articulate the "cultural politics of difference" in more creative and emphatic ways.[7] The emergent regimes of cultural production enable social actors to mobilize popular movements and cultures that facilitate new modes of intervention in the reproduction of society.

So before discussing black filmmaking specifically, it is necessary to address some of the shifts in the production of popular film that created the conditions for its deployment. The arrival of filmmakers like Matty Rich, Leslie Harris, or Spike Lee on the commercial film stage was not simply based on their talent or cinematic vision; it was also made possible by the conditions and processes that continue to transform the industrial image-making landscape in general and the production of film specifically. The cinema is a high-risk industry that has developed flexible production strategies in order to maintain a competitive edge in a burgeoning consumer culture saturated with a seemingly endless stream of popular media products.

The Big Picture: Flexible Accumulation and the Formation of the New Hollywood

The movies are a business enterprise which is governed by the primary goal of all businesses: making money. The unpredictability of the future preferences of moviegoers, however makes a business subject to much more risk than many other industries. . . . As innovations are introduced and the environment changes, the "landscape" of the industry adapts, with the "chameleonlike" majors managing to maintain their dominance in the marketplace.
      GARTH JOWETT AND JAMES LINTON; S8

Sociologists interested in studying popular media culture avoid evaluative debates on its aesthetic worth or ideological operations and choose instead to examine media as a manufactured object produced in and by social organizations.[9] As a result, sociological studies of media directed their critical gaze toward examining the organizational systems, gatekeeping processes, and economic/marketplace considerations that facilitate the production of popular media products. The availability of cultural goods to the public depends largely on the market structure and organizational environment of *specific industries.* As a result, cultural production cannot be reduced to the preferences of either mass audiences or individual producers. The organizations and individuals who create cultural products must constantly battle the uncertainty of market structures. In fact, new patterns of consumption, shifts in public mood, and newly arising popular movements keep the producers of popular culture uncertain and constantly guessing about what it is that consumers will both prefer and patronize. Because the production of film is such an expensive enterprise, the industry is especially sensitive to technological, social, and economic change.

For much of its early history, the production of film operated under the rigidities of the classical Hollywood system, typically referred to as the "studio era." This system was dominated by powerful individuals who controlled virtually all phases of production. Moreover, as Los

Angeles became the filmmaking capital of the world, it also evolved into an exclusive sphere of cultural production that restricted access to the technological expertise, material resources, and networks necessary to participate in the culture of filmmaking. The studio era is often regarded as the most notorious regime of popular film production.[10] Filmmaking under the guidance of this production regime resembled the assembly-line techniques that characterized much of early industrial capitalism. The directors, writers, performers, and technicians, for example, were hired by studio moguls to make specific types of movies. Some of the salient features of this system included long-term contractual agreements, stringently enforced genre conventions, and the rigid typecasting of performers. In addition, several studios became associated with certain filmic styles and genres.[11]

But the popular film industry has always been marked by instability and change. According to film historian David Bordwell, the Hollywood mode of production began showing signs of change as early as the 1930s.[12] The shift to more advanced forms of capital accumulation and organization played a central role in the restructuring of the film industry. Bordwell contends that shifts in the modus operandi of capitalism strengthened rather than loosened previous organizational structures by reasserting the hierarchies of management. This reinforced the extensive control of the management hierarchy, particularly the power wielded by tactical experts whose knowledge of the technology and work process placed the production of popular film in their control. In the 1930s, the organization of the film industry shifted from the studio model to the production-unit system. This form of management control usually placed a small group of men in charge of supervising six to eight films per year. Film supervision included assigning the writers, director, and actors. In addition, each individual focused on a specific genre, leading to both organizational and creative rigidity.

A major blow to the dominance of the studio system was the antitrust suit that forced the major film companies to divest themselves of exhibition activities. Prior to 1948, the majors owned both the films and the theater exhibition sites, thus creating full vertical integration and eliminating any significant competition in the production, distribution, and exhibition of films. As Robert Strick writes, "[T]he Paramount case opened distribution and exhibition channels to independent producers by prohibiting such practices as 'block booking,' collusion by distributors on clearance and run, zone arrangements[,] . . . discriminatory pricing arrangements, and fixing admission prices. It created a more competitive market in both production and exhibition."[13]

Further, by the 1950s, signs of an industry in a state of flux and transition became evident as the majors began a long and arduous process of reinventing and repositioning themselves in the business of media entertainment. The film industry's adoption of more flexible production strategies was a necessary response to social change forces that were beyond the control of popular film executives: population shifts, especially suburbanization; changing recreational habits and patterns of consumption; and particularly, intense competition with television. Prior to the impact of television, other social changes were beginning to erode the cultural and economic hegemony of the film industry. Soon after World War II, the film industry was devastated by a recession that lasted for ten years.[14] During this period, movie attendance decreased by half, a large number of theaters closed, and industry profits dropped precipitously. The postwar recession in movie profits was caused, in large part, by white out-migration to the suburbs and the baby boom, which focused consumer spending on family-oriented products like home ownership, appliances, and automobiles. Residing in communities away from the downtown-centered location of most movie houses, suburbanites began to develop consumer habits that focused on new leisure activities.

The ascendancy of television as the primary source of popular media entertainment weakened the industry even further. The availability of television created new patterns of movie attendance. The changes in consumption forced the film industry to seek out and satisfy specific tastes and locate more specialized audiences.[15] Rather than continue a system committed to long-term production, fixed costs, and structural rigidity, film companies shifted instead to more flexible modes of productivity. Because television is generally considered "free" entertainment, film content had to differentiate itself from the "safe" programming logic of television. From the beginning, the film industry had always raised the suspicions of moral entrepreneurs committed to regulating sexual desire, social behavior, and gender boundaries.[16] However, the loosening of strict production codes and the implementation of a new rating system in 1966 broadened the subject matter explorable in mainstream filmic discourse and also established greater product differentiation from television by placing a greater emphasis on sexual and violent imagery especially. Thus, the film industry was able to reinvent itself in large measure by swiftly adapting to changing social mores and values about sexuality and the human body, and emergent youth countercultural trends.

Organizational, economic, and social changes since the 1960s continue to restructure the production, distribution, and reception of popular film. Whereas the production context of commercial films was once dominated by film companies devoted exclusively to film production, filmmaking currently takes place within the organizational context of colossal corporate entities. Some film companies became part of conglomerates through mergers with larger corporations outside the culture industries, while other film companies created their own conglomerate organizations through diversification.[17] The move toward conglomerate ownership allows film companies to diversify capital investments, thus expanding their financial resources while minimizing investment risks in film. This rise of conglomerates accelerated the demise of what remained of the studio system—an insular entity exclusively engaged in filmmaking—and introduced new hierarchical divisions in the film industry.

The new hierarchical arrangements replaced, for example, studio moguls with producers and directors as principal agents in the film production process. No longer restricted to long-term contractual agreements, filmmakers (i.e., producers, writers, directors) spend much of their time and energy "making deals" with film companies.[18] Box-office success allows filmmakers to select from and work with a number of different film distributors, thus creating greater independence and flexibility than was typical during the first few decades of film production. In sharp contrast to the studio era, the most successful producers and directors now roam as powerful "free agents," able to command vast resources (and salaries) from film distributors. Many movie projects are assembled now by producers who piece together all of the various elements necessary to make popular movies. In addition, film directors play a central role in each of the three phases of project development: preproduction, production, and postproduction. Unlike the studio era, directors are generally not hired with the expectation that they will carry out the cinematic vision of an industry mogul. The successful film director is both an artist and a politician.[19] While the management hierarchy has changed, film remains an intensely bureaucratic industry; hence, film directors must still negotiate studio obstacles in the filmmaking process by maneuvering in ways that maximize budgetary resources, creative control, and cooperation from studio executives in marketing their films.

The most tenacious problem facing the producers of popular media is the uncertainty of demand for cultural products.[20] And because of the high cost of film, market uncertainty is especially troublesome. As film studios have become integrated into larger corporate systems, one of the ways in which they combat market instability is by utilizing the skills of marketing specialists. This response to a vast and uncertain consumer market has also reconfigured the film production hierarchy: marketing specialists are accorded a strong and powerful management role in the production of popular film.[21] In fact, it is usually a team of marketing specialists who select and determine which films get financed, produced, and distributed, based essentially on their perceptions of audience desire and popular trends.

The principal goal of the marketing specialist is to determine if a demand—or more appropriately, a consumer market—exists for any film production under consideration. Marketing specialists, then, must deal with the constant pressure of market uncertainty caused by widespread variability in consumer taste preferences and desires, which often leads to unpredictable patterns of consumption.[22] The film industry has discovered that postwar patterns of moviegoing strongly suggest that people go to see specific movies movie rather than the movies in general. This was a marked shift from the prewar patterns of moviegoing, when attendance, especially before television, was a routine leisure activity. The industry relies on a broad array of sophisticated marketing techniques that are carefully employed to generate interest in a film and attract potential moviegoers to the theaters. For example, the industry historically has used the "star system" and technological innovations to stimulate moviegoing. However, recent strategies variously include more sophisticated consumer research instruments and data, merchandise promotions and tie-ins, press kits, television and newspaper advertising, popular music culture, and new technological achievements in computerization.[23]

The timing of a film's release is also an important consideration. The film industry knows, for example, that box-office receipts are most lucrative during certain periods throughout the year. Thus, deliberately calibrated release patterns are designed to take advantage of increased film attendance during the summer months and winter holiday season. Despite the attempt to harness the practice of scientific market research to the industry's ends, the sheer constancy of market uncertainty continues to make it extremely difficult to identify and select successful products. Most producers of popular film product admit that there is no science, no certain way, to guarantee that a movie will generate meaningful interest from moviegoers. As a result, the industry operates greatly on the theory of *precedence.* In other words, the films that are most likely to get produced tend to be based on what kinds of films have been most successful—that is, profitable—at the box office in the past.

An additional feature contributing to the change in the landscape of film production is the growth in exhibition sites. The expansion of exhibition outlets is driven by three factors: residential population shifts, new marketing strategies, and technological advances in communications media. One of the most definitive changes in the industry is the spread of the multiplex theater. Multiplex theaters are comprised of several minitheaters sharing a common main entrance, concession stand, washrooms, and projector booths. Multiplexes are able to house as many as sixteen theaters at one central location, thus broadening the space for movie exhibition.[24] In 1976, only 10 percent of the U.S. indoor theaters were of the multiplex variety. By the late 1980s, the vast majority of theaters were multiplexes.[25] Multiplexes quickly became new social arenas of fun and entertainment, adjusting to the unpredictable but steady growth of consumer culture. Most notably, multiplexes tend to be located near public spaces where people congregate to shop—especially consumer-oriented locations like shopping malls.[26]

The construction of multiplex exhibition sites is also influenced by post–World War II patterns of residential segregation: most of the new theaters are located in middle-class residential areas inhabited by college-educated and suburban families. Central to the motivation behind the multiplex phenomenon is the attempt by entrepreneurs in theater exhibition to recapture large portions of the audience lost during the apex of suburbanization.[27] But another film exhibition species is on the horizon, the megaplex.[28] These new theater complexes are even larger than their multiplex predecessors, and they also represent the move to add theme-park–like amenities to the moviegoing experience.

Furthermore, technological innovations in communications media drive the growth of ancillary markets like cable television, pay-per-view, and home video.[29] Indeed, the rise of ancillary markets has altered the production and box-office strategies practiced by film distributors. The growth of these markets produces additional outlets from which film distributors can generate revenue. Unlike the period that preceded the rise of the ancillary markets, the "life span" of a movie is more open-ended, consumable well after its theatrical run. Cable television and pay-per-view are especially attractive distribution outlets because film companies do not have to print several thousand copies for theater and home-video rentals. The growth of these markets gives film companies more flexibility and allows them to compete for consumers who prefer to view movies at home.

Finally, the production of commercial film has been significantly reshaped by the maturation of a more robust independent film movement. Traditionally, independent filmmaking has been characterized as any filmmaking activity—production, distribution, exhibition—that takes place outside the formal parameters of Hollywood. The lack of access to large sums of capital and distribution are the main factors that differentiate the independent filmmaking sector from Hollywood. Whereas the creative environment for a filmmaker working within a major film company is bolstered by the deep pockets of conglomerate ownership, an independent filmmaker, in contrast, generally works in a more impoverished environment. The independent filmmaker collects capital through a variety of alternative means: art grants, foundations, bank loans, private investors, and local fund-raising efforts. However, one of the benefits of the independent circuit is the elimination of corporate intrusion in the creative processes of filmmaking. Artistic control reduces the pressure to make films that are intensely formulaic in terms of both form and content. Because independent filmmakers generally do not have access to budgets that allow for elaborately designed action scenes and special effects, this environment tends to encourage greater narrative and filmic innovation.

The sphere of independent film production is not only more vigorous, it is also more organized. Dissatisfaction with the insularity, lack of creativity, and cost-prohibitiveness of Hollywood serves as a major impetus for developing alternative networks and organizations that support independent filmmaking. A variety of organizations at both the local and national level have been created to enhance film production and exhibition by independent filmmakers. Also, a varied menu of events like the Sundance Film Festival, the New York Film Festival, the Philadelphia Festival of World Cinema, and the Austin Gay and Lesbian Film Festival gives the independent film movement greater vitality and the work of independent filmmakers wider exposure.

There are a number of factors that interact to enliven the culture of independent filmmaking. For example, independent filmmakers benefit from better access to the equipment and technological expertise required to produce film. Film equipment can be rented, leased, or more easily purchased. Also, the improvements in technology and equipment allow higher-quality films to be made with lower budgets. Moreover, greater access to film training and expertise enlarges and enhances the independent filmmaking community. Film training during the studio era, for instance, was dominated by apprenticeship and nepotism, thus making it difficult to gain access to the technological and artistic expertise required to make film. Training for the film profession and the paths of entry into the field today are not as restricted. In fact, many colleges and universities offer film classes and degree programs, ranging from film history and criticism to film production. The widespread availability of film training in the United States prepares many aspiring filmmakers for entry into other film- and video-making industries that may not necessarily be associated with the mainstream film industry. Thus, many aspiring filmmakers cultivate their skills in less capital- and labor-intensive endeavors like music video and advertising. Widely available film training and exposure to more expressive modes of cinematic address invigorate the independent film movement by creating productive spaces for groups traditionally excluded from substantial participation in the production of film.

Finally, the cultivation of the independent film circuit and the enlarged sphere of exhibition venues also provide an entrepreneurial niche for independent distributors and film entrepreneurs.[30] Independent distributors, unlike the majors, focus *exclusively* on disseminating low-budget feature-length films. Independent distributors target specialized segments of the moviegoing population. A typical audience targeted by indies, for example, might include older, more discerning moviegoers.[31] But independent distributors may also exploit certain thematic trends or cult film genres that appeal to young moviegoers. Independent distributors incur lower costs, produce more nonformulaic films, and offer directors more creative control than the majors. Prior to the merger mania of the 1990s, independents did not belong to conglomerates; hence, they tended to be more vulnerable to periods of economic slowdown and fluctuating patterns of film attendance.[32] However, a recent wave of media mergers and the commercial and critical success of independent film companies have led to the purchase of independent distributors by corporate entertainment outfits interested in further diversifying their product offerings.[33]

The gap between the independent film circuit and Hollywood is gradually closing, due mainly to the flexibility of the latter. Shifts in popular culture trends force the producers of media products to seek out and service new spheres of consumption. Film historian Thomas Schatz writes that the New Hollywood produces basically three classes of movies: the blockbuster, the mainstream A-class star vehicle, and the low-cost independent/specialty film.[34] The "blockbuster mentality" compels film executives to seek out film projects that are much less expensive in order to exercise some degree of thrift and reduce financial risks. The specialty film fits this requirement precisely. In order to simultaneously increase output while minimizing expenditures, many of the major film companies frequently "pick up" or finance small-scale independent film projects.[35] This strategy facilitates greater product differentiation and enables swift adjustments to changing market demands and popular tastes. Over the last couple of decades, the major film distributors have relied on smaller independent film companies to create some of the product they distribute. In this scenario, the smaller independent film companies assemble the creative personnel, develop script and film content, and control much of the creative process, while the distributor usually supplies the capital. But in exchange for supplying capital, the studio often manages to assert some demands on the creative process, particularly as it relates to enforcing budgetary restrictions and monitoring potentially volatile content.

In general, the climate for making films has changed from the rigid days when studio moguls controlled all phases of production. Several factors have combined to transform the landscape of popular film production. The reorganization of the film industry takes shape within a global media environment in which change and volatility have become the norm. Indeed, the cultural landscape is marked by new patterns of consumption; intricate shifts in population demographics; and the development of new media systems and services like satellite television, ancillary markets, and Internet computing. In addition, the commercial film industry is altered by the growth of the independent film industry, which has been heartened by wider access to film training, new distribution and exhibition outlets, and the rise of second-tier film distributors. The film industry must continually adopt more flexible regimes of capital accumulation, organization, and production in order to remain competitive in a fiercely expanding cultural marketplace. Because of the high cost of film production, the film industry is especially vulnerable to market uncertainty, technological innovations, and downward economic trends. The industry must constantly reinvigorate theatrical movie attendance by differentiating itself from its principal competitors, which include but are not limited to network and cable television. Finally, the expansion of consumer culture demands seeking out untapped niches of consumption. As a result, the culture industries have been forced to develop a more differentiated conception of their prospective audiences and the kinds of product offerings they make available to them. It is, then, within this context that we can account for and understand the changing social and organizational currents that create fissures for the production of specialty films like "black cinema."

The New Hollywood and the Production of Black Cinema

If within the next thirty years, America is going to be predominantly a nation of color, then white studio executives had better begin to understand who their consumer is going to be.

WARRINGTON HUDLIN[36]

Historically, both film and television have denied African Americans substantive participation as producers and content providers.[37] Whereas much of television's early commercial history was dominated by the three major networks, fissures in the production of film have enabled African Americans to establish a filmmaking practice that functioned apart from the mainstream industry.[38] So while the principal focus of this study is on the post-1986 formations of African American filmmaking in the arena of commercial cinema, I do not want to suggest that this is the only period of distinction. In fact, black filmmaking practices in the United States have a rich and diverse history.

The production of black cinema corresponds with historically specific social, economic, political, and cultural currents. For African Americans, a number of barriers have limited their access to both the material resources and the technological expertise required for full participation in the industry. Despite these barriers, however, African Americans have long understood the significance and power of cinema as a popular medium of communication and entertainment and consequently have fought diligently to carve out a distinct and relevant cinematic practice. Dating as far back as the early 1900s, when a group of African

Americans collectively mobilized their resources in order to respond to D. W. Griffith's *Birth of a Nation,* efforts to play a meaningful role in the production of popular film have been marked by struggle and historically specific circumstances.[39] It is possible, for example, to discuss at least four distinct formations of African American filmmaking that can be determined to have a particular identity, set of characteristics, and historically situated intentions: race movies, blaxploitation, independent filmmaking, and the independent/commercial trend, which is my primary focus.

Race Movies

The earliest formations of a black American filmmaking practice began to take shape during the opening decades of the twentieth century. Film historians and critics now refer to the movies made during this period as "race movies." Race movies were made specifically for emergent black urban audiences.[40] The great black migrations dramatically reconfigured the American social, political, and cultural landscape. In due course, the massive shift of black Americans from a rural to an urban-based population established the context for the creation and reception of new popular cultures, new consumption habits, and leisure activities for African Americans. Whereas the production of movies targeting black audiences signaled the growth of a black urban population, more important, it also signaled the ability of this group to financially support a small film industry. Starting in 1915 with the Lincoln Film Company, small black film companies began to appear in many heavily black-populated cities like Chicago and Philadelphia.[41]

One of the most celebrated filmmakers associated with this period is Oscar Micheaux. Micheaux worked in both the silent and sound eras. He was also one of the first to recognize that black movies could be entertainment vehicles for a mass black audience.[42] As a result, he often engaged in extensive promotional campaigns to attract sizable audiences for his films. Well before Melvin Van Peebles and Spike Lee arrived on the film industry scene, Micheaux realized that the volatility of race and racism could make for both compelling and entertaining film content and also attract the interests of potential filmgoers. In reality, Micheaux was probably more entrepreneur than filmmaker. Like many black businessmen and -women during the first half of the twentieth century, Micheaux responded creatively to the rigid enforcement of racial segregation.[43] Black entrepreneurs sought ways to exploit segregation by creating businesses that catered specifically to African Americans, who were prohibited from routine participation in American cultural life.

The full vertical integration practiced by the major Hollywood studios eliminated any serious competition in exhibition, so producers of race movies often had to screen their films in second-tier theaters, lodges, churches, and private homes. And since there was no formal distribution system to disseminate and exhibit their work, many of the filmmakers carried their movies from city to city in order to gain access to potential moviegoers. In many ways, race movies represent an important cultural and political response to the presence of segregation—de facto in the North and de jure in the South. Prior to 1965, blacks were not welcome in mainstream movie theaters. Public spaces and accommodations were rigidly governed by segregation. In fact, up until the 1960s, three patterns of segregation influenced black moviegoing practices and facilitated the production of race movies: black-only theater houses, segregation by time, and segregation by seating.[44] Segregation assured the producers of race movies a limited, but identifiable audience.

While the bulk of these films have been heavily criticized for their mimicry of Hollywood film genres, technological inferiority, compliance with bourgeoisie values, and perpetuation of the color-caste politics of the era, race movies mark the origins of a cinematic practice controlled, partially, by African Americans.[45] And while the production of race movies took place completely outside the parameters of Hollywood, it also involved black and white cooperation. Ironically, the demise of this era of black filmmaking was accelerated by the burgeoning civil rights movement: a philosophical shift that emphasized integration and assimilation rather than economic development as the way to achieve racial equality. The civil rights movement employed a number of different protest strategies in its efforts to challenge legalized segregation. The discriminatory practices of movie theaters were also targeted. Throughout the 1950s and 1960s, organized social movements began to challenge segregation laws directly. By the mid-1960s, civil rights legislation legally prohibited theater owners from restricting attendance and seating patterns on the basis of race. According to film historian Thomas Cripps, race movies were trapped by the waning of antebellum racial customs.[46] Blacks and liberal whites alike viewed the production of race movies as reproductive of the racial inequities targeted by their protest efforts.

Another factor that contributed to the decline of race movies was the production of Hollywood films featuring African Americans. The bulk of these films fit the musical variety that specialized in showcasing black musical, singing, and dancing talents.[47] Moreover, the production of Hollywood theatrical releases that featured black entertainers reflects a general shift toward more diversification in the types of movies Hollywood was beginning to distribute. The industry was able to adjust to a changing commercial culture landscape by appealing to audiences across racial groups. The cultivation of black celebrities (i.e., Harry Belafonte, Dorothy Dandridge, and Sidney Poitier), elaborate sets, and new technologies (color and sound, especially) began to attract large numbers of black moviegoers.

Blaxploitation

Between 1969 and 1974, the popular film industry produced over sixty or so action-oriented films that featured African Americans. Commonly referred to as the blaxploitation era, this particular period in American film history has its own distinctive set of characteristics. These films are harshly criticized for their intensely narrow representation of African Americans, technological inferiority, and formulaic structure. Ironically, this black film boom was energized by two creative pieces of African American film work: Gordon Parks's *The Learning Tree* (1969) and Melvin Van Peebles's controversial maverick film *Sweet Sweetback's Baadasssss Song* (1971). These two films introduced to Hollywood the notion that black-theme movie product could generate respectable box-office revenue and also signaled the importance of black patronage to the film industry. Yet even though this particular wave of cheaply made movies targeted black audiences, the trend was largely controlled by white film executives and directors. In addition, industry production strategies imposed formulaic conventions in order to accelerate the production of genre remakes, of which the gangster/action movie was most profitable. Thematically, the films generally focused on a black hero/heroine who was strong enough to successfully fight off antagonists who threatened ghetto communities. As David E. James accurately points out, however:

> [T]he utility of that image was compromised and almost entirely countered by the displacement of attention away from the properly political analyses of the situation of Black people and from the possibilities of ameliorating it by systemic social change. By focusing the problem of the ghetto exclusively on local crimi-

93

nal issues, blaxploitation spoke directly to the everyday experience of its audience; but its generic conventions—the redress of wrong by the superhero vigilante
rather than by community control; the portrayal of
corruption as a police or Mafia aberration rather than
as endemic and structural; the backhanded glorifica-
tion of heavy drugs, prostitution, and other forms of
self-destruction that sublimated resentment rather
than channeling it in socially useful directions; and a
chauvinist, macho anti-intellectualism—allowed for a
vicarious release of anger in ways that threatened the
power and prejudice of neither the state nor its local
institutions.[48]

Blaxploitation filled a number of voids concurrently. For example,
social, cultural, and generational shifts within the African American
community generated momentum for the formation of new collective
racial identities articulated perhaps most vehemently by the militant
posturing of black power ideology. Dissatisfaction with nonviolent protest strategies, the slow pace of racial change, the deterioration of urban
communities heavily populated by African Americans, and the repopu-
larization of black nationalism created a "black awakening."[49] The emergence of a quasi-radicalized black protest movement, energized mainly
by a younger generation of African American leadership, began to articulate a more aggressive critique of American society, thus distancing
itself from the integrationist politics of the civil rights vanguard.[50] The
new assertive political posturing also gave birth to new-style politics (the
Afro) and conceptions of self ("Black is beautiful!") that began to transform the social production of black popular and expressive cultures.[51]

As film scholar Ed Guerrero meticulously argues, blaxploitation appealed to the new sensibilities made possible by this awakening.[52] The
concentration on black heroes defeating corrupt white police officials
and Mafia men, for example, undoubtedly appealed to a younger generation of African Americans, who experienced the frustrations of urban rebellions, police repression, and a heightened racial backlash. The
films also reflect both the gender and generational dimensions of this
awakening. As young African American male leadership began to question the efficacy of traditional civil rights leadership, it proposed in its
place a hypermasculinist form that privileged male leaders over female

leaders.[53] Arguably the most persistent problem in the blaxploitation film was the superstud characteristics used to code black masculinity.[54]

A second void filled by blaxploitation is more closely associated with the transitions that were beginning to force the popular film industry to undergo reorganization during this period. Between 1969 and 1971, the major film companies experienced huge financial losses.[55] For much of its history, the film industry has always had to make adjustments in order to keep pace with the rhythm of social, economic, and cultural change. The dramatic cultural and economic shifts that marked the 1960s and the 1970s provided new challenges and demanded new responses. The social and political conflicts of the period intensified generational cleavages. Youth rebellion was expressed in numerous ways, and the culture industry sought ways to exploit (and contain) its most exuberant manifestations.[56]

The mid- to latter part of the 1960s and early 1970s was a period of serious economic transition and uncertainty for the film industry as the realities of "white flight" from increasingly volatile cities altered the profile of moviegoers accessible to the owners of theaters located in many downtown districts. Demographic shifts in the population meant that theater owners had to appeal to a growing concentration of young, black, urban moviegoers.[57] Blaxploitation was, in part, a swift response to a changing racial geography and market that allowed the film industry to recoup some of its financial losses during this period of transition by shifting some of its resources to the production of films that targeted young black moviegoers.

The demise of the blaxploitation film wave is probably the result of pressures applied from within the African American community and a focused commitment by the industry to win back many of its (potential) moviegoers now living in suburban communities. Indeed, as James H. Miller points out, one of the ironies and paradoxes of cinematic history between 1968 and 1974 is that the commercial success of black-oriented films led to their demise.[58] According to many black film critics, Hollywood producers recognized the economic potential of the black moviegoing audience but also understood that they did not have to make blaxploitation-type films to gain its patronage. Jesse Rhines writes that "from 1969 through the middle 1970s, white-owned distribution companies released an average of fifteen films per year featuring blacks." By the middle to late seventies, though, the production of black-theme films declined sharply. Discussing this trend, Rhines adds, "[B]etween

1975 and 1985 the theatrical release of films by African Americans, or films featuring African Americans in significant roles, averaged fewer than two a year." [59]

Black Independent Filmmaking

The hierarchical structure of the commercial film industry is dominated by rigid gender and racial arrangements. Much like the creation of race movies, black independent filmmaking is also a cultural and political response to the exclusivity of Hollywood. This particular cinematic practice can best be described as an attempt to establish an alternative set of resources, networks, and institutions in order to provide African American filmmakers with opportunities to practice their craft. The bulk of African American filmmaking operates mainly on the independent circuit. In general, these films are not "picked up" by film companies for distribution and, as a result, are limited to peripheral or nonrevenue exhibition sites like film festivals and public television. The largest and arguably the most innovative body of African American filmmaking, then, goes largely unnoticed due to the inaccessibility to venues that produce large audiences.

The black independent film movement developed its most definitive features in the 1970s. Ironically, this race-conscious surge in film production was a cultural and political by-product of the liberal commitment to integration that framed the logic of the civil rights movement in the 1960s. Committed to the ideal of integration as the key to ameliorating racial inequality, the civil rights movement weakened the development of black-owned and -operated enterprises. The move away from black industry further diverted resources and cultural leadership away from an already weakened black film industry.

However, one of the main tenets of the civil rights movement emphasized education as a way to improve the social and economic plight of African Americans. Consequently, black enrollment in colleges and universities began to increase dramatically. Miller argues that the independent black film movement developed out of the educational reforms made possible by the civil rights movement. Increased black enrollment in colleges and universities coincided with the greater availability of film history and film training in higher education. The convergence of these factors created the first serious opportunity for African Americans to gain access to the technological expertise and filmmaking styles that inform the creative process of filmmaking.

In general, black independent film tends to gravitate toward one of two categories: narrative and documentary.[60] The narrative film developed its unique contours from the movement that black film critic Clyde Taylor has called the "LA Rebellion."[61] It was out of this collective effort that a group of newly trained independent black filmmakers residing in Los Angeles began to reexamine the relationship between narrative film, counterhegemonic cultural politics, and black cinema. Taylor has defined this movement as an effort to establish definitions, the drafting of manifestos, the excited exchange of ideas and techniques, the revisionist review of historical legacies, and the self-conscious awareness of being players on a historically distinct stage. It is also within the arena of black independent cinema that a self-consciously black feminist filmic practice has been carefully cultivated.[62] Because film is an intensely male-dominated sphere of cultural production, the independent circuit is virtually the only available venue for black women filmmakers.

The documentary film is usually produced to educate and inform viewers about specific topics. Over the last decade or so, the documentary work of African American filmmakers has become more visible due mainly to the Public Broadcasting System, cable television, and home video. One of the most successful black-owned film production companies, Blackside, specializes in producing film and video products that are both educational and historical.[63] The contours of African American documentary film work are also diverse. For instance, the work of Marlon Riggs has been equally inspirational and provocative. Riggs has used the documentary form to explore the complex interaction between race and late nineteenth- and early twentieth-century popular culture (*Ethnic Notions,* 1986); the popular rise of television and the industry's ongoing struggle to keep pace with a constantly shifting racial landscape (*Color Adjustment,* 1991); and the complex relationship between racial identity, gender, and sexuality in the African American community (*Tongues Untied,* 1991, and *Black Is . . . Black Ain't,* 1995). And while Riggs's work is clearly representative of the documentary form, his filmmaking style also incorporates nonconventional modes of film and video production to include performance and autobiography as well.[64]

A second African American–led independent film movement consisted of black filmmakers primarily from the East Coast. In 1978, the Black Filmmaker Foundation (BFF) was established.[65] The BFF took on the responsibility of building an organization that could redress the institutional disenfranchisement of black filmmakers and audiences. According to the brochures compiled by the BFF, it is a product of the political and artistic consciousness that developed in the late 1960s and early 1970s. Many of the filmmakers affiliated with the BFF received their film training and education through university admissions policies and government programs that targeted traditionally underrepresented groups.[66] The BFF attempts to provide a range of activities, including workshops, seminars and conferences, exhibitions, a skills bank, and employment listings for its members. Black independents, during this period, began to view themselves as a collective group engaged in a historically specific episode of cultural struggle.[67]

Despite these important formations, black independent cinema still remains largely unnoticed and underfunded. This particular cultural practice is enlivened by the wide availability of film training, access to film equipment, and the creation of organizations like the BFF. The lack of funding, however, weakens the institutional support systems for black independent filmmaking. And one of the main sources of funding for independent artistic expression in the United States—government funding of the arts—is shrinking as a result of fiscal constraints and a conservative political hegemony committed to exercising greater control over the popular cultural sphere. Moreover, black independent film remains marginal and therefore invisible because it has limited access to highly visible exhibition venues. While there have been some notable individual successes from the black independent film movement—Spike Lee, for example—the future direction of black independent cinema remains hopeful, but also uncertain.

Black Commercial Independents

After Spike Lee's successful independent feature *She's Gotta Have It,* a small class of black independent filmmakers began to experience greater access to the vast resources of the first- and second-tier film distributors. As I discussed above, film directors and producers operate as free agents who spend much of their time developing film projects and then shopping them around to the various studios. Thus, as the cultural marketplace continues to expand and develop new appetites, sensibilities, and popular trends, these shifts compel a move toward some variation in the product distributed by film companies. The most important distinction between noncommercial and commercial black independent filmmaking is that the latter benefits from access to commercial film industry resources and, most notably, production and marketing budgets, distribution, and theatrical exhibition. The creative process of black filmmaking takes on a precisely different character when it is practiced within the corridors of the commercial film industry. Black filmmakers must not only negotiate the typical obstacles that confront most filmmakers, but in addition, they must successfully navigate the racial hierarchies of the industry.

Still, despite vast and obvious period differences, the formations of late twentieth-century black filmmaking bear striking similarities to the pioneering efforts of the first generation of black filmmakers. Both practices were driven in part by entrepreneurial priorities. The fact that black independent filmmakers seek out ways to translate their creative labor into profit-making ventures does not mean that the promotion of black culture and politics is irrelevant but that the chance to carve out a niche in a burgeoning media entertainment culture is, too, a preeminent factor. Some of the more innovative filmmakers have established small independent production companies that enable them to mobilize the resources necessary to take advantage of newly arising opportunities in independent feature film distribution, cable television, music video, and other multimedia services more effectively. The small independent companies allow filmmakers to establish alternative networks and organizations while maintaining a relationship with the distributors of film and other media products.[68] The motives for organizing independent production companies are simultaneously entrepreneurial and political. In the role of entrepreneur, black filmmakers attempt to create and sustain small-scale enterprises that create a variety of media products and services. But the creation of small media production outfits is also driven by political motivations: the development of resources and institutions that enable African Americans to carve out a small niche in the creation of popular media products and consequently play a more active role in shaping the new mediascape. Furthermore, this formation of entrepreneurship positions blacks to assert a modicum of control over media content. Discussing this particular trend in African American media production, filmmaker Spike Lee insists:

> Nowadays, there are more and more black artists who
> are in control of their work. That is the difference.
> Black artists are in control of their work, they're setting
> up their own corporations, they don't have white
> people doing everything for them, ripping them off.
> I mean, this is a conscious decision that everybody's
> making. What they have come to realize is that power
> comes from control, and you have to be in control of
> your art. You know, we don't want any more of this

99

Morris Levy shit, you make a million dollars for somebody else and you end up broke. Them days gotta
be over.[69]

Lee's comment reveals a very important shift in the logic governing
African American media production: whereas black protest efforts
throughout most of the twentieth century urged the communications
media industry to create more "positive" representations of African
Americans, post–civil rights era protest trends emphasize asserting more
creative, administrative, and organizational control over the resources
that govern the production and content of popular media products. But
Lee and his contemporaries are not the first generation of African Americans to employ this strategy. As I discussed above, the producers of race
movies struggled to create their own media organizations; however,
their efforts took place within a historical context that enforced severe
limits on their ability to act as meaningful players on the field of popular
media production. Thus, the more assertive attitudes of African Americans do not necessarily reveal a more sophisticated approach to the production of media as much as they point to a rapidly expanding media
culture and marketplace and the loosening of racial barriers, which create more opportunities to respond creatively to racism.

Take, for instance, the market-segmentation strategy. Market segmentation divides potential consumers into identifiable segments and
then aggressively targets them. Groups are divided into various segments based on a range of criteria, such as age, race, class, region, and
gender. Most marketing analysts agree that, in order for segmentation
to succeed, a group must first be identifiable, measurable, accessible, and
substantial enough to generate profits. Segmentation has become increasingly important to the producers of goods and services, mainly because it allows them to penetrate target audiences with some degree of
precision in order to increase the sales of their products. In reality, the
notion of the "mass media" obscures the specialized tendencies of media production in the postindustrial information economy. The producers of media products are seldom interested in large, undifferentiated
groups of consumers. Instead, they are increasingly committed to servicing specialized segments of the consumer population. One of the immediate implications of this strategy is that traditionally overlooked
groups—blacks, Latinos, gays and lesbians—are now more likely to be
targeted.

In the rapidly expanding global marketplace, the most successful producers of goods and services must be able to identify and serve as many different spheres of consumption as possible. Thus, as the social and economic status of many African Americans continues to improve, the group's participation as consumers in the mainstream economy has warranted special attention. Whereas the popular culture industries once ignored black consumers, many have developed specific marketing campaigns to win their patronage. Efforts to appeal to black consumers, however, are marked by a high degree of uncertainty and unfamiliarity. Marketing specialists are basically misinformed about the social and economic factors that pattern African American consumption.[70] As with other segments, trends in African American consumption vary according to gender, age, region, and class differences and are therefore difficult to predict.

One distinct variation in African American consumption is patterned by age. While I discuss this subject in greater detail in chapter 6, it is important to note that youth play a pivotal role in the production of cultural goods like popular film and music. Youth markets are attractive because the group's income is mostly disposable.[71] The culture industry is especially responsive to youth subcultural practices that inspire the creation of new collective identities and popular trends that drive consumer behavior. The evolution of hip hop, for example, has been shaped by new repertoires of cultural production that also invigorate youth consumption. Indeed, many black filmmakers have incorporated some of the expressive motifs of hip hop into their work in order to develop film product that appeals to the industry's staple audience: youth.

But the post-1986 resurgence of African American–directed feature-length films also corresponds with the structural changes that continue to reorganize the production of commercial cinema. One of the most significant breakthroughs for African American filmmakers has been the rise of the independent film distributor.[72] The proliferation of black film product in the late 1980s and early 1990s is largely attributable to the growth of independent distribution. Unable to compete with the majors, independents are more likely to produce and distribute small-budget feature films. In addition, independent distributors are more likely to seek out "fresh" material that can be differentiated from the imitative and formulaic cycles that tend to dominate film production in Hollywood. For instance, because the majors are less likely to risk breaking new genres or innovatively styled films to their mainstream audience, independents are able to market products like "black cinema" as a moviegoing experience that differs from the standard menu of films served by the majors. Further, as film costs continue to escalate and the majors fight to maintain a constant flow of product output, the growth of the ancillary and international markets allows independents to carve out important niches in film distribution.

The early nineties black film boom was also stimulated by more flexible systems of production in Hollywood. Continued success for the major film companies is predicated on their ability to respond to and exploit the popularization of product innovations and trends that emerge from the spirit and vitality of the independent film movement. Greater flexibility in production allows the majors to incorporate film genres and styles that originate outside the mainstream film industry. For example, after the success of *She's Gotta Have It* (Island Pictures), *Hollywood Shuffle* (Samuel Goldwyn), and *House Party* (New Line Cinema), the major film companies gradually began to include African American–directed features as part of their product offering, mainly in the form of the low-budget specialty film. In fact, the majority of black-directed films distributed by the majors since 1986 are produced at costs well below the average Hollywood film. For the major film distributors, the specialty film creates greater product diversity while simultaneously controlling costs.

Several other factors also work to alter the relationship between African American filmmakers and the commercial film industry. First, access to film training creates a class of filmmakers literate in the history, styles, and production techniques of cinema. As a result of higher rates of college attendance and graduation, many African Americans involved in the production of film (i.e., writers, directors, producers) have acquired cultural capital in the form of advanced degrees, thus facilitating greater access to professional careers in the media industry. Moreover, changes in the music industry—most notably, the growth of the music video industry—also forge new avenues of access to film- and video-making experience. For example, the Hughes brothers, producers of *Menace II Society* and *Dead Presidents,* started their professional careers directing music videos for West Coast rap groups.[73]

Finally, market segmentation gives African American filmmakers an advantage in developing specialized feature-length films to serve specific segments of the moviegoing population. Indeed, as filmmaker Warrington Hudlin contends in his statement earlier in the chapter, the drive toward market segmentation makes servicing the desires and tastes of black audiences a greater priority. Like many of his contemporaries, Hudlin believes that black filmmakers are in a unique position to produce the kinds of products that Hollywood must begin making available to an increasingly segmented marketplace. Because film is especially open to entrepreneurial efforts, some black film directors and producers have been able to achieve periodic success. Those who have enjoyed the most success have been able to develop and "pitch" their product ideas to studio executives and secure the capital necessary for production.

Black filmmakers, like entrepreneurs in general, are not so much actors producing change but rather actors who react to and exploit a rapidly changing social world. Part of making sense of the commodification of black cinema is to study more directly how African American filmmakers move to take advantage of the structural changes that reorganize the terrain of popular media culture and production. It is within the context of an ever-expanding popular media landscape that many young African Americans have developed a different view of themselves, their social world, and their role within that world as active makers of history rather than passive victims of history. The production of black cinema constitutes an important theater of struggle for the articulation of African American cultural and representational politics.

In part 2, I consider the role that filmmaker Spike Lee performs in this emergent theater. The section is organized into two chapters. Chapter 4 examines the organizational environment, production strategies, and spirit of entrepreneurship that structure the production of films created by Lee. Chapter 5 explores how Lee exploits the volatile terrain of race relations in order to create provocative film narratives about American life along the color line. Lee's strategic intervention on the field of popular culture is indeed emblematic of how broad structural changes in the production of media enable new regimes of cultural production to take shape.

PART TWO

4 Producing the Spike Lee Joint

One of the harsh truths of American business for blacks, particularly those who work in concert with large white distribution entities, has been that all these young black entrepreneurs have had to make peace with the white power structure, one way or another. . . . [L]acking the means of distribution and independent funding, these African American minimoguls inevitably find themselves working with multinational white institutions that have traditionally remained hostile to sharing power with us.

NELSON GEORGE[1]

Without question, Spike Lee typifies the entrepreneur who has transformed marginality—in this case, his status as an African American and independent filmmaker—into a source of opportunity by responding, in innovative fashion, to social, economic, political, and cultural changes. Lee has adroitly turned the ironies of late twentieth-century capitalism to his own professional advantage by exploiting the public's ongoing fascination with blackness. The filmmaker's cultural and representational politics, however, take place within the context of a commercial culture landscape that continues to produce new spaces of cultural production and specialized media products for a vast consumer market. Between 1986 and 1995, Lee wrote and directed eight feature films. This type of back-to-back productivity is an uncommon accomplishment in the fast-paced, constantly evolving world of popular film production. The fact that a young African American independent filmmaker produced so many feature-length films is even more rare.

Throughout his filmmaking career, Lee has struggled endlessly to challenge Hollywood axioms about the commercial and critical potential of black cinema. Moreover, the filmmaker openly acknowledges the political nature of popular film production and has strategically maneuvered to call into question the racial barriers that characterize the commercial film industry. Like most successful filmmakers, Lee has learned how to negotiate an industry that is concerned mostly with controlling costs and reducing risks in its efforts to accumulate large profits. Lee has also been forced to wrestle with an industry that has only recently begun to open its doors to black filmmakers and their products.

In this chapter, I discuss some of the organizational processes and production strategies that situated the merchandising and dissemination of films created by Lee. In 1986, Lee emerged as a breakthrough success. As a result, Lee soon began to play a crucial role in the commercial revitalization of black cinema. Ironically, Lee's success in the commercial film industry represents the norm rather than the exception in popular film production. The filmmaker's formula for success—film narratives that hinge on social and racial conflict—became a commercially successful product/genre innovation that many film studios began to incorporate, in varying forms, into their lineup of film products. But like any successful idea or product innovation that surfaces in Hollywood, Lee's formula would also be subjected to the organizational routines and production strategies that process and manufacture *all* popular film products.

Spike Lee and Independent Filmmaking

*Getting the money to make a film being an independent
filmmaker has got to be one of the hardest things to do. . . .
I might have to find a job that pays something in the
meantime.*

SPIKE LEE[2]

Most analysts agree that Lee's first feature film release, *She's Gotta Have It* (*SGHI,* 1986), established the precedent for the reemergence of black cinema as a viable commercial product. The production of *She's Gotta Have It* occurred completely outside the operations of Hollywood and indicated that a feature film with an all-black cast could be both commercially and critically successful. In several respects, the making of *SGHI* runs counter to the production logic that governs the New Hollywood. The film, for example, was made without union support, insurance, or location permits. It was also especially small in scope, crew, and payroll. Principal photography for the film was completed in twelve days with a nine-member crew. Further, the main shooting location was limited to one site—a studio apartment atop a restaurant. Also, there was no elaborate promotional campaign, television advertisements, or music sound track to build interest in the film. In addition to writing, directing, producing, and acting, Lee rented a six-plate editing machine to cut and edit the film from his own apartment.

As with most independent efforts, the crew was able to take advantage of many of the fissures that energize the culture of independent filmmaking. Lee and his cinematographer, Ernest Dickerson, rented the equipment necessary to make the film from local shops. The availability of technologically improved equipment allows independent filmmakers to make higher-quality films without incurring high costs. Also, in preparation for the film, some of the crew members participated in seminars given by the Association of Independent Video and Filmmakers and the Black Filmmaker Foundation. A number of different organizations designed to aid independent filmmaking provided information on how to write screenplays, cast for films, perform production designs, edit, and finance potential projects.

As is the case with most independent films, the biggest obstacle in the production of *SGHI* was lack of financial capital. The initial funding for the film was collected from a wide range of formal and informal sources. Initially, Lee applied to several film foundations and arts service organizations for funding. Production grants from these federal and private sources are not meted out liberally. Despite the autonomous status of independent filmmakers, a number of obstacles must be skillfully negotiated in order to obtain funding from these organizations.[3]

While he received a few small grants, Lee also attempted to attract private investors and limited partnerships in order to finance the completion of the film. Despite the small scope and low costs of independent films, a substantial capital investment is required to finish films in the postproduction phase.[4] The film business, in general, is risky, and the financing of independent projects is an especially risky investment. Lee discovered that securing private investments was as difficult as securing grants for the arts. Four weeks after the completion of principal photography, Lee screened a rough cut of the film for potential investors and local journalists. The event was a small success insofar as it generated a few small private investments. Lee also pursued informal sources to collect additional funding. The filmmaker mailed out over fifty letters to friends, family members, and other acquaintances asking for private donations. The personal donations, few in number, ranged from $100 to $2,000.

If lack of access to capital is the major source of difficulty for independent filmmakers, lack of access to exhibition venues must rank a not-so-distant second. Major film festivals are important exhibition sites for independents primarily because they are able to generate press coverage and also attract potential distributors for films produced outside Hollywood. *SGHI* was accepted to the San Francisco Film Festival and was the only American film, in 1986, accepted to the prestigious "Director's Fortnight" at the Cannes Film Festival in France. In San Francisco, the film was popular with audiences and received favorable reviews in the local press. Several independent film distributors seeking new and affordable product to release expressed interest in purchasing both the domestic and foreign rights to distribute *SGHI.* Lee eventually selected Island Pictures as the distributor for *SGHI* because of how it had handled other small independent features. Also, according to the filmmaker, Island recognized that a black movie market existed and committed to developing a strategy to attract it.

After signing a distribution deal, both Lee and Island had to devise a skillful, yet inexpensive, release strategy for the film. The timing and release strategy for *SGHI* was carefully calculated. After screening the film at Cannes, Island decided to bypass the New York Film Festival and go for an early August opening. The rationale behind the strategy was to target the period in between the two busiest seasons of film attendance, the summer and holiday months. The film company recognized that the bulk of press coverage for movies takes place during these two periods. Rather than compete with elaborately budgeted films, an early August release date was selected in order to minimize competition for press coverage. Unable to finance a national advertising campaign for *SGHI,* Island relied instead on the media gatekeeping institutions to generate "free" publicity for the film. These institutions are crucial subsystems in the operations of the culture industry because they link media products to their intended audiences. As a sociologist of culture notes, "[T]he diffusion of cultural goods is either blocked or facilitated at this strategic checkpoint."[5] Both *SGHI* and Lee benefited from local and national media publicity. For instance, in the markets where *SGHI* was released, the local newspapers ran lengthy features.[6] In addition, nationally circulated periodicals like *Time* and *Newsweek* ran favorable reviews of the film. *NBC Nightly News* even ran a complimentary light-hearted news story on the film.

Part of Lee's appeal as good "copy" for the press was the public persona he was beginning to strategically craft.[7] In interviews for various newspapers and magazines, Lee candidly expressed his dislike for the Hollywood establishment and, in particular, the industry's representation of African Americans. Lee heavily criticized movies like *Soul Man* and also voiced concern about the portrayal of black men in the film *The Color Purple*. Lee's frontal assault was in fact strategic and intentional to the extent that he understood that such a position generated enormous publicity while also building a strong base of black support.

The distribution strategy for *SGHI* was also carefully planned. The initial theatrical "run" for *SGHI* was exclusive: the 300-seat New York Cinema Studio One served as the test market. Slow distribution strategies are generally employed to cultivate market appeal by maximizing the effects of good word-of-mouth advertising. After a successful two-week run in New York City, the ensuing release pattern was gradual and limited.[8] The next three markets—San Francisco; Washington, D.C.; and Chicago—had two main variables in common: young black moviegoers and a sizable concentration of moviegoers accustomed to attend-

Table 4.1. *Variety* Box-Office Reports for *She's Gotta Have It* (Island, 1986)

Week	Week's Reported Box Office ($)	Cumulative Reported Box Office ($)	Screens	Week's Average $ per Screen
1	50,000	50,000	1	50,000
2	85,200	142,287	2	42,600
3	157,000	314,402	5	31,400
4	330,800	654,790	10	33,080
5	290,800	918,867	14	20,771
6	462,900	1,390,198	33	14,027
7	494,600	1,888,851	40	12,365
8	380,300	2,256,664	38	10,007
9	365,500	2,634,389	42	8,702
10	252,909	2,870,283	38	6,655
11	166,951	3,039,279	35	4,770
12	152,437	3,189,735	29	5,256
13	142,000	3,342,703	36	3,944
14	111,300	3,458,743	28	5,059
15	101,820	3,566,663	21	4,848
16	141,350	3,709,375	24	5,889
17	78,500	3,787,124	12	6,541
18	56,300	3,841,309	9	6,255
19	38,800	3,880,148	11	3,527
20	32,400	3,917,427	7	4,628
21	38,000	3,959,157	4	9,500
22	44,000	4,010,938	4	11,000
23	36,500	4,046,741	4	9,125
24	19,000	4,065,394	2	9,500

ing art movies and film festivals. The film was gradually released in other markets that shared similar characteristics.

An examination of *Variety*'s list of top-fifty box-office receipts suggests that *SGHI* was remarkably successful for a low-budget specialty film (see table 4.1). In its opening week, *SGHI* was listed thirtieth. The film peaked as high as seventh—during its seventh and eighth weeks—for an extremely high dollar-per-theater average.[9] The film remained on *Variety*'s top-fifty list for a surprising twenty-four weeks and eventually grossed over $11 million (foreign receipts included). Island Pictures purchased the rights to *SGHI* for a reported $400,000.

Spike Lee and the Commercial Film Industry

Successful filmmakers are distinguished not only by a command of their medium but also by their political savvy. They know how to manipulate the studio system to their advantage, or at least how to negotiate the bureaucratic pitfalls they will encounter. They must know how to assemble an attractive package of story and stars, how best to pitch it to studio executives and how to build momentum and support for their projects.

MARK LITWAK[10]

In order to minimize risk and prudently navigate market variability, the film industry operates principally on the theory of precedence. Therefore, one of the ways in which studio executives allay fears concerning market uncertainty is to imitate successful feature films. The theory of precedence is also applied to assess the value of screenwriters, performers, producers, and directors. A filmmaker's value, in short, is as good as his or her last film. After the commercial success of *SGHI,* Lee emerged as a "hot" commodity. Both the film and the public image he constructed laid the foundation for a commercially successful formula: entertaining movies canvassing the contemporary rhythms of African American life while also privileging important social issues. Lee discovered a "hook," and the industry displayed early signs that it was willing to bite.

The transition from independent to commercial film, however, created a dramatically different environment for the filmmaker. Balancing his personal cinematic imagination with marketplace considerations emerged as a principal source of tension. Due to the fact that independent filmmakers work outside the commercial film industry, they seldom worry about corporate interference or if their films will play well for large audiences. But once an independent filmmaker begins working with the large film distributors, he or she must deal with studio executives' efforts to keep production costs low and produce a finished product that can appeal to as wide an audience as possible. Whereas studio executives are focused on controlling costs, filmmakers usually have a different set of priorities: they tend to be concerned with securing sufficient studio resources to both make and market their films. The successful filmmaker, then, must demonstrate a command not only of his or her craft but also of the studio politics that inevitably intrude on the filmmaking process. For African American filmmakers, the necessity to function simultaneously as artists/businesspersons requires even more finesse because their film projects typically represent unfamiliar territory for film industry executives. Filmmakers, more generally, cannot be satisfied with being good artists. They must also be able to articulate to studio heads why they think their prospective film projects should be financed.

Despite the commercial success of *SGHI,* Island executives expressed concerns about the cost of Lee's second feature film, *School Daze.* Unlike the filmmaker's first feature, *School Daze* required large exterior and interior sets, choreographed dance performances, and a more elaborate production design. Lee submitted a $5 million budget. Island executives placed a $3 million ceiling on the project and began to express concerns that it was "overly ambitious." In order to control costs, Island proposed scaling down the scope of the project by cutting some of the musical numbers. In addition, the film company wanted to select and supervise the hiring of the production manager, coproducer, and candidates for other important management positions. Lee refused to scale down production, and as a result, Island decided not to finance *School Daze.* Through a negative pickup deal, Columbia Pictures financed *School Daze* for a reported $6.5 million.

After the movie was first screened for Columbia executives, it was suggested that the next screening be for a recruited audience. Test screenings in Hollywood are a customary method of assessing the strengths and weaknesses of a prospective feature film release. Early screenings allow studio executives and filmmakers to evaluate a film's potential appeal by collecting audience feedback. The city of Philadelphia was chosen because of its large black population and also because of the successful theatrical run of *SGHI.* The requested demographic profile for the recruited audience was 65 percent black and 35 percent white. In total, 335 persons attended the test screening; all but 17 were black. The film was still a work in progress at the time of the screening but played well for the mostly black audience. Studio executives recommended that the next recruited screening contain a larger percentage of whites. At the end of the screening, a questionnaire was handed out to each audience member.[11] Some of the conclusions from the initial test screening read as follows:

- *School Daze* played quite well to this mostly black Philadelphia audience, generating a 34% Excellent rating (norm is 20% "Excellent"), a total Highly Favorable rating of 83% (Norm is 60%), . . . and a 76% "Definitely" recommend score (norm is 45%).
- The movie played well above Averagely Well to younger (under 25) moviegoers and above Averagely Well to older moviegoers. All of the sex/age groups provided well above average "Definitely" recommend scores.
- The results of this screening indicate that *SD* plays quite well (at least for a predominantly black audience). It also plays well to all sex/age groups and particularly well to all younger audience members.[12]

The film was screened a week later at a large multiplex theater located in a suburban shopping mall in Paramus, New Jersey.[13] The audience was younger and had a higher proportion of whites. At the end of the film, the audience members were asked to fill out the same questionnaire used for the original test screening. Some of the conclusions from the second test screening were as follows:

- *School Daze* did not play very well to this racially mixed Paramus audience, receiving considerably lower ratings and recommendation scores than it did at the first, predominantly black screening.
- Overall, the movie received a 14% "Excellent" rating (norm is 20% "Excellent") and below average total highly favorable

   ratings of 48% (norm is 60%) . . . and a below average "Definitely" recommend score of 35% (norm is 45%).
- From black audience members, the movie received slightly
   above average "Excellent" ratings of 23% and somewhat above
   average highly favorable ratings of 67% . . . and an above average "Definitely" recommend score of 54%. In contrast, whites
   gave below average "Excellent" ratings of 27% . . . and an extremely low 12% "Definitely" recommend score.
- As before , the movie was most enjoyed for its story about
   black campus life (mainly by black audience members), its humor, its message about prejudice, and the entertaining manner
   in which these elements were combined. However, many more
   audience members at this screening (both blacks and whites)
   criticized the movie than at the previous screening, mainly for
   being too long and slow (both blacks and whites) and, at times,
   confusing (more whites than blacks). In addition, some whites
   described the movie as being difficult for them to relate to because it was "too black."[14]

The industry rarely ignores low scores from test screenings. Consequently, film executives generally expect the director to make changes
in the film in accordance with the data collected from the screenings. In
the case of *School Daze,* the test screening results required that Lee alter
the original version of the film in several ways. For example, because
audiences consistently commented that the film was too lengthy, *School
Daze* was shortened. The Philadelphia cut was 2 hours and 25 minutes;
the final test cut was reduced by some 38 minutes. The final version ran
a fast-paced 1 hour and 58 minutes. Two scenes were dropped after audiences referred to them as too confusing and ambiguously inserted into
the narrative. For reasons that are quite different, studio execs and filmmakers consider test screenings to be an important part of the production process. The test screenings presented an opportunity for the
studio to improve playability by making film content more accessible to
moviegoers. For Lee, the test screenings were an opportunity to gauge
which filmic techniques work best with the audience.[15]

   Unlike his first feature film release, Lee had to grapple with industry concerns regarding how his creative work would play for a much
broader audience than the one that fueled the success of *SGHI*. And although Lee claimed that his primary objective was to make films about

and for African Americans, he would have to concede that part of the price of doing business with large film distributors was that he also had to give some consideration to how his films played with potential white moviegoers. In exchange for financial capital, the studios often impose their own priorities on the creative process in order to create product that will appeal to large segments of the film-going audience and, as a result, return a handsome profit on their financial investment.

Censoring the Spike Lee Joint

Lee's first two feature films were marketed by their respective distributors as comedies. However, the narrative and thematic structure of each film strongly resisted the genre label. According to the film director, *SGHI* and *School Daze* were marketed as comedies in order to make them more palatable and less threatening to potential white audiences. Lee's third feature, *Do the Right Thing* , in contrast, created an entirely different set of studio-related dilemmas due to the tone and dramatic intensity of the film—more specifically, its ambiguous and controversial representation of American race relations. While preparing for the production of *Do the Right Thing,* Lee was confronted with an explicit act of studio censorship. Censorship by studio executives is common but generally subtle in form. More often, writers, producers, and directors exercise discretion during the creative process.[16] But occasionally, studio execs find it necessary to cut a scene, rephrase a piece of dialogue, or alter some other element considered too risky. This filtering process is an example of how the creative process is routinely purified by industry gatekeepers as a means of staying within the normative boundaries of dominant social and cultural values.

Prior to the production of *Do the Right Thing,* Lee decided to reserve final-cut approval. In theory, final-cut approval is a contractual agreement that permits a filmmaker to exercise substantial control in determining film content and finished product prior to distribution.[17] His final-cut approval of *Do the Right Thing* was immediately challenged by Paramount Pictures, the film's original distributor. The company expressed serious concern that the script's ending was too volatile and could possibly incite black moviegoers to "riot." As a precondition for financing the film, Paramount insisted that specific scenes be reworked and the ending "softened." Lee refused to relinquish final-cut approval and also rejected recommendations to alter the film's ending. Seeing no end to the impasse, Paramount refused to bankroll production of the film. Lee submitted scripts to two other major film companies. Studio executives from a competing distributor declined to move on the project, stating that the scope of the film did not justify Lee's projected $10 million budget. However, another studio, Universal, accepted the script, but only committed to a $6.5 million budget. Rather than run the risk of having all prospective deals fall through, Lee accepted the Universal offer with the contractual stipulation that he would retain final-cut approval.

But the censorship of Lee's representational politics is not limited to Hollywood studio executives. As Lee began to move from the obscurity of independent filmmaking to the high visibility of commercial filmmaking, he became subject to the policing apparatus of not only the studio but also the African American community. In addition to grappling with studio executives, Lee has been forced to contend with the complex and often unforgiving scrutiny and high expectations of African Americans. The shift from the filmmaking margins to the commercial mainstream transformed Lee into a visible vehicle for expressing racial pride—subjecting him to demands that were almost impossible to satisfy. Lee's arrival on the popular filmmaking stage saddled him with enormous responsibilities as the African American community expected him to correct what it often regarded as a constant barrage of "negative" black imagery.

However, in those cases when Lee's film narratives prescribed critical depictions of African Americans, his representational politics brought him into conflict with some segments of the black community. For example, while filming *School Daze,* Lee was confronted with explicit acts of censorship by black college officials and administrators. Lee wanted to use his alma mater, Morehouse College, as the main location for principal photography.[18] Midway through the shoot, however, the colleges associated with Atlanta University Center decided to bar Lee's production team from filming on their campuses. School officials and administrators expressed concern that the film would "portray a negative image of Black colleges" and African Americans in general.[19] Moreover, the administrators stated that they did not want sex or certain divisive issues in the black community addressed in the film. Some officials even demanded to read the script before deciding to grant the filmmaker permission to use their campus as a shooting location. Lee labels this form of policing black filmmaking the "positive image trap." He refused many of the administrators' demands and completed photography at locations where he was able to obtain permission. In some cases, though, the filmmaker resorted to some of the guerrilla instincts he displayed while filming *SGHI* and shot at preferred locations without permission.

Historically, the censorship of black image production by other African Americans is the result of a middle-class corrective ethos that seeks to restrict the representation of African Americans to images presumed to be more "positive" or in concert with bourgeois notions of respectability. Moreover, the administrators' attempt to censor Lee's cinematic vision of black American life reflects what Kobena Mercer has described as the "social engineering" approach to black cultural production. Basically, this approach views black image making as a practice that should be devoted to promoting more positive representations of African Americans. Thus, a film like *School Daze* that focused on numerous contentious issues within the black American community generated serious concern for an older generation of black college administrators who themselves remain committed to the notion of promoting respectable—or in other words, bourgeois—images of blackness.[20]

Distributing the Spike Lee Joint

*I don't want to duplicate what happened to a lot of the
black filmmakers of previous generations in front of me—
and some from today as well. . . . When I was in film
school, I would see these guys who had spent four or five
years, and sometimes even longer, trying to raise money for
their films. And these were often good films. But they were
seen, if they were seen at all, as nothing but a blip on the
screen before the public. If anything, we would end up
seeing them at a screening at a museum, or at a university,
or during Black history month, and that's all. But I knew
I didn't want hundreds of people to see my films. I wanted
millions of people to see my films.*

SPIKE LEE[21]

In addition to providing financial capital, the first- and second-tier studios are able to distribute feature films widely. The financial superiority of the majors enables them to saturate theaters and generate enormous publicity and potential audience interest in a film. For many African American filmmakers, lack of access to distribution deals restricts the dissemination and reception of their creative work. So even though Lee's shift to the commercial film industry meant dealing with test screenings, studio politics, public scrutiny, and battles over budgets, he benefited immensely from the exposure that the major film companies can generate when they decide to utilize their marketing and distribution muscle. Lee decided early during his transition that, despite all the difficulties, the majors could give him the one thing he would never achieve on his own: access to millions of moviegoers.

But because Lee's films tend to have the production values, scope, and style of specialty films, the distribution logic governing the dissemination of his movies is notably distinct. *School Daze,* for example, opened in thirty markets and on 221 screens. By comparison, Touchstone Pictures released *Three Men and a Baby* on 1,615 screens the same weekend. The release date of the film, February 12, fit in between the two most active film-going seasons. *School Daze* ranked in *Variety*'s top-ten box-office reports during its first four weeks and peaked as high as sixth during its second week on the charts. In its fourth week, the film covered its costs. After a six-week theatrical run, the dollars-per-theater average remained strong—$9,028—but the studio reduced the number of screens by nearly 30 percent, from 95 to 68. By week fourteen, the film was no longer listed on *Variety*'s fifty top-grossing films chart.

Columbia employed a limited advertising campaign for *School Daze.* Both Lee and his film were trapped in a web of studio politics due to changing leadership. During the period before the film's release, the studio changed presidents. *School Daze* was viewed as a priority of the prior leadership; thus, the new studio hierarchy displayed an ambivalent attitude toward the film. The new president did not believe *School Daze* was a viable box-office product and limited the budget allocated for paid advertisements. The studio, for instance, neglected the black print media. Lee charged that Columbia's marketing division failed to properly study the moviegoing habits of blacks and also failed to do its homework on the audience demographic that supported *SGHI*.[22] According to Lee, the company decided to put him on the road—twenty-one cities in twenty-one days—to promote the film through guest appearances in the major markets. The promotional strategy was rather simple: use Spike Lee, literally, as the principal means for selling the film. In today's world of film marketing, the primary strategy usually calls for direct advertising through television ads and promotional tie-ins that generate public awareness and interest in a film. Columbia's release strategy and meager promotional effort suggest that the company was not interested in developing the film's full commercial potential but only in turning a quick profit on the low-budget feature. Still, despite limited distribution and poor studio support, *School Daze* was one of the few films that turned a profit for Columbia in 1988.

Universal Pictures' distribution strategy for Lee's third feature film, *Do the Right Thing,* differed sharply from Columbia's treatment of *School Daze.* First, the film was released during the summer season. The summer is an important season for the film industry because the primary moviegoing audience—young teens and adults—is away from school. In the summer, film companies generally release movies that have the potential to draw huge crowds and box-office receipts. *Do the Right Thing* was Universal's main entry in the 1989 summer box-office derby.[23] The timing of the release also suggests that Lee was beginning to establish himself as a formidable "player" on the field of popular culture who was able to compete for consumer dollars.[24] The news media focus on Lee and *Do the Right Thing* accelerated the filmmaker's meteoric rise to celebrity status.

In its first full week, *Do the Right Thing* opened on 361 screens and peaked two weeks later on 534 screens (see table 4.2). *Batman,* by contrast, opened on 2,194 screens the same summer. In its second week of nationwide release, but limited distribution, *Do the Right Thing* began to turn a profit. Initial box-office receipts from the film were impressive; the average dollars per screen was one of the summer's highest. Universal, unlike Columbia, ran television and radio advertisements and also actively targeted black moviegoers by using the black press. And despite its release as a low-budget specialty film, *Do the Right Thing* was the most talked about film of 1989. The film received extensive press coverage. Lee contends that some of the additional publicity had a negative impact. According to the filmmaker, potential white moviegoers stayed away from the film because of the media's claim that *Do the Right Thing* encouraged blacks to riot. By week seven, *Do the Right Thing* was exhibited on 178 screens, nearly 70 percent fewer than its third-week peak. The *Variety* box-office reports also suggest that the bulk of the revenue was generated in the first five weeks of the film's theatrical run.

Between 1986 and 1991, Lee's commercial appeal grew substantially. In 1986, *SGHI* opened in one theater and peaked at 42; in 1991,

Table 4.2. *Variety* Box-Office Reports for *Do the Right Thing* (Universal, 1989)

Week	Week's Reported Box Office ($)	Cumulative Reported Box Office ($)	Screens	Week's Average $ per Screen
*	3,563,535	3,563,535	353	10,095
1	2,916,960	8,848,045	361	8,080
2	3,017,880	13,447,106	498	6,060
3	2,090,610	16,905,541	534	3,915
4	1,514,265	19,418,306	471	3,215
5	1,064,650	21,203,891	398	2,675
6	687,470	22,371,871	322	2,135
7	397,830	23,113,836	178	2,235
8	318,585	23,647,801	176	1,810
10†	289,170	24,681,806	238	1,215
11	302,560	25,102,176	248	1,220
12	221,580	25,424,581	232	955
13	169,150	25,655,211	199	850
15†	94,720	25,926,301	148	640
16	30,210	25,972,051	114	265
17	22,855	26,004,026	80	286

*Opening-weekend reported box office.
†Weeks 9 and 14 not reported.

Lee's fifth feature film—*Jungle Fever*—opened on 636 screens nationwide and peaked at 844 (see table 4.3). A close examination of the box-office reports compiled by *Variety* suggests that Lee's films were immensely popular, especially for low-budget, moderate-release specialty films. As table 4.4 indicates, each successive product increased in budget, number of screens, and box-office gross receipts. The average budget for his first five feature releases is $7.68 million. The average theater gross from these movies was three times the cost of production, $20 million. The major film companies discovered that doing business with Lee was good business.

Despite his reputation as a controversial black filmmaker, Lee's first five features played well with a broad spectrum of moviegoers: black/white, youth/adult, male/female, multiplexes/art theaters. The reasons for this are as varied as they are complex. For instance, Lee's films have generally been popular with black and white youth when he has been able to skillfully align them and his public persona with the popular rhythms and sensibilities of youth culture. Lee has also used music and music video as promotional devices. The filmmaker has often crafted movie sound tracks that consciously tap into the varied popular music

Table 4.3. *Variety* Box-Office Reports for *Jungle Fever* (Universal, 1991)

Week	Week's Reported Box Office ($)	Cumulative Reported Box Office ($)	Screens	Week's Average $ per Screen
1	7,953,180	7,953,180	636	12,505
2	7,552,210	15,505,390	773	9,770
3	5,612,600	21,117,990	844	6,650
4	2,569,880*	23,687,870	825	3,115
5	2,797,910	27,406,235	720	3,885
6	1,409,460	29,315,695	578	2,438
7	858,825	30,174,520	411	2,089
8	501,635	30,676,155	235	2,134
9	335,855	31,012,010	165	2,035
10	221,875	31,233,885	125	1,775
11	257,250	31,491,135	147	1,750
12	145,410	31,636,545	131	1,110
13	102,500	31,739,045	125	820

*Weekend reported box office.

Table 4.4. Compilation of Films Directed by Spike Lee (1986–93)

Film	Budget ($)	Maximum Screens	Domestic Box-Office Receipts ($)
She's Gotta Have It	175,000	42	11 million
School Daze	6.5 million	224	18 million
Do the Right Thing	6.5 million	534	28 million
Mo' Better Blues	11 million	572	24 million
Jungle Fever	13 million	844	33 million
Malcolm X	34 million	1,249	45 million

cultures of the African diaspora. Sound tracks from a Spike Lee joint have included genres as diverse as rhythm and blues, jazz, reggae/dance hall, hip hop, go-go, and gospel.

Moreover, both the style and the content of Lee's films have allowed him to play well in both multiplex theaters and art movie houses. On the one hand, Lee's ability to keep his cinematic antennae in tune with popular youth cultures and shifting social currents enables him to maintain his appeal with the film industry's most reliable set of customers. On the other, Lee's willingness to use the arena of popular film to explore complex social problems like racism allows him to tap into that stream of moviegoers who prefer films that are more intellectually stimulating and engaging. And yet the director's films tend to perform more strongly as limited releases, losing some of their earning power when spread thinly across a wide number of screens. This further suggests that Lee's popularity, while strong and consistent, is also concentrated.

The filmmaker would test his popularity and capacity to reach beyond his concentrated market of moviegoers in the production of the biographical picture *Malcolm X*. In fact, the production strategies employed for the film differ substantially from Lee's earlier projects; thus, I would like to discuss it separately.

From Specialty to Spectacle: Producing the *Malcolm X* Biopic

During my first meeting with Warner Brothers, I had tried to explain to them that this was a big, big film, that this was an epic film. Epic in period. Epic in length. And epic films cost money.

SPIKE LEE[25]

Even before production began, Lee envisioned his biographical picture *Malcolm X* to be a spectacular production. Unlike his first five feature films, Lee desired an elaborate production effort for *Malcolm X*. But the production and making of the movie illuminate the tenuous relationship between studio politics, black cinema, and the creative process.

Ironically, the difficulties Lee experienced with the production of *Malcolm X* were partially attributable to the scattered success of popular films directed by him and other African Americans during the early 1990s. As a result of his box-office success, a number of studios turned to distributing black-theme films. In the studios' rush to discover their own version of Spike Lee, though, a precarious imitative cycle of movies began to take shape in the early 1990s. During the same time Warner Brothers had decided to green-light the production of *Malcolm X,* the most profitable films made by African Americans tended to be ghetto action pictures, which cost very little to produce. To a large degree, the industry's conception of commercially viable black cinema was limited to this important, yet narrow, wave of films, which tended to draw much of its popularity from the proliferation of gangsta imagery in American culture. Consequently, the popular film industry established rigid criteria for films written and directed by African Americans. By the early 1990s, studio support for black cinema was essentially restricted to films that exploited the contemporary rhythms of black youth popular culture. As I discuss in detail in chapter 6, these films cost very little to produce and often covered expenditures in their second or third week of theatrical run. Moreover, these films enforced hardened formulas that severely limited the thematic thrust of black cinema.

Lee's production design for the film *Malcolm X,* however, far exceeded the industry's rigid treatment of films with black subject matter. Lee's frustrations and ambivalent relationship with the popular film industry are fueled, in part, by the industry's narrow conceptualization of black cinema. Discussing the difficulties he experienced while producing *Malcolm X,* the filmmaker states:

> They still feel—I'm talking about the major Hollywood
> studios—that white movie goers here in America are
> not interested in films with black subject matter. . . .
> The studios have no respect for the buying power of
> the Black market, no belief that other people are interested in the films we make. They would like for us to
> believe that the people who are interested in, say a
> Spike Lee film, have no idea that they together form
> a market. We have to prove the same thing over and
> over to the studios, again and again and again. So as
> filmmakers we face the same glass ceiling that our
> brothers and sisters in white corporate America face
> every day.[26]

In his production of *Malcolm X,* Lee would again challenge Hollywood axioms about the thematic scope and market potential of black cinema.

Warner Brothers had purchased the film rights to *Malcolm X* nearly twenty-five years before the project was financed and distributed as a feature-length film. As many as five scripts had been written and rejected by the studio during that time.[27] In addition, the studio had difficulty finding a suitable director for the project. Like most film ideas pitched to the Hollywood establishment, the project remained untouched and on the shelf. But after the project had sat dormant for twenty-five years, executives from Warner Brothers expressed interest in producing the film. What was different about the commercial cultural landscape in the early 1990s that reinvigorated studio interest in the project?

First, and obviously, executives believed the project could turn a profit for the studio. But the decision to finally make the film was facilitated by noneconomic factors also. The processes that influence which products are disseminated by the culture industries are based on the management hierarchy's *perception* of the cultural marketplace. To be sure, the most successful companies are the ones that respond swiftly to change. Warner Brothers' decision to finance *Malcolm X* was driven by several factors external to the organization. For example, Academy Award winner Denzel Washington had established himself as a talented actor with box-office appeal. Spike Lee, who was not the film's initial director, had positioned himself on the cutting edge of black cinema. And perhaps most important, black youth had created a popular culture based on Malcolm X as a symbol of race pride and cultural resistance. By the early 1990s, the renewed interest in Malcolm X sparked a proliferation of rap songs, caps, T-shirts, books, and posters that saturated the popular cultural world of black youth. It was the popularization of Malcolm X and his attractiveness to black youth that both Warner Brothers and Lee sought to exploit.

From the beginning, the production of the film was hindered by studio strife and politics. First, there was the difficult task of selecting a director for the project. Warner Brothers chose a white filmmaker, Norman Jewison, initially. The filmmaker had received critical acclaim for his cinematic adaptation of a successful Broadway play about African American soldiers in the 1940s. But many African Americans protested his assignment to the project, claiming *Malcolm X* should be directed by an African American. Public pressure included a letter-writing campaign as well. Lee also began to publicly denounce the choice of Jewison as the director. Lee used the symbolic capital he had accumulated as a popular African American icon to position himself for the project. Lee met with Marvin Worth, the man who had optioned the film rights to Warner Brothers, to discuss the possibility of directing the film. After a meeting between Lee, Jewison, Worth, and studio executives, Jewison decided to resign from the project. It was soon decided that Lee was the best director for the project.

A second source of tension was the budget allocated for production. Lee's three feature films prior to *Malcolm X* had been financed and distributed by Universal. But because Warner Brothers owned the film rights to *Malcolm X,* he would have to work in a different organizational environment. Studio execs immediately rejected Lee's initial $34 million budget proposal. Warner Brothers offered $18 million plus the film's foreign rights, which were purchased by Largo Productions for $8 million. Despite the insufficient funding, Lee refused to downsize the project, which included extensive preproduction work in the form of interviews and research; a rigorous two-year production schedule consisting of principal photography in New York City, Saudi Arabia, Egypt, and South Africa; a set design that required the creation of twelve sets; over four hundred crew members; a cast of two hundred principals; and the orchestration of thousands of extras.[28] In addition, the postproduction schedule required, among other things, editing over two years' worth of footage into a feature-length film. The enormity of the project created serious problems.

A third source of tension was creative control. Lack of sufficient capital imposed serious limitations on Lee's creative vision. Lee argued that, in order to do justice to the complex trajectory of Malcolm X's life, the film would need to exceed three hours in length. Warner Brothers wanted a two-hour-and-fifteen-minute film. Studio executives prefer shorter films. According to industry research, lengthy films reduce the number of screenings per day, thus reducing potential box-office revenue. Lee charged that the success of films like *Dances with Wolves* (Orion Pictures) and *JFK* (Warner Brothers), both of which ran more than three hours, proved otherwise. In addition, Lee expressed concerns about the studio's desire to conduct test screenings. The filmmaker feared that even a slightly unfavorable score from test audiences would threaten his creative independence. Lee's three pictures prior to *Malcolm X* were each distributed by Universal. Whereas Lee's directorial and administrative style with Universal had been, to a large degree, autonomous, the filmmaker charges that his working relationship with Warner Brothers was, in contrast, adversarial. Discussing his battles with the executive brass at Warner Brothers, Lee writes:

> Corporations do business. I'm usually able to get along with the people I do business with. I have a relationship with them, like at Universal, but that was not the case at Warner Brothers. Their offices are run very differently. Universal is really a good situation for me because it's a hands-off situation. They let me alone. They let me make my films. And they never failed to turn their profit. I've never had somebody meddle as much as Warner Brothers has with me so far. . . . Of

course, I realize I never made a $33 million film at Uni-
versal, either. So the higher the stakes, the more the
studio wants to have a hand in the creative filmmaking process.[29]

But studio executives were not the only element of discord that
threatened to subvert Lee's cinematic interpretation of the former civil
rights leader's life. Lee's creative license was vehemently challenged
from various segments of what he surely expected to be a decisively
supportive African American community. Much as it had with *School
Daze,* the African American "image police" expressed concerns regarding Lee's personal agenda and his unmitigated desire to merchandise
black culture.[30] In fact, his presence as the director of the film generated intense protest from some circles and raised a number of questions.
For example, some of Lee's most adamant and vocal critics charged that
Lee's agenda was self-serving and strictly committed to self-promotion of
the filmmaker's career in the entertainment industry.[31] Others expressed
concerns regarding how Lee would represent Malcolm X. For example:
Would the film present Malcolm X as a street hustler, pimp, and drug
user? Would Lee explore Malcolm's sexual relationships with white
women? Some African Americans demanded that Lee de-emphasize the
zoot-suited, street-hustling days that characterized part of Malcolm's
young adult life. In addition, the Nation of Islam's leader, Louis Farrakhan, attempted to influence the filmmaker's portrayal of Malcolm's life.
More specifically, Farrakhan voiced concern about how Lee planned to
portray the antagonism that erupted between Malcolm X and the founder of the Black Muslim movement, Elijah Muhammed.[32]

In the end, however, financial matters far outweighed all other concerns. The film ran overbudget, and Warner Brothers refused to finance
the completion of the project. As a result, a completion bond company
had to assume responsibility for production. The bond company is the
guarantor to make sure a film is completed in compliance with the script
agreed to by the creative personnel and studio. It is the company's job
to ensure that the final product meets the high quality expectations of
the industry. But the bond company wanted Lee to scale down the re-
maining production schedule, which included shooting scenes in Egypt
and South Africa. After several disagreements, the bond company, too,
refused to supply the capital necessary to finish production.

Lee soon found the future status of the film hanging in the balance.

In addition to completing the shooting schedules, the postproduction phase of the project—which included, among other things, editing, sound mixing, and music recording—was a major task. The production crew had compiled nearly a year and a half of film footage, which now needed cutting into a neatly packaged final cut. Trapped in a battle of wills, the studio and the bond company decided to let the film linger indefinitely, complaining that both costs and the filmmaker were spiraling out of control. It was at this time that Lee began to denounce Warner Brothers publicly. Lee feared he might lose discussions conducted in the shrouded secrecy of boardroom corridors, so he decided to make the battle public. He soon released press statements and then scheduled a press conference. He reminded the press that Oliver Stone's production of *JFK*, which was also distributed by Warner Brothers, was also a three-hour film that ran overbudget. Lee claimed before the press that the budget and production problems he faced were in fact customary. He framed the issue in the following manner: was the production of *JFK* more important than the production of *Malcolm X*? Why was Warner Brothers willing to flex its financial muscle for *JFK* and not for *Malcolm X*? Lee's answer was simple and strategically designed to generate public attention: racism. Lee charged that despite his track record of critically and commercially successful films, studios continued to treat him unfairly by restricting him to low production budgets. He argued that white directors with little or no experience or, in other cases, box-office blunders were given $40 million to $50 million budgets to make their films.

In many ways, Lee's comments about the industry were accurate, to the extent that they pointed to a larger problematic: the difficulty black filmmakers faced establishing themselves in ways that enable them to command resources and respect from the commercial film industry equal to those of their white peers. Despite the popularity of black expressive cultures, the culture industry still remains reluctant to abolish all of the barriers that prevent full participation by blacks as producers of popular media products. This is perhaps most true of the film industry. The production of popular film is arguably the most prestigious of the most prominent popular media cultures and is certainly the most expensive. Thus, the film industry has been quite deliberate in its treatment of black filmmakers and the films they wish to produce. In addition to dealing with serious thematic and genre restrictions, black filmmakers have been forced to accept especially low production budgets. The primary obstacle confronting Lee was the lack of industry commitment to sustaining a black film production trend that moves beyond the limited parameters of youth-inflected ghetto narratives.

Lee's use of the news media was a strategic gamble. As far back as *She's Gotta Have It,* Lee understood that because he was a marginal player in the culture of Hollywood, coverage from the press was analogous to paid publicity. Lee calculated that the use of the press in this instance, however, was one of the few options available to him to fight back against the intransigence of Warner executives. Eventually, Lee was able to raise money to complete the film by making personal appeals to wealthy black entertainers.[33] Without their support, the project would have remained suspended indefinitely.

Despite the numerous production dilemmas, a number of factors indicate that *Malcolm X* was packaged, released, and marketed as a potential blockbuster. First, the finished product was packaged to assure a PG-13 rating. This was important insofar as it allowed the film to target young moviegoers especially. In one of several interviews with major periodicals, Lee openly claimed, "I've never made a PG-13 film before, ever. We did not want to give parents nor schoolteachers nor educational systems an excuse why this film cannot be used as a class trip, or why it could not be a part of their curriculum."[34] Lee's attempt to appeal to young moviegoers, families, and educators undoubtedly influenced his cinematic interpretation of Malcolm X. Indeed, one of the main criticisms of the film charged that the representation of Malcolm X was intentionally diluted and made nonthreatening. The decision to present a figure who could appeal to and entertain a large movie audience was not entirely Lee's. This decision had actually been made some twenty-five years prior to production when Warner Brothers purchased the film rights to *The Autobiography of Malcolm X.* Gitlin's assessment of the production logic that governs the television industry is also applicable to the film industry. The national entertainment industries, he argues, are committed to keeping their movies compact, narrow, and simplified. Further, he writes: "Indeed, coherence is defined as narrowness, and not just in the thinking of the writers but audiences, too. It is the dramatic aesthetic that prevails in this culture. Such conventions are shared, not imposed. When they are shared long enough and deeply enough, they harden into the collective second nature of a cultural style."[35] In his analysis of the production of movies made for prime-time television, Gitlin concludes that both the creative personnel and the audience gravitate toward thematic and stylistic conservatism. Lee's decision to make an epic biographical picture made it even more difficult to deal with the intricacies of Malcolm X's life and times. The dominant narrative structure of the biopic, by nature, tends to elevate historical figures over historical context, thus presenting historical struggle as a conflict between Herculean male individuals.[36]

A second indication that the film was released as a potential blockbuster was the broad-base audience Lee attempted to recruit, evidenced by his elaborate use of the media gatekeeping institutions. For each specific movie product, filmmakers must create an audience image—that is, an imaginary market of potential moviegoers.[37] Segments of the African American moviegoing population were, of course, the primary target audience. Lee conducted interviews and appeared on the cover of several magazines that target black consumers. Black newspapers were also saturated with information about the film. In addition, Black Entertainment Television (BET) presented numerous specials that targeted youth and adult audiences separately. During a lecture tour at historically black colleges, Lee proclaimed the need for African Americans to support the film. Furthermore, the filmmaker carefully designed a variety of promotional tie-in products featuring the "X" symbol that was widely popular among African American youth.

But Lee also worked diligently to create a link between the film and potential white moviegoers. A variety of media sources targeting white consumers were used for promotion. For example, mainstream news periodicals ran cover and feature stories on the film. The movie was also featured on the cover of mainstream specialty consumer magazines like *Esquire* and *Rolling Stone.* In addition, the filmmaker made guest appearances on television programs—*Larry King Live, Niteline,* and *60 Minutes*—that provided access to large white adult audiences. MTV was an important vehicle for growing the interest of white youth. Both MTV and BET ran heavy rotations of the music video *Revolution*—from the movie sound track—performed by the rap group Arrested Development. The producers of *Malcolm X* realized that, in order to turn a profit (the final tab was $34 million), it was necessary to recruit a wide audience. The challenge to produce a box-office hit requires that a filmmaker appeal to different segments of the moviegoing population in order to maximize the size of the potential audience.

Finally, wide distribution also suggests that the film was treated as a potential blockbuster. The film was released near Thanksgiving Day,

Table 4.5. *Variety* Box-Office Reports for *Malcolm X* (Warner Brothers, 1992)

Week	Week's Reported Box Office ($)	Cumulative Reported Box Office ($)	Screens	Week's Average $ per Screen
1	14,564,862	14,564,862	1,124	12,958
2	12,542,372	28,837,396	1,249	10,042
3	5,367,287	33,911,081	1,249	4,297
4	2,851,055	36,578,188	1,249	2,283
7*	3,087,774	45,174,542	1,110	2,969
8	1,201,114	46,283,041	1,040	1,356
9	NR†	NR	880	NR
10	353,297	47,542,013	266	1,328
11	187,688	47,720,963	122	1,538
12	116,163	47,822,994	79	1,470
13	NR	NR	33	NR
14	48,596	47,913,823	47	1,034
15	41,607	47,954,144	34	1,224
16	27,979	47,981,176	25	1,119

*Weeks 5 and 6 not reported.
†Not reported.

during the high-traffic holiday season. It opened on 1,124 screens and soon peaked at 1,249 (see table 4.5). Reported box-office revenue the opening weekend exceeded $14 million. *Time* magazine reported that "the film grossed $2.4 million its first day, a whopping 66% more than Oliver Stone's *JFK.*" The film's high dollar-per-theater average was impressive during the first three weeks. By week four, *Malcolm X* grossed over $36 million. But the film began to lose some of its box-office strength subsequently. By mid-January, the film was on 1,040 screens, but the dollar-per-theater average dropped considerably. By week ten, the number of screens had been reduced to 266. During the film's final nine weeks, according to the *Variety* reports, *Malcolm X* grossed less than $2 million. By film industry standards, the box-office performance was average at best. The film did not lose money, but its failure to demonstrate "legs"—that is, perform well at the box office for an extended period of time—was surprising considering the amount of hype and prerelease publicity.

Malcolm X received, by far, the most publicity of any film in 1992. The struggle to produce *Malcolm X* created even greater media interest than usual. The film had all the necessary dramatic elements coveted by the media gatekeeping institutions; thus, it generated enormous free publicity. So what happened? First, there were some disputes about box-office receipts. It appears as though several theaters attributed ticket sales from *Malcolm X* to other films. But perhaps most important, it appears as though Lee's attempt to move from the specialty to potential blockbuster film was a miscalculation of his market potential. The film demonstrates that, while Lee's market appeal is strong, it continues to be concentrated.

But the movie did generate nearly $50 million in domestic sales, a noteworthy feat for a black-theme, period film. Lee's struggle to broaden the thematic and commercial scope of black popular film must also be viewed in historical context. The commercial success of black cinema in the early 1990s was buoyed mostly by the box-office dollars of young moviegoers. As a result, those movies that successfully linked themselves to the popular rhythms of youth culture tended to perform strongly at the box office. The staple audience of black cinema, young moviegoers, is less likely to turn out in large numbers for films that stretch beyond the pleasurable confines of the symbolic world they create for themselves. *Malcolm X* was a period piece, a biographical picture that was not easily assimilable to the contemporary currents of youth popular culture. For example, while the movie sound track contained a rap song, the bulk of the music consisted of period songs from the sixties. Consequently, it was difficult to use the sound track as a promotional tie-in product that could appeal to youth in particular. Black music is still the most popular, prestigious, and profitable African American expressive culture. Thus, to the extent that Lee could not harness the powerful appeal of black music to the film, much like the ghetto action films discussed in chapters 6 and 7, it was difficult to generate and sustain interest.

Finally, the enormous amount of time and energy Lee invested in the production and marketing of *Malcolm X* also revealed his increasing commitment to establishing himself as a major player on the field of commercial culture—a commitment that demanded that the filmmaker master the roles not only of artist/filmmaker but of entrepreneur/businessperson as well. Much like one of the most enduring figures of "race movies," Oscar Micheaux, Lee understood the need to market both himself and his films in an assertive style. In the case of Lee, though, he also enjoyed certain opportunities that simply did not exist for previous generations of black filmmakers. Thus, Lee fully recognized that, in the age of media cross-fertilization and infotainment, his success as a filmmaker could be enhanced by gaining access to popular resources beyond the arena of popular film.

Spike Lee and the Accumulation
of Symbolic Capital

There is a nationalist underpinning to his financial and creative activities, yet Spike has no problem doing business with corporate America. She's was very much a guerrilla enterprise that was distributed by Island, then a maverick studio. Ever since, Spike has worked with major studios and national advertisers. Is there a contradiction in this? Only if your head is still stuck in the '60s. In the face of modern corporate infotainment monoliths, the most realpolitik counterstrategy is to be in business with as many as possible. Diversifying protects you against cooptation by any single corporate entity or industry. With revenue flowing in from commercials, books, music videos, and merchandising, Spike has some major cushion should Hollywood get tired of his methods or his mouth.

NELSON GEORGE[38]

Lee's success as a filmmaker can be partially attributed to his entrepreneurial endeavors external to the production of film. Lee, like most African American filmmakers, has had to contend with low budgets and modest marketing campaigns. Typically, a studio will release a black film in specific markets, with the hope that a few people will see it, like it, and then generate interest through word of mouth. Indeed, African American filmmakers pose an intriguing dilemma to studios: despite the popularity of black cultural productions, executives are still careful to invest only the minimum amount of dollars necessary to produce a film. So because the film industry remains lukewarm at best about black cinema, the entrepreneurial practices of individual filmmakers, then, emerge as an important feature in their efforts to carve out a successful niche in the popular culture industry.

Despite the specialized scope of his films and the meager promotional efforts undertaken by studios, Lee has successfully navigated his marginality by practicing an assertive brand of entrepreneurship. He transformed his marginal status as a black independent filmmaker into a diverse and multifaceted commercial enterprise. To be sure, the filmmaker's movement into other spheres of commercial culture has enabled him to develop cross-promotional tie-ins that both invigorate and broaden his commercial appeal. For example, Lee's association with the Nike shoe company and Michael Jordan broadened his base and established him as a "player" on the terrain of American popular culture. In addition, his music recording company and music video productions allow him to keep a finger on the pulse of the most popular and dynamic form of African American expressive culture.

This cross-promotional strategy represents an exercise in good business acumen. By spreading himself across the popular cultural landscape, Lee increases his visibility and attaches himself to popular trends that enliven his commercial viability. According to cultural critic Nelson George, Lee's entrepreneurial practices function as a buffer, shielding him from the unpredictable world of filmmaking generally and the marginal status of black filmmakers specifically. Lee's entrepreneurial practices also perform a strong promotional function. The commercial viability of most films relies on promotional tie-ins that stimulate audience interest. Merchandising is a crucial aspect of marketing in the New Hollywood. As Graeme Turner asserts, "popular film is rarely presented to its public as a single product or commodity."[39] Film, more generally, is a composite commodity, incorporating a plethora of merchandise that serves both a promotional and economic function. Promotional merchandise comes in various forms: sound tracks, music videos, apparel, toys, books, posters, and even the Internet. Although he is often criticized for his use of promotional tie-in–related strategies, Lee's emphasis on merchandising is not unique; in fact, it represents an industry rule that has been evolving at least since the 1950s, when film producers realized that rock 'n' roll music could be employed to make movies more attractive to young filmgoers. Lee's use of other media and commercial endorsements accords him both the prestige and the symbolic capital necessary to compete in the vast and ever-changing world of popular media culture.[40]

While Lee's merchandising efforts are not especially unique, what the filmmaker merchandises is distinctive: a peculiar mix of black cultural resistance and identity politics. Because studios limit the promotion budget for specialty films, Lee often relies on his public image as a controversial filmmaker to carve out a market niche and attract media publicity. In the process, the filmmaker dexterously exploits the volatility of race. In essence, he effectively turns his fight against institutional racism into a cause célèbre that is equally riveting, strategic, and problematic. Lee openly acknowledges that "controversial or political subject matter can work well at the box office."[41] Volatile subject matter functions as both a political gesture and a promotional tactic. The film-maker's cultural politics and productions, for example, invoke race pride ("Stay black!") while commercializing it at the same time ("Buy black!"). The emergence of a viable black culture industry, in this instance, is freighted with sharp contradictions: Lee appropriates resources from the dominant culture industry to establish a base (Forty Acres and a Mule Filmworks) from which to launch commodities (films, books, clothing, inspirational speeches) that vigorously enunciate what Cornel West characterizes as the "new cultural politics of difference." And yet, this form of politics is also market-mediated and therefore vulnerable to shifts in the commercial and cultural landscape.[42]

Perhaps the most striking feature of Lee's ascendancy in the sphere of popular culture is how he negotiates the institutional and racial barriers that partially structure the popular film industry. By constantly berating the institutional racism that permeates the culture of Hollywood, the filmmaker uses his peripheral status to achieve, among other things, final-cut approval, studio financing, and media publicity. In truth, Lee has transformed what is generally believed to be a major obstacle for aspiring black filmmakers—film industry racism—into an enterprise that facilitates greater access to the social sites and resources central to the production of popular film. The manner in which he lobbied to get the directorial assignment for *Malcolm X* is an example. Lee turned the weight of industry indifference toward black filmmakers and their creative work against itself in an attempt to compel studio executives to "do the right thing." In the case of the production for *Malcolm X,* this meant securing provisions for a large budget and all of the professional amenities that accompany the production of widely distributed prestige films. While Lee did not receive everything he demanded, he did gain some measure of control over a highly anticipated and much publicized feature film.

Also, by openly criticizing the racial politics of the film industry, Lee has articulated the need for black filmmakers to be able to exercise control over their creative labor. For Lee, one important dimension of his filmic projects has been his constant struggle to maintain final-cut approval over his films. One of the primary sources of tension for filmmakers working in the commercial film industry is the struggle to exercise some measure of creative independence. Ironically, Lee's strategic indictment of the film industry has enabled him, more often than not, to exercise creative control over his work. But in the process of struggling for creative independence, Lee has been forced to make concessions, too. Most notably, he often works within the parameters of rigidly enforced budgetary restrictions, thus limiting the scope of many of his films.

And yet, despite being limited to the low-budget specialty film, Lee has managed to turn his creative independence into a distinctive style of cinematic discourse. In the course of making and marketing his films, Lee has cultivated a representational strategy and directorial signature that compel a consideration of how the formation of black American filmmaking can be deployed to engage, if not occasionally oppose, competing discourses about race and the culture wars that drive the social and political struggles of the period.

5 Spike's Joint

Presently in America a war is being fought. Forget about guns, planes, and bombs, the weapons from now on will be the newspapers, magazines, TV shows, radio, and FILM. The right has gotten BOLD, bolstered by their squashing of Ice-T's COP KILLER, any piece of art that doesn't hold the party line is subject to attack. It's war in the battleground of culture.

SPIKE LEE[1]

Spike Lee's call to arms along the cultural fault lines of American society is strikingly reminiscent of Patrick Buchanan's infamous declaration of the "culture wars" during the 1992 Republican Party convention. And although the sphere of popular media is, first and foremost, a vastly growing entertainment industry, Lee's comment correctly suggests it is also a fierce theater of social and political struggle. Like the producers of rap music, black filmmakers struggle to mobilize a cultural and representational politic that engages the shifting features of postindustrial black life and the rising tide of racial conservatism. Lee, like other participants in a growing black culture industry, has maneuvered to exploit transformations in the industrial image-making landscape that produce spaces for the commodification of expressive cultures that derive much of their energy and popularity from the fertile reservoir of black youth culture.

From the very beginning of his commercial filmmaking career, Lee has viewed the popular cinema as a stage for dramatizing the racial themes, plots, and subplots that structure American history, culture, and everyday life. In addition, the filmmaker has made more explicit the political nature of popular film entertainment and the manner in which African Americans have been excluded from any significant participation in its production. While Lee has been careful to associate with a variety of media cultures—television advertising, music video, music recording, and book publishing—his role as an independent filmmaker has been the driving force behind his ascendancy in American popular culture.

Filmmaking is not a random creative process. It involves making choices not only about the social world but also about *how to represent* the social world. Filmmaking is a distinct site of discourse, action, and production. A seemingly endless combination of techniques, styles, and aesthetic strategies informs the filmmaking process and enables distinct repertoires of representation. The mimetic qualities of cinema enable filmmakers to reconstruct their social world in ways that can work either to interrogate or to legitimate dominant social, economic, and political relationships. In many instances, a symbolic discourse like film can do both simultaneously. And as Michael Ryan and Douglas Kellner remind us, "[T]he representation of the social world is political and [the] choice of modes of representation instantiates differing political positions toward it. Indeed, every camera position, every scene composition, every editing decision, and every narrative choice involves a representational strategy that embeds various interests and desires. No aspect of film merely reveals or depicts 'reality.' Rather, films construct the social world in very specific ways."[2]

In this chapter, I discuss some of the distinctive filmmaking strategies that give style, structure, and significance to the ways in which Lee has strategically intervened in the world of popular film production. I consider, for example, how he manipulates specific elements of the cinematic apparatus—sound, movement, camera angles, editing, character development, and story-plot—to reimagine and re-represent the nuances of late twentieth-century black life. First, I explore the filmmaker's treatment of the hierarchical divisions and class tensions that structure African American communities. Second, I discuss Lee's attempt to represent and problematize the black American middle-class experience. Next, I assess the filmmaker's interrogation of "whiteness." In the final section, I discuss some of the expressive modes of cinematic authorship that give this filmmaking practice a distinct signature.

Differentiating Blackness

What makes you think a whole group of people have to be alike?

ESTHER ROLLE[3]

One of the most significant features of what Wahneema Lubiano refers to as the "Spike Lee Discourse" is its primary thematic locus: the interior spaces that organize the African American social world.[4] According to film scholar Ella Shohat, Lee skillfully appropriates the resources of popular film to rewrite the dominant narratives of all-black–cast films that are typically symptomatic of the subordinate status of African Americans from the dominant culture.[5] Shohat contends that one of the most important aspects of Lee's success is his attempt to reclaim the symbolic territory of popular film as a prologue to engaging dominant discourses about the broad range of social experiences that characterize the lives of African Americans.

In *School Daze,* for example, Lee constructs a fictional black college, Mission College, as the context for exploring how the politics of color, gender, and class militate against the making of a politically uniform and harmonious African American community. The film narrative presents the African American social world as a fragmented and contested sphere composed of numerous hierarchies and conflicts that operate somewhat independently from spheres of interracial conflict. In fact, one of the primary criticisms leveled at the film and its director was that it put on display many of the tensions that historically have created deep divisions and antagonisms within the African American community.

The film's opening credits coordinate two distinct elements in filmic discourse—the photographed image and music—to establish a context for interrogating the mythic claims of a monolithic African American community. The film begins in documentary fashion, combining both still photos and the Negro spiritual "I'm Building Me a Home." Whereas the Negro spiritual signifies unity, community, and the struggle by African Americans to establish autonomous spheres in which to practice community and assert a distinctive cultural identity, the still-photo montage illuminates the varying experiences and identity politics that proliferate within the African American community.[6] For example, the montage neatly juxtaposes contrasting political figures like Frederick Douglass, Booker T. Washington, and Marcus Garvey; cultural icons like

Paul Robeson and Ella Fitzgerald; sports heroes ranging from the concil-
iatory Joe Louis to the politically outspoken and robust Muhammad Ali;
and protest politics like the nonviolent civil rights movement and the
militant gestures expressed by the Black Panthers. The montage con-
denses the passage of time and, more important, conveys the idea that,
despite efforts by African Americans to "build a home," this struggle has
created enduring social and political divisions within the African American population. Moreover, the montage suggests that there is no such
thing as a black monolith or a single black experience, but rather a plu-
rality of identities and experiences that produces a broad range of political interests, ideologies, and expressive cultures.

In *School Daze,* Lee orchestrates a number of different characters
to animate the diverse range of interests and experiences in the black
American community.[7] Characters function primarily as the field of
action for articulating social and political discourses that are juxta-
posed against other characters. When analyzing popular cultural discourses like film, it is important to keep in mind that a character is often
constructed in relation to other characters in order to generate narrative conflict and tension. Each character, then, represents a distinct field
of discourse that performs a particular symbolic function in the narrative. The additional power and attraction of cinema, of course, is that
spectators see and hear the author's construction of characters.[8] We
see, for example, the author's choice of costuming, makeup, movement,
and environment. Also, we hear dialect and sound perspective used to
provide additional layers of meaning that facilitate our "reading" or
comprehension of each character. This method of analysis demands
that characters not be read as realistic figures but rather as animated
constructs that mobilize and put on display certain values (individualism) as well as certain ideological discourses (patriarchy). Conflict between characters is essentially conflict between competing values and
ideologies.

How does Lee construct an array of characters to both organize and
animate his cinematic critique of the social and political cleavages at
work in the African American community? The film is dominated by
two fraternities, the Gamma Phi Gamma fraternity and the "Fellas." The
two fraternities are differentiated primarily by socioeconomic class and
political orientation. On the one hand, the Gamma fraternity is an ensemble of characters who accentuate the values, interests, and experiences of the black bourgeoisie. On the other, the Fellas are an ensemble
of characters who give voice to the values and experiences of the black

working class. Fraternities are the social organizational site for the elaboration of male cultures and generally encompass a range of activities that can be oriented toward service, economic, or social needs. Fraternities were created to meet certain needs in the transition from boyhood to manhood and also perform many functions of a family.[9] Historically, the African American college fraternal orders have functioned as a source of racial unity and resource mobilization.[10] However, fraternal organizations are as much exclusive as they are inclusive. Black fraternal life, then, has also been symptomatic of the class cleavages that both reflect and reproduce political divisions within the African American community.

Lee communicates the middle-class status of the Gammas visually. For instance, members live in a spacious fraternity home, drive foreign cars, and wear stylish clothing. In addition, as the film unfolds, the viewer learns that members of the fraternity come from legacies of college-educated parents who were also members of black Greek-letter organizations. Many of the scenes are edited in a narrational fashion that counterposes the different class positions of the two fraternities. The working-class status of the Fellas is also communicated visually. We see, for example, that the characters live in a cramped dorm room, share an old automobile, and wear clothes that are less stylish than their counterparts. Further, members of this fraternity, as one of them explains, represent the first in their respective families to attend college. The competing values and political orientation of the two fraternities often place them in conflict as each attempts to dominate this fictional world of African American life and culture. The fracturing of black politics and community develops along two opposing poles in *School Daze:* on the one hand, the Fellas are committed to racial uplift through the practice of resisting African American complicity in the continuation of class stratification, while the Gammas, on the other, are committed to racial uplift through the incorporation and practice of middle-class values. It is the ideological tension between these two opposing value systems that creates conflict and motivates action in the story-plot.

The signature character from the Fellas, Dap Dunlap, represents a fissured black nationalist position. His character is informed by his role as a campus activist and, more specifically, the antiapartheid politics popularized in the mideighties. The viewer's introduction to Dap occurs in the opening sequence of the film, as he delivers a speech from the front steps of the administration building on campus. Throughout the narrative, Dap is generally involved in some type of protest or at-

141

tempting to mobilize students in opposition to the traditions that govern everyday campus life and university administration politics. Dap's Afrocentric paraphernalia animates his black nationalist orientation. Further, he is figured as an outsider, a nonconformist who struggles to subvert the main goal of college institutions, which is to prepare students for successful entry into a compliant, middle-class lifestyle.

Julian, the leader of the Gamma fraternity, is Dap's ideological antithesis. Julian conforms to the central tenets and middle-class notions of respectability. He frequently voices his disapproval of Dap's campus politics, labeling him an embarrassment to college administrators and students in general. Whereas Dap is devoted to disrupting tradition, Julian is primarily interested in continuing tradition. His costuming is distinctly middle-class and suggests a privileged background. These elements, then, construct the two young African American men as motivated by divergent interests, goals, and class experiences.

Dap and Julian dominate the narrative, figuratively and literally. The majority of the scenes, close-ups, dialogue, and story-space is devoted to these two characters. They are indeed the cause-and-effect agents motivating action, story conflict, and plot development. As a result, the narrative structure and operations of *School Daze* are sharply gendered. The female characters are clearly marginal in this filmic dialogue about intraracial social and political tensions. Whereas the men dominate the foreground, the women tend to occupy the background of this fictional world. Thus, the spheres of conflict and scenarios that dramatize the dynamic struggles and divisions within the African American community are imaginatively figured, by Lee, as the dominion of men. Lee's cinematic portrayal of the black American social world elides the voices of black women and, as a result, fails to devote substantive narrative time and space to their experiences.[11]

And while the voices and experiences of black women are indeed marginalized in *School Daze,* there are one or two sequences in which women are featured as the source of narrative action. For example, one sequence is a dance performance titled "Good and Bad Hair," which highlights the two central female character discourses in the film, the "Jigaboos" and the "Wannabees." The Jigaboos are characterized by their earthy, "natural" look and strong identification with black identity. The women are typically dark-skinned and sport Afrocentric hairstyles. Similarly to the Fellas, the Jigaboos are represented as members of the working class. Alternatively, the Wannabees (want to be white) are demarcated by their intense internalization of European-informed standards of beauty. Generally light-complexioned, the women wear colored contact lenses (typically, blue or green); hair extensions to emulate long, straight hair; and other cosmetic accoutrements that alter, according to Lee's logic, their "natural" look. The Wannabees, like the Gammas, embody the interests of the black middle class. The women are often well dressed, drive expensive cars, and live in nicely furnished apartments.

The Jigaboos and the Wannabees function as the primary vehicle through which Lee attempts to problematize the issue of skin color antagonism.[12] While colorism within African American communities has worked historically as an instrument of division, Lee's treatment of the issue in *School Daze* is underdeveloped, thus making it symptomatic of the problem rather than critical of the problem. Perhaps one of the most striking aspects of the Spike Lee Discourse is that the filmmaker oftentimes mistakes putting a social problem on cinematic display for a form of critique in and of itself. In the context of the narrative politics of *School Daze,* the Wannabees' stylization of the female body is considered Eurocentric and therefore self-deprecating and "unnatural."[13] Lee figures the Wannabees as less racially conscious and authentic than their female counterparts. It is precisely this type of racial *essentialism,* or rigid notions of what constitutes blackness, particularly in his early work, that generated such sharp criticism of Lee's cultural and racial politics.[14]

Considering that Lee's critical gaze is occasionally clouded in the film, especially his gender and sexual politics, he does offer, however, a sharper critique of the class differences *within* the African American community that operate as a constant source of conflict prohibiting a monolithic experience based simply on race. In addition to the class-coded conflict between the two male fraternities, Lee explores other dimensions of class tension. One example occurs in the sequence between the Fellas and a group described in the film credits as the "Local Yokels." The "Locals" represent the majority of African Americans who do not attend college. They are also resentful of Mission College students, who often look down on them. The conflict between the working-class fraternity members and a group of local working-class blacks appropriately emphasizes how class divisions in the African American community often lead to conflict.

On campus, the working-class Fellas are constantly engaged in conflict with middle-class students. However, away from campus, the Fellas are redefined as middle-class and aloof from the experiences of working-class blacks by the Locals. After a slight altercation between the Fellas and the Locals in a fast-food restaurant, the former attempt to return to campus but are confronted by the latter. The ensuing dialogue in the sequence is instructive (remarks of members of the Locals are italicized):

Dap: Brother, what do you want?
Spoon: We ain't kin.
Leeds: And we're not your brother. How come you college motherfuckers think y'all run everything?
Booker T: Is there a problem here?
Spoon: Big problems.
Moses: I heard that.
Leeds: You come into our town year after year and take over. We wuz born here, gone be here, and gone die here, and can't find jobs because of you.
Monroe: Dap, can we go?
Leeds: We may not have yo ed-u-ca-tion, *but we ain't dirt either.*
Dap: Nobody said all that.
Leeds: You Mission punks are always talking down to us.
Dap: I'm sorry you feel that way, I really am.
Leeds: Are you black?
Eric: Take a look in the mirror.
Dap: You got a legitimate beef, but it ain't with us.
Leeds: I said, are *you black?*
Dap: Don't ever question whether I'm black. In fact, I was gonna ask yo' country BAMA ass, why you put those drip-drop chemicals in your hair?
Leeds: I bet you niggers think y'all are white. College don't mean shit, y'all niggers, and you gone be niggers forever, just like us . . . niggers!
Dap: You're not niggers.

From the Locals' perspective, there is no difference between Mission College students: they are all disdainful of poor and working-class blacks. The Fellas are repositioned by the Locals as a part of the same social hierarchy the fraternity purports to resist. Leeds's question, "are you black?" is posed in an accusatory tone and basically reclassifies the Fellas as blacks who "wannabee" white—that is, disassociated from working-class blacks and their struggles. In this context, the perception of class difference and privilege assumes greater saliency than race. In addition, the dramatic tension in this sequence is complemented by a strategic use of *mise en scène.* In the cinema, *mise en scène* refers to how visual elements are choreographed and arranged on-screen in correspondence with a thematic idea. One of the dominant visual motifs used in *School Daze* to symbolize conflict is two people positioned in an "in your face" profile. This particular sequence is framed by a medium shot that allows the spectator to fully see the spatial arrangements of the characters. Lee's management of screen space signifies class tension and conflict as the Locals are lined up in an angle that positions them in conflict with the Fellas.

Lee's politicization of popular film discourse earned him critical acclaim and the uninvited role as African American spokesperson. The filmmaker's emergence in the late 1980s did bring to the terrain of commercial cinema a distinct style of discourse about the shifting contours of race in postindustrial American culture. Before Lee, and even after him, the handful of theatrical releases that featured African Americans were generally comedies or popular music vehicles that rarely explored the more intriguing and dramatic aspects of African American life. In *School Daze,* Lee accurately presents the black American community as fractured internally by a number of differences—differences of class, color, generation, gender, and region. But while Lee's politicization of popular film represents an important form of intervention, his cinematic imagination generally tends to privilege the experiences of men over women. In this microcosmic black world, Lee fails to represent the experiences of women in ways that break from prevailing gender discourses and render them problematic.

One of the interesting conditions of Lee's popular ascendancy is that it took place with few other African American filmmakers on the commercial scene. As a result, Lee became the focus of both celebration and scrutiny. Perhaps more so than any other filmmaker, Lee's representational politics, and especially the gender dimensions, have been heavily criticized. In reality, the cinema is a male-dominated sphere of cultural production. Traditionally, women have been relegated to the role of sexualized object, although more women are challenging the gender hierarchies that structure film production. Lee's primary goal has been to challenge and demystify the ways in which Hollywood movies, to use Ed Guerrero's book title, "frame blackness."[15] But in the process of doing so, the filmmaker has not been as sensitive to the ways in which the commercial film industry also frames gender and sexuality. Inasmuch as the black press has often celebrated his work, and the mainstream press has often policed his cultural politics, feminist critics have challenged the notion that Lee's cultural politics are, in fact, oppositional. But unlike other filmmakers, Lee has not been detached from this criticism. The filmmaker's loose affiliation with the world of scholarly and cultural criticism has compelled him, for example, to reconsider his representation of gender.[16] In some of his later work, Lee has acknowledged the need to create more nuanced representations of women in his films and also be more critical of how he represents blackness.

Interrogating Blackness

What is at issue here is the recognition of the extraordinary diversity of subjective positions, social experiences and cultural identities which compose the category "black." . . .
The question of the black subject cannot be represented without reference to the dimensions of class, gender, sexuality and ethnicity.

STUART HALL[17]

Lee's cinematic exploration of the contradictions, tension, and hierarchies that shape the interior spaces of the black social world is also a dominant thematic motif in his 1991 feature film release *Jungle Fever*. In this particular film, Lee constructs a narrative that suggests that race is a fluid, contradictory, and unstable locus of identity. Further, *Jungle Fever* suggests that individuals must often negotiate a complex array of identities. The film complicates the experience of race, by suggesting that other formations of identity also influence how individuals experience the social world.

According to Hall, one of the most significant dilemmas in creating representations that effectively interrogate dominant representations of blackness is "not only the absence or marginality of the black experience, but also, its simplification."[18] For African American filmmakers, the struggle to resist the simplification of the black experience has created a tremendous burden and responsibility. This burden of representation creates pressure to produce films that strike the black viewing public as both "positive" and authentic representations of African American life. Such a project is, of course, impossible given the range of experiences and identities that make up a vast and diverse African American population. Still, the most persistent challenge confronting black cultural producers calls for them to replace "negative" images with "positive" images.[19]

The alternative challenge confronting black cultural producers is to abandon the call for more bourgeois-styled images and cultivate, instead, a cultural politics that invests in the idea that the representation of the social world is irreducible to the positive or negative image conundrum. The representation of blackness is more complicated than the prescriptions typically championed by the black image police. Indeed, as Hall reminds us, individuals are always negotiating various kinds of differences—race, gender, class, age, sexuality. Further, he adds:

> [T]hese antagonisms refuse to be neatly aligned; they are simply not reducible to one another; they refuse to coalesce around a single axis of differentiation. We are always in negotiation, not with a single set of oppositions that place us always in the same relation to others, but with a series of different positionalities. Each has for us its point of profound subjective identification. And that is the most difficult thing about this proliferation of the field of identities and antagonisms: they are often dislocating in relation to one another.[20]

To be sure, a necessary breakthrough in black representational politics is the struggle to create images that are not simply inversions of negative stereotypes. The more formidable struggle is to create representations that recognize that the experiences of African Americans are shaped by different identities, positions, and social contexts. In other words, the challenge confronting more nuanced forms of representational politics is to explore how everyday black experiences are shaped not only by race but also by other formations like class, sexuality, gender, and age.

Despite all of the criticism that has been directed at Lee over the years, very little of it acknowledges that he has given, albeit in occasionally problematic ways, some consideration to creating film narratives that engage the complex ways in which blackness is experienced and socially constructed. In *Jungle Fever,* the character Flipper Purify comes exceptionally close to animating a discourse that articulates a multipositioned subject; that is, a character whose different identities—gender, sexuality, race/ethnicity—do not cohere neatly or remain impervious to external forces and the shifting contours of everyday life.

The creators of film employ a number of strategies when constructing characters. One important element is the selection of names possessing appropriate meanings and/or connotations to help personify the character. *Flipper,* for example, connotes movement and instability;

indeed, a fractured subject. Moreover, Flipper embodies the frustrations and volatile position of the black middle class.[21] *Jungle Fever* vigorously problematizes the black middle-class experience. Whereas the black urban poor have been the subject of numerous inquiries and television news narratives, very little critical attention, by comparison, has been devoted to middle-class African Americans. It is as if the problem of "race" only affects the black poor and working classes. And in those instances in which popular media culture devotes time and space to the treatment of the black middle class, it is often in terms that obscure the role race plays in their lives. Take, as a case in point, the portrayal of black middle-class life in the television situation comedy.

Historically, the inclusion of African Americans in television programs has been problematic and contentious.[22] Gitlin posits that the current motives for whitening television have shifted from the crude racial prejudices that shaped the origins of the medium to a kind of market calculation that restricts black representation on television.[23] While black dramatic or serious subject matter is customarily excluded from the face of prime-time television, blacks have generally served as excellent vehicles for comedy. Without question, the domestic situation comedy has been the dominant genre in the medium's representation of African Americans. Because the producers of commercial television are generally timid when it comes to engaging explicitly racial themes, the sitcom is an ideal site for constructing blackness precisely because, as Stephen Neale and Frank Krutnik write, "racial difference is made acceptable within the parameters of the traditional family unit."[24] Whereas the popular film industry has gravitated toward grim pseudorealistic portrayals of black ghetto life, the television industry has moved in a different direction instead: toward idealized portraits of black middle-class domesticity.[25]

During the 1980s, *The Cosby Show* rewrote the rules governing the television industry's representation of African Americans. The program dominated the eighties television landscape, revived the domestic sitcom, and emerged as *the* paradigm for the prime-time depiction of black middle-class life. As Henry Louis Gates Jr. asserts, "[T]he show's unprecedented success in depicting the lives of affluent blacks has exercised a profound influence on television. . . . 'Cosby's' success has led to the flow of TV sitcoms that feature the black middle class, each of which takes its lead from the 'Cosby Show.'"[26] The sitcom's representation of black family life clearly broke important ground in American cultural history by shifting the parameters of television's portrayal of black familial life.[27]

But in the process of reconfiguring the scope of black faces on television, the popularity of the sitcom also facilitated an imitative cycle that gravitated decisively toward the presentation of a nonproblematic black middle class. This trend became the television industry's equivalent to one of the most prominent and reactionary themes of the 1980s: the declining significance of race.[28] The new black sitcom, more often than not, ignored the pernicious manner in which race and racism penetrate the lives of the black middle class.[29] Ironically, and as Herman Gray contends, the programs provided a surreptitious critique of the black urban poor that paralleled the growing influence of social conservatism. Gray suggests that TV's fictional characterization of black middle-class identity as positive, affluent, and attractive confirms the notion that upward mobility in American society is open to all who demonstrate the right cultural values and behavior.[30] Further, Gray contends that the repetitious portrayal of successful black middle-class families suggests that the black urban poor are impoverished because they "live differently and operate with different attitudes and moral codes from everyone else."[31]

But like all sitcoms, *The Cosby Show* and its imitators were limited, first, by their narrative structure and, second, by their placement within the prime-time television lineup. The limits of the sitcom are the limits of the genre. Comedic situations rarely permit an incisive treatment of serious social and political issues.[32] Generally speaking, sitcoms adhere to formulaic strategies that enforce serious limitations on both character and plot development. The dominant narrative structure of the sitcom consists of three components: exposition, complication, and resolution.[33] The conventions of the domestic sitcom are subjected to a recurring process of destabilization/restabilization and rely upon a happy resolution of the complication that temporarily disrupts narrative equilibrium. Furthermore, the nucleus of the paradigm is invested in the notion that the bourgeois nuclear family is the model of normality and the solution to most social problems.

Finally, the location of the domestic sitcom in the TV lineup imposes strict topical limitations. The early-evening time slot reserved for the sitcom precludes serious and dramatic treatment of subject matter because it targets a young, adolescent viewing audience. Presumably, then, the later time slot in the prime-time schedule tends to program for a more mature audience. In this sense, then, to paraphrase the novelist Herbert Gold, the proliferation of black middle-class family situation comedies in the 1980s tended to "be about happy people with happy problems."[34]

However, if television's portrayal of the black middle class revolves around happy people with happy problems, Spike Lee's portrayal in *Jungle Fever* is a sharp contrast, to the extent that it revolves around complicated people with complicated problems. Cinema is a fiercely visual medium; thus, it magnifies the power of the image. *Jungle Fever* is organized around a rather dynamic play on cultural symbols that foregrounds the visual vocabulary of film (i.e., *mise en scène,* lighting, color, costuming, artifacts). The film does not break new ground in its deployment of visual elements, but it does successfully arrange these elements in correspondence with the intentions of the filmmaker: to explore the volatile interaction between race, class, gender, and sexuality in American culture.

A number of visual cues, for instance, are inserted to solidify Flipper's middle-class status: home delivery of the *New York Times,* a spacious and elegantly furnished brownstone home, black art, and nicely fitted suit-and-tie ensembles that animate his corporate status. Despite the *Cosby Show*–like similarities, Flipper's middle- and professional-class status is constantly renegotiated in relation to a number of different circumstances. Most important, in contrast to the unproblematic treatment of the black middle class in the television sitcom, Flipper's experiences are routinely problematized. Flipper is forced to negotiate different circumstances that do not consistently privilege his status as a handsomely paid architect.

In fact, different contexts compel Flipper to negotiate different identities that are frequently inscribed on him. While at work, for example, Flipper is positioned primarily along the axis of race. For instance, early in the film, when asked about work, the character replies: "I'm just a struggling black man in a cruel and harsh white corporate America." It is clear that while his contributions to the architectural firm that employs him are significant, his future status as partner in the firm is treated with ambivalence. In this context, Flipper's character is defined in relation to the two white partners who own the firm. The first sign of conflict develops when Flipper's request for a black secretary is ignored by the two partners. One of the partners is openly antagonistic toward his request and accuses him of coming "dangerously close to reverse discrimination." The notion of reverse discrimination is immediately challenged by Flipper when he poses the question "Why am I the only person of color working in this firm?" The central conflict between Flipper and his white counterparts is specified clearly: the precarious status of blacks who gain entrance into predominantly white, upper-middle- and middle-class professions. Flipper is at once assimilated and marginalized.

The conflict between them is further accentuated during a meeting to discuss Flipper's future with the firm. The visual organization of the sequence is an example of how film, when used efficiently, can communicate laconically. Rather than use the conventional shot/reverse shot method employed most often to accompany lengthy dialogue in film scenes, Lee opted instead to film the meeting in one long take, a sequence shot, with no editing or close-up camera angles.[35] The spatial arrangement of the characters in this sequence signifies the power imbalance between the partners and Flipper. They are seated at the opposite ends of a large conference table. In addition, the camera is noticeably unsteady, thus sharpening the dramatic tension between the characters. The constant movement of the camera symbolizes the instability many black professionals experience in white corporate and professional settings.[36] Dissatisfied with his future prospects for becoming a partner in the firm, Flipper angrily submits his resignation.

Later in the film, Flipper experiences a near-fatal altercation after he is confronted by two white police officers. In this situation, Flipper's identity is repositioned along the axis of race *and* gender. While Flipper is engaged in a playful boxing match with his white female lover, an onlooker mistakes the lighthearted skirmish for an assault. In a furious charge, two white police officers subdue Flipper and force him into a submissive position by pointing a gun to the back of his head, a clear and obvious act of intimidation. Angie, Flipper's lover, naively screams that he is her lover. Flipper, realizing that racial norms and sexual mythology generally abhor intimacy between black men and white women, nervously replies, "We are just friends." The officer reluctantly removes the gun from his head. As Flipper turns to face the officers, the camera shifts to a subjective point of view using a handheld camera shot. During the subjective point of view, the camera is placed behind the character's eyes and allows the spectator to view and experience the same visual phenomena observed by the character. Handheld camera shots are often ragged and shaky, thus exaggerating movement. The subjective point of view shot in this sequence is used more for psychological than aesthetic purposes: it invites the spectator to experience Flipper's terror. In this context, Flipper is forced to negotiate a set of subjective positions that have little to do with his class and professional status. The sequence underscores how identities are constantly defined and redefined, changing often in relation to social context. Furthermore, the sequence suggests that individuals do not always choose or determine how others will construct them. In this sequence, Flipper is forced to deal with the residual effects of society's criminalization of African American males. Moreover, the sequence displays how racialized perceptions are often inscribed on the body in ways that can negate a consideration of other subjective positions. In this case, Flipper's professional and middle-class status are muted entirely.

If Flipper's identity is positioned along the axis of race in relation to the white partners and the police officers, his identity is repositioned primarily along the axis of class in relation to his brother Gator Purify. One of the most intriguing dilemmas in America since the 1960s has been the concurrent expansion of the black middle class and the black urban poor. As a result, the increasing trend toward occupational differentiation has led to greater forms of social and economic polarization *within* the African American community.

The narrative tension between Flipper and Gator symbolizes the increasing class division that differentiates the everyday experiences of the black middle class from those of the black urban poor. Throughout the film, Gator is strategically positioned outside the spheres of middle-class life, thus generating a range of critical commentary regarding the growing social and economic chasm that distinguishes the postindustrial experience of the two groups. Most of the scenes in which Gator appears configure him as an intrusive force that repeatedly disrupts the confines of black middle-class domesticity. In sharp contrast to Flipper, the costume design for Gator is raggedy and soiled, his hair unkempt. In addition, he is habitually nomadic—a place of residence is never established; hence, the spectator can surmise he is probably homeless. Finally, Gator is unemployed and also addicted to crack cocaine.

The scene that most vividly dramatizes the conflict between Flipper and Gator is the Taj Mahal sequence. In this sequence, a dolly shot follows Flipper, a symbol of black middle-class success, as he searches for Gator, a symbol of black urban poverty and despair. Sometimes called a tracking shot, this film technique is executed by placing a camera on a moving vehicle that can follow alongside the events taking place on-screen. The shot is used in this instance to follow Flipper as he navigates his way down an urban ghetto street. Traveling shots in the cinema can serve an important symbolic function. Rather than rely on a few visual clichés to portray this inner-city block, Lee chose instead to construct a social world that juxtaposes a broad spectrum of inner-city residents. Within this same block, we see, for example, a street-corner minister, prostitutes, homelessness, idleness, drug dealers, working people, and affectionate couples, all coordinated to signify the dual vitality and dislocated status of inner-city communities.

The movement of the camera is especially active, shifting fluidly between subjective and objective cinematic point-of-view shots. In the subjective point of view, as noted above, the camera is placed behind the character's eyes literally and allows the spectator to view and experience the visual phenomena viewed by the character. In contrast, quick cuts to an objective point of view reposition the spectator at a distance, thus permitting a voyeuristic gaze at Flipper as he travels along this inner-city block. The tracking shots used to follow his journey help to prolong the suspense of his search. Further, the medium-range panning shots allow the spectator to follow Flipper's eyes and view the phenomena he views.

But it is not only the visual techniques and strategies that make this particular scene especially thick and descriptive in cinematic terms. The selection of music is equally informative—Stevie Wonder's "Living for the City." In film, music is often used to convey meaning and/or establish mood. The lyrics of this particular song address the social, economic, and political struggles that confront black men and women as they attempt to negotiate the hostile terrain of the postindustrial city. Music is an important element that enables filmmakers to add texture to images. The use of this 1970s popular song produces an intriguing discourse that subtly transcends the period features of this 1990s popular film: the dialogue between image and music situates the concentration of urban social and economic dislocation as an enduring feature of the post–World War II landscape.

As Flipper enters the Taj Mahal, described by one character in the film as "the crack hotel for drug addicts," both he and the spectator come face-to-face with the ravages of urban poverty and the burgeoning drug economy. The Taj Mahal is greatly exaggerated, but much of popular film is, in order to forcefully articulate a thematic idea. The exchange between Flipper and Gator is unpleasant, but the clash between the two characters can be read symbolically as a clash between the black middle class and the black urban poor. Flipper, a cinematic metaphor of black middle-class success, is forced to acknowledge the devastating impact of economic dislocation on poor black communities and the lives of many of their inhabitants. And even though it is expressed subtly, the subtext of the film is stridently antithetical to the black family situation comedy insofar as it emphasizes the increasing significance of race in the lives of the black middle class. In the relationship between Flipper and Gator, Lee appears to be suggesting that the black middle class is at least partially implicated in the deterioration of poor black lives and that their preoccupation with professional success and achievement has also come at a great price: the abandonment of the urban poor and their continued struggle for social and economic justice.

In general, Lee's treatment of Flipper's identity as unstable and variable across different social contexts demonstrates a degree of maturity in his cinematic imagination and representation of blackness. The character posits that no single subjective position—race, class, gender—is fixed or impervious to external forces. Rather, these identities are fluid, inherently volatile, and continually remade in social contexts over which individuals seldom have any control. To the degree that Lee is especially cognizant of the ways in which blackness is represented, he has deployed the commercial film apparatus to reconsider the representation of whiteness, too.

Reversing the Gaze: Interrogating Whiteness

One change in direction that would be real cool would be the production of a discourse on race that interrogates whiteness. It would just be so interesting for all those white folks who are giving blacks their take on blackness to let them know what's going on with whiteness. In far too much contemporary writing . . . race is always an issue of otherness that is not white; it is black, brown, yellow, red, purple even.

BELL HOOKS[37]

Many feminist film critics call attention to the significance of the "look," or gaze, in cinema. There are basically three looks in the filmmaking and viewing experience. First, the camera's look as it records the filmic events and action; second, the audience's look at the image and action that take place on the screen; and third, the look the characters exchange within the film.[38] Feminist film critics maintain that the dominant look in cinema is, historically, a gendered gaze. More precisely, this viewpoint argues that the dominant visual and narrative conventions of filmmaking generally fix "women as image" and "men as bearer of the image." I would like to suggest that Hollywood cinema also frames a highly particularized *racial* gaze—that is, a representational system that positions blacks as image and whites as bearer of the image. One of the most potent elements of the burgeoning visual media culture is its capacity to shape how people look at—and therefore vicariously experience—the social world around them. As a result, one of the most intriguing possibilities of black filmmaking is the opportunity to create a countergaze that struggles to produce alternative ways of looking at—and possibly even experiencing—the world. The practice of black filmmaking signals an important moment insofar as African Americans shift from the passive object of the look in cinema to the active and creative agent who frames the look.

Cultural critic bell hooks contends that cultural criticism's fascination with race often assigns this system of classification to Asians, blacks, or Latinos, but seldom to whites. The catchall phrase "people of color" further suggests that "race" is something with which whites do not have to grapple.[39] Moreover, historians of U.S. popular cultural history have placed great emphasis on how blackness has been represented largely within the context of the white imagination.[40] Thus, to the extent that public discourse and the popular media tend to foreground an explicit recognition of blackness, they oftentimes conceal any such recognition of whiteness. Ignoring and therefore not naming the broad array of privileges and manifestations associated with whiteness only serves to fortify its power and presumed naturalness. One important shift in academic discourse is the turn toward a more explicit interrogation of how whiteness is lived, constructed, and reproduced.[41]

While Lee's cultural politics have been devoted to representing blackness, the filmmaker has also created some provocative representations that mobilize a distinctive discourse on the meanings and complexities of whiteness. The filmmaker's first two feature films deal exclusively with black thematic matter and black characters. However, in his third feature film release, *Do the Right Thing,* a critique of American race relations, Lee explores new representational territory: the cinematic representation of "whiteness." During the release of the film, Lee was bombarded with questions that probed how difficult it was for him to create white characters for the film. Underlining this question, however, is the assumption that black filmmakers are unable to think creatively about the experiences of "whiteness" and are therefore only capable of imagining filmic worlds that construct representations of African Americans. Despite his public persona as an ardent supporter of black films, Lee's filmic treatment of white subjects can be described as politically charged but not necessarily polemical. The filmmaker has struggled to create a broad range of white characters in his films that also avoids counterstereotyping and simplification.[42] *Do the Right Thing* is a good illustration.

One of the central thematic dilemmas that partially structures the film is the lack of economic vitality that depresses central-city African American communities. The few spheres of economic activity to be found in this fictional community are not controlled by blacks. The main site of commerce is Sal's Famous Pizzeria, owned by and named for one of the film's central characters. Sal, a white Italian, is a multi-accented character. Sal's attitude toward the blacks in the community is a combination of attachment, paternalism, mistrust, and hostility. With blacks whom he regards as nonthreatening, he is affable and pa-ternalistic. For example, Sal habitually pays the local drunk a dollar for sweeping the front of his restaurant. He also employs an individual, Mookie, from the neighborhood to hand-deliver pizzas. His general at-titude toward Mookie is a combination of paternalism and mistrust. On the one hand, Sal believes he is doing Mookie a favor by simply employ-ing him (Mookie's friends are unemployed); on the other hand, he does not permit him to assume a major role in the operations of the restau-rant. Whereas Sal is repeatedly positioned behind the register and gen-erally handles the exchange of money, Mookie never handles the cash register.

In the case of both the drunk and Mookie, Sal's paternalism is a stra-tegic negotiation of his economic presence in the community and func-tions as a buffering device to maintain good standing. But the pizzeria is at once an economic and a cultural resource. Sal decorates the restaurant with a "Wall of Fame," which features popular Italian Americans like Robert De Niro, Sylvester Stallone, and Liza Minelli. Sal is very much a patriarchal figure and governs the daily operations of the pizzeria. At one point in the film, Sal claims, "There is no freedom here. I'm the boss!" Individuals who intrude upon Sal's economic and cultural terri-tory are viewed in hostile terms.

The conflict between Buggin' Out and Sal is illustrative of this point. The former recognizes the "Wall of Fame" and poses the question to Sal, "Why aren't there any black people up on the wall?" Sal immediately replies, "This is my pizzeria and Italian Americans on the wall only." Buggin' Out begins to protest the fact that, while Sal celebrates Italian American expressive culture, the bulk of his customers are black; hence,

"Since black people spend *much* money here, we do have some say." Sal threatens Buggin' Out with a baseball bat. The bat is a symbol of racial violence against African Americans and is an obvious reference to the escalation of racial hate crimes throughout the eighties.[43] A similar confrontation erupts between Sal and another black youth, Radio Raheem. When Raheem enters the restaurant carrying a boom box blasting loud rap music—a motif that symbolizes the more assertive forms of black youth expressive culture—Sal angrily interprets this as an intrusive, if not violative, gesture. In this sequence, the oblique camera angle is employed to dramatize the tension and also animate Sal's view of Raheem. The use of extreme close-up shots enlarges and accentuates Sal's distorted view and the personal anxiety he experiences about Raheem and his rap music. Oblique angles are tilted shots that disrupt the transparency of filmic discourse and generally serve as a form of authorial intrusion to suggest tension, disruption, or anxiety. In this case, the oblique angles and extreme close-ups are used for psychological purposes and communicate, via the visual grammar of film, Sal's distorted perception of Radio Raheem as a threat to his economic and cultural space.

One of the most interesting debates that crystallized after the film's release centered around the question of whether or not the character Sal was racist. Unfortunately, the premise of the question was misinformed, and as a result, the trajectory of the debate was woefully misguided. A more productive question, for example, might have pondered: How does Sal's character invite a more subtle understanding of the complex and oftentimes contradictory contours of whiteness in general and white racism in particular? Some critics argued that the conflict between Sal and the black youth in the film actually trivialized racism.[44] First, this critique was often informed by a literal rather than symbolic reading of the film. Second, it also misses one of the sharpest commentaries of the film: the extreme and volatile nature of racial antagonisms that percolate just below the surfaces of everyday life and their power to transform seemingly small, if not insignificant, incidents into serious expressions of hostility.

Do the Right Thing operated more at the level of allegory and symbolism. Thus, if we view Sal and the black youths in the film as vehicles for expressing some of the shifting racial moods and sensibilities of the late twentieth century, then the politics of the film become much more dynamic and discernible: the intensification of racial tension between black youth, downwardly mobile whites, and institutions of social control.

Sal's struggle to keep the pizzeria financially solvent resonates with the postindustrial anxieties of white lower-middle-class families. As Robert Chrisman accurately contends, "Sal is the quintessential petit bourgeois who must operate within the ethnic enclaves America creates for its non–Anglo Saxon constituencies."[45] It is within the context of a rapidly changing economic order that working-class whites are marginally permitted to share in the benefits of white privilege. The black youth in the film, much like the nationwide perception of black youth in general, constitute a threat to the social order and maintenance of white privilege. Sal's response to Radio Raheem and his sonic boom box animates the hostile response to black youth that has become more vehement during the political evolution of social conservatism.

But Lee struggles to create a film narrative that at least acknowledges some of the nuances of white racial attitudes. For example, Sal's son, Pino, is virulently racist in his attitude and behavior toward blacks. He openly displays hostility and constantly refers to blacks as "niggers," "animals," and "apes." Pino demonizes all blacks in general. He is embarrassed by the family's association with "niggers" and wants to relocate the business. Throughout the film, Lee constantly juxtaposes various representations of whiteness. During one scene, Sal and Pino engage in a candid and intimate discussion about race. The face-to-face positioning of the two implies that there are different sides of whiteness and further makes the point that not all whites view blacks in similar terms. The representational politics are subtle, but Lee does open up space in the black popular cultural imagination to avoid the counter-stereotyping of whites.

Despite Pino's disdain toward African Americans, he enjoys black popular culture. In a rather well conceived and memorable scene, Lee explores how whites and blacks often derive pleasure from similar sources of black popular culture, but for fundamentally different reasons.

Mookie: Pino, who's your favorite basketball player?
Pino: Magic Johnson.
Mookie: Who's your favorite movie star?
Pino: Eddie Murphy.
Mookie: Who's your favorite rock star? Prince?
Pino: The Boss . . . Bruce!
Mookie: Pino, all you ever talk about is nigger this and nigger that, and
 all your favorite people are so-called niggers.

Pino: It's different. Magic, Eddie, Prince are not niggers . . . I mean are not black . . . I mean, they're black but not really black. They're more than black. It's different.

For Pino, black athletes and entertainers "are not niggers"; they're "different." To be sure, the growing popularity of many black performers among white audiences is partially attributable to the crossover strategies that have emerged since the postwar social transformations in American popular culture. Blacks who place a priority on crossing over generally play down the notion of racial difference in order to appeal to white consumers. Moreover, crossover personalities may avoid taking public positions on divisive social issues so they will be less likely to alienate whites. Whereas blacks appeal to whites because they often mask their blackness, these same performers are appreciated by black audiences for specifically racial reasons: historically, black audiences derive pleasure from black popular culture icons because they represent a source of race pride and achievement despite the continuation of racism.[46] The dialogue between Mookie and Pino suggests that popular culture functions as a site of pleasure even though different groups produce meanings that comply with the needs of their own subcultural identities and desires.[47]

Stylizing the Cinematic Apparatus

Check the technique.

ERIC B AND RAKIM[48]

Spike Lee's varying approaches to filmmaking and the techniques that he employs are especially stylized. Like most filmmakers, Lee struggles to create a signature style that differentiates his films from others. In the course of his commercial filmmaking career, he has incorporated an array of filmmaking repertoires, demonstrating in the process a tendency to resist rigid adoption of the classical forms of popular film production and narration. Lee's stylization of the apparatus constitutes a form of authorial expressivity. This distinctive approach to directing cinema occasionally intrudes upon the filmmaking process by interrupting, violating, and subverting some of the norms and conventional modes of representation that dominate the aesthetic organization of classical film. Moreover, as I discuss below, the more expressive forms of author-ship create a very different film-viewing experience for spectators.

The classical Hollywood cinema is the most influential model of film-making practice in the world. This particular mode defines the character-istics and aesthetic codes that normalize the art of filmmaking in Ameri-can cinema. In truth, the narrative structure, camera work, and editing in the cinema have adhered to essentially the same rules throughout the history of modern American filmmaking. The classical model refers to a pattern of representational norms that have evolved over time, shifting now and then in relation to technological, organizational, and social changes but nevertheless retaining many of its core features.[49]

In a rather informative essay, Peter Wollen outlines the central char-acteristics of classical cinema and what he posits as its antithesis, coun-tercinema.[50] The values and techniques of the latter, according to Wol-len, oppose the orthodoxy of the former. A close examination of Lee's filmmaking style suggests that he strategically incorporates some of the elements defined by Wollen as part of the countercinema filmmak-ing practice. What are some of the ways in which Lee resists the norms and values that typically govern the production of the classical para-digm? First, it is important to note, however, that, like most filmmakers who make feature-length films for theatrical distribution, Lee functions mostly *within* the norms that regulate the production of popular film. For instance, his portrayal of Malcolm X adhered to many of the basic rules and conventions that structure the Hollywood biographical pic-ture. But it is equally important to note that the filmmaker has also com-bined experimental and nonconventional methods of cinematic au-thorship in some of his most memorable work.

The classical cinema paradigm privileges the notion of transparency over foregrounding. Whereas the logic of transparency attempts to ob-scure the constructedness of the fictional world represented on-screen, foregrounding, conversely, attempts to make the construction of the film world more explicit. Most movies produced by the Hollywood ma-chine are governed by the notion of realism, a transparent approach to filmmaking. Discussing the realism style in American popular film cul-ture, film scholar Louis Giannetti writes: "[W]e rarely notice the style in a realistic movie; the artist tends to be self-effacing. Such filmmakers are more concerned with *what's* being shown rather than how it is ma-nipulated. The camera is used conservatively. It's essentially a recording mechanism that reproduces the surface of tangible objects with as little commentary as possible. . . . The realistic cinema specializes in art that conceals art."[51]

To be sure, Lee's cinematic politics have never invested firmly in the notion that he was presenting spectators a nonpartisan, objective view of the world. In fact, his intentions have been, in part, to stake out a particular set of claims on the nature of race relations, and the post-industrial experiences of blacks especially, and manipulate the technology of film production to articulate those claims. Part of carving out this space has also meant developing a style of filmmaking that has been as striking and imaginative as his goal of both gaining and maintaining access to the resources of the major culture industries. Lee's politicization of popular film entertainment, then, has been especially strategic and intentionally provocative. In many of his films, for example, he has often refused to comply with the idea of transparency, preferring instead to practice a method of filmmaking that foregrounds his own authorial presence and distinctively marks his filmmaking signature. Giannetti discusses this manner of filmmaking as formalism and writes: "The formalist cinema is largely a director's cinema: Authorial intrusions are common. There is a high degree of manipulation in the narrative materials, and the visual presentation is stylized. The story is exploited as vehicle for the filmmaker's personal obsessions. . . . This style of cinema deals with ideas—political, religious, philosophical. . . . Its texture is densely symbolic."[52]

On the one side, the features of realism are less noticeable; the filmmaker strives to disguise the constructedness of the story-world presented on screen. On the other, the director strives to unveil the transparency of filmmaking. Still, the idea of realism dominates the production of popular film and television. Considering that classical cinema is at best moderately self-conscious, Lee's approach to filmmaking is determinedly self-conscious, often acknowledging his stylized use of the cinematic apparatus. While some view Lee's filmmaking techniques as gratuitous or self-serving, they nevertheless represent a form of authorial action, a form of agency that contests the intensely regulated forms of cinematic authorship that customarily obscure the fact that all forms of media are a socially constructed, manipulative view of the world.

Take, for example, Lee's use of characters directly addressing the spectator—a consistent narrative motif throughout his early work. This type of address is seldom used in classical cinema, mainly because it interrupts the flow of film events that take place on-screen. In addition, full frontality in cinema ruptures traditional story-space boundaries that generally position the spectator more fully as a voyeur. In the case of classical cinema, characters only address other characters *in* the film. In *Do the Right Thing,* Lee jump-cuts to a sequence that features the character direct-address device. In the sequence, the camera cuts to five different characters who utter racial epitaphs. The sequence is both a playful and serious experimental technique that disorients the normal film-viewing process: jump cuts are deliberately abrupt editing transitions that disrupt the continuity of narrative time and space. Direct character address also establishes a more personalized experience of film viewership by repositioning the spectator as a more active participant in the film-viewing process. As a result of this technique, characters speak directly to spectators.

Furthermore, the narrative structure that defines much of Lee's filmography is antithetical to the norms of classical cinema. The dominant narrative structure usually constructs a single story-plot that contains, according to Wollen, "a unitary homogenous world." In this system, the organization of narrative adheres to a basic formula: the introduction of a harmonious setting; the insertion of a conflict that disrupts the equilibrium; the climatic clash, which generally places the protagonist in some sort of contest; and finally, the restoration of a harmonious world. The narrative structure in the typical Spike Lee Joint, however, privileges multiple story-plots over the single-story-plot formula. In other words, the filmmaker generally deploys the film-within-a-film device, which fractures the primary story-plot. Consequently, his film narratives tend to develop acute fissures. So instead of constructing a single homogenous world, Lee opts for creating a filmic world in which a polyphony of issues, conflicts, and enigmas seem to proliferate unabashedly.

Perhaps Lee's most decisive break from the classical style of filmmaking is the manner in which his film narratives tend to close. Because the classical paradigm generally privileges the notion of a single story-plot, the primacy of this style lends itself to easy resolution and narrative closure. Discussing narrative closure in classical cinema, Bordwell writes:

> [W]e can see it as the crowning of the structure, the logical conclusion of the string of events, the final effect of the initial cause. This view has some validity, not only in the light of tight constructions that we frequently encounter in Hollywood films but also given

> the precepts of Hollywood screenwriting. Rulebooks
> tirelessly bemoan the pressures for a happy ending and
> emphasize the need for a logical wrap-up. . . . Thus an
> extrinsic norm, the need to resolve the plot in a way
> that provides "poetic justice," becomes a structural
> constant.[53]

The happy-ending cliché is arguably the most dominant narrative motif in Hollywood film. Indeed, one of the most taken-for-granted belief systems in Hollywood is the notion that, in order for a film to be a box-office success, the narrative must be compact, simple, and easily resolved. Moreover, industry insiders strongly believe in making uplifting, "feel-good" movies, which generally translates into a neat resolution of narrative conflict. But the tendency to resolve conflict reaffirms dominant ideological values like individualism and patriarchy and further suggests that heroic, often male, deeds are the solution to social problems.[54]

Yet narrative closure in the Spike Lee Joint is intentionally resisted. Rather than asserting a harmonized world at the end of his films, Lee repeatedly subverts this industry rule by choosing to end many of his film narratives on the curvature of several question marks. This strategy leaves the film/text open-ended and subject to multiple interpretations. At the same time, though, this strategy can also generate discomfort for filmgoers accustomed to narrative closure. Take, for example, the following conclusion of a test screening survey from Lee's second feature film, *School Daze:* "[T]he majority of audience members felt negatively about the ending, finding it confusing, too abrupt and unresolved. Similarly, some audience members (both blacks and whites) complained that the story and the message were confusing."[55] The results of the survey suggest that when moviegoers are exposed to open-ended film narratives, it violates their perception of what constitutes coherence and clarity, thus making the film-viewing experience unpleasant in some instances.

An excellent example of this open-ended structure is, of course, the intensely debated *Do the Right Thing.* The film ends abruptly and declines to resolve the multiple enigmas that motivate conflict and action in the story-plot. In fact, one of the main charges leveled against the film was that Lee raised many issues regarding the volatility of racism but failed to propose any solutions. This critique is, of course, inspired by a set of spectatorial norms accustomed to narrative resolution. The conclusion of *Do the Right Thing* does in fact leave the spectator pondering several questions—for example: What happens to Sal and his pizzeria? Did Mookie "do the right thing" by initiating the destruction of the pizzeria? Did Raheem's death justify burning and looting Sal's property? Is black rage against white property a legitimate expression of political resistance? Whose political philosophy was right, Martin Luther King Jr.'s or Malcolm X's? Paraphrasing Wollen, it can certainly be said that—with its endless counterposition of characters, conflicts, and issues—*Do the Right Thing* can best be understood as an arena, a meeting place in which different discourses encounter each other and struggle for supremacy. The film, according to conventional wisdom, is unfinished and therefore open to a seemingly inexhaustible number of different spins and interpretations. But to the extent that narrative aperture intentionally invites the production of meaning, it also encourages dialogue. Spectators are forced to create their own ending(s) and therefore ponder the many questions the film deliberately refuses to answer. Finally, narrative aperture correctly suggests that complex social issues are *structural* and not *personal;* hence, heroic acts by individuals cannot resolve them. It makes the crucial point that happy endings only exist in the imaginary fantasyscapes of Hollywood.

Lee's recombination of both conventional and more expressive forms of cinematic authorship is indicative of what some film scholars argue is the emergence of a "New Hollywood." The New Hollywood rests, in part, upon technological innovations that facilitate a more definitive break from the dominant conventions and approaches to narrative in the cinema by creating new possibilities in the areas of sound mixing, camera movement, and photography, for example. The New Hollywood is greatly influenced by the European art cinema, which typically employs, according to Bordwell, Staiger, and Thompson, "a looser, more tenuous linkage of events than we find in the classical film."[56] The art cinema generally creates multidimensional characters rather than one-dimensional characters whose traits tend to be overwhelmingly "good" or "bad." Further, Bordwell, Staiger, and Thompson maintain that, whereas characters in the classical cinema have clearly defined traits and characteristics (i.e., heroes and villains), characters in the art cinema lack clear definition and objectives. This new style in Hollywood is generally associated with a generation of film school graduates who have enjoyed tremendous success in the commercial arena employing more expressive forms of cinematic authorship—Martin Scorsese, Francis Ford Coppola, and Robert Altman, to name a few.[57]

Rather than supplant the classical style, art cinema has been as-similated into the dominant paradigm. While participants in the New Hollywood can be described as stylists, they tend to work within the paradigmatic structure of the classical model. Bordwell, Staiger, and Thompson remind us that, despite the achievements of the new stylists, the classical premise of time and space remains powerfully in force, with only subtle alterations. Moreover, the emergence of celebrity direc-tors reinvigorates theatrical film-going, which, in turn, strengthens the popular movie industry and, ironically, the classical paradigm. Lee's styl-ization of the apparatus, then, appears to be part of a broader, albeit subtle, trend in the commercial filmmaking industry. The filmmaker's own carefully crafted image as an icon of black popular culture, in fact, stimulated interest in other black American–directed films that are more committed to the dominant conventions of film production. So despite Lee's neo–black nationalist image, the stylistic choices that mark his un-conventional filmmaking techniques are rooted in the trends and val-ues of European art cinema.[58] Lee's approach to commercial filmmaking is as much a by-product of the genre hybridization of the classical, art, and exploitation styles of filmmaking as it is a decisive shift in the logic of black cultural production or any particular form of black resistance.

Lee's breakthrough success was made possible by several interre-lated factors. First, the production, distribution, and consumption of popular media products have changed dramatically during the latter decades of the twentieth century. Technology not only accelerates the production and distribution of products; improvements in technology also make access to communications media resources slightly more democratic than in previous periods. Thus, new players have been able to occupy small niches in the industrial image-making landscape. And while new communication technologies and the information economy do not threaten the hegemony of capitalism or the global spread of cor-porate influence, they have, albeit inadvertently, created space for the mobilization of new cultural practices and movements that creatively contest social and political domination.

In many ways, the renewal of black filmmaking was made possible by the innovations and growing popularity of the hip hop movement. Hip hop redefined the presence and vitality of black youth culture in the popular cultural landscape. More important, it forged new territories and spaces for African Americans to assert greater control over the shap-ing and reshaping of the popular culture scene. Consequently, young African American filmmakers who have harnessed the creative energy and spirit of hip hop to their own cinematic imaginations have gained limited access to the corridors and resources of commercial cinema. Spike Lee, to be sure, has responded in an innovative fashion to the changing cultural landscape. He understood that, in order to become a formidable player on the field of popular culture, it was necessary to align himself with some of the more popular movements and sensibilities of the youth scene. Lee's strategic use of hip hop culture certainly enlivened his filmmaking career. But while he has been careful to incorporate some of the expressive elements of hip hop, he has not limited his cultural politics to the sensibilities of the youth movement. The filmmaker, as I have discussed above, has politicized the sphere of popular film production in ways that also move beyond the priorities and preoccupations of hip hop.

Finally, because Lee was responding to rather than creating changes in the popular culture landscape that facilitated his arrival on the cultural stage, his imprint on the production of black cinema, while obviously important, must not be viewed as dominant. In reality, the scope of black cinema broadened far beyond its most distinguished icon in ways that not even he could contain, direct, or anticipate. By the early 1990s, the most dominant characteristics of black commercial cinema were not associated with the neo–black nationalist racial politics and expressive techniques that defined the typical Spike Lee Joint but rather with the popular rhythms of gangsta rap and the proliferation of ghetto imagery in American culture.

PART THREE

6 Producing Ghetto Pictures

Capitalism and its images speak directly to desire for its own profit. But in that very process it breaks down or short-circuits limiting customs and taboos. It will do anything and supply any profane material in order to keep the cash tills ringing. . . . Modern capitalism is now not only parasitic upon the puritan ethic, but also upon its instability and even its subversion.

PAUL WILLIS[1]

Black pathology is big business.

ISHMAEL REED[2]

Despite its social and economic marginality, the postindustrial ghetto performs a dynamic role in American culture. However alienated it may be, the ghetto is very much a central part of American society, a potent symbol in the cultural landscape, and a pervasive, if not dominating, feature in our national imagination. In a variety of instances, the postindustrial ghetto has become a virtual centerpiece in the growth of several industries. Since the 1980s, for example, prison construction, crime management, private security systems, local and national television news, advertisements for consumer goods (Nike and Reebok are two high-profile examples), professional basketball, and the popular music and film industries have one thing in common: their recent growth and economic fortunes have been built, at least partially, on the basis of their unique affiliations with the social transformations that characterize postindustrial ghetto life.

The notoriety and commercial success of *Do the Right Thing* catapulted Spike Lee into the glare of the media spotlight. The news media soon figured Lee as the representative icon of black cinema. Lee became the personification, the filter through which a very complicated and diverse cultural practice was rendered intelligible. To be sure, the focus on Lee was not entirely unjustified. However, Lee's role cannot be described as dominant. In fact, the most popular trend of black American–directed feature-length films during the post-1986 resurgence of black cinema—the ghetto action film cycle—is not necessarily associated with Lee.[3] This particular wave of films devoted much of its narrative power almost exclusively to the perilous relationship between young, poor black males and the postindustrial ghetto.

As I shall argue in the next chapter, the urban ghetto film cycle represents an extremely complex form of social discourse and is therefore irreducible to uniform "readings," genre or otherwise. Genre affiliation is used to categorize a broad and often imposing inventory of film production (e.g., western, horror, science fiction). This does not mean, however, that films associated with a particular genre or cycle are ideologically static. The term *genre* is most useful as an analytical device that allows media analysts to order the vast amount of material produced in Hollywood. Typically, the term suggests that certain core symbolic elements exist to establish a linkage between a specific group of films and their respective audiences. For instance, plot structure, setting, and character types can work to establish a genre film identity.

In reality, genre lines are often blurred, disrupted, and/or recombined, thus making *genre* a difficult term to sustain analytically. Because genre boundaries are so fluid, it is not uncommon for a film to belong to two or more genres simultaneously. It is important to note that, while I identify these films as part of an observable Hollywood production cycle, the variation between them is striking. In spite of the fact that the films tend to pivot around the social and economic dislocation of young black males, the narrative organization and visual vocabulary of the film cycle are many-sided and cut across different genres and filmmaking conventions. This particular cycle of films ranges from John Singleton's coming-of-age tale *Boyz N the Hood* (1991) to the Hughes brothers' consciously gangster-styled *Menace II Society* (1993). A more useful change in perspective, then, does not focus so much on the enforcement of rigid genre boundaries but rather on why specific film narratives or subject trends take shape. Rather than debate genre distinctions between these films, I want to focus on the social context for the production, distribution, and consumption of African American–directed "hood" movies that began regularly flowing out of Hollywood in the early 1990s.

The repetitious production of popular film narratives centered on the inner-city experiences of young black males during a period championed by the Black Filmmaker Foundation as a "renaissance in black cinema" provoked intense criticism and reinvigorated charges of racism in Hollywood. A broad spectrum of critics, scholars, and even black filmmakers repeatedly posed the question, "Given the complexity of black American life, why would Hollywood limit its representation of blacks to films that glorified youth violence, gang culture, and antisocial behavior?" But rather than view the film industry as engaging in a deliberate and strategic conspiracy to demonize blacks, I want to suggest that the production of the film cycle was the consequence of a complex web of social, economic, and cultural factors.

To be sure, the popular rise of the ghetto action film cycle illuminates the complex relationship between the social transformations that characterize post-1960s black youth culture and the changing dynamics of popular media production. Since the production of commercial film is a specific sphere of cultural production, it is necessary to appreciate the social and organizational contexts that enabled the making of this particular film cycle. In this chapter, I argue that the repetitious production of ghetto-theme action films in the 1990s was a swift response by the commercial film industry to three crucial developments: the perversely prominent rise of the postindustrial ghetto in the American popular and political imagination; a reconfigured popular culture economy and youth marketplace; and finally, the commercial vitality of hip hop culture in general and the popularization of gangsta rap music specifically.

Blaxploitation Revisited, or Business as Usual?

All of Spike's films have been blaxploitation films, all our films in the future are going to be blaxploitation films, all of John [Singleton's] films are going to be blaxploitation films because they make money. They're exploiting something from black culture to make money. Bottom line, every film made is an exploitation, in a sense.

ALBERT HUGHES[4]

During several interviews to promote their first feature film, *Menace II Society,* Albert and Allen Hughes often expressed utter disdain toward the claim that their film was simply a replay of 1970s blaxploitation. In retrospect, the blaxploitation era has become notorious for its greatly exaggerated and typically burlesque configurations of blackness. In general, blaxploitation refers to a wave of Hollywood films produced between 1970 and 1974. This particular wave of films was an attempt by the film industry to appeal to the new sensibilities and cultural mood shifts created by the black power awakening of the late 1960s.[5] Albert Hughes's remark above is noteworthy because it compels us to consider an important question: Is the production of black cinema any more or less exploitative than the production of popular film in general?

By the early 1990s, film narratives exploring black male youth culture and the postindustrial ghetto proved to be extremely competitive at the box office, generating enormous sums of money for major and independent film distributors. The cycle of films performed remarkably well across different film exhibition seasons. For example, *Variety* reported that the most cost-effective film released during the 1991 spring season was "Warner Brothers' hit *New Jack City* with its $43.6 million gross in eleven weeks making it the only major picture for the period to break even from domestic theatrical release alone."[6] Unlike most films, *New Jack City* generated a notable profit margin between the Christmas season and summer months, typically a less lucrative film-going season. Discussing the summer opening of *Boyz N the Hood, Variety* reported that the film "had an opening-weekend success unparalleled by any other black made film. And its per screen average, $12,091, was higher than that of *Terminator 2: Judgment Day.*" The enormous commercial success of *New Jack City* and *Boyz N the Hood* fueled an imitative cycle that eventually produced over twenty similarly packaged feature-length films between 1991 and 1995.

However, any serious contemplation of why ghetto-theme action pictures ascended in popularity must also look outside the internal operations and economics of Hollywood. The industry's sudden interest in and exploitative turn to ghetto narratives was a swift response to new market opportunities and popular appetites made possible by the currents of social change. The association of the term *exploitation* with African Americans conjures up ideas of unfair, even racist, treatment. In the case of film, for example, the expression *blaxploitation* was added to our critical cultural vocabulary to refer to the wave of commercial films produced in the early to mid-1970s that targeted black urban moviegoers. My association of the term *exploitation* with the 1990s film cycle, then, should be carefully delineated.

Exploitation films are neither recent nor new to Hollywood. As far back as the early twentieth century, exploitation films have been immensely popular with moviegoers.[7] Over the years, exploitation films have come in many genre forms, appealed to different segments of the moviegoing population, and capitalized on a mixture of topics and social trends. The teen and youth film is one specific example of exploitation product. Discussing the most salient attributes of this distinct trend in popular film production, Doherty writes:

> As a production strategy, the 50's exploitation formula typically had three elements: (1) controversial, bizarre, or timely subject matter amenable to wild promotion; (2) a substandard budget; and (3) a teenage audience. . . . Movies of this ilk are *triply* exploitative, simultaneously exploiting sensational happenings (for story value), their notoriety (for publicity value), and their teenage participants (for box office value). Around 1956, "exploitation film" in this sense had become fairly common usage within the industry.[8]

The film industry's shift to "teenpics"—that is, movies produced primarily for consumption by young moviegoers—was a response to a precipitous drop in film-going and the fracturing of the movie audience. By the 1950s, films marketed directly to youth or exploiting themes specific to youth were surfacing with great frequency.

There is no single definition of exploitation films. In fact, the term is admittedly imprecise. Before the social and cultural eruptions of the 1960s, exploitation films were once regarded as low-prestige entertainment that gratuitously displayed violence and sexual titillation. The exploitation film was especially important to the commercial viability of small, independent film distributors, which were forced to turn to sensational material in order to carve out a market niche. However, by the 1960s, changes in censorship standards and shifts in audience tastes enabled prestige film distributors to incorporate much of the sex and violence that was typically associated with marginal filmmaking cultures. Moreover, film scholar Martin Rubin asserts that it was during this period of social ferment that genre realignment began to blur the lines of distinction between exploitation, art, and commercial films.[9] He attributes the collapsing of genre boundaries to a social, cultural, and economic climate that forced the commercial film industry to adopt new production strategies in order to remain viable in a culture that was undergoing substantive change. Films that were more sexually charged and/or violent enabled the film industry to again distinguish itself from the more conservative tendencies of television entertainment and also respond to serious social and cultural permutations.

Rubin argues that exploitation films are defined by a number of prestige-negating factors related to quality of content, production, and exhibition. However, many of the prestige-negating factors outlined by Rubin do not adequately define the ghetto action films of the 1990s. For instance, many of these films achieved critical acclaim, suggesting that film content was, in a few cases, well thought of by industry insiders, critics, and movie audiences. The most obvious example is John Singleton's *Boyz N the Hood,* which received wide praise and two Academy Award nominations.[10] Also, Matty Rich's *Straight Out of Brooklyn* (1991) received special recognition during its run at the prestigious Sundance Film Festival. Moreover, most of the films were exhibited in high-traffic multiplex theater sites. And as I discuss in detail below, there was a carefully calibrated effort by the studios to market these films to a rapidly changing youth and international market, further suggesting that industry executives took their earnings-making potential seriously. What, then, makes this specific wave of films exploitative?

The evolution of the ghetto action film cycle is consistent with the recent social and economic history of film production in the United States; hence, it is not especially unique. Nevertheless, as with all popular consumer goods, these films circulated within a historically situated social milieu. The resonance of the film cycle was conditioned by the social and economic transitions that reorganize postindustrial ghetto life and, more crucially, the social construction of the "underclass" as a peculiar source of voyeuristic pleasure and a means for articulating racial backlash. It is within this social context that the film cycle develops its most conspicuous exploitative features.

In addition to obvious economic imperatives, the production decisions made by culture industry executives are also based on their discernment of what the public is most likely to be attracted to. Film industry executives, for instance, choose from an almost endless reservoir of scripts and movie ideas thematic content that conforms to their own values and imprecise calculations of consumer tastes. This selection process makes product development an enormously challenging practice.[11] In the process of navigating the difficult waters of market uncertainty, culture industry executives routinely survey the social landscape and are constantly on the lookout for emergent trends, cultural mood shifts, and newsworthy topics that could possibly translate into marketable film products.

So while it is certainly true that the formation of the ghetto action film cycle was economically motivated (as I discuss below, the films were usually profitable), its short-lived vitality was also nourished by the currents of social change. This particular film cycle amassed much of its popular and commercial vigor as a result of the central position that the postindustrial ghetto holds in the larger popular imagination. The symbolic efficacy of the ghetto is freighted with sharp contradictions. On the one hand, the ghetto has emerged as the dominant locus of social problems according to leading public opinion polls. For instance, public concern about crime, welfare, and decaying moral values invariably invokes the ghetto. On the other hand, the language, fashions, cultural productions, and allegedly nihilistic lifestyles associated with ghetto youth seem to give life to the production of new popular culture trends in the United States.[12]

Some film scholars maintain that a crucial trait of the exploitation film is its high level of context dependency.[13] It seems, then, that at least one pattern of the exploitative ethos is films that seek to cash in on timely and sensational subject matter that grips public attention. Consequently, the thematic requirements typically resonate with public fascination over some topic, issue, or event. The elaboration of this particular production strategy has its roots in a commercial film industry committed to constantly locating new thematic frontiers to conquer in addition to devising new promotional strategies in order to continually reinvigorate theatrical film-going and maintain its economic vitality in a competitive global cultural marketplace.

The ghetto action film cycle was both timely and sensational. The cycle's most poignant, popular, and problematic themes were based on the social and economic dislocation of poor inner-city youth. This particular film cycle was premised on a production strategy designed to serve an audience already titillated with and primed for action-oriented narratives about the deterioration of America's inner cities. Hollywood's decisive turn to ghetto-theme action pictures was symptomatic of a broader shift in post–civil rights era racial discourse: the fantastic and wildly distorted notion that poor black youth constitute the core of America's social, economic, and moral crisis.

Moreover, the commonsense ideas that define "authentic" urban ghetto life conform neatly with two elements that commonly arouse American popular appetites: sex and violence. For example, young African American men "strapped" (armed with guns), "gangbanging" (killing each other), and "slingin'" (dealing drugs) became staple images of the ghetto film cycle. In addition, young "unwed" (read immoral) African American women with children and "welfare-dependent" were obligatory representations of life in the "hood." The visual vocabulary of the genre, then, drew heavily from the nation's collective lexicon of commonsense ideas connected with "blackness" and urban ghetto life. As historian Jacqueline Jones points out, this view of the inner city reflects American values and priorities. She writes: "[S]ensational stories about the 'underclass' resonated within a white middle class caught up in its own fascination with sex, violence, and alcohol and drug abuse."[14] Lurid representations code the ghetto as not only dangerous but different and exotic, too. The menacing specter of ghetto youth culture became *the* exploitative hook that made the production of this particular film cycle both timely, sensational, and oddly enough, more easily marketable.

Whereas the urban ghetto film cycle generated pleasure for many, it was a source of moral panic and a sign of black pathology for others. Take, for example, the mainstream news media's collective response to the film wave. The most prominent news narratives developed an accusatory tone: ghetto action films targeting young moviegoers encouraged violence and juvenile delinquency. While many journalists wrongly speculated that *Do the Right Thing* would spark misconduct, random outbreaks of violence did occur at the opening of *New Jack City, Boyz N the Hood,* and *Juice.* Many of the major news media organizations devoted substantial press coverage to these incidents and further fueled public perception that the popular media worsened an already too violent inner-city youth culture.[15] Tricia Rose contends that the policing of black popular culture has become synonymous with the increased surveillance of black youth in general.[16] Politicians seeking election year votes, for example, make fighting black youth expressive cultures tantamount to fighting crime. In many ways, though, the more intense policing of popular culture is also a response to the growing fascination of white youth with blackness.

Selling Out: Hip Hop Culture and White Pleasure

*Black kids want to be sold out, as in there ain't no more
records left, no more tickets for the concert. . . . Being a
starving artist is not that cool in the ghetto.*
                                    RUSSELL SIMMONS[17]

*Who's pushing the rawest rhymes to No. 1 on the charts?
For years now, the largest volume of hip hop albums has
been sold to white suburban kids who've deposed heavy
metal and elevated hip hop to the crown of Music Most
Likely to Infuriate My Parents. The suburban rebellion—
its record-buying tastes, its voyeurism of what too often it
views as "authentic black culture"—has contributed to the
primacy of the gangsta-rap genre.*
                                    FARAI CHIDEYA[18]

In addition to the precarious rise of ghetto imagery in American culture,
the repetitious production of ghetto-theme action movies reflected the
flexible priorities of film production in the face of a changing popular
culture landscape. The film industry, similar to other popular culture
industries, invests enormous resources in servicing specialized markets,
and young consumers especially. The adolescent and young adult market constitutes the core audience for Hollywood film. This trend dates
back to the middle 1950s, when, according to Doherty, Hollywood realized that youth could sustain impressive box-office revenue alone and
to the exclusion of adults.[19] The emergence of the American teenager as
a major participant in consumer culture in the 1950s accelerated the
ascendancy of movies targeting youth.

The increased prominence of youth in the consumer economy was
due in part to the social transformations that indelibly marked postwar America. At the end of World War II, youth benefited from two
developments that greatly differentiated their experiences from those
of previous generations of youth. First, they enjoyed a growing and
robust economy. In addition, this economy was buoyed by an expanding consumer culture driven by new electronic media technologies and
unprecedented economic mobility. Second, the postwar boom also afforded youth greater control over their own financial resources. Unlike

youth during the depression or war years, youth in the 1950s could allocate more of their personal income to discretionary means and consumption. The 1950s situated important changes in U.S. popular cultural history. For example, the pop radio format, phonograph, transistorized radio, and independent record labels reorganized the production, distribution, and consumption of popular music. It was also during this period that the broader insertion of television into American domestic life stimulated unprecedented cultural changes.[20] In their own way, both the music and television industries eventually developed production strategies to appeal directly to youth. More generally, this new popular cultural landscape gave rise to the formation of an enlarged youth marketplace that further enabled youth to create and maintain a separate social world that existed outside immediate adult supervision. And although racially segregated neighborhoods, schools, and public accommodations persisted, the juvenilization of the popular culture industry provided the shaping context for greater social intercourse between black and white youth that was difficult to control.[21]

While youth continue to occupy a dominant position in the film industry's production logic, how this translates into film product is by no means a static or even predictable process. It is important to note, then, that commercial cultural formations are shaped by historical particularities that continually refigure youth subcultures and popular trends. As a result, the film industry must constantly modify its production strategies and product offerings in order to remain popular with successive generations of youth. The ghetto film cycle was Hollywood's attempt to exploit historically specific mood shifts in youth popular culture. In addition, the core symbolic attributes of the film cycle strategically incorporated expressive elements from hip hop's predominantly youth constituency.

The primacy of hip hop in the post-1980s commercial cultural landscape is a complex process that demands greater detailing than I can provide in this study. The evolution and vitality of hip hop demonstrate, at once, the unpredictability of popular cultural formations and their power to produce change by enabling distinct mood shifts, giving shape to new identities, and establishing distinct modes of cultural production. Rap music is the most prominent symbol of hip hop culture. No matter the state of public opinion, rap music is a multilayered expressive culture that encompasses an expansive range of subgenres, stylizations, gendered performances, and consumers. As with most emergent popular music trends, the major record companies did not immediately appreciate or understand the commercial potential of rap.[22] Many skeptics speculated that rap was simply a passing fad. Thus, the music industry's response to the earliest signs of rap's commercial potential in 1979 was mild at best.

By the middle to late 1980s, however, the breakthrough success of groups like Run DMC and Public Enemy signaled the crossover potential of rap. Historically, black music genres that perform well on the pop music charts achieve greater market credibility and wider circulation because of the potentially lucrative sums of money white patronage can generate. The growth and popular appeal of rap groups facilitated an important link between the new trends configuring black youth expressive cultures and the larger popular culture scene. Moreover, the increasing popularity of rap performers gave powerful credence to the idea that hip hop culture could be variously packaged and successfully marketed to white youth.[23]

To be sure, the ability of rap music to cross over into a broader sphere of youth consumption was crucial to its eventual absorption into other arenas of popular cultural production. But any discussion of the incorporation of rap into mainstream commercial culture must certainly address what Herman Gray characterizes as the profound shifts that began to reorganize the production, representation, and wider circulation of blackness in the 1980s.[24] Commercial culture emerged as one of the most frequent and visible spaces for circulating claims and counterclaims on the meaning(s) of blackness. This shift is perhaps most vividly evident in the popularization of blackness on the Music Television network (MTV). Indeed, MTV's problematic inclusion of black youth expressive cultures (especially, music, dance, and fashion) elucidates the broader shifts that refigured American commercial culture in the 1980s—more precisely, the increased presence and intensification of black bodies across the global popular cultural landscape.

By the late 1970s, media analysts generally agreed that cable television was one of *the* primary growth industries in communications media technology. The growth of cable television reflects the trend toward specialization, narrowcasting, and market segmentation that continues to characterize the more flexible and commonplace forms of popular media production. The innovators of MTV were driven by one main goal: to develop a programming concept designed specifically for a youth aggregate. It was their belief that the television industry had not yet developed a network idea that was committed to servicing the 12- to

34-years-of-age demographic exclusively. Moreover, the creators of MTV were interested in combining the strengths of radio and television to create, in essence, a visual radio station with youth appeal.

After long and laborious debate, the twenty-four-hour music network was launched in 1981.[25] Similarly to other popular cultural formations in U.S. history, MTV has not been insulated from the racial sensibilities that pervade the larger society. For example, as a result of the narrowcast philosophy, MTV executives elected to limit the network's format to rock music. This decision led to the adoption of a policy that customarily denied black rhythm and blues performers access to the new music network. The structure of the format quickly generated controversy.

By 1983, MTV was emerging as a significant force in the revitalization of an economically depressed popular music industry.[26] Initial research revealed that MTV was successfully reaching its target market. Also, according to R. Serge Denisoff, one study reported that 63 percent of the respondents stated that they purchased an album after seeing an act perform on MTV. The network was well on its way to becoming the national popular music radio station the United States never had. But MTV's new role as music industry gatekeeper did not come without its share of problems. It was precisely because the network was able to break new acts and music genres to a national audience almost overnight that the exclusion of black music videoclips became even more contentious.

MTV's decision to exclude blacks was a combination of market calculation and racism. The executive hierarchy maintained that the network's core viewership consisted of rock music aficionados. In other words, the executives postulated that because the network's primary target was white youth, the insertion of blacks into the format would alienate its predominantly white constituency and, most important, jeopardize the commercial viability of the network. Thus, it was a form of institutional rather than crude racism that prohibited any significant black presence on the network.[27] MTV executives claimed their decision was motivated not by race but by market forces and audience tastes they did not control. But this kind of market assessment hinges on a set of cultural assumptions about what is and is not marketable. Thus, what are typically computed as bottom-line economic considerations are often *socially* determined. Consequently, the decision to exclude blacks was not simply based on economics; it was also informed by the constellation of industry commonsense ideas and practices specifically re-acting to and based on what *whites* would find pleasurable.

Roughly six years later, though, the decision-making calculus of MTV brought to light dramatic changes both in the network and in the larger orbit of popular culture. The network hierarchy not only reversed its decision to exclude blacks; it began to develop black music genre–specific programs to, in the words of one MTV executive, "superserve a portion of the audience that likes black music."[28] A critical question, of course, is, *Why* did the network change its original position? More to the point, what was different about the cultural landscape in the late 1980s that persuaded MTV to stop viewing black popular culture as a commercial liability? This question, however, was not unique to MTV. In fact, network television, the film industry, college and professional sports, and other culture industries developed strategies and formulas throughout the 1980s to fit black expressive cultures, audiences, and creative personnel into their production schedules.[29]

In the case of MTV, several factors compelled format changes. First, during the 1980s, the crossover appeal of blacks in popular music (Michael Jackson, Whitney Houston), television (Bill Cosby), and film (Eddie Murphy) strongly suggested that black entertainers were primary sources for white pleasure. Thus, pressure from within the popular music industry to play the music videoclips of crossover acts like Michael Jackson became more vehement.[30] Second, MTV became, in many ways, a victim of its own success. As a result of its immense popularity, the emergence of rival music videoclip service providers sparked competition. MTV executives recognized that, in order to remain on the cutting edge of youth popular culture, it was necessary to refashion its programming concept. Whereas the network was once exclusively a music video service, it has developed a broader spectrum of youth-appeal programs, including live concerts, sports, game shows, fashion, and animation.

Finally, and most important, social and political currents throughout the decades of the eighties and nineties produced profound changes in the lives of youth that demanded that the network undergo serious changes in order to simply remain relevant. Although MTV was once considered a novel experiment, its executives are increasingly mindful of the critical space the network now occupies in the world of youth culture and politics. For instance, the network's "Rock the Vote" and "Choose or Lose" campaigns are strategic efforts to translate its popularity into a relevant political voice for the generational concerns of its youth constituency.[31] In addition, the various programs on HIV/AIDS awareness and sexual behavior are further indication of the network's attempt to keep its finger on the pulse of the rhythm of social change. In short, MTV executives gradually began to understand that their particular business—youth culture—was acutely political and extended far beyond the parameters of rock music and white suburban youth.

MTV's embrace of black popular culture, then, can be partially viewed as elemental to the strategic move to reposition the network in relation to a youth universe that is constantly evolving and developing new sensibilities. Television networks, too, practice what are often called "identity politics" in an effort to differentiate themselves from competitors.[32] Thus, in its ongoing effort to remain "fresh," MTV could no longer continue to ignore the creative energy that was dramatically altering the demeanor of black youth cultural politics. By the late 1980s, hip hop culture was rapidly emerging as a crucial sphere of youth discourse, contouring not only the popular cultures of many black and Latino youth but the larger youth body politic. Even more, hip hop was becoming a fountainhead of youth rebellion and cultural production. In truth, many of the enduring attributes of rap seem to fashion ingredients that are central to the MTV ideal: the music is dynamic, continually evolving, irreverent, and most of all, stylishly in vogue and therefore extremely marketable.

But it is crucial to understand the significance of MTV and its relationship to American youth culture. First, it is important to note that MTV does not create new popular cultures; as a result, its capacity to change the cultural landscape is, in fact, limited. However, to the extent that MTV functions as a very visible circuit that transmits what are typically local or regional subcultural trends to a national and global audience, the network does greatly influence the tenor of popular culture. MTV's strength rests mainly upon its capacity to energize and magnify emergent popular cultural formations and therefore enlarge their scope and commercial viability. MTV gives what are essentially local and regional cultural trends—grunge rock, alternative rock, gangsta rap—a national flavor and broader sphere of influence.

MTV broadened the market for rap by directly projecting hip hop culture into the homes of white youth.[33] Moreover, as rap began to grow in popularity and develop a broader youth constituency, the vocabulary of the music also acquired additional accents, styles, and narrative innovations. Whereas New York City was once the undisputed epicenter of rap music production, it was clear by the late 1980s that the rap industry landscape had changed dramatically from the formative years dominated by rappers, producers, and independent labels operating principally out of New York City. Two definitive breaks within the production of rap were West Coast expansion and the evolution of hardcore rap, or what is more commonly labeled "gangsta rap."

Gang$ta Inc.

They're effective because they're ghetto.

RUSSELL SIMMONS[34]

By the early 1990s, *gangsta rap* had become a household term used widely by politicians, journalists, and civic and religious leaders who were, in their own way, concerned that the intensification of sexual and violent imagery in popular culture was largely responsible for what was broadly perceived as an erosion of traditional values and escalating youth crime and drug use. Gangsta rap has been routinely singled out as an example of how popular culture allegedly promotes antisocial values and youth nihilism. This particular subgenre of rap evolved as a distinct performative style in the 1980s and is most often associated with the California hip hop community. However, Robin D. G. Kelley reminds us that the inspiration for what is now merchandised as gangsta rap has its origins in early East Coast hip hop.[35] The hard-core trend, what some innovators would later call "reality rap," was intimately related to the rhythms of postindustrial change that reshaped the social and economic character of largely segregated black working-class communities like south-central Los Angeles and east Oakland. In the context of disintegrating black urban life, structurally conditioned idleness, poverty, a burgeoning illegal drug economy, and the disciplinary ethos of "the war against the poor," gangsta rappers purported to give voice to the alienation and rage experienced by many young, dislocated black males. Gangsta rap's initial breakthrough took place in the flourishing underground music cultures and entrepreneurial ghettos of poor and working-class black and Latino youth. Many of the O.G.'s (original gangstas) drove from city to city and distributed their music from car trunks. As the hard-core style gradually began to surface from its underground roots, it was at first considered too explicit and as a result not amenable to merchandising. However, gangsta eventually supplanted message, Afrocentric, pop, and other subgenres of rap as the most commercially viable hip hop product in the early 1990s.[36]

Three factors contributed significantly to the rapid proliferation of "studio gangstas" and the successful merchandising of the hard-core style: new technology in the production of popular music; changing musical tastes and youth trends; and the spirit of entrepreneurship practiced by small, independent rap labels. First, the new music-recording technologies, especially multitrack recording systems, enabled producers of the gangsta style to create a music that was unusually thick and descriptive. The use of auditory cues like street sounds, screeching car chases, gunfire, police sirens, sound bites from television news reports, and sample dialogue from popular gangster films gave the new style a cinematic texture that bolstered its claims of "keeping it real," or in other words, authentic. Second, because each successive generation of youth seeks out different forms of music with which to identify, change is a permanent theme in popular music culture. Popular music trends are volatile primarily because the core audience consists of young teens whose taste can and often does vary. The film and music industries are especially sensitive to trend shifts in youth culture. Thus, the identification of many youth with the sensibilities of the hard-core style (i.e., sartorial design, hairstyles, language) stimulated the creation of products designed to exploit this particular mood shift in youth culture.

Finally, the role of entrepreneurship in the popular rise of gangsta rap cannot be overstated. Historically, the popular music industry has incubated entrepreneurial enclaves and mini–music moguls who make their mark by recording marginal music styles and cultures that have not yet broken into the mainstream music market. Unlike film production, for example, music recording is not inherently cost-prohibitive. But because major record companies are less likely to invest in music genres that have little or no market exposure, the cultivation of hard-core rap was left to the operators of small, independent labels located on the fringes of the music industry. Without a doubt, it is one of the greatest ironies that an enduring and celebrated tradition in American capitalism—entrepreneurship—was largely responsible for transforming hard-core from an underground, peripheral subculture to a mainstream, multimillion-dollar enterprise.

The most successful producers of consumer products first understand the need to identify trend shifts and popular appetites and, second, develop ways to swiftly serve them. Eric Wright (also known as rapper Eazy E) and Jerry Heller were two of the first to develop a coherent strategy for the successful production and distribution of hard-core rap.[37] In fact, it was both their record label, Ruthless Records, and group NWA (Niggers with Attitude) that propelled the hard-core style into the center of American popular culture. Wright and Heller successfully attained a distribution deal that broadened the appeal of hard-core beyond the local, underground youth cultures of Los Angeles and Oakland. Discussing his own vision and business acumen, Wright acknowledged that the distribution deal performed two crucial tasks: it afforded Ruthless Records the ability to distribute product quickly enough to exploit emergent trends while at the same time maintaining creative independence.[38] The latter was especially crucial to the producers of gangsta rap. Creative independence and their small size provided the insulation and freedom to record with essentially no fear of corporate interference or censorship. However, as hard-core began to break into the mainstream, the explicit lyrics generated an enormous backlash. Intense public scrutiny, warning labels, congressional hearings, and general moral condemnation sought to assert greater control over the production, distribution, and consumption of gangsta rap. But the greater scrutiny also created free publicity and, as many producers of gangsta rap soon experienced, increased sales.

Suge Knight, the cofounder of the independent label Death Row Records, also successfully mined the lucrative field of hard-core. A *New York Times Magazine* cover story on Knight reported that, between 1992 and 1996, Death Row "sold more than 15 million records and grossed more than $100 million."[39] In the magazine, journalist Lynn Hirschberg asserts that the real genius of gangsta rap entrepreneurs is their ability to shape and package ghetto culture for consumption by the youth of America. Much of Death Row's early success was built on the popularity of two gangsta rap celebrities, Dr. Dre and Snoop Doggy Dogg. Ever mindful of the need to maintain Death Row's innovative edge and hard-core image, the popularity of the label was strengthened after Knight recruited the popular yet enigmatic Tupac Shakur.[40] Further, Brian Cross makes the crucial point that the debate over the content in hard-core rap obscures the primary motivation for its increased production. To the degree that it was genuinely original, the innovators of the new rap style were more interested in cultivating the economic prospects of explicit rap lyrics than in producing authentic narratives about life in the postindustrial ghetto.[41]

The gangsta style can be partially viewed as a marketing pose—a strategic device to carve out a small but potentially lucrative niche in a vast popular culture marketplace. In many ways, the creators of hard-core were carrying out a strategy that is now common in the age of music video culture—image management. Indeed, one of the most significant influences of music video on popular music production is the ever-increasing significance of a carefully packaged style and image. This trend has given the rap enterprise several faces and varying styles from which to choose. For example, the influential group Public Enemy altered the rap landscape by meticulously orchestrating a selective range of symbols to effectively shape and market a specifically black nationalist worldview. Thus, the difference between Public Enemy's neo–black nationalist pose and Ice-T's gangster pose lay not so much in their attention to image making and performance but rather in the type of image and worldview they both tailored for the popular culture marketplace. Indeed, many of the O.G.'s understood that the new style was well suited for servicing a marketplace that was developing a seemingly insatiable appetite for sex and violence. Moreover, the proliferation of "studio gangstas" and associated rap labels illustrates the segregated conditions that structure the culture industry: for many young black working-class males, the gangsta genre was perceived as their only possible avenue for entrance into the popular music industry. The employment of this strategy, however, was not unproblematic insofar as it played on, and also exploited, the alleged social pathologies of poor ghetto youth.[42] Moreover, access to the technology and production sites of hard-core is overwhelmingly dominated by men. Thus, the creative environment out of which the music was produced is a predominantly male domain that privileges male pleasure and dominance.[43]

The meteoric rise of gangsta rap is all the more intriguing because it occurred contrary to conventional music industry logic. Gangsta rap sales grew rapidly and impressively even though it was virtually excluded from radio airplay, one of the most important promotional venues for popular music. In spite of numerous barriers, and much to the discontentment of the larger society, gangsta rap successfully penetrated the mainstream music market. The 1991 NWA album *Efil4zaggin* ("Niggaz4Life" backward) represented a breakthrough moment in the popular ascendancy of the hard-core style. *Efil4zaggin* debuted in the number two position on *Billboard* magazine's pop music charts. The following week, the album held the number one position, which meant that it was the biggest-selling album in the country.[44] *Billboard*'s Top Pop Albums chart is determined by the SoundScan accounting system, which based chart placement on the number of national sales electronically scanned per week. This system of measurement is notable because it provides a portrait of music sales from music chain stores located predominantly in suburban shopping malls. Much to the surprise of music industry analysts and music chain store managers (and probably even the producers of hard-core), the lofty sales of gangsta rap were driven mainly by white youth purchasing CDs and cassette tapes from suburban shopping centers.[45]

It was, then, the successful marketing of hard-core and the ensuing expansion of rap's consumer market that built the foundation for the rise of tie-in commodities and other cross-promotional uses.[46] Although the expansion of rap's appeal did not signal the erasure of the racial, class, and gender boundaries that structure the youth marketplace, it did, nevertheless, reveal significant shifts: specifically, young white males were emerging as major consumers of black popular cultural products. It was this reconfigured popular culture marketplace that the film industry inevitably noticed. Still, a significant challenge lay ahead: how could the producers and gatekeepers of popular film harness rap's energy and movement into a broader sphere of youth consumption?

The ghetto action film cycle emerged as the film industry's swift response to a rapidly changing youth culture and marketplace. This response was not unprecedented to the extent that it was a direct effort to appeal to the film industry's most stable market—young moviegoers—even if it was based on social currents that were clearly not of the film industry's own making. The job of film industry executives was to select scripts that translated the popular appeal of hip hop, and especially hard-core, into salable film product. If minimizing risk is one of the central principles in developing media product for mass consumption, it should come as no great surprise, then, that film industry executives embraced film projects that could be directly marketed to a cross section of youth by appropriating the language, style, and sensibilities of hip hop culture, and especially the allure of hard-core.

Ghetto Paradise

When Hollywood realized that white kids were really into rap—and don't kid yourself, that's the audience the studios are really lusting for—a little light went on: "Hey we can make money from black culture!"

ELVIS MITCHELL[47]

How pivotal was the popularization of hip hop culture in general, and gangsta rap specifically, to the production of the ghetto action film cycle? Before the financing of feature-length commercial films can be seriously contemplated, a number of basic questions must be satisfactorily answered. First, what is the market potential for a proposed film project? That is to say, does an identifiable audience exist for the film? Second, how much will it cost to produce, distribute, and market the proposed project? Third, where will the financial resources to produce the film come from? For example, in the case of high film production costs, outside financing is sometimes necessary.

The market demand for popular film is typically unstable and difficult to predict. Despite all of the work that goes into conceiving, producing, and distributing films, many fail to generate profits for their respective studios. The commercial success of rap music in general, and gangsta rap specifically, established an identifiable and targetable market. The ghetto action film cycle relied heavily on accompanying sound tracks that featured rap music as well as the casting of rap performers. Rap music culture, in this instance, was typically employed as a promotional tie-in, thus appealing to an already established youth market with some measure of precision. Pop music and music videoclips are important promotional vehicles for films. The popularity of music video makes provisions for new film industry marketing strategies: the release of most films that target young audiences is generally preceded by an accompanying music video. This strategy, for instance, was skillfully employed to market the 1983 film *Flashdance*.[48] In addition to rap music sound tracks, the casting of rap performers in film production has also become a common industry practice.[49] This tie-in promotional strategy develops a direct cross-marketing link to popular trends in hip hop culture.

The commercial film industry is constantly seeking out new ways to make product available. At the same time, however, controlling the escalating costs of film production is a serious priority, too. Because film production costs are so high, studios also need to find lower-budget productions in order to fill out their annual inventory of product release. The drive to cut costs compels the managerial hierarchy to seek out films that can yield the highest return on investment. The logic governing the production, distribution, and marketing of the ghetto action film wave runs counter to the blockbuster ethos that has been rapidly inflating film production costs since the middle 1970s. Film financing in Hollywood is a complex process that often involves package deals that include both domestic and foreign investors in order to cover the costs of elaborate productions. In the case of the ghetto action films, though, because production costs were relatively low, the studios were able to fund them internally without outside or foreign financing.

For example, the average cost of the cycle's three most commercially successful films was $5 million, a figure that falls exceedingly under the typical Hollywood film.[50] Furthermore, the average domestic box-office receipts collected from these same three films, $43 million, far exceed what the film industry considers a successful return on investment. It is this investment-to-profit ratio that evokes the specter of seventies blaxploitation by sharply reproducing the black cinema/white profit formula.[51] The production of the nineties ghetto action film cycle followed a typical pattern: almost uniformly, the film studios enforced extremely low budgets, limited distribution, and inexpensive marketing campaigns that were generally linked directly to rap music. This black cinema/corporate profits scenario indicated that, while the industry was eager to appropriate the most popular elements of black youth expressive culture, it would do so in terms that prescribed extraordinarily low capital investments, thus making production relatively risk-free and even a limited theatrical run a moneymaking endeavor.

Likewise, the release/exhibition pattern for many of the films suggests that distribution costs were tightly controlled and a specialized audience targeted. The release pattern for *Boyz* is a good example (see table 6.1). Columbia Pictures released the film during the summer, a season that aggressively targets young moviegoers who are out of school. The film opened on 829 screens and peaked at 917 screens nationwide. While not distributed as widely as the megablockbuster *Terminator II* (which was released that same summer on 2,400 screens), when compared to other African American–directed feature films, the release pattern is moderately wide. The number of screen exhibitions also suggests that the film was exhibited in both urban and suburban theater complexes.

The marketing scheme for *Boyz* suggests that the film was produced with a specifically youth market in mind. According to Columbia Pictures President Frank Price, the marketing campaign sought primarily a young black audience. Price defined the movie's secondary audience as "young whites, primarily those who listen to music like that in the film."[52] The exit polls conducted by the studio suggest that *Boyz* attracted an audience across the country that was equal parts white and black; thus, the film was successful in reaching its primary and second-

Table 6.1. *Variety* Box-Office Reports for *Boyz N the Hood* (Columbia, 1991)

Week	Week's Reported Box Office ($)	Cumulative Reported Box Office ($)	Screens	Week's Average $ per Screen
1	15,229,280	15,229	829*	18,370
2	10,915,613	26,144,893	901	12,115
3	7,290,748	33,435,641	917	7,950
4	5,444,015	38,879,656	881	6,129
5	3,462,542	42,342,198	830	4,172
6	3,007,780	45,349,978	895	3,360
7	2,234,760	47,584,738	911	2,453
8	2,120,846	49,705,584	856	2,478
9	1,718,714	51,424,298	911	1,887
10	1,338,458	52,762,756	908	1,474
11	1,147,733	53,910,489	847	1,355
12	805,513	54,716,002	707	1,139
14†	292,361	55,513,362	226	1,294
15	244,134	55,757,496	232	1,052
16	203,268	55,960,764	191	1,064
17	229,330	56,190,094	188	1,220

*By contrast, the blockbuster *Terminator II: Judgment Day* opened on 2,400 screens.
†Week 13 not reported.

ary audiences, which were predominantly young (and probably male) moviegoers. The table further indicates that, within its first five weeks of theatrical exhibition, *Boyz* accumulated over $42 million, a brisk and impressive return on Columbia's $6 million investment in producing the film.

In addition, a look at the box-office reports for *New Jack City* (table 6.2), *Straight Out of Brooklyn* (table 6.3), and *Menace II Society* (table 6.4) reveals variation in the distribution of ghetto action films. Both *Boyz* and *New Jack City* were distributed by major studios, which may explain why the number of screens and the box-office revenue were high. The majors have deeper pockets, and their distribution muscle enables them to saturate theaters with their respective products. *New Jack City* enjoyed an extremely high average dollars per screen performance. The film opened on 862 screens and peaked at 905, an exceptionally high number of screens for a black-directed celebrityless vehicle. Like many of the films from this genre, *New Jack City* produced immediate and impressive box-office revenue, over $33 million during its first five weeks of theatrical release. The film reportedly cost $6 million to produce.

The distribution strategy for *Straight Out of Brooklyn* and *Menace* developed sharply different characteristics. The fact that these films were

Table 6.2. *Variety* Box-Office Reports for *New Jack City* (Warner Brothers, 1991)

Week	Week's Reported Box Office ($)	Cumulative Reported Box Office ($)	Screens	Week's Average $ per Screen
1	10,031,036	10,031,036	862	11,636
2	7,777,155	17,808,191	887	8,767
3	NR*	22,255,826	905	4,915
4	5,461,360	29,608,714	905	6,034
5	3,775,351	33,384,065	872	4,329
6	2,800,173	36,184,238	865	3,237
7	2,421,835	38,606,073	845	2,866
9†	1,407,996	41,739,157	631	2,231
10	1,062,666	42,801,823	568	1,870
11	828,112	43,629,935	428	1,934
12	531,833	44,161,760	217	2,450
13	488,754	44,650,522	205	2,384
14	329,242	44,979,764	170	1,936
15	319,784	45,299,548	154	2,076
16	523,437	45,822,905	246	2,127
18‡	432,428	46,703,007	183	2,362
19	196,653	46,899,660	136	1,445
20	281,257	47,180,917	119	2,363
21	215,176	47,396,093	84	2,561
24§	49,977	47,624,353	36	1,388

*Not reported.
†Only weekend gross reported for week 8.
‡Week 17 not reported.
§Weeks 22 and 23 not reported because the movie was not listed in the weekly box-office reports. It is uncertain whether this was due to its not having grossed enough to make the top-60 list.

distributed by small independent film companies helps to explain the variation in strategies. First, *Straight* was distributed by Samuel Goldwyn, a second-tier film distributor. In addition, the film was produced on a shoestring budget. Indeed, part of the film's appeal was the fact that Matty Rich appeared on a popular radio station in New York City to solicit donations to finance the film. He also used the credit cards of his mother and sister, making the film for $300,000. It was only after a successful screening at the Sundance Film Festival that a distribution deal was secured. Given the low-budget features of the film, Samuel Goldwyn opted to go for a very small and limited release schedule. The film was released only in select markets and only after word-of-mouth advertising had been established. It peaked at 75 screens. Unlike *Boyz,* for example, the film was exhibited primarily in art theater houses rather than the high-traffic multiplex theaters that specialize in exhibiting the more expensive and heavily marketed film products.

Table 6.3. *Variety* Box-Office Reports for *Straight out of Brooklyn*
(Samuel Goldwyn, 1991)

Week	Cumulative Reported Box Office ($)	Screens	Week's Average $ per Screen
1	88,886	5	14,994
2	200,540	9	12,406
3	259,653	9	6,568
4	373,529	20	5,694
5	507,140	17	7,859
7*	1,608,407	75	5,993
8	1,798,321	65	2,922
9	1,966,754	57	2,955
10	2,113,425	61	2,404
11	2,223,500	50	2,197
12	2,331,680	39	2,467
13	2,422,688	37	2,459
14	2,469,898	26	1,815
16*	2,516,210	37	1,252
17	2,556,362	34	1,181
18	2,590,997	34	1,018
19	2,616,586	24	1,066
20	2,656,131	38	1,041
22*	2,712,293	12	1,688

*Weeks 6, 15, and 21 not reported.

Menace was released nearly two years after the successful box-office run of *Boyz* and *New Jack City.* Although *Menace* came near the end of the ghetto action film cycle's popular peak, the film still managed to generate handsome profits. Whereas *Boyz* opened on 829 screens, *Menace* opened on half that number, 464. This suggests that, from the beginning, the film's distributor, New Line Cinema, would employ a different release strategy: one that would neither anticipate nor seek the remarkable performance of *Boyz.* Because New Line was a small independent film distributor (it was eventually purchased by Ted Turner and is now a part of the Turner Broadcasting/Time Warner entertainment media empire), it did not have the resources to saturate theaters with *Menace;* thus, it, too, elected to target a more limited market. The film was still able to turn a quick profit. While the film cost about $3 million to make, it generated more than three times its production costs in only its second week of theatrical release. By the sixth week, *Menace* had earned over $20 million at the box office. The film also demonstrated what the industry calls "legs." That is, it produced strong box-office revenue over the course of an extended period of theatrical release.

Table 6.4. *Variety* Box-Office Reports for *Menace II Society*
(New Line Cinema, 1993)

Week	Week's Reported Box Office ($)	Cumulative Reported Box Office ($)	Screens	Week's Average $ per Screen
1	4,952,947	5,696,985	464*	10,674
2	4,529,884	10,226,869	513	8,830
3	3,680,049	13,906,918	540	6,815
4	2,929,037	16,855,955	570	5,139
6†	2,172,251	21,400,121	552	3,935
7	1,451,889	22,852,010	430	3,376
8	1,421,567	24,273,577	392	3,626
9	903,280	25,176,857	335	2,696
10	612,921	25,789,778	245	2,502
12†	339,125	26,529,102	145	2,339
13	244,926	26,774,028	124	1,975
14	148,993	26,923,021	89	1,674
16‡	89,677	27,139,926	81	1,107
17	257,184§	27,378,462	224	1,148
18	146,647	27,545,013	146	1,004
19	117,082	27,622,195	110	1,064
20	69,332	27,131,527	69	1,005

Cliffhanger (Tri-Star) opened on 2,333 screens and *Super Mario Brothers* (Buena Vista) on 2,081 screens.
†Weeks 5 and 11 not reported.
‡Only weekend box office reported for week 15.
§*Variety* reported a 187% increase in box-office receipts. *Menace* demonstrated what the industry calls great "legs," meaning that it was able to sustain its box-office appeal over an extended period of time.

Overall, the tables suggest that the ghetto action film cycle was extremely successful at the box office, producing substantive profits in only a few weeks of theatrical release. This perhaps more than other factors explains its repetitious and accelerated production. Moreover, the release patterns of the movies discussed above suggest that the genre was exploited by both major and minor film distributors. And though the two employed different distribution strategies, both were able to cash in on the popularization of ghetto action films. In general, the majors tended to go for moderately wide releases and substantial profits while the minors opted for smaller release patterns that still generated noteworthy profits.

It is important to note that the nineties ghetto action film cycle was not the film industry's first effort to exploit the growing vitality of rap music. In the early to mid-1980s, rap's commercial success inspired the production of a handful of films.[53] The production, marketing, distribution, and consumption of these early films, however, vividly illustrate how rap and its market greatly expanded between the eighties and nineties. Take, for example, Warner Brothers' rap musical *Krush Groove* (1985). Similar to many of the nineties hip hop–inflected films, *Krush Groove* not only emphasized rap music but also employed rappers as principal actors.[54] In the mid-1980s, rap's market was primarily young black urban teenagers. The release/exhibition pattern for *Krush Groove* further illustrates that the film industry's attempt to take advantage of the emergent youth culture targeted a modest, predominantly African American market. The film peaked on 519 screens. The opening-weekend reported box office for *Krush Groove* was $2,905,293. The film was a commercial success, able to turn the $3 million it cost to produce into an eventual gross of $15 million. By contrast, *Boyz N the Hood* peaked at 917 screens and grossed over $15 million its opening weekend! According to the director of *Boyz,* John Singleton, the film grossed over $100 million in combined domestic and international box-office receipts. The enormous success of *Boyz* clearly demonstrates how the consumer market for rap and tie-in commodities—in this case, popular film—grew substantially between 1985 and 1991 to include, in addition to black youth, suburban youth and a growing international market, too.

This shift in consumer demand also reflects a more decisive transition in the production, distribution, and consumption of black popular culture. In an industry that operates on the theory of precedent, the box-office appeal of hip hop–influenced films like *House Party, New Jack City,* and *Boyz N the Hood* with young white moviegoers inspired a new ethos that placed the production of black cinema on a decidedly different course. Whereas the production of rap-inflected films in the mid-1980s predominantly targeted young black teens, the production of rap-inflected films in the 1990s imagined a wider and potentially more lucrative market of black, white, and international moviegoers. Black popular film, from this perspective, is packaged not only for black consumption and pleasure but, more important, for white consumption and pleasure. This trend in popular cultural production distinguishes the ghetto action film cycle from the blaxploitation boom of the 1970s. Moreover, this trend also illuminates the important transformations that remap the racial and class boundaries of the youth marketplace and subsequently give what is packaged as black popular culture a more prominent position in the commercial culture landscape.[55]

However, to comprehend the ghetto action film as a product rigidly controlled by the commercial film industry and market demographics simplifies the popular rise of the film cycle. In addition, such a perspective precludes the possibility of viewing the film cycle as a cultural formation committed, in part, to the labor of ideological struggle. Despite the film industry's swift incorporation of the cultural politics associated with hip hop culture, the film cycle also represents an important site of black youth agency. The representational politics of the film cycle are dialogically related to the controlling discourses that produce meaning(s) about blackness and postindustrial ghetto life. Moreover, this particular formation of cinematic discourse vigorously engages a historically specific experience—the social and economic dislocation of black youth. Consequently, the thematic ideas, cinematic techniques, and stylistic conventions that define the film cycle give this historically situated formation of African American filmmaking enormously complex ideological configurations—a subject to which I turn next.

1 The Ghettocentric Imagination

All these black, ghetto-centered action flicks must necessarily differ in subtle ways from the standard studio product. While they all adhere to the images, editing, and sounds of action formula, they also implicitly undermine Hollywood's inherent tendency to repress or co-opt resistant or oppositional social perspectives in its films. . . . Rather than think of these films as the cause of violence, we should view them as vehicles through which society's racial contradictions, injustices, and failed policies are mediated. They are the artist's examination of, and dire warnings about, a society in which African Americans are, in terms of statistics, worse off today than before the civil rights movement. And though the news is bad, the blame resides with the social order in its totality, not the cinematic vehicle that delivers the news.

ED GUERRERO[1]

The most provocative films associated with the ghetto action film cycle are typically described as excessively violent, misogynist, and straight-up nihilist. But the representational strategies that give the cycle its creative shape demand more subtle analysis. My goal is not to negate critiques of this filmmaking trend (I offer some, too) but rather to explore the ways in which this particular formation of popular film culture engages a larger orbit of racial discourse. The films from the ghetto action cycle not only compete and circulate among each other; indeed, these films circulate among a broad universe of music videos, television programs, news journalism, literature, and even political discourses, which each struggle to figure the representational landscape that renders postindustrial ghetto life more comprehensible.

In chapters 1 and 2, I discussed some of the dominant representations of the postindustrial ghetto. Even though dominant discourses perform a pivotal role in shaping the outlines of racial discourse, they do not necessarily assert total authority over the ideological sphere. Counterdiscourses are typically deployed to produce and circulate alternative meanings about the social world. In this chapter, I consider how the representational politics employed in the ghetto action film cycle strive to produce new interpretations of the lived experiences of poor black youth. Any serious examination of the postindustrial ghetto as a contested symbol must, first, aim to understand the context out of which this particular formation of ideological struggle takes shape. The coding of cultural symbols like the urban ghetto, for example, is inherently unstable, contentious, and historically specific. The study of the cultural landscape, to be sure, should never simply be about "reading" texts or symbolic objects like film. A text-only approach reduces a vast cultural landscape to a flow of anchorless symbolic materials located outside the boundaries of social and historical struggle. The most challenging task is to interrogate the historical terrain upon which symbolic materials are both created and circulated. Furthermore, it is important to note that the formation of the symbolic sphere animates the ongoing struggle to determine the body of ideas, claims, and representations that achieve commonsense status and, as a result, penetrate the everyday and taken-for-granted ideologies of any given historical moment.

Even though removed from the more official circuits of political power, the tenor of black youth popular culture continues to have a political resonance. Popular media culture, too, is a terrain on which the processes of social and political struggle are in constant operation. The most popular sites of representation—film and television—engender their own historical particularities and dimensions of struggle. Racialized cultural objects like the *black* ghetto become fiercely charged locations of ideological struggle as competing cultural producers struggle to assign them meaning. It is within the context of a historically specific dialogue about race, youth, and urban poverty that the ghetto action film cycle generates its most poignant and problematic features.

The ghetto action film cycle represents a dynamic site of ideological production. Despite the dominance of themes and imagery that seem to comply with popular notions of youth villainy, many of the films from the cycle mobilize complicated meanings about the lived experiences of postindustrial ghetto life. Moreover, this particular filmmaking practice is structured by a historically specific *ghettocentric imagination.* The expressive culture of black youth loosely organizes a worldview that cultivates varying ways of interpreting, representing, and understanding the changing social, economic, and political contours of ghetto dislocation. This historically specific imagination approaches what Raymond Williams describes as a certain "structure of feeling."[2] Arguably, this distinct structure of feeling or generational mood shift has achieved a dominant position in the larger orbit of black popular culture. In fact, some critics maintain that the preeminence of ghetto-centricity in black youth discourses elides more nuanced representations of the African American experience.[3]

Ironically, black youth popular discourses and mainstream representations of the urban ghetto are not entirely asymmetrical. For instance, both treat inner-city blight—violent crime, familial disorganization, and drug and welfare dependency—as the core experience of black America. But black youth believe that the popular mediascape functions as an all-important site for giving voice to their ideas about ghetto dislocation.[4] Whereas the producers of rap music have struggled to rearticulate the lived experiences of poor youth, filmmakers have likewise waged a similar struggle. In the following pages, I focus on the cinematic elaboration of this historically conditioned youth discourse. First, I explore Albert and Allen Hughes's strategic deployment of the gangster film. More specifically, I consider how the Hughes brothers tailor the gangster genre to fit the historically specific experiences of late twentieth-century ghetto youth poverty. Second, I examine how urban ghetto space is recoded. One of the foremost themes that resonates throughout the ghetto action picture is the idea that poor black urban communities are locations of entrapment and repression. In the final section, I explore how the makers of this film cycle reproduce common-sense discourses about the (dis)organization of black familial life. Paradoxically, the gender politics of the film cycle are typically structured in terms that militate against the resistive thrust that partially characterizes the oppositional intentions of this filmmaking practice.

Postindustrial Ghetto Life from a Young G's Perspective: *Menace II Society* as Counter(?) discourse

Gangster/crime films continue to be made and hold their own in the marketplace. The genre remains a viable framework for getting something important said. Its basic material continues to attract talented people who give it expres-

sive force and creative shape. Its durability attests to its cultural importance. The genre has survived because the issues it addresses have always been central to the American experience, because its formal properties have given them a clarity of outline and lucidity of exposition, and because it has been infinitely flexible in adapting itself to shifting social and cultural conditions. It has played an important role in both forming and reflecting the American imagination.

JACK SHADOIAN[5]

The emergence of "gangsta rappers" not only signaled a new marketing posture; it also opened space for the production of a distinct trend and form of youth discourse. Historian Robin D. G. Kelley argues that the gangsta subgenre in rap was never merely a celebration of gang violence.[6] For Kelley, the "gangsta" motif enabled narratives that struggled to penetrate and reverse the dominant racial discourses that criminalized black youth.[7] During the early 1990s, a surge of popular movies — *New Jack City* (1991), *Straight out of Brooklyn* (1991), *Boyz N the Hood* (1991), *Juice* (1992), and *Menace II Society* (1993) — represented the filmic incorporation of the hard-core trend popularized by the producers of gangsta rap music. In these and other feature-length commercial films, the postindustrial ghetto functioned as the principal setting for film production and narrative pleasure.

Menace is one of the more aesthetically and ideologically provocative entries from the cycle. The Hughes brothers immerse the spectator in the fictional world of young teens who rely on street crime to negotiate the hostile environment and circumstances of ghetto dislocation. But rather than romanticize youth criminality, the Hughes brothers aim to create a cinematic world that constructs a compelling framework for understanding why some poor youth turn to crime and violence. The film's representational strategies are profoundly political. Its most enduring thematic attribute, to be sure, is the relentless critique of a social and political system that continues to reproduce young "menaces to society." The creators of *Menace* ruthlessly explore the volatile relationship between black youth culture and the postindustrial ghetto terrain. As a result, the film is an elaborately arranged set of characters, sequences, and dialogue that attempts to think critically about black youth alienation in the interstice between the *liberal structuralist* and *conservative behaviorist* analysis of the black urban poor.[8]

Although *Menace* embodies the transformations that contour black

199

youth popular discourses, the film also illuminates an important feature of change that marks the broader popular culture landscape: the intensification of violence in American film and television.[9] As African American filmmakers have become more literate in the techniques and history of cinema, they tend to draw from and expand on a vast system of conventions, genres, and stylistic choices. The Hughes brothers' stylized presentation and aesthetic organization of *Menace,* for example, are influenced by the commercial rebirth of the gangster film. The urban gangster/crime film is an enduring genre in American popular culture and has typically exploited the perceived chaos of America's ethnically and racially diverse cities.[10]

Despite the enduring presence of the gangster genre in American popular film culture, its deployment must be understood as fluid and constantly developing historically specific meanings. The genre has been shaped by numerous factors: public fascination with real-life gangsters, censorship, and technological innovations in film production, especially sound.[11] Shadoian asserts, however, that the basic structure of the genre is "ready made for certain kinds of concerns" that mainly reflect the tension between America as the land of opportunity and corporate hegemony. According to Shadoian, the core thematic requirement of the gangster film is inherently devoted to societal conflict. He writes:

> [T]he gangster is not the same as an outlaw; he specifically violates a system of rules that a group of people live under. He is the product of an advanced, urban civilization. In Westerns, by contrast, the conflict is often outside the realm of a social system as such, although it may bear upon it. It concerns the individual versus the land. . . . In the gangster/crime film, meanings emerge, whether deliberately or not, about the nature of society and the kind of individual it creates. By definition, the genre must shed light on either the society or the outcasts who oppose it, and by definition, the gangster is outside, or anti, the legitimate social order. The gangster/crime film is therefore a way of gaining a perspective on society by creating worlds and figures that are outside it.[12]

If we accept this definition as an essential premise of the gangster film, an immediate question emerges: What type of perspectives on American society and the individuals it creates do the Hughes brothers attempt to construct?

Despite the persistence of strong genre expressions, the vocabulary of the gangster film is rearticulated as various filmmakers assert their distinct accents on the genre. The commercial success of *Menace* clearly points to the durability of the genre and its ability to adapt to, engage, and remain relevant to the shifting contours of American social life. While the Hughes brothers rigorously studied the gangster films of Brian De-Palma and Martin Scorsese, their particular elaboration of the genre subjects a historically specific societal conflict—the hypersegregated status of ghetto communities and the impoverishment of black youth—to cinematic exploration.[13]

Menace brings to cinematic life what Cornel West describes as the nihilistic threat that increasingly pervades poor black communities. According to West, nihilism is "the lived experience of coping with a life of horrifying meaninglessness, hopelessness, and (most important) lovelessness. This usually results in a numbing detachment from others and a self-destructive disposition toward the world."[14] The notion that black youth culture is nihilistic is both popular and widespread. At the same time, though, this notion also generates serious questions and concerns. Two of the most powerful and eloquent retorts against the black nihilism claim have been put forth by Stephen Steinberg and Eric Lott.[15] Steinberg maintains that the emphasis on the allegedly nihilistic lifestyles of black youth—crime, drugs, and other negative behaviors—comes perilously close to endorsing the view that deviance is the primary culprit in the deterioration of poor black urban life. Elsewhere, Lott charges that the dismissal of black youth popular culture as nihilistic obscures the radical potential and political critique articulated in the creation of rap and black cinema.

The ensuing debate over nihilism is, in truth, complicated. On the one hand, West is right to call into question those elements of black life—especially homicidal violence and misogynistic practices—that aggravate the already blighted conditions of ghetto dislocation. On the other hand, Steinberg's contention that the emphasis on black nihilism shifts critical scrutiny away from the social, economic, and political structures that are implicated in everyday ghetto life is legitimate, too. Ultimately, Steinberg's razor-sharp critique urges anyone concerned about the plight of black youth to guard against what he calls "semantic infiltration." Thus, one of his concerns is that the ideas of even a progressive activist and public intellectual like West can be appropriated and employed to embolden those discourses that work at pathologizing blackness.

Menace unabashedly participates in the nihilism debate. The film's central character, Caine, animates the collective experience of black youth who must live daily with the humiliation and alienation brought on by the profound transformations of postindustrial ghetto life. West adds that, while this threat is not new to black America, its late twentieth-century manifestation feeds on poverty and shattered cultural institutions. Throughout the film, Caine is, in fact, loosely anchored to many of the primary cultural institutions—family, school, religion. But poor black youth and their values, as Carl Nightingale maintains, are not completely dislocated from mainstream society. Popular media entertainment culture, for example, connects Caine to sensationalized models of masculinity and also teaches him the status rewards of conspicuous consumption. In fact, Caine's everyday practices are governed by his desire for upward mobility, mainly through the acquisition of material goods—jewelry, cars, designer clothes—that confer status and prestige, according to mainstream values.

On the surface, this particular character—Caine—fits the *master-status-determining characteristics* that inscribe black youth as members of the "dangerous classes."[16] For instance, Caine sells drugs and commits robberies, violent murders, and carjackings. It is, of course, precisely these forms of youth delinquency that color popular perceptions of crime.[17] One of the risks, then, of creating a character like Caine is that it does, to some degree, reinscribe many of the dominant codings and representations that figure young black males as dangerous and criminal. In addition, because the cinema is such a visually saturated medium, images tend to dominate how audiences interpret and produce meaning from the characters portrayed on-screen.

But as Seymour Chatman writes, "[F]ilms are particularly versatile in exhibiting the unspoken inner lives of characters laconically."[18] The cinematic apparatus provides numerous elements that enable filmmakers to introduce subtle attributes that nuance their construction of characters. According to Chatman, whereas *flat* characters are direct and teleological, *round* characters are agglomerate.[19] Round characters are marked by numerous traits, some of which may even seem incongruous. With round characters, Chatman argues, "[w]e come to anticipate, indeed to demand, the possibilities of discovering new and unsuspected traits. Thus, round characters function as open constructs, susceptible of further insight. Our 'readings out' are not limited to the actual period of immediate contact with the text. . . . The great round characters seem virtually inexhaustible objects for contemplation."[20] Caine, I would like to suggest, is more round—that is, open-ended—than a *prima facie* reading may discern. More important, how does the Hughes brothers' open-ended construction of Caine enable the spectator to discover new insights about poor black youth that counter the staple, controlling representations of young black males?

A prominent feature of the ghettocentric imagination is its ability to foreground the worldviews of black youth. In *Menace,* one of the main methods of privileging the perspectives of youth is the incorporation of the *voice-over technique.*[21] The voice-over authorizes Caine as *the* primary source for narrative transmission. The voice in cinema is generally considered subordinate to the image. The hierarchical placement of the visible above the audible is not uniquely specific to the cinema but is symptomatic of a more general late twentieth-century cultural production logic that is emphatically creating a vast visual culture. But sound constitutes an important arena of discursive activity in the cinema. Moreover, much like the image, sound can also be manipulated. Indeed dialogue, music, and sound effects can be arranged to create mood or context or symbolize character traits.

The voice-over technique in *Menace* is significant because it gives Caine—a symbol of black youth social dislocation—a prioritized voice and privileged position. Moreover, the displacement of the voice-over from a localizable body outside the story-world visualized on-screen endows the voice with a certain authority.[22] The Hughes brothers use the voice-over technique, for example, to communicate directly to the spectator Caine's thoughts on poverty, the surveillance of black youth, and the lack of meaningful economic opportunities for the poor. In the process, an important barrier in the spectatorial process is subverted: rather than exclusively address the characters in the film, Caine also addresses the spectator. Caine's voice works mainly as a figurative instrument articulating the frustrations and disappointments of poor black youth. The spectator is invited to make sense of the social and economic transitions that reshape postindustrial ghetto life from Caine's point of view. Positioning Caine both inside and outside the story-world presented on-screen allows the character to speak authoritatively on the crisis scenarios that implicate many poor black youths. Caine's voice, quite simply, then, presides over this fictional representation of life in the hood.

From the opening sequence, the Hughes brothers bring to the center of their cinematic world the crimes and behaviors of poor black youth that overwhelmingly dominate current debates about youth delinquency, criminal justice, social policy, and race. The film begins with the central character, Caine, and his friend O-Dog purchasing beer from two local Korean vendors. An unpleasant exchange between the two young men and the Korean couple culminates with O-Dog's violently killing both storekeepers at gunpoint range.[23] From the film's opening frames, the spectator is immersed in a fictional whirlwind of unbridled youth rage and violence.

As the two young men depart the convenience store, the Hughes brothers employ the *flashback* technique and insert footage from the 1965 Watts urban uprising. Why would the filmmakers invoke the Watts uprising? The flashback technique in film is generally employed to supply the spectator with important background information preceding the chain of events that move the story-plot toward narrative closure. Initially, this abrupt rupture of time and setting is unsettling, but it allows the authors to contextualize the 1990s ghetto landscape. In this instance, the flashback technique introduces a seminal period of events in post–World War II U.S. race relations: the swelling of urban uprisings in the 1960s that reflected the withering of the civil rights movement, its inability to ameliorate inner-city blight, and the ensuing backlash against black protest.

The Hughes brothers chose to insert a series of black-and-white newsreel footage that includes burning buildings, armored tanks, federal troops, police dog attacks, acts of police brutality, and defiant black citizens. Black-and-white film stock is often used to signify the past. The newsreel footage gives the film a hybrid documentary/commercial texture. Typically, the documentary addresses real people and real events rather than fictional people or events. The documentarist believes she or he is providing commentary on a real world that already exists rather than a fabricated world constructed by the filmmaker. Giannetti writes that, "implicit in the concept of documentary is the verb to *document*—to verify, to provide an irrefutable record of an event."[24] Further, Giannetti reminds us, however, that documentarists, like fictional filmmakers, "are not just recorders of external reality[;] . . . they shape their raw materials through their selection of details."[25] The manner in which the newsreel footage is expressively reedited does not pretend to be a neutral act of documentation. The Hughes brothers' selection of detail emphasizes racial terror and state-sanctioned force. The inclusion of the footage documents an important link between the 1990s ghetto landscape and

the tumultuous social and political climate of the 1960s. The juxtapo-
sitioning of these two time periods suggests that any representation of
the post–civil rights generation of poor youth must also consider the
racial and historical antagonisms that structure their lives. The quasi-
documentary strategy enhances the Hughes brothers' capacity to blur
the distinctions between the fictional and real world, thus endowing the
film with the power of realism.

Like most popular film narratives, *Menace* is organized by a series of
conflicts. For example, the film is partially structured along the theme
of intergenerational tension.[26] Caine is portrayed in sharp contrast to
his grandfather. The relationship between the two characters illuminates what sociologist Elijah Anderson describes as the erosion of the
"old head" as an authority figure in black urban communities. An old
head, Anderson writes, "is a man of stable means who was strongly committed to family life, to church, and, most important, to passing on his
philosophy, developed through his own rewarding experience with
work, to young boys he found worthy. He personified the work ethic
and equated it with value and high standards of morality; in his eyes a
working man was a good, decent individual."[27] The primary role, then,
of the old head was to equip young boys with a value system that emphasized hard work, family life, and religion. Anderson maintains that,
while old heads once occupied a position of authority in the black
community, this is no longer true. Due mainly to social and economic
transformations in urban ghettos, the traditional old-head figure has
lost prestige and credibility as a role model. According to Anderson, one
of the most important factors in this loss of status is the glaring inaccessibility to meaningful employment for black youth. Anderson argues,
"[W]hen gainful employment and its rewards are not forthcoming, boys
easily conclude that the moral lessons of the old head concerning the
work ethic, punctuality, and honesty do not fit their circumstances."[28]
For many poor African American youths, the moral urgings emphasiz-
ing patience and religious faith are generally viewed as antiquated and
irrelevant means of improving the material conditions of their lives.

A sequence in which Caine, O-Dog, and the grandfather converse is
especially revealing. Both the dialogue and shot composition of the sequence bring the notion of intergenerational conflict into sharper focus.
The placement of characters and other visual weights, in addition to
camera angles and the composition of image, are symbolically coded
strategies of representation controlled by the director's manipulation of
screen space. As Chatman argues, there is no predetermined rationale

for the arrangement of these weights; they are all *choices* made by the director. The choices made by the Hughes brothers in this sequence are noteworthy. The grandfather is seated in a chair across the room from the two teens. The *shot–reverse shot* technique that accompanies the dialogue exaggerates the physical distance between the figures on-screen. The exaggerated physical separation symbolizes the ideological and generational chasm that separates Caine and O-Dog from the grandfather.

Also, the dialogue in this sequence articulates distance and conflict. The grandfather attempts to exercise moral authority by invoking passages from the Bible. It is also interesting to note that, throughout the film, the grandfather is photographed with little camera movement. This representational strategy equates the grandfather not only with an elderly lifestyle and dated critiques of black deprivation but also with immobility and acquiescence to social inequality. The dialogue in the scene is informative:

Grandfather: Now what I want to talk to you about is the trouble you've been getting into. . . . Boys, the lord didn't put you here to be shooting and killing each other. It's right there in the Bible, Exodus 20:13, "thou shall not kill."

Caine: Grandpa, I ain't never killed nobody.

Grandfather: Oh, I doubt that. . . . And Kevin [O-Dog], I've heard stories about you.

O-Dog: Sir, I don't think God really cares too much about us, or he wouldn't put us here. I mean look at where we stay at. Its all fuc . . . It's messed up around here.

Grandfather: You don't have any belief, boy. The lord don't care about who's got the biggest house . . .

We then hear Caine's voice.

Caine (voice-over): My grandpa was always coming at us with that religion. And every time, it would go in one ear and out the other.

Cut to Caine and O-Dog leaving the apartment.

Caine: Sorry about that, man. Grandpa can get carried away with that Bible and shit.

O-Dog: Hell, yeah. He be in church every Sunday, huh?

Caine: Faithfully. I mean sitting there praying to a white Jesus.

O-Dog: Man, black people got too much damn religion as it is.

Caine: That's what I'm saying.

The grandfather, in this sequence, is clearly attempting to exercise his moral authority as an old-head figure, but the disinterested body language of Caine and O-Dog indicates the approach is futile. The strained dialogue focuses the spectator's attention on the broad generational cleavages that define the relationship between the two black teens and the grandfather. On the one hand, the grandfather believes religious faith is crucial to the recuperation of black life, whereas Caine and O-Dog, on the other hand, reject religion as a viable option for transforming their lives. Moreover, the sequence suggests that the grandfather has, at least to some degree, accepted the practice of ghetto dislocation, while, on the contrary, the misguided vigor of the young men both confronts and doubts its legitimacy.

The ambivalence toward Christianity reflects the sense of hopelessness that constitutes a core feature of the worldview of many black youth whose window of opportunity for social and economic mobility has become increasingly narrow. But the rejection of religious faith is not limited to Christianity. Caine and O-Dog also reject more pseudoradical religious doctrine—most notably, that of the Nation of Islam. One of the supporting characters in the film, Sharif, symbolizes the religious organization. For instance, Sharif is often costumed in colors—red, black, and green—and paraphernalia emblematic of the black nationalist politics of the organization. In addition, he constantly berates Caine and O-Dog for their use of alcohol and drugs. According to Sharif, drugs are poisonous substances designed to control and/or destroy African Americans. Sharif's Farrahkanian political views are routinely dismissed by Caine as hollow rhetoric. During the spectator's initial introduction to Sharif, Caine, in voice-over commentary, describes him as an "ex-knucklehead turned Muslim. He was so happy to be learning something he liked, he kept coming at us with it. He thought Allah could save black people . . . *yeah, right!*"

The cynical rejection of old-head authority, religion, and black political ideology is strongly reactionary. Caine and O-Dog view politics and religion as meaningless, an inefficient means of achieving what poor blacks should be most concerned with: improving the immediate material conditions of their lives. Moreover, this ideology demonstrates how increasing social and economic distress has led black youth to reject the primary institutions responsible for imparting the core ideological values that partially shape individual belief systems and behavior. The failure of black cultural and political life to penetrate specific segments of the African American population foregrounds important questions about the identity politics articulated in the ghettocentric imagination.

Caine and O-Dog vividly animate what Elijah Anderson discusses as the formation of a different identity structure among post-1960s black youth.[29] According to Anderson, the militant attitudes of the late 1960s imbued black youth with a hyperpoliticized sense of racial pride, and as a result, black identity and self-concept have undergone significant revision.[30] He writes:

> With raised consciousness, the young, unskilled black worker often perceives himself useful only to the most exploitative employer, in the most menial of jobs, and then receives little or no job security, advancement, benefits, and at times no pay. With the increased emphasis on self, young blacks are tending to be more selective about the jobs they will perform, and often will not accept employment and work conditions they consider to be demeaning. This attitude appears in striking contrast to that of an earlier generation of blacks, many of whom accepted almost any available work.[31]

The refusal, then, to comply with the division of labor and the moral urgings of religious doctrine establishes a greater likelihood for participation in alternative social networks like the underground economy.[32]

In contrast to dominant discourses about crime, the authors of *Menace* portray the decision to become a part of the underground economy as a rational rather than strictly delinquent choice. Martin Sanchez Jankowski's ethnographic study of gangs in urban America asserts that youth decide to participate in criminal activity for a variety of reasons, basing their decisions on a rational calculation of what is best for them and the improvement of their financial well-being.[33] *Menace* creates a fictional world that suggests that Caine's decision to participate in legally prohibited acts is the result of a cost/benefit decision-making process. Caine's primary motivation is to become socially and economically mobile, to improve his material status. It is critical to note that this perspective does not excuse the horrific actions of Caine and especially O-Dog; rather, it provides an alternative framework for understanding *why* participation in the underground economy is regarded as a viable option by some individuals. Perhaps one of the most compelling achievements of *Menace* is the film's ability to avoid both a self-righteous condemnation and romantic celebration of youth criminality.

Take, for example, the scene in which Caine produces crack cocaine from the powdered substance. The Hughes brothers combine expressive lighting, the montage style of editing, gangsta rap, and the voice-over technique to give this particular sequence a strategic function in the film. All of the symbolic materials in cinema — camera, speech, gestures, written language, music, color, lighting, costume, and sound — function narrationally.[34] Narration in this sequence positions Caine as both a victim *and* predator of the urban ghetto. The expressive application of lighting is notable. The apartment where Caine prepares the crack cocaine "rocks" is moderately lit. The constant darkness that fills the room illuminates, for the spectator, the fact that Caine is operating in the underground world. Further, the montage style of editing conveys the passage of time as Caine prepares his product. The preparation of crack is presented as a delicate process that requires the mastery of specific skills acquired primarily in the underground sector. The editing moves the spectator through the detailed precision necessary to produce the substance.

The choice of music, the gangsta rap song "Dopeman," provides an additional layer of meaning. The lyrics describe dope dealers as lecherous entrepreneurs who supply illegal substances to a community of desperate drug addicts. The composition of the sequence skillfully portrays the dilemma that confronts black youth like Caine: whereas participation in the underground economy is an attempt to gain advantage over a social and economic system that has little use for poor youth beyond menial labor, this lifestyle also establishes a counterideology that functions mainly to exacerbate the already wretched conditions of ghetto poverty. In his discussion of barrio youth and the crack cocaine economy, one ethnographer concludes that this emergent street culture is "a complex web of beliefs, symbols, modes of interaction, values, and ideologies that have emerged in opposition to exclusion from mainstream society. . . . [It] is not a coherent, conscious universe of political opposition but, rather, a spontaneous set of rebellious practices that in the long term have emerged as an oppositional style."[35] *Menace* explores how the oppositional culture of young street hustlers, ironically, reproduces rather than transform their peripheral status.

But rather than simply map Caine as a flat, one-dimensional predator, the strategic use of the voice-over marks him as a complicated figure instead. Caine's thoughts while preparing the crack cocaine are directly communicated to the spectator. The character explains his decision to operate in the underground economy as follows: "[W]orking for minimum wage was never my style. I like making big dollars. I learned how to mix drugs when I was little. . . . Heroine, cocaine. All of it." For Caine, the underground economy is a vehicle for gaining access to income and the highly coveted material goods that circulate in a vast consumer economy. The underground world is also a location where his skills as a hustler can be most effectively practiced. Caine cannot imagine a life outside the one in which he is immersed. Even a friend's proposal to relocate to Atlanta fails to excite Caine, as he emphatically tells the friend, "[Y]ou act like Atlanta ain't in America. *They* don't give a fuck!" "They," in this instance, refers to mainstream society and his suspicion that the only thing awaiting him in the legitimate economy is menial labor, poverty, and further degradation. Caine is convinced that his opportunities for upward mobility outside the informal economy are limited. Like many poor youth, Caine believes he has no real stake in the society and therefore nothing to lose by practicing a criminal lifestyle. This counterideology is a reaction against a society that provides few opportunities for black youth mobility and has instead become increasingly committed to hard disciplinary methods that continue to drive the imprisonment of black youth toward unprecedented rates.[36]

Finally, Caine's disdainful disposition toward society, and the ghettocentric ethos more generally, is emblematic of a broader conflict that gives the demeanor of black expressive culture a dynamic design: the problematic relationship between capitalism and the racial arrangements that structure the everyday experiences of poor black youth. Gilroy asserts that the multidimensional facets of black youth expressive culture are "manifested in the confluence of three critical, anti-capitalist themes that have a historic resonance in Diaspora culture and can be traced directly and indirectly back to the formative experience of slavery."[37] For Gilroy, these thematic elements form a whole but nonprogrammatic politics. He writes: "[T]he first theme deals with the experience of work, the labor process, and the division of labor under capitalism. It amounts to a critique of productivism—the ideology that sees the expansion of production forces as an indispensable precondition of the attainment of freedom. In opposition to this view of production, an argument is made that sees waged work as itself a form of servitude."[38] For Gilroy, black youth expressive cultures—especially dance and music—create spaces away from wage labor and celebrate the body as an instrument of pleasure rather than an instrument of work. Black historical memory works, in this instance, to equate wage labor with the "peculiar institution" of slavery. My focus on the gangsta theme in late twentieth-century black youth discourse develops a position that is greatly informed by Gilroy but proposes an alternative view instead.

One of the primary ideological themes in the ghettocentric imagination is indeed the critique of the racial division of labor. The scattering of industry away from inner-city communities has created chronic levels of underemployment/unemployment for poor ghetto youth. The few occupational opportunities that do exist tend to center around wage labor in the service sector. Typically, these jobs are menial, transitory, low in prestige and wages, and offer little if any opportunity for social and economic mobility. Labor in general, and menial labor especially, works to discipline how individuals are harnessed to institutions of social control. Not only does work reproduce the material conditions of society; work also performs important ideological functions in modern capitalist societies. For example, work is synonymous with status, prestige, manliness, and individualism. In many ways, then, the disdainful attitude toward work and the formal economy is a serious rejection of core societal norms and values.

As I argued in chapter 2, the cultural practices of black youth are not anticapitalist and, in fact, reproduce rather than subvert the idea of capital accumulation. In *Menace,* the Hughes brothers' strategic rewrite of the gangster film genre suggests, however, that, although black youth do not reject *all* forms of work, they are growing increasingly hostile toward menial labor that they define as imprisoning and humiliating. It is, then, precisely because access to the formal economy and meaningful employment is so limited that the underground sector, an annihilative alternative, strikes youth like Caine as a viable option.

Caine's refusal to participate in the legal economy and comply with the arrangements of social subordination is in fact complicated. More important, the Hughes brothers' representation of youth dislocation brings to the arena of popular film entertainment a provocative discourse that animates the changing world and worldviews of poor black youth. Ultimately, Caine's refusal to "slave" in the formal economy and his decision to "hustle" in the informal economy hint that black youth are not necessarily against capitalism; rather, they are against the subordinate positions and economic disadvantages to which capitalism restricts them. The creators of the film suggest that, to the extent that capitalism is unable to adequately incorporate poor youth, it will continue to produce young "Menaces II Society." Finally, and from this cine-matic point of view, the audience is invited to contemplate the ways in which society and hyperghettoization rather than nihilism are impli-cated in youth criminality.

Reimagining the Hood: Cinematic Space and the Politics of Symbolic Inversion

When we open our eyes today and look around America
we see America not though the eyes of someone who has
enjoyed the fruits of Americanism. We see America through
the eyes of someone who has been the victim *of American-*
ism. We don't see any American dream, we've experienced
only the American nightmare. We haven't benefited from
America's democracy, we've only suffered from America's
hypocrisy. And the generation that is coming up now can
see it and are not afraid to say it. If you go to jail so what?
If you were black you were born in jail.

MALCOLM X[39]

The above epigraph by Malcolm X is important for two reasons. First, his interpretation of American society as a site of imprisonment reso-nates with the collective experiences of poor African American youth in the 1990s. Thus, it explains, in part, their fascination with the slain leader as a symbolic source of racial pride. Second, it also sheds light on the changing nature of oppositional practices in African American cul-ture: the shift from clandestine to more assertive critiques of racism. His-torically, the means by which African Americans could engage in open forms of resistance, symbolic or material, has been constrained by the potential threat of white retaliation. While it is true that the opposi-tional posture of black youth expressive culture is cloaked in a perfor-mance aesthetic, it nevertheless demonstrates how black youth move against racial subordination in more confrontational forms.

One of the most persistent themes that gives shape to the ghetto-centric imagination is the representation of the urban ghetto as a site of repression and entrapment. This particular recoding of urban ghetto space is a critique of the hyperghettoization of poor black Americans.[40] The ghetto action film cycle suggests that the status differential between the black urban poor and more upwardly mobile social groups is also reflected in certain types of spatial arrangements that sustain prevailing class and racial hierarchies. This interpretation of space permeates the cinematic elaboration of the ghettocentric imagination and serves as one of the main circuits of ideological critique. In the ghetto action film, spatial relations are represented as power relations.

In the cinema, filmmakers can employ various elements to construct what David Bordwell classifies as *scenographic* space. This notion of space, the film scholar writes, "is the imaginary space of fiction, the 'world' in which the narrative suggests that fabula (i.e., story) events occur."[41] Moreover, this imaginary fictional space in the cinema can be constructed on the basis of both visual and auditory cues.

In *Boyz,* film director John Singleton explores how urban space shapes postindustrial ghetto life. In many ways, Singleton's authorial style demonstrates a commitment to the basic aesthetic and narrational principles that govern classical cinema. The classical style is mostly characterized by its paradigmatic organization and obedience to a historically constrained set of more or less likely options.[42] Singleton's affinity for classical cinema, however, does not necessarily preclude the possibility of devising a representational politic that bears the marks of ideological struggle. For example, the black working-class setting in *Boyz* symbolizes entrapment. Broadly speaking, the entrapment theme enunciated in the ghettocentric imagination reflects on the effects of social and spatial isolation of black urban communities. Social isolation excludes the urban poor from both the formal and informal networks that circulate information about employment and other opportunities for upward mobility.[43]

Singleton's development of the entrapment theme is subtle but informed. The theme is particularly relevant to the three central characters that motivate narrative action—Tre, Ricky, and Doughboy. The three young males experience social isolation differently. So while *Boyz* is organized on the basis of the classic "coming-of-age tale" popular in American storytelling, Singleton creates a fictional world that nuances how this popular narrative style is applied to young African American males. By juxtaposing sequences of the young men operating in different spheres of black life, the narrative shifts fluidly across the different territories that variously situate the everyday experiences of inner-city youth.

The sequence involving the football recruiter (Crump) is a good illustration of how the *classical-cutting* editing technique juxtaposes the distinct ways in which Ricky and Doughboy (two brothers) are entrapped by their isolated environment.[44] As the recruiter approaches the house, he is met by a group of young men on the front porch:

Dooky: What college you from?
Crump: I'm from USC.
Monster: Yo, man, you gotta have a scholarship to go to SC?
Crump: No, but it helps.
Monster: Yo, you think you could hook me up with a scholarship?
Crump: What do you do?
Monster: I use to play baseball . . .

The conversation is abruptly ended by Doughboy, who then ushers the recruiter inside the home. The recruiter is interested in meeting Ricky, a high school football standout.

As a talented athlete, Ricky represents the commodity/preferential status of black bodies in a consumer culture impassioned with black male athleticism. Moreover, Ricky's preoccupation with sports draws attention to a growing crisis in some spheres of black youth subculture—the overdevelopment of athletic skills to the exclusion of developing academic skills. Like many young African American males, Ricky believes that collegiate athletics is a direct pipeline to professional sports, a lucrative contract, and prestige. Sports is viewed as a way out of the ghetto, a vehicle for upward mobility.[45] The recruiter's comment that the prospects for a professional athletic career are minimal is directed toward Ricky and the spectator. Furthermore, after the recruiter informs him that he will have to take the college entrance exam, Ricky begins to have doubts about attending college. Lacking confidence in his scholastic abilities, he experiences an acute sense of entrapment and anxiety about his future.[46]

In the same sequence, Doughboy and his friends are positioned outside the house—a symbolic reference to their peripheral status as young men rendered idle and obsolete in a society that provides shrinking opportunity for poor youth. The seamless style of classical cutting in this sequence, as Giannetti notes, "breaks down the unity of space, analyzes its components, and refocuses our attention to a series of details."[47] The editing technique refocuses the spectator's attention to the different worlds inhabited by Ricky and Doughboy. Throughout the film, despite his role as a petty drug dealer, Doughboy is fashioned as a young man with a voracious appetite for reading. Moreover, he often thinks philosophically about issues ranging from creation versus evolution to incarceration. The recruiter's lack of interest in Doughboy signifies a disturbing trend in the relationship between black youth and collegiate institutions: universities are far more likely to locate athletic rather than academic talent in poor black communities.[48] Whereas Ricky is entrapped by delusions of sports fame as a means of escape, Doughboy, despite his academic potential, is entrapped by a life of diminishing opportunity.

The idea that the postindustrial ghetto suffocates the lives and opportunities of poor African American youths reverberates throughout Matty Rich's *Straight Out of Brooklyn.* This interpretation of space is evoked in almost every frame, shot, and sequence. Unlike John Singleton and Spike Lee, both graduates of prestigious film schools, Rich's screenwriting and directorial style are markedly rough and unpolished by feature film standards. But interestingly enough, the grim technical features of the film compliment the filmmaker's intentions to represent ghetto life as confining, dark, and painful. In a number of interviews, Rich discussed how the film served as a therapeutic exercise for him, an opportunity to deal creatively with the personal frustration of growing up in the impoverished Red Hook housing projects in Brooklyn, New York.

The visual cues selected to give the construction of space solidity create a narrative paradigm that powerfully expresses the idea that ghetto isolation severely restricts black mobility. For example, the opening *establishment shot* focuses the spectator's attention on the exterior of the Red Hooks housing project in Brooklyn. Establishment shots are visual cues used by filmmakers to assist the spectator in postulating where narrative action takes place. The exterior shot of the housing project not only represents a physical location but also codes it with specific meanings.

Symbolically, Rich codes urban ghetto life as a condition of social, economic, and physical imprisonment. For instance, the main characters in the film work in the most menial sectors of the service economy. Furthermore, the interior shots that situate life inside the housing project employ frames that are tight and enclosed. The proxemic patterns between characters also accentuate the idea that life in the projects is tenaciously confining. The narrative is a powerful coding of urban ghetto life and explores the combination of despair, humiliation, deprivation, and anger that poor African Americans must negotiate throughout their everyday lives.

Moreover, the ghettocentric imagination also produces representations of the urban ghetto as a theater for state coercion and militarization. The critique of postindustrial ghetto life, in this instance, is a direct reference to the surveillance operations that deploy coercive technologies against ghetto communities as a means of exercising greater control. This theme is, of course, dialogically related to "law-and-order" discourses and the intensification of force used to discipline black youth perceived to be wildly terrorizing the streets. The overemphasis on crime, drugs, and violence by politicians and the news media creates what Mike Davis describes as an "imaginary class relationship, a terrain of pseudo-knowledge and fantasy projection."[49] This imaginary relationship codes black youth as dangerous and also authorizes the deployment of military-style tactics and technology as necessary for the maintenance of social order. But the use of force also relies on an equally vigorous ideological project for legitimization. Sharp racial and gender coding devices shape the surveillance strategies of society's formal institution of social control, the police and other law-enforcement agencies. As Anderson writes:

> [O]n the streets color-coding often works to confuse
> race, age, class, gender, incivility, and criminality, and
> it expresses itself most concretely in the person of the
> anonymous black male. In doing their job, the police
> often become willing parties to this general color cod-
> ing of the public environment, and related distinc-
> tions, particularly those of skin color and gender,
> come to convey definite meanings. Although such
> coding may make the work of the police more man-
> ageable, it may also fit well with their own presupposi-
> tions regarding race and class relations, thus shaping
> officers' perceptions of crime "in the city." Moreover,
> the anonymous black male is usually an ambiguous
> figure who arouses the utmost caution and is generally
> considered dangerous until he proves he is not.[50]

The methods for controlling crime develop an informal *and* formal policy of disciplining black males.

Boyz poignantly critiques this method of social control. The interrogation of Ricky and Tre by two police officers is a good example. The spectator has been supplied with a number of cues sufficiently characterizing the two teens as ordinary youth with good intentions. But the two officers define the young men according to the prevailing master-status characterization of young black males, which interprets their

youth, race, and gender as signs of potential danger . As the two officers —
one white, the other black—approach the vehicle, their weapons are in
a ready position, prepared to respond to the slightest hint of resistance.
One of the officers asks Tre if he possesses any weapons or drugs. The
officer handles Tre roughly and intimidates him by pointing a gun to his
head. Further, the officer assumes the young men belong to one of the
local gang sets and refers to them as "no-good niggas." What is most interesting about this sequence is Singleton's reversal of a dominant code:
rather than portray the white officer as openly hostile and aggressive, it is
the black policeman—Officer Coffey—who personifies society's disdain
and repulsion toward black youth. The code reversal effectively demonstrates the pervasiveness of the master-status-determining characterization of young black males as dangerous criminals. The subtle reversal also
makes reference to what Davis describes as the "*black*lash" against youth
criminality.[51]

Singleton also critiques the militarization of black urban communities through the skillful deployment of offscreen sound. As Bordwell
notes, auditory cues, like visual cues, can invite the spectator to construct story-space in specific ways. Sonic space can also be instrumental
in solidifying the spatial context in which narration takes place. As is
the case with the arrangements of visual weights, the filmmaker's selection of details in arranging acoustic materials, while generally less obvious, is also an important element of filmmaking manipulation that
creates a (sound) perspective that gives the film additional layers of
meaning.[52]

In *Boyz,* a dominant motif structuring the representation of space is
the selection of offscreen sounds associated with the coercive technologies of the state—police sirens, helicopters, and other surveillance mechanisms. This particular use of offscreen sound complements Singleton's
interpretation of the postindustrial ghetto by allowing him to manipulate sound perspective spatially. The constant intrusion of forceful and
threatening sounds from police surveillance suggests that black communities are targets of military-style combat. Throughout the film, this
use of offscreen space is accompanied by shots of blacks engaged in nonthreatening acts, suggesting that the entire community is wrongfully
criminalized.

Finally, this interpretation of space brings to the sphere of black
cinematic discourse a second theme identified by Gilroy as central to
the oppositional ethos of black expressive culture.[53] The second theme,
he writes, is "a critique of the capitalist state revolving around a plea for

the disassociation of law from domination, which denounces state brutality, militarism, and exterminism."[54] This particular theme depicts the coercive technologies of the state as an illegitimate means of social control that violates black bodies and communal life. In *Menace,* for example, the police are figured as hostile agents who routinely step outside the legal boundaries of law enforcement to discipline black youth. This form of image reversal performs an important imaginative function: the state rather than black youth is criminalized. This particular coding of the postindustrial ghetto differs vastly from the dominant representational politics that figure this same spatial system as a site of lawlessness and moral decay.

The Limits of the Ghettocentric Imagination: Black Familial Life and the Crisis of Black Masculinity

Current discussions about the plight of the black urban poor are overwhelmingly focused on the instability and changing structure of black familial life. The nature of black family life has long been a topic of discussion in academic discourse.[55] However, since the middle 1960s, the shifting patterns of black familial life have become a central focus of journalists and politicians, too. Generally speaking, popular and political discourse charges that the organization of black families is incompatible with the nuclear family model.[56] More recently, the deleterious effects of urban dislocation—drug addiction, violent crimes, teenage pregnancy, and welfare dependency—have reinvigorated speculation about the vitality of black families and also their role in the social reproduction of the urban poor.

The often-cited Moynihan Report is crucial to any contemporary discussion of black family life because the "findings" offered from the report anticipated the racial, gender, and class themes that would eventually exercise tremendous influence over how black culture and familial life are typically understood. The report concluded that the structure of family life in the black community constituted a "tangle of pathology . . . capable of perpetuating itself without assistance from the white world," and that "at the heart of the deterioration of the fabric of Negro society is the deterioration of the Negro family. It is the fundamental source of the weakness of the Negro community at the present time."[57] Further, the report argued that the matriarchal structure of black culture weakened the ability of black men to function as authority figures. This particular notion of black familial life has become a widespread, if not dominant, paradigm for comprehending the social and economic disintegration of late twentieth-century black urban life.

The ideas generated by the report have been broadly appropriated. The conservative elaboration of the report, for instance, refashions the "culture-of-poverty" thesis as the primary means for understanding the current plight of the urban poor. Social conservatives argue that the erosion of traditional values, combined with the aberrant behavioral norms intrinsic to ghetto culture, reproduce the social ills afflicting the urban poor. The deterioration of black family life, according to this view, establishes a lifestyle in black communities that perpetuates a culture of dependency, deviance, and danger.

This particular interpretation of black familial life is not, however, unique to social conservatives; it also informs the broader sphere of commonsense ideology. To be sure, the belief that ghetto pathology is the direct cause of social and economic dislocation pervades public policy, electoral politics, popular media discourses, and lay public opinion. Popular media representations, for instance, play a discernible role in solidifying the belief that black culture is predominantly matriarchal and consequently inferior according to the presumptions of patriarchy. Most television programs featuring African Americans typically employ the matriarchal model as the basic formula for narration. This formula is especially true of the genre most likely to feature African Americans, the family situation comedy. A historical survey of blacks in television sitcoms suggests that the representation of African American family life fits a common pattern: a family unit led by a single female head of household; the father is customarily absent.[58] And while it is true that black female-headed households have rapidly increased since the 1960s, the trend is not uniquely African American.[59]

The notion that black familial life is largely responsible for ghetto poverty pervades the cultural landscape. This particular representation of black life achieves its hegemonic position precisely because it is able to appeal to the larger society as common sense and therefore indisputable. Moreover, African American filmmakers are not insulated from the gender and racial assumptions that organize the dominant representations of the black urban poor. Although black filmmakers posture themselves as oppositional, their representational politics and, more specifically, the ways in which they imagine black life on film can be characterized as reactionary and susceptible to penetration by the ideas of social conservatism. The gender politics that shape the imaginations of black familial life in the black action ghetto film cycle vividly illustrate this point.

Take, for example, Matty Rich's representation of gender and black family life in *Straight Out of Brooklyn*. Rich's construction of the father fails to challenge prevailing gender ideologies. In the film, the father's inability to locate meaningful employment severely restricts his ability to make significant contributions to the family household economy. Much of the internal grief and external fury experienced by the father is aggravated by his personal struggle to grapple with his status as a failed patriarch. The father's frustrations are paramount to the narrative because Rich—the writer and director—complies with the hegemonic definitions of the nuclear family model by subscribing to the patriarchal tenet that the *natural* role of the father is that of the breadwinner. Rich's construction of the father animates what Arthur Brittan terms the "crisis in masculinity." Brittan writes:

> From the perspective of men-in-general, the concept "crisis" involves the realization that their power and authority can no longer be taken for granted. If their power is challenged, then a dominant group is in a crisis situation. It begins to look around for explanations and rationalizations which allow it to understand and cope with the new situation. . . . The "crisis of masculinity," then, is about the generalized feeling among men-in-general that they are no longer capable of fully controlling the world. They have lost their collective nerve, their self-assurance, their sense of certainty.[60]

While the statement above is instructive, it is also too reductive. The statement offers two broad generalizations that misrepresent the complicated and shifting contours of male gender identity: first, it presupposes that *all* men are in a state of crisis; second, it presupposes that all men experience the crisis in a similar manner. The formation of masculinity cuts across several interlocking territories—race, class, age, and of course, sexuality. Because varying forms of masculinity exist, different crises are also manifest. For example, the crisis may differ substantially for black and white, poor and rich, young and old men, or gay and straight men.

In *Straight Out of Brooklyn,* the father's inability to command high-wage labor renders him powerless and undermines his household authority. It is under these conditions that some men find it difficult to cope with their powerlessness and begin seeking compensatory means for reasserting an already fractured masculinity. Violence is often employed as an immediate solution to their personal difficulties. In Rich's narrative, this faulty attempt to recuperate a fragile gender identity is made by the father. The fact that Rich presents domestic abuse is not inherently problematic. The fact that the narrative fails to adequately interrogate domestic abuse is, however, severely problematic. *Straight Out of Brooklyn* subscribes to the prevailing logic that black male abuse of black women is the result of racial rather than gender hierarchies. Thus, what is specifically a site of gender conflict is coded as a by-product of racial conflict. According to the narrative, domestic abuse is primarily the result of the father's frustrations with white racism and not his privileged status as a male in a patriarchal culture. The film fails to consider that, while the father is subordinated in the public sphere, his male status grants him a position of dominance and authority in the private sphere of the family household.

Moreover, Rich's construction of the mother/female counterpart perpetuates the "superstrong black mother" controlling image discussed by Patricia Hill Collins.[61] According to Collins, in their attempt to counter white representations of black womanhood, black cultural producers present the superstrong mother figure capable of enduring a formidable interlocking system of race, gender, and class subordination. In Rich's narrative, the mother courageously endures deferential roles at both work and home. As a temporary worker, the only employment available to her is domestic service. Throughout the film, she accepts the embarrassment of routinely visiting the New York Department of Labor in order to locate new domestic service assignments. Her search for employment symbolizes her strength and determination to help provide the family with economic resources. In the private sphere, the mother tolerates her abusive husband. In fact, the mother explains the father's violent and abusive demeanor as a valid compensatory means for expressing his frustrations with a white world that denies him the accoutrements of patriarchy. Her focus on the father's difficulties in the labor market suggests that the father's battle with racism is more urgent than her own personal battle with an abusive husband and occupational immobility.

Additionally, one of the strongest critiques of *Boyz* focuses on the gender politics that inform this popular film narrative about postindustrial black life.[62] While Singleton is clearly attempting to create a narrative that counters dominant media representations of young African American males, many of his core thematic ideas comply with the patriarchal assumptions of social conservatism. The film's characterization of black familial life is particularly vulnerable to this charge. As in most forms of classical narration, Singleton juxtaposes characters that are ideologically antithetical. In *Boyz,* the portrayal of black familial life is personified by two parental figures: Furious Styles and Ms. Barnes. Whereas Furious embodies responsible parenting, conversely, Ms. Barnes embodies the pitfalls of irresponsible parenting. The narrative presents Furious as an affectionate parent who owns his own business. Ms. Barnes is presented as disinterested in her children and lazy, and there are no cues that she is employed. Whereas Furious imparts moral education by teaching his son right from wrong, Ms. Barnes is seldom portrayed in an educative or authoritative role. Finally, narrative closure in *Boyz* reaffirms the idea that single-parent *fathering* leads to successful child development (Tre graduates from high school and attends college), while single-parent mothering, on the contrary, leads to unsuccessful child development (Ricky and Doughboy are both the victims of homicidal conflict). Collins describes Singleton's representation of this externally defined controlling image of black motherhood with remarkable precision:

> Like the matriarch, the welfare mother is labeled a bad mother. But unlike the matriarch, she is not too aggressive — on the contrary, she is not aggressive enough. While the matriarch's unavailability contributes to her children's poor socialization, the welfare mother's accessibility is deemed the problem. She is portrayed as being content to sit around and collect welfare, shunning work and passing on her bad values to her offspring. . . . African Americans can be racially stereotyped as being lazy by blaming welfare mothers for failing to pass on the work ethic. Moreover, the welfare mother has no male authority figure to assist her. Typically portrayed as an unwed mother, she violates one cardinal tenet of Eurocentric masculinist thought: she is a woman alone.[63]

Singleton's characterization of black parenting fails to mobilize a discourse that effectively counters the common assertion that the presence of male authoritative figures in black households is the solution to ameliorating youth unemployment, crime, and alienation. Further, the narrative politics of *Boyz* imply that mothers on welfare are to blame for the delinquent behavior of inner-city boys.[64]

Singleton's symbolic configuration of Furious is important for two reasons. First, this portrait of black fatherhood in a working-class community adds a dimension to the representation of black familial life that is ordinarily omitted from popular and public discourses.[65] For Singleton, Furious serves as an *educative* role model for the film's primary target audience—teenage and young adult black males. Furious, then, can be "read" as an alternative representation of black masculinity, one that differs greatly from the versions characteristically portrayed in popular culture. For example, Furious talks affectionately with his son about sex, the rigors of life, and the need to support black-owned enterprises. Furious also performs child-rearing and other domestic duties traditionally associated with females and mothering. The portrayal of a black father actively involved in child rearing counters the dominant notion that black men are customarily absent and negligent.

But an alternative reading of Furious is far less favorable. One of the pivotal scenes in the film takes place when the mother (Reeva) relinquishes her son, Tre, to Furious and states, "[H]e is yours now. I've done all I can do, but I cannot teach him how to be a man." The basic assertion in this sequence—and the film in general—is that women are unable to teach young boys how to be responsible, productive male adults. Singleton's effort to celebrate the idea of black fatherhood is symptomatic of a larger problematic in gender ideology: the assumption that the formation of an affirmative and productive identity for male children is naturally transmitted from the father. The idea that it takes an adult male to teach a young boy how to be a "man" is not unique to *Boyz;* this "father knows best" logic pervades American culture.

Despite the fact that *Boyz* featured a gangsta rap celebrity (Ice Cube), a rap music sound track, and was immensely popular with youth, the film was praised by conservative politicians and journalists. The immediate question, of course, is, Why would conservatives endorse a hip hop–inflected film like *Boyz*? The answer points directly to the gender presuppositions that penetrate the film's ideological core. California Governor Pete Wilson's approval of *Boyz* suggests that the film's representation of black familial life resonates affirmatively with the patriarchal claims of social issues conservatism. Discussing the urban uprisings in Los Angeles after the acquittal of four police officers charged with the beating of motorist Rodney King, Wilson offered the following statement on the May 3, 1992, broadcast of *This Week with David Brinkley:*

> I think everybody in America should see the film *Boyz N the Hood.* In that movie, a *strong* [emphasis added, throughout this quote] father makes the difference for his teenage son, a nineteen-year-old boy about to rush back out and try to avenge his best friend who has just been gunned down in a mindless, senseless gang war. And this *strong* father literally and figuratively puts his arms around his son and says, "I won't let you go out into the street. I'm not going to let them kill my son." Now what that movie says is that we need a *strong* father and that welfare is no suitable replacement for that.

Wilson's statement is freighted with assumptions about race, gender, and class. His repeated reference to a "strong" father figure suggests that single mothers, and especially those receiving welfare, are weak and inadequate authority figures. For Wilson, *Boyz* is an exemplary corrective solution to black youth social and economic dislocations because the film reiterates the conservative mantra that black familial pathology is the main culprit of youth crime and violence. Black families in general and black boys specifically *need* fathers in the household. The claim "boys need their fathers," as Brittan argues, is born out of popular ideology, not fact. Both Wilson and Singleton make the assumption that if male children do not identify with male authority figures, they will experience severe social problems. The film, much like popular debates about urban poverty, fails to address the more crucial dilemma facing many black youth: the increasing likelihood of living in poverty (children under the age of eighteen account for 40 percent of the poor).[66] Poor children do not need male adult figures as much as they need adults, male or female, who can provide them access to health care, quality housing, and education.

The specter of black familial pathology also drives the narrative work in *Menace.* The Hughes brothers effectively demonstrate the effects of urban dislocation on black familial life but fail to adequately address some of the structural causes. One of the initial household sequences in the film offers narrational cues that supply the spectator with background information regarding Caine's childhood. The household sequence is shot in warm, expressionistic colors and lighting. The perpetual darkness and red hues in the household portray Caine's familial life as the equivalent to "hell on earth." Caine's father, for example, sells drugs, gambles, and commits violent murders in his presence. In addition, his mother is characterized as a heroin addict who eventually dies of an overdose. As a young teen, Caine vividly recalls that his father "taught" him how to operate in the underground economy. Both parents are vilified as malevolent role models. The Hughes brothers present black familial life as an incubator of deviant values and behavioral norms that gives birth to criminality and public villainy.

Menace bears out the claim that black familial disorganization is the most crucial factor in the reproduction of ghetto poverty and youth delinquency. Conservative journalist George Will's endorsement of the film hinges specifically on its representation of black familial life. In a nationally syndicated column, Will contends that *Menace* is "therapeutic" and "so relentlessly realistic" that it "strengthens the spectator's resolve to enforce domestic tranquillity." [67] Further, Will writes, "Caine is shown as the essentially unparented child of an addictive mother (soon dead of an overdose) and a murderous father who guns down a man during a living room card game. The movie's unrelievedly bleak message is that the intergenerational transmission of violence will continue." For Will, *Menace* is cinematic evidence that the most compelling problem afflicting the urban poor is parental irresponsibility. Although it may be unwittingly, the Hughes brothers' coding of black familial life, nearly three decades later, refashions Moynihan's contention that the black family is a "tangle of pathology" that is "the fundamental source of the weakness of the [African American] community at the present time." More important, the fact that the film was made by two young African American filmmakers certainly serves to embolden this particular claim on blackness.

Rather than develop a representational politic that reverses the pathology paradigm, the creators of the ghetto action cycle tend to construct filmic worlds that reinforce this popular interpretation of black familial life. The gender politics of the ghetto action film cycle also reveal how deep the stream of conservative commonsense racial ideology flows. Moreover, the failure to challenge the rising tide of conservative hegemony is not insignificant, insofar as filmmakers like John Singleton, Albert and Allen Hughes, and Matty Rich, just to name a few, are often celebrated for their "authentic" representations of postindustrial ghetto life.

Ghetto Reelness: Black Filmmaking and the Authenticity Impasse

Filmmakers are members of society, and, as such, are no less subject to social pressures and norms than anyone else. Furthermore all filmmaking occurs within some social context. . . . [F]ilms are rarely the product of a single person. . . .

ROBERT C. ALLEN AND DOUGLAS GOMERY[68]

In spite of its overwhelming and obvious entertainment function in a vast popular culture marketplace, the ghetto action film is typically viewed by critics, the news media, and filmgoers as an authentic portrayal of ghetto life. Indeed, one of the most fascinating developments of the film cycle's reception is the notion that this group of popular movies represents official transcriptions of the lived experiences of poor black youth. African Americans working within the ghetto action genre cycle, for instance, are typically viewed as documentarists capturing the grim realities of postindustrial ghetto life rather than professional filmmakers who skillfully deploy the conventions of popular film production to gratify moviegoing audiences easily titillated by violent and sexual imagery.

The label *black filmmakers* is a widely accepted feature of our popular cultural vocabulary. Indeed, no other group of feature filmmakers is racially identified to the extent that African Americans are. It is, after all, far less common to identify Steven Spielberg, Oliver Stone, or Penny Marshall as "white" filmmakers. Moreover, the label suggests that a specific body of films points to a specific group of filmmakers and formation of discourse.[69] The label, in addition, differentiates black cinema from other popular films and sources of entertainment. The label also distinguishes African American filmmakers as a distinct class of authors. This system of classification has enabled a select group of African Americans to carve out a small niche in the production hierarchy of commercial film. This same system of classification, however, also tends to restrict the ability of African Americans who desire to experiment with film genres and narrative conventions that may fall outside the narrow parameters of what the popular film industry typically regards as viable black cinema.

Because the ghetto action film is generally associated with African American filmmakers, the genre cycle is widely perceived as an authentic representation of urban ghetto life. Michel Foucault reminds us that authorship is a dynamic creative process rather than a purely individual exercise. His question "What is an author?" is important because it suggests the need to rethink the context and creative processes of authorship.[70] According to Foucault, "the author" is a Western cultural invention wedded to the notion of individualism; thus, it conceals the extent to which the imaginative reconstructions of the social world are drawn from a dynamic social landscape that exists external to the author.[71] The cinematic worlds created by filmmakers take shape within the context of a shared symbolic and material landscape. This view suggests that filmmakers do not operate within an isolated social milieu.

The common belief that black filmmakers produce veritable representations of the African American experience tends to attribute their creative skills to a specific criterion: race. Their "blackness," in short, is viewed as the primary source of their artistry. As a result, African American filmmakers are not viewed as independent and creative professionals who devote substantive time and energy to cultivating the skills necessary for participation in the film industry. Instead, African American filmmakers are looked upon as a monolith who benefit from a racial experience that *naturally* enables them to produce film narratives about black life. This limited appreciation of black filmmaking talent helps to explain why African Americans are often confined to low budgets and film genres that fail to illuminate the diversity of African American life.[72]

This reception of African American–directed feature films is partially attributable to film studio marketing strategies and news media narratives that stressed the allegedly true-to-life qualities of the ghetto film cycle. This wave of films was often promoted by studios and defined by the news media as realistic rather than interpretive portrayals of urban ghetto life. In this instance, cinematic style, aesthetics, and the racial composition of the filmmakers were each central to defining this particular formation of discourse as authentic. Take, for example, New Line Cinema's promotional campaign for *Menace*. After a successful initial box-office performance, the film studio developed a second promotional campaign that included the following print copy: "This is the Truth. This is what's Real." Indeed, part of the film's enthusiastic reception among film audiences and critics was attributable to the belief that the Hughes brothers had produced a film that illustrated the purport-edly nihilistic lifestyles of black youth with candid precision.

Film critics and news journalists often characterized movies from the ghetto action film cycle as original and factual, but harrowing, portraits of black poverty. To be sure, thanks to the film wave's repetitious por-traiture, youth gangs, violent crimes, and drug-related incidents were widely embraced as incontestable indicators of African American life. During the early 1990s, black filmmakers emerged as newsworthy sub-ject matter. Both the print and television news devoted large amounts of space and time to the commercial film industry's revitalized interest in the film projects developed by African Americans. One of the persis-tent themes that emerged from the wave of news media coverage was how black films provided a unique look into black American life. For example, a *CBS Evening News* reporter described a Los Angeles youth group's field trip to see the film *Boyz N the Hood* as "anything but an ordinary escape to a summer movie. It was more like a field trip in their own backyard."[73] Similarly, an ABC news story discussing the surprise success of Matty Rich's *Straight Out of Brooklyn* concluded by saying that, while the filmmaker's next project was uncertain, the film would defi-nitely "draw on his own life and the streets he knew so well."[74]

The widespread assertion that African Americans are *naturally* able to produce "realistic" representations of ghetto life is informed by the pe-culiarities of an inherently flawed racial logic. Cultural critic bell hooks maintains that this viewpoint tends to ignore the class positionality of Af-rican American filmmakers. She argues that the most prominent African American cultural producers enjoy a class status that provides them ac-cess to powerful and popular resources like the communications media. Moreover, she urges critical analysis "of a cultural marketplace wherein blackness is commodified in such a way that fictive accounts of under-class black life in whatever setting may be more lauded, more market-able, than other visions because mainstream conservative audiences de-sire these images."[75] hooks's comments are noteworthy because they suggest that certain types of representations of blackness are more likely to be merchandised, not because they are necessarily real but rather be-cause they fit neatly with the prevailing commonsense characteriza-tions of black life.

Should black filmmakers be expected to produce "realistic" depic-tions of African American life? Moreover, is such a cultural politic itself realistic or even plausible? Representation of the social world includes making choices not only about what to represent but also about how to represent it. Unfortunately, the emergent debate regarding the ghetto action cycle has gravitated toward questions of "realness" and authenticity. However, the crucial issue is not how real cinematic representations are but how filmmakers (and other cultural producers) negotiate a complex field of commonsense ideas that seek to render late twentieth-century ghetto life more comprehensible. For example, does the creative labor of African American filmmakers produce alternative narratives for making sense of urban ghetto life? Do their representational politics counter or reproduce the dominant ideological strategies that inform how the experiences of ghetto dislocation are understood? By privileging these types of questions, the focus shifts from a concern with cinematic accuracy and locates this formation of popular film discourse in relation to a broader orbit of discourses struggling to dominate how youth dislocation, for example, is made sense of.

Similarly to all creative agents, black filmmakers work in historically determined situations. The way in which they experience, understand, and represent the world, then, is always socially constituted. In fact, the representational politics practiced by black filmmakers develops a dialogic relationship with other socially circulated discourses. In addition, black film directors, wittingly or unwittingly, participate in a constantly evolving dialogue about race in a social and economic world that is becoming increasingly fragmented along racial lines. The creative production of black cinematic discourse can function to refute, supplement, or affirm competing discourses about the lived experiences of African Americans.

I do not want to suggest that black film directors are obligated to disorganize dominant racial ideologies. I raise the issue because many black filmmakers adopt the position that their representational politics are, at least, sensitive to the need to challenge the dominant representations that distort the African American experience. Indeed, the reason the news media and the general moviegoing audience believe that black film is authentic discourse is partially attributable to the kinds of claims on blackness made by African American filmmakers.

In truth, many black filmmakers promote their films by remarking that when they are behind the cameras, viewers receive a more authentic portrayal of black life. This view subscribes to the notion that African American–based representations of black life are "realistic" rather than ideological. This assertion, however, is misleading to the extent that it obscures the constructedness of black film production. It would be wrong to suggest that African American filmmakers do not possess certain sensibilities and nuances that enliven their cinematic depictions of black life. But it is equally problematic to assume that their representational politics are only informed by the experience of race. Black filmmaking strategies are also informed by how filmmakers experience their gender, class, and sexuality. Moreover, black filmmaking strategies are shaped by commercial decisions that seek to appeal to the changing appetites of the cultural marketplace.

The practice of resisting the dominant, or commonsense, ideologies of a given period is difficult work because it requires a fundamental reworking of the belief systems that facilitate how members of society think about and experience their social world. The ghettocentric imagination has created the energy and opportunity for black youth to gain greater access to popular communications media resources like film, television, and music, but does it promote an alternative worldview? In other words, does this complex body of ideas and representations create counterdiscourses that effectively contest dominant viewpoints of the postindustrial ghetto? In short, is this particular structure of feeling, this historically distinct cultural practice, sufficiently oppositional?

My examination of the ghetto film cycle suggests that it recombines oppositional and hegemonic ideas about black American life. The ghettocentric project both critiques and reproduces dominant racial discourses. That is to say, while some of the thematic ideas that structure the genre cycle reimagine ghetto life in ways that contest dominant discourses, other themes central to the film cycle fail to imagine ghetto life in ways that counter the commonsense terrain of racial and gender ideology. For example, the recoding of the postindustrial ghetto as a site of entrapment and state repression reverses the dominant claims on blackness that criminalize ghetto communities. This particular idea suggests that the coercive strategies and technologies deployed to discipline black youth are illegitimate, violative, and excessively punitive. On the other hand, the gender politics of the ghetto film cycle tend to reinscribe dominant ideas about the failure of black parents and their role in the intergenerational transmission of poverty and urban dislocation. This thematic motif buoys the notion that the black urban poor suffer mainly from behavioral pathologies that ultimately cause and reproduce social and economic dislocation.

In my view, what makes black cinema an important site of cultural production is its capacity to animate a broad range of discourses that circulate throughout the African American community. One of the main reasons black filmmakers receive so much attention from the popular and academic press is because popular film is a prestigious sphere of production. Black filmmakers are not insulated from the dominant discourses that seek to portray ghetto life in ways that lean toward moral condemnation. Throughout this book, I have suggested that the representational politics of black filmmaking take their shape in relation to a complex sphere of discourses about black American life. Indeed, the body of films discussed here suggests that the larger terrain of black industrial image making is connected to historically specific "culture wars" struggling to dominate commonsense definitions of black life. Moreover, the ensuing "culture wars" are not insignificant insofar as they constitute an important theater for shaping commonsense ideologies about American life near the close of the twentieth century. Black popular film discourse participates on an enlarged terrain upon which various forms of social, political, and ideological struggle take shape.

Finally, participation on the popular cultural field cannot, alone, produce substantive change in the material lives of black Americans. But the fields of rap music and film production do suggest that African Americans develop ideas about and representations of black life that occasionally break from dominant representations. Moreover, this suggests that the energy for mobilizing other forms of social and political intervention does exist. Black popular culture discourse suggests that subordinated populations are able to develop alternative ways of imagining their own experiences, ways that call official discourses into question—news media, political speeches, and legislation. The ascendancy of black popular cultural forms also suggests that African American cultural producers have been able to amass large measures of symbolic capital. The obvious question that comes into view, though, is, Can African Americans translate increased symbolic capital, largely on the terrain of popular media culture, into political and economic capital that can begin to reverse some of the disturbing trends that define black American life specifically and U.S. race relations more generally?

Epilogue

The Culture Industry and the Hip Hop Generation

The landscape of popular media culture continues to be made over by the fierce currents of social and technological change. During the early 1990s, a successful stream of black American–directed films produced a glimmer of hope that a black filmmaking practice might actually find a secure niche in the production hierarchy of commercial cinema. Thus, in 1991, the release of over twenty black films generated extensive press and academic attention. And while those films were only a small fraction of the total films released from Hollywood that year, their number was greater than the number of black-directed feature films released during the entire previous decade. It was also in 1991 that several observers began flirting with the prospect that the ascendancy of a small cadre of black filmmakers represented the first real chance to break through the barriers that had long prohibited substantive participation by blacks in the production of cinema. In a *New York Times Magazine* cover story, writer Karen Grigsby Bates presented a number of questions concerning the popular ascent of black film directors and Hollywood's sudden interest in their feature film projects. One of the more intriguing questions Bates posed was, "[G]iven Hollywood's fickle nature and short attention span, will the filmmakers have the opportunity to become part of the Hollywood power structure?"[1] In other words, Bates was openly contemplating whether the increase in black commercial features represented the collapse of industry barriers or whether black filmmakers were simply the flavor of the moment.

If black cinema was on the move during the beginning of the 1990s, then its status by the close of the decade could only be described as nearing a crossroads as questions regarding the vitality of black cinema have emerged once again. Ironically, the successful run of the ghetto action film cycle simultaneously invigorated and limited the prospects for black film production in the 1990s. The commercial success of films like *Boyz N the Hood* spawned an imitative cycle that flooded the silver screen with images of postindustrial ghetto life. Much like its gangsta rap counterpart, the ghetto action film cycle imposed serious limitations on the

black film narratives that industry executives viewed as viable and therefore suitable for investment. There was virtually no space for popular
film narratives that did not comply with the hardened formulas of the
ghetto action film cycle. And while ghetto-themed films created space
for commentary on the lived experiences of poor black youth (mostly
males), the repetitious production of the cycle pushed other narratives
about black life off of the commercial culture map, thus making the het-
erogeneity and complexity of black life less visible.

For example, the writer and director of *Love Jones* (New Line Cinema,
1997), Theodore Witcher, developed the idea for the film in 1991, the
year that movies like *New Jack City, Boyz N the Hood,* and *Straight Out
of Brooklyn* began to dominate the image of black cinema. *Love Jones*
represents a sharp break from the thematic and aesthetic contours of
gangsta-style film narratives. However, Witcher experienced difficulty
convincing the industry to consider this particular cinematic portrayal
of black life, primarily because the setting, characters, and story differed
so greatly from what the studio regarded as a viable "black" film.

Approaching the twenty-first century, black popular culture is undergoing yet another series of transitions. As the backlash against the
proliferation of ghetto action flicks intensified, speculation regarding
the future of black cinema has ensued. For example, the successful adaptation of Terry McMillan's popular novel *Waiting to Exhale* drove some
industry observers to conclude that films about the black middle class
will populate the silver screen and thus begin compensating for the
overproduction of ghetto action film narratives. But popular culture
never works this predictably. In addition to centering on black middle-
class life, *Exhale* privileged the representation of black women. Because
the most visible forms of black popular culture have focused primarily
on the precarious relationship between young black males and the postindustrial ghettoscape, the everyday lives of young black women have
been greatly obscured. Despite a strong performance at the box office,
Exhale has not yet spawned a new production logic or cycle.

I have maintained throughout the pages above that commercial
film production in the United States is governed by the theory of precedence. Consequently, the likelihood of any new conceptualization of
black cinema's evolving into a new production cycle is contingent upon
whether or not box-office viability can be established. Because Hollywood constantly seeks out new ways to reinvent itself, new trends and
cycles continue to emerge. Throughout the 1990s, the major film distributors have gravitated even more decisively toward megablockbuster

action films. In the meantime, smaller independent film distributors have been forced to rely on smaller-budgeted features. It appears as though specialty product like black cinema is even more marginal in the production priorities of the current filmmaking landscape. Given the current conditions, black filmmakers have been forced to begin rethinking their relationship to the commercial film industry.

Perhaps no filmmaker reflects this reality more than Spike Lee, who has seen his star gradually fade in recent years. While no one person is singularly responsible for the new trends that take shape in popular culture, Lee was nevertheless central to the commercial revitalization of black cinema in the late 1980s and early 1990s. Once regarded as unflappable and masterful at circumventing the racial barriers that partially structure the New Hollywood, Lee has been forced to rethink his presence on the commercial film landscape.

Since the production of his highly anticipated but modestly successful biographical picture *Malcolm X,* Lee's films have not performed well at the box office. His declining box-office appeal reflects a combination of three factors: first, his miscalculation of the market appeal of black cinema; second, the commercial supremacy of ghettocentricity; and third, the volatile nature of popular culture more generally and its relentless appetite for change. Whereas Lee was certainly mindful of the popular hegemony of ghettocentric themes, his personal vision of black cinema often deviated from the conventions of the youth expressive culture as well as the kinds of films that came to define black cinema in the early to middle 1990s.

Despite his past success and inclination for self-promotion, Lee has experienced serious difficulty getting his recent film projects financed by studios. For example, *Get on the Bus* (1996), a film focusing on the journey of a group of African American men traveling by bus to the Million Man March, was privately financed. Moreover, the scanty budget and short shooting schedule for the film resembled Lee's maverick effort to produce *She's Gotta Have It.* Also, in anticipation of the fiftieth anniversary of the historic breaking of the color barrier in the modern era of professional baseball, Lee publicly discussed his desire to make a biographical picture based on the life of Jackie Robinson. But again, no studio demonstrated interest in the project. The difficulty Lee began facing around 1995 in getting his films financed highlights just how dramatically the relationship between African American filmmakers and the commercial film industry had changed since 1991. Despite a successful track record, he finds himself once again on the extreme margins of the film industry. His rise and gradual decline highlight the peculiarities of race and its imprint on popular American culture. It is very unlikely that a white filmmaker with talents similar to Lee's would be facing such industry barriers.

Admittedly, part of the problem facing black filmmakers is the market uncertainty that makes all film production a risky enterprise. Historically, black cinema has thrived on its ability to attract black urban moviegoers. Exactly what proportion of the film-going audience blacks represent is debatable. An abundance of anecdotal claims assert that blacks represent a disproportionately high share of the moviegoing population. If this is true, then it is perhaps one of the great ironies that blacks are not going to see black-themed films. A cursory glance at box-office report data suggests that black films tend to lag significantly behind similarly budgeted mainstream product. Because blacks have less disposable income than their white counterparts, it is not that surprising that black films perform poorly.

Moreover, as ghetto film scripts have lost their commercial vitality, industry executives are now left holding defunct formulas that once enabled them to translate the popular idioms of gangsta rap into film product. So to the extent that hip hop is undergoing its own transformations, this will certainly reconfigure the contours of black popular film, too. Hip hop has made important interventions on the terrain of popular culture. Yet it is difficult to deny that the supremacy of the youth-informed culture has imposed serious limitations on the aesthetic and commercial possibilities of black cultural production insofar as the sensibilities and mood shifts of hip hoppers have asserted considerable influence over which cultural products are perceived as authentically black and commercially viable.

Furthermore, black popular culture has also undergone serious transformation on the terrain of network television. More recently, signs of resegregation in both household viwership patterns and network programming give strong indication that the relationship between African Americans and the television industry has entered another phase. For instance, a recent report concluded that black and white households watch very different television programs. The report found that of the top twenty-five shows watched in black and white households, only three appeared on the same list: *ER* (NBC), *Monday Night Football* (ABC), and *60 Minutes* (CBS).[2] Moreover, the fall 1996 lineup for network television revealed that black-themed shows were conspicuously absent. The three longest-running networks—ABC, CBS, and NBC—included only two series with predominantly African American casts in their respective lineups. The FOX network, once the hub of 1990s network programming for (young) black audiences, included only four such programs in its lineup.

While the lack of programming on the three longest-running networks is certainly troubling, the lack of programming on FOX was particularly noticeable because the network relied heavily on "black-appeal" programming—*In Living Color, ROC, South Central, Martin, Living Single, New York Undercover*--to build its network identity and establish its commercial viability. FOX is the network most watched by African Americans. Yet in the process of establishing itself as a major player in the production of network television programming, FOX has gradually moved away from the expressive cultures of African Americans in order to achieve a more mainstream status.

Whereas the four major networks have abandoned the themes and styles of black popular culture, the two upstart mininetworks—Warner Brothers (WB) and United Paramount Network (UPN)—have made them central to their efforts to join the elite ranks of network television. Black-appeal programs have become a staple product in the lineups of both WB and UPN. The two mininetworks featured a combined twelve "minority-themed" programs in their fall 1996 lineups. Like FOX, it appears as though both will rely on popular trends from black expressive culture as a strategy for establishing an audience base, commercial viability, and a competitive position from which to launch future programs. But while WB and UPN can be applauded for their inclusion of blacks, serious questions have been raised regarding the quality of programming. Several of the programs—*The Wayan Brothers* and *Homeboys from Outer Space*—have been heavily criticized for their slapstick comedy routines and burlesque-style caricatures of blackness.

In many ways, these shows indicate that, by the late 1990s, even the "hard-core" facade made so popular in the iconography of gangsta rap had been refashioned and customized to fit the comedic programming priorities of the upstart mininetworks. In their battle to move into the ranks of network television, both rely heavily on formulaic sitcoms that center on life in the "hood." Preliminary indications suggest that the strategy may be working. Between 1996 and 1997, WB's ratings climbed 13 percent and UPN's rose 6 percent while three of the four established networks dropped in terms of number of households. For the two upstarts, their growth was especially pronounced among teens and men and women in the 18-to-34 aggregate.

Like all popular cultural trends, gangsta imagery began to show signs of erosion even as it was reaching the zenith of its commercial success during the middle 1990s. In fact, a combination of public scorn, new methods of containment and censorship, youthful exuberance, and high-profile celebrity deaths gradually undermined the appeal of the gangsta motif. So as we approach the end of the 1990s, an emergent question comes into view: Is there any life in black popular culture after ghettocentricity? In other words, as the gangsta motif loses its commercial viability, what is on the immediate horizon for black cultural and representational politics? The question is especially relevant to both film and television representations because both sites are so closely linked to the expressive cultures of black American youth. And to the extent that black popular media culture has been overwhelmingly dominated by the sensibilities and mood shifts of the hip hop generation, we can anticipate future production trends to be influenced by them also. So any serious effort to contemplate the future of black popular culture requires a wider contemplation of the social, economic, and political world black youth inhabit. For better or worse, it has been the creative interventions of the hip hop generation that have determined the greater public visibility and commercial viability of black popular culture.

Whereas most of contemporary debate regarding youth focuses on "Generation X," African Americans have been largely erased from this historically specific construction of youth. But if the Generation X discourse highlights issues and trends that are specific to white youth, then the recent and explicit recognition of the "hip hop" generation foregrounds the increased influence of black youth on American culture. By their very nature, youth cultures develop styles, modes of expression, and practices that arouse the concerns and surveillance mechanisms of the adult culture. Still, it is difficult to recall a youth cultural movement that has generated the multilayers of public scorn, social control, and resentment aimed toward hip hoppers.

It comes as no great surprise that, as hip hop culture has become synonymous with black youth, a groundswell has emerged to challenge its popular hegemony. More recently, the media spotlight has turned its glare on the hip hop generation. In the process, the labeling devices, terms, and images used to construct this particular segment of youth dovetail, in many ways, with the broader currents of racial conservatism and the rearticulation of blackness. More specifically, how has dominant discourse made sense of the hip hop generation?

Take, for example, the March 17, 1997, issue of *Newsweek* magazine, which devoted a cover story to the changing contours of black American life. The overall tone of the lifestyle feature illustrates the hysteria that defines the popular media's sudden interest in the hip hop generation. The widely read newsweekly framed its coverage with the following setup: "Black families in the 90's are divided, as whites were in the '60s. And hip hop is their Vietnam." The story goes on to claim that the new generation gap cleaving the African American community threatens to tear it apart. Moreover, rap is portrayed as the signature voice of the hip hop generation—a voice that is described simultaneously as disrespectful, hostile, and lacking hope.

Like journalism in general, the article emphasizes the extremes: a mother listening to gospel music in one room while her son listens to gangsta rap in a separate room. In addition, credentialed experts are quoted to legitimate some of the basic claims of the piece. For example, black youth are accused of "pointing fingers" and inflating the importance of racism in their alleged failures. Psychologist Alvin Poussaint asserts that, even though racism was "nastier" for previous generations of youth, the hip hop generation complains more about racism. The tone of the article essentially maintains that the barriers limiting black youth achievement are not societal or structural in nature and that the problems confronting them—a lack of respect for their elders and the rules of mainstream society—are primarily self-inflicted.

More generally, the article colors hip hoppers in sharp contrast to an impressive pantheon of black political and cultural leadership. For example, the hip hop generation is portrayed as an affront to the dreams and aspirations of civil rights leaders—most notably, Martin Luther King Jr. The article derides the hip hop community for the creation of a culture that lacks "continuity or hope" and goes on to describe its youthful members as persons who are "about thriving in Armageddon, not transcending it."

Included in the issue was an editorial piece by the magazine's contributing editor Ellis Cose, whose goal was to provide a counterportrait of black youth as smart, respectful, and ambitious. But in the process of enlarging the public's perception of black youth, Cose also reinscribed dominant representations of hip hop. Hip hoppers are described by the usually perceptive Cose as thuggish, slang-speaking, and disinterested in achievement. The point is not that the imagined community of hip hop does not have its share of delinquent youth or problematic values but rather that its constituents are far more dynamic and heterogeneous than news media discourses convey. Cose's aim to challenge widespread assumptions about black youth was a well-reasoned complementary to what he certainly recognized as a flawed cover story. However, the fact that he elected to showcase a youth who did not identify with hip hop legitimated, ironically, the magazine's deprecatory treatment of the many youth who choose to align themselves with the cultural movement.

The pejorative labeling of hip hop—and by association, black youth—is pervasive. Indeed, a new commonsense discourse is currently being fashioned that is mainly premised on the vilification of hip hop—and by association, black youth. And though I accent the *Newsweek* article, in reality, it is emblematic of a broadening consensus in the United States: the fantastic notion that black youth are the primary culprits in the erosion of public civility, personal safety, and respect for law and order. This view of black youth and hip hop culture, for example, informs news media narratives.

The news media's interest in the hip hop generation is influenced more generally by a set of conventions that rigidly organize how, when, and under what circumstances African Americans become newsworthy. For example, hip hop emerges as newsworthy only when it can be pegged to the pathology narratives customarily deployed by news workers to construct images of postindustrial black life. At various moments, the news media have exploited tragic and/or controversial flashpoints in order to paint very broad and distorting brush strokes that villainize the hip hop community. Some of the more recent episodes include the dispute between then (1992) presidential candidate Bill Clinton and Sista Souljah and, of course, the tragic murders of rappers Tupac Shukur and Notorious B.I.G. Thus, to the extent that these types of incidents project icons of black youth popular culture into wider public view, the news media exercise considerable influence over how public opinion forms its views of the hip hop generation.

Rap music has been especially targeted in the "culture war" offenses waged by various moral crusaders who contend that the music is antisocial and dangerous to the moral health of its youthful audience. For instance, in 1995, one informal coalition composed of two politicians (Senators Daniel Lieberman [D-Connecticut] and Sam Nunn [D-Georgia]) and political activists (William Bennet and C. Delores Tucker) launched a campaign that targeted twenty popular music acts, eighteen of which were rap groups. The coalition ran radio advertisements and initiated a letter-writing campaign against what it termed the music industry's reprehensible decision to sell children records that, in the coalition's words, "glorify murder and drug use and that celebrate the beating and raping of women." And while the antirap crusade has focused principally on gangsta rap, the ramifications of this initiative extend well beyond this particular subgenre. The evolving crusade against hard-core rap emboldens a larger campaign directed against the cultural practices popularized by black youth and the creative confidence they now exude in the face of immense social, economic, and political transition.

Generational image making abounds throughout the twentieth century. For example, popular discourses about baby boomers, hippies, and yuppies are familiar parts of the nation's historical memory. More recently, the term *Generation X* has been offered to capture the lived experiences of the post–baby boom generation. Generation Xers are variously figured as angry, frustrated, apathetic, and technologically literate. Inasmuch as popular narratives about American life develop period features, they also intersect with historically specific ideas about race, gender, and class. Thus, these socially constructed discourses are essentially produced with white, middle-class youth in mind.

And while contemporary narratives and popular representations of white youth vary, the discourses constructing black youth pivot tightly around the core assumption that they constitute a threat to the secure maintenance of mainstream social life. The policing of youth is by no means a recent phenomenon. However, the manner in which African American youth are policed in the context of late twentieth-century American life is arguably more elaborate and pernicious. Whereas the portrayal of white youth as disaffected slackers may require more stringent forms of motivation, the contrasting view of black hip hoppers as deviant requires more punitive responses from the adult world.

To be sure, as some of the more irreverent aspects of hip hop— most notably, the once-burgeoning gangsta motif—began to impose indelible marks on the public's image of the hip hop generation, the assault against black youth has intensified. In addition, the elaborate efforts to control and label the expressive cultures of black youth developed momentum after it was established that white youth constituted a substantial market for hip hop–related merchandise and sensibilities. The popular diffusion of hip hop throughout American culture has increased the surveillance strategies employed to contain and disparage the youth subculture.

Although gangsta iconography grips the attention of most hip hop antagonists, the historical and industrial context situating the making of this expressive culture is typically overlooked. The symbolic contours of the hard-core style are shaped largely by the creative skills and imaginations of working- and lower-middle-class black youth. The identification of many black youth with ghetto street culture is based, in part, on the lack of access to mainstream institutional life. In many ways, the decisive move toward gangsta iconography was as much a response to limited opportunity *within* the culture industry as anything else. I do not intend to ignore the problematic aspects of the gangsta project. Certainly, the hypermasculinist style and misogyny that became elemental to certain strands of gangsta exploited and also reproduced widely shared views of black youth as criminal-minded and dangerous. However, I am arguing that insofar as occupational mobility within the culture industry is severely limited, some black youth gravitate toward the most marginal (and problematic) sites of hip hop as a way of gaining access to the resources of popular media culture and production. Because the culture industry is rigidly segregated along the lines of race, class, and gender, it enforces a narrow range of possible career choices available to black youth. The proliferation of studio gangstas, then, is connected to the fact that so many black youth are isolated from the informal networks and opportunity structures that facilitate mobility in the culture industry. Still, and more problematically, the proliferation of studio gangstas also reflects how young black males gain a modicum of public visibility and symbolic capital by popularizing discourses that emphasize the desire to exploit and control their female counterparts.

One of the main reasons that the popular music industry is such a preferred site for most working-class black youth is because entry into the film and television industry is substantially more difficult. Whereas the production of film may require access to film training or expensive equipment, the production of music is comparatively less cost-prohibitive. And yet even while working-class black youth can manufacture a demo tape in the basement of their homes, the popular music industry remains racially segregated in terms of genre, style, and consumption. For many working-class black youth, hard-core became a preferred base for cultural production because, first, it was ghettoized and therefore accessible to them and, second, they exercised considerable control over its expressive content.

The idiom of demonology was expressed to fit the rising popularity and accelerated production of gangsta. Gangsta rappers, for example, have become very easy targets for politicians seeking to shore up voter support by striking a tough pose against the youth culture. More generally, youth cultures are vulnerable to the whims and anxieties of the adult world. Youth cultures necessarily generate discomfort from a varying range of authority figures—parents, police, clergy, and politicians. Throughout the middle to late twentieth century, youth cultures have been viewed as rebel cultures that threaten social equilibrium. The potential for threat is heightened once questions of race (i.e., black and/or Latino), class (working class), or sex (females) are thrown into the mix. Thus, at least since the 1950s, as a result of technological innovation, postwar affluence and the rise of a consumer economy, and a gradual reconfiguration of the racial landscape, the popular cultures of black youth have been more closely monitored.

The belief that the expressive cultures of working-class black youths corrode the norms and values of the mainstream is certainly not unique to hip hop. Still, the policing of the hip hop generation develops features that are distinct from other periods and regimes of social control. Moreover, the efforts employed to control the popular cultures of black youth parallel how black youth are surveilled and controlled more generally in the late twentieth century. Thus, to the extent that the electronic dissemination of black youth expressive cultures threatens socially contrived boundaries, it necessitates varying repertoires of social control. Some of the more recent episodes include warning labels on popular music products, congressional hearings, the V-chip, and widely publicized antirap campaigns and political speeches. These and other efforts are only partially based on concern about the erosion of public civility or popular culture's effect on the values and development of the nation's children. These efforts are also designed to exercise more effective control over a generation of African American youth who are creatively mobilizing around a rapidly changing cultural landscape and against a rising conservative racial hegemony.

Finally, if bashing the hip hop generation has developed into a vast symphony of voices, I would like to trumpet a discordant note. Despite all of the pessimistic statistics, predictions, and sloganeering that reference them as "endangered species," black youth have been remarkably resilient and equally brilliant in the face of serious societal change and conflict. In the wake of the massive migrations that repopulated America's central cities, black youth have been caught in the middle of unprecedented economic, demographic, spatial, and political transformation. The city landscapes on which so many black youth now come of age have become the great American wastelands of the late twentieth century as more upwardly mobile families and industry have moved farther and farther away.

And while contemporary narratives typically construct black youth as a source of national crisis, history will undoubtedly be more generous because the sheer determination that governs their cultural practices compels such treatment. Let us not forget that, in the midst of widespread urban dislocation, working- and lower-middle-class black youths have been central players in the creation of a popular expressive culture that is now global in scope, tenaciously dynamic, and incredibly fertile. The often-expressed view that hip hop is void of hope and full of nihilism is artificial at best. The entrepreneurial spirit, creative energy, and optimism that drive the inventive terrain of hip hop production adamantly belie this view. One of the most remarkable aspects of the emotional and productive investments black American youth have made in the formation of hip hop is the forming of a cultural movement they control even while mainstream society is becoming more impenetrable for large segments of working-class youth. Hip hop is their terrain mainly because they struggle so courageously for it—in which case, it will continue to be defined according to how they experience and negotiate a very complex world. Hip hop culture bears the imprints of how black youth struggle to understand, enjoy, and represent the world they profoundly experience. Thus, to see them struggle to turn the misery and pain of social and economic marginalization into a vibrant expressive culture vividly illustrates how aggrieved populations struggle to remake society in ways that make their everyday lives more empowering, rewarding, and pleasurable even in the face of seemingly insuperable odds.

Notes

Introduction

1. Roberts (1993, 92–93).
2. Fass (1977) explores the formation of early twentieth-century youth culture.
3. See Newman (1987) for a discussion of black-appeal radio programming and its growth and relationship to black culture. See also Barry Gordy's (1994) account of the origins of Motown Records and its relationship to shifts in black urban culture. Nightingale (1993) discusses, for example, the role of black teen magazines and the syndicated dance music show *Soul Train* in the further elaboration of black celebrity promotional vehicles.
4. For a history of the rise and fall of public space and public amusement, see Nasaw (1993).
5. For an intriguing discussion on the relationship between black population shifts and the transformations of black popular music culture, see Lipsitz (1990).
6. Lott (1993) discusses the racialized patterns of desire and imagination that informed the production of minstrelsy. For an analysis of early forms of popular film culture and constructions of blackness, see Rogin (1996).
7. This quote is from an interview with Stuart Hall conducted by Lizbeth Goodman (1993).
8. This quote is from Wood (1993, 63).
9. Film criticism and analysis operate on many levels. The focus on narrative addresses the storytelling aspects of filmic discourse. Moreover, the emphasis on apparatus seeks to better understand and appreciate the technological specificity of film production and discourse. Finally, the focus on ideology seeks to understand how the cinema is a site where ideas, values, and images are (re)produced. See Rosen (1986) for a more complete treatment.

Chapter One

1. Hall (1987, 9).
2. Rubin (1994, 240–41).
3. Hall and Jacques (1990, 11).
4. Murray (1990), Lash and Urry (1987), and Harvey (1989) discuss some of the dominant aspects of economic reorganization and the new postindustrial capitalist order.
5. See Harvey (1989).
6. See Coontz (1992) for a discussion of the relationship between the postwar boom, middle-class growth and prosperity, and federal government subsidies.

7. For another discussion of the interaction between new modes of capital accumulation and cultural life, see Lash and Urry (1987).

8. For a more detailed discussion of the economic tension that compromised the industrial economic order, see Harvey (1989, 141–71).

9. This mode of accumulation is characterized by: the organization of economies of scope featuring specialized production; flexibility with respect to labor processes, especially short-term and temporary labor; specialized patterns of consumption; the rise of the service sector economy, displacing the industrial sector; and the weakening of labor unions and the collective-bargaining power of labor.

10. Bluestone and Harrison (1982, 6) posit that the "essential problem with the US economy can be traced to the way capital—in the forms of financial resources and of real plant and equipment—has been diverted from the productive investment in our basic national industries into unproductive speculation, mergers and acquisitions, and foreign investment."

11. For a discussion of the impact of downsizing on American workers, see New York Times (1996). This book was based on a special series report that originally appeared in the daily edition of the *New York Times*.

12. Sugrue (1996) focuses on the massive restructuring of postwar Detroit and its impact on patterns of racial segregation, race relations, and urban poverty.

13. See Hall and Jacques (1990).

14. The absorption of women into the service sector economy is dominated by placement in low-wage, short-term, and service-oriented labor that provides little, if any, economic security.

15. Meier and Rudwick (1979) explore the racial tensions that shaped labor organizations like the United Auto Workers in Detroit.

16. For a good discussion of the urban and labor history of African Americans, see Barron (1971). Also Bonacich (1972) provides a theoretical discussion of the labor market segmentation of black and white workers.

17. Stern's (1993) critique is a sharp reply to those who contend that ghetto life before the 1960s was substantially more organized and viable.

18. Massey and Denton (1993) discuss a broad range of factors that facilitated the formation of black ghettos in the twentieth century.

19. Wilson argues that the most distinctive feature defining black urban ghettos in the 1980s and 1990s is that "for the first time in the twentieth century most adults in many inner-city ghetto neighborhoods are not working in a typical week" (1996, xiii).

20. For instance, women's rights organizations began to challenge the patriarchal norms, values, and cultural practices that reproduce gender inequalities. Both the Equal Rights Amendment (ERA) and reproductive rights emerged as major political struggles articulated by women's organizations. Moreover, the values and social mores that regulated sexual behavior and orientation were contested and further highlighted social and generational tensions. And Mexican Americans also began challenging regimes of authority that continued to subjugate their communities (Muñoz 1989).

21. For an extended discussion of the emergent social and economic crises that besiege many lower-middle-income and middle-income families, see, for example, Newman (1988) and Rubin (1994).

22. Quadagno (1994) discusses how the antipoverty programs of the Lyndon B. Johnson administration became linked with the civil rights movement and, as a result, African Americans. Thus, the white backlash against affirmative action, the racial integration of residential neighborhoods, and school busing also included a declining commitment to the welfare state.

23. Omi and Winant (1994) provide an excellent theoretical and practical analysis of the dynamic interplay between race, social change, and politics.

24. Lipsitz (1995, 379).

25. For a more detailed discussion of the erosion of the New Deal era and Democratic Party politics, see Fraser and Gerstle (1989) and Balz and Brownstein (1996).

26. Edsall and Edsall (1992, 35–36) note that prior to the 1960s, according to public opinion polls, most Americans did not view either of the major political parties as more or less likely to advance the cause of racial equality. However, by 1964, public opinion polls began to change, as many Americans began to view the Democratic Party as more likely than the Republican Party to advance the cause of racial equality.

27. Edsall and Edsall (1992) and Lind (1996) discuss the racialization of the two major political parties.

28. Rusher (1984) discusses the contours of conservatism in the 1950s.

29. The presidential campaigns of Barry Goldwater, George Wallace, and Richard Nixon each emphasized countersubversive themes that attempted to redefine American identity in very exclusive terms. These political themes carved out important territory and created space for the cultivation of neoconservative popular ideologies and also served as the framework for remapping the contours of racial discourse. Each political figure would articulate specific themes that were reappropriated and reworked by conservative cultural producers. See, for example, Edsall and Edsall (1992), Carter (1995), and Reider (1989).

30. For an additional discussion of the rise of these three groups, see Pinkney (1984) and Omi and Winant (1994).

31. See Viguerie (1980) and Peele (1984) for additional treatment of 1960s conservative politics.

32. Edsall and Edsall (1992) argue that, in the arena of electoral politics, the two major parties practice two distinct tactics in their struggles to win over voters: the "air war" and the "ground war." The former is essentially the deployment of electronic media and political advertisements to package candidates and political ideas For a discussion of political advertisements, see, for example, Diamond and Bates (1992) and Jamieson (1992a and 1992b). The "ground war" is the use of more locally driven resource mobilization in the form of phone banks and mailing lists to appeal directly to potential voters. Whereas the "air war" tends to be less fractious and divisive, conversely, the ground war is usually nastier and more divisive because it is generally conducted outside the spotlight of the news media glare.

33. Reed (1996) discusses the efforts of the Christian Coalition to shape American politics and culture.

34. More so than any other factor, this contingency of religio-conservative crusaders distinguishes American political conservatism from other forms that

are also gaining in importance around the world. West (1991) argues that it was the religious component of Reaganism, for example, that distinguished it from the rise of Thatcherism in Great Britain.

35. The sphere of electronic media—radio and, most specifically, television—has become a central location for accentuating the voice of the religious right. The proliferation of televangelism allows church leaders to greatly expand their audience and the efficiency of their countersubversive offense against what they perceive to be the moral decay of American secular life. For more on this phenomenon, see, Ferre (1990).

36. The rise of conservative think tanks like the Heritage Foundation and Empower America plays a huge role in the shaping of public policy. For example, the conservative assault on the welfare state was both renewed and strengthened by Heritage Foundation Fellow Charles Murray's *Losing Ground* (1984). Essentially, Murray argued that the social programs of the 1960s and 1970s worsened trends in ghetto poverty and should therefore be dismantled. Moreover, William Bennet's affiliation with Empower America has given him a new and highly visible stage from which to attack popular culture. For a discussion of Empower America, see Frantz (1996).

37. Vedlitz (1988) outlines some of the ideas and myths that shape neoconservative perspectives.

38. Efforts to control the scope and demeanor of popular culture transcend political party affiliations and cut across a wide group of public figures, including former education secretary William Bennet and elected officials ranging from former vice president Dan Quayle to President Bill Clinton and former senator Bob Dole. Child advocates like C. Delores Tucker and Tipper Gore have also expressed concerns about the nature and content of popular music culture.

39. Stuart Hall uses the Gramscian term *historical bloc* rather than the classical Marxist term *ruling class* to discuss the complexities and diverse composition of power and domination operating in advanced capitalist societies. See Hall (1987, 7). Rather than claim that the neoconservative project is dominated by a specific "ruling class," we can say that it is composed of numerous political subjects and groups struggling to assert their distinctive moral, social, economic, and political agendas.

40. See Lamont (1992, 9–13). Also, for a sociological analysis of social boundaries and the making of social inequality, see Lamont and Fournier (1992).

41. Rogin (1987) considers the countersubversive dimensions of Ronald Reagan's public career in both entertainment and politics.

42. Jamieson (1992a, 65–66).

43. Susan Faludi (1991) maintains that the conservative right has also mobilized in strategic ways to contain the rise of feminist politics.

44. Walters (1991, 142) discusses the implications of conservative hegemony for African Americans and politics.

45. See Gramsci (1971) for an elaboration of the term *war of position.*

46. For instance, conservatives did this by not opposing the idea or principle of racial equality. Rather, they targeted their resources and resistance toward federal policies and judicial decisions that attempted to move beyond the

principle of equality and toward social policies that aimed to produce equality of results.

47. Grossberg (1992) discusses the relationship between everyday life, popular culture, and politics.

48. Kazin (1995, 262).

49. Edsall and Edsall (1992, 174).

50. There is an expansive literature exploring the influence of Reaganism on American culture and politics. For example, see Dallek (1984), Morreale (1990), and Wills (1996).

51. Dallek (1984).

52. Hall defines this as "the attempt to 'educate' and discipline the society into a particularly regressive version of modernity by, paradoxically, dragging it backwards through an equally regressive version of the past" (1987, 2).

53. For an excellent discussion of the relationship between Reaganism, television news, and the war on drugs, see Campbell and Reeves (1994).

54. Kazin (1995).

55. My analysis of Reaganism has been greatly informed by lengthy conversations with Jimmie Reeves. I have come to understand that what is popularly described as Reaganism is as much a cultural phenomenon as it is a political or an economic one. It was in many ways a historically specific articulation of national identity and purpose in reaction against the constantly evolving social, economic, and demographic shifts that continue to propel the United States toward the twenty-first century.

56. For a discussion of the rhetorical devices employed by Reagan, see Stuckey (1990).

57. Omi and Winant (1986, 61–62). For a more recent and elaborate update of their groundbreaking work on the racial formation process, see Omi and Winant (1994).

58. For a lengthy discussion of the "rebirth" theme used to guide Reagan's 1984 reelection campaign strategy, see, for example, Morreale (1991). Morreale critiques the campaign spots and political biographical film that sought to position Reagan as the guiding force in the process of national restoration and renewal.

59. The social and political context of law-and-order discourses is outlined by Scheingold (1984).

60. Hall (1987, 137).

61. Omi and Winant (1994) define racialization as the process by which racial meaning is attached to a previously racially unclassified relationship, social practice, or group.

62. O'Reiley (1989) discusses in particular the covert operations of J. Edgar Hoover and the FBI against black organizations like the Black Panthers and the Student Nonviolent Coordinating Committee. Hoover argued that these groups and others like them represented a genuine threat to American national security, thus necessitating the use of militarylike operations to defeat the more radicalized aspects of the black civil rights movement.

63. This is most noticeable in the sphere of electoral politics. Take, for ex-

ample, the Willie Horton strategy developed by Republican Party campaign officials in 1988. This strategy first emerged in media politics in 1968. As Edsall and Edsall (1992) write: "[T]he Wallace campaign shaped a new right-wing populism and a new symbolic language for the politics of race, a symbolic language allowing politicians to mobilize white voters deeply resentful of racial change without referring specifically to race" (p. 78). According to the authors, the added dimension of race "gave new strength to themes that in the past had been secondary — themes always present in American politics, but which had primarily lacked, in themselves, mobilizing power" (p. 98).

64. D. Carter (1996, 11).

65. According to Gordon (1991) the primary impetus for this shift is the vigorous rise of social conservatism in American political life. Gordon produces an insightful analysis of how the issue of crime fueled a resource retrenchment in social spending and a rights retrenchment in policies of coercive control.

66. Davis (1997, 264–79).

67. See, for example, Becker (1963), Lemert (1972), Schur (1971), and Quinney (1974).

68. Lusane (1991) contends that the drug crisis in inner cities is a combination of domestic and international conflicts. Further, he contends that because the war focuses mainly on inner-city drug dealers and users, the initiative is essentially a war on poor black and Latino youths.

69. Eagleton (1991) considers several functions of ideology in addition to legitimation.

70. Campbell and Reeves (1994) argue that the "war on drugs" became the political equivalent to England's "enemy within" crisis, which politicized questions of citizenship by developing an exclusive definition of Englishness that focused some of the country's frustrations, anxiety, and fear about worsening social and economic conditions against a common enemy — immigrants of color. In the United States, young, urban African American and Latino/Latina Americans have become the target of immense social and political antagonism that aggravates the deteriorating conditions of race relations.

71. Reiman (1996) outlines some of the most commonplace myths about crime and crime-control efforts.

72. For an excellent critique of the nuclear family and the nostalgia trap, see Coontz (1992).

73. Eagleton (1991, 59).

74. Eisenstein (1982) contends that the New Right's attempt to stabilize the patriarchal "nuclear family" develops both antifeminist and racist tendencies. She adds that the attempt to reestablish this familial mode of organization is also outmoded due to structural changes in the political economy and the contested status of traditional gender roles.

75. Edsall and Edsall (1992, 174).

76. Lawrence (1983) examines the crucial role that popular conceptions of the family play in the production of hegemonic ideologies.

77. The notion that the marriage-based heterosexual family is pivotal to the maintenance of civilization also drives the Defense of Marriage Act, which codifies into law the option for states to refuse to legally recognize and constitution-

ally protect gay and lesbian marriages performed in states where such unions may be legal.

78. For an intriguing analysis of how race overshadows consideration of class deprivation and also enlivens attacks against policies designed to aid the poor, see Franklin (1991).

79. Collins (1991) examines a number of economic and political issues related to the plight of African American women.

80. Ibid., 76–77.

81. The term *culture of poverty* was coined by Oscar Lewis (1968). Lewis based his discussion of the poor on his observation of poor families in rural Mexico. For Lewis, the poor developed a cultural lifestyle that was adaptive to the conditions and environment of poverty. Whereas Lewis argued that the values and behavior of the poor were adaptations to poverty, the appropriation of his thesis has been inverted by conservatives, who argue that the culture and behavior of the poor produce social and economic inequality.

82. For a comparison of the culture of poverty with social Darwinist thought, see, for example, Steinberg (1982) and Lind (1996).

83. The post-1960s outline of this debate was greatly informed by the infamous Moynihan report. See Moynihan (1965). While the report was intended to offer some recommendations to strengthen black family life and move the "Great Society" program forward, it actually served an alternative purpose: the weakening of the welfare state. The report's focus on black familial disintegration as the primary agent and cause of racial inequality was co-opted by neoconservative policy makers to undermine the welfare state. Moreover, the gender politics of the report were critical of black mothers, who were characterized as overpowering matriarchs who subverted male authority. For a critique of the report's conclusions about black women, see Giddens (1984, 325–36).

84. For an example of this argument, see Will (1990). Essentially, Will places the blame for the problems of the black ghetto squarely on the shoulders of young black mothers, who, in his words, don't know how to mother. For Will, the major cause of intergenerational poverty among urban blacks is the inability of mothers to inspire their children with the right values and drive necessary to thrive in a democratic society.

85. Winant (1997, 105).

86. Mercer (1991, 427).

87. Ibid., 426.

88. Reider (1989).

89. For a more detailed critique of whiteness as a racial signifier, see Frankenberg (1993) and Roediger (1991).

90. Grossberg (1992).

91. Feiler (1996, 19, 20).

92. This quote is taken from a *Time* magazine cover story on the popular rise of country music. See Painton (1992, 65).

93. The dimensions of racial and gender ideologies in the big-budget action-adventure genre are discussed by Pfeil (1995), Jeffords (1994), Guerrero (1993), and Sklar (1994).

94. Some argue that talk radio and television as well as the Internet democ-

ratize the new information landscape because they enhance widespread citizen participation. For example, the Internet is an information frontier that has led to a profusion of local and personal (as well as corporate) regimes of information and entertainment production. At the same time that the Internet has created unprecedented space to circulate news and information, it has also enlivened the proliferation of antigovernment, militia, and white-supremacy groups—groups that are in essence concerned about the perceived encroachment of blacks on the privileged terrain of white material advantage and, more precisely, the sense of lost prestige, power, and authority on the part of many white men.

95. Tricia Rose (1994b, 7) contends that the new SoundScan tracking methods underestimate the music consumption of blacks because they are more likely to purchase music from street vendors or stores not affiliated with the larger suburban chains.

96. For a brief but informative history of the transformation of country music and the genre's soaring profits throughout the middle 1980s and early 1990s, see, Scherman (1994) and Cusic (1995).

97. See Applebome (1996, 241).

98. For a more complete description of the demographic shifts in country music consumption, see, for example, Schone (1991) and Stark (1994).

99. Morris (1992, 5) provides a detailed discussion of country music listeners.

100. The three programs that appeared on the lists of black and white households were *ER* (NBC), *60 Minutes* (CBS), and *Monday Night Football* (ABC). The report also concluded that white television viewers are more likely to watch programs like *Friends* (NBC) and *Seinfeld* (NBC), whereas black television viewers are more likely to watch programs like *Martin* (FOX) or *New York Undercover* (FOX). The BJK&E Media group, a marketing research firm, produced the report. The report's findings were discussed in *Mediaweek,* April 22, 1996, 30.

101. Grossberg (1992, 79).

102. See Feiler (1996).

103. Painton (1992, 66).

104. See Applebome (1996). Egerton (1974) and Carter (1995) also assert that American values, politics, and culture are being southernized.

105. The roots of country music are connected to the birth of southern rhythm and blues music. For a more detailed discussion of the contributions of black musical styles to country, see Thomas (1996).

106. Gray (1995, 35).

Chapter Two

1. Kelley (1997, 224).

2. Herman Gray (1995) contends that commercial media culture is a primary site for producing discourses about and representations of blackness.

3. See Brain's (1994) theoretical discussion of the relationship between the production of symbolic artifacts and the reproduction of social relations and social-political hierarchies.

4. Hall (1981b) discusses the theoretical tension between these two positions.

5. Hall (1992, 24).

6. Gray (1995, 2).

7. Hall and Jacques (1990, 17).

8. This is a quote from a popular rap song by the Goodie Mob (1995).

9. For some good examples of this genre of scholarship, see Hebdige (1979), Willis (1977), Frith (1981), Lipsitz (1990), Gilroy (1993), Gray (1995), Rose (1994b), McRobbie (1991), and Boyd (1997).

10. Kelley (1994b, 11).

11. See Griswold (1994).

12. Swidler (1986).

13. For a more elaborate discussion of what Raymond Williams refers to as dominant, emergent, and residual forms of culture, see Williams (1977).

14. For a more elaborate critique of the dominant ideology thesis, see Abercrombie et. al (1980).

15. For an example of this view, see Wilson (1987).

16. For a succinct, yet informative, discussion of the transformation of urban life and the construction of postindustrial cities, see Katz (1989, 124–84).

17. Schor (1991, 39–41).

18. For engaging explorations on the schooling of black and poor Americans, see Kozol (1991). Kirschenman and Neckerman (1991) discuss the discriminatory hiring practices of employers against black youth. Anderson (1980) also addresses the racially inflected tensions black youth face on the job site. For a discussion of the self-esteem and confidence of poor black youth, see Nightingale (1993).

19. The Center for the Study of Social Policy (1992) reports that the United States has a greater percentage of its youth living in poverty than other advanced capitalist nations.

20. M. Davis (1992, 306).

21. Center for the Study of Social Policy (1992) and Lerner (1995).

22. Edsall and Edsall (1992).

23. Wattenberg (1995).

24. For a full discussion of the three phases, see Gans (1995).

25. A variety of symbol handlers and cultural producers have played a role in the making of the "underclass" label. While the work of social scientists and politicians has been important, the news-reporting conventions and visual strategies employed by the national news media played a crucial role in the broad circulation and use of the label. In 1977, *Time* magazine ran a cover-story feature on the "underclass." The photos accompanying the story focused primarily on black and Latino poor inner-city residents. Also, in 1978, ABC News produced a prime-time news-story feature that focused on dislocated youth and the escalation of juvenile delinquency. The feature was titled "Youth Terror: The View behind the Gun." Moreover, what is interesting about this news piece is that it is unnarrated. The producers of the program elected to create a documentary-style news report that certainly appealed to viewers as an authentic representation of black and Latino youth dislocation. In the late 1980s, CBS News produced the feature "The Vanishing Black Family," which also visualized the "underclass" for television

viewers. To be sure, black and Latino youth have been central in the creation and visualization of the label. For analysis of the formation and politics of the label, see Katz (1991 and 1989), Gans (1995), and Lemann (1991).

26. The culture-of-poverty position essentially argues that the poor suffer not from structural and economic problems but rather from cultural deficiencies. The emphasis from this perspective is on family history, lifestyles, and the behavior of the poor. The term itself was born from the work of anthropologist Oscar Lewis (1968), who coined it to describe the rural poor in Mexico. The concepts behind the term, however, have been fashioned to discuss and explain the poor in the United States. Whereas Lewis developed the term to discuss how the poor adapt to impoverished conditions in ways that tend to facilitate the reproduction of poverty, the manner in which conservatives have claimed and the defined the culture-of-poverty discourse seems to blame impoverished conditions on the culture and behavior of the poor. For a critique of the term, see, for example, Katz (1989 and 1991), Wilson (1987), and Steinberg (1981).

27. For a full discussion of the public arenas model, see Hilgartner and Bosk (1988).

28. Gordon (1994, 125–26).

29. Katz writes, "[T]he term underclass offers a convenient metaphor for use in commentaries on inner-city crises because it evokes three widely shared perceptions: novelty, complexity, and danger. Conditions within inner cities are unprecedented; they cannot be reduced to a single factor; and they menace the rest of us. The idea of the underclass is a metaphor for the social transformation embedded in these perceptions" (1991, 3).

30. To be sure, the specific manner in which the news media work to suppress their ideological dimensions in the selection, organization, packaging, and presentation of news is also crucial. For example, Campbell (1991) stresses that TV news stories operate as "narratives" that follow familiar boundaries of plot, character, setting, problem, resolution, and synthesis. Tuchman (1979) and the Glasgow University Media Group (1980) focus on how filmic conventions tend to legitimate news's claims of representational facticity. Hall (1981a) argues that television news conceals its ideological operations by offering itself as authentic visual transcriptions of the "real world."

31. Campbell and Reeves (1994, 38).

32. For studies of how the news media construct images and definitions of race, see, for example, Hartman and Husband (1981), Dijk (1987), Entman (1990 and 1994), and Jacobs (1996). The growing body of literature suggests that the news media typically address issues of racial conflict and protest rather than racism.

33. For a discussion of the function of the news media, see Gans (1979, 290–99).

34. Ericson, Baranek, and Chan (1987) examine how the news media produce images and definitions of deviance.

35. TV news can be viewed as a form of popular culture due, primarily, to its role in TV entertainment and the formulaic conventions that news workers employ. During the last few decades, many of the local news media affiliates have adopted a strategy referred to by some critics as "If it bleeds, it leads." This is a

reference to the fact that producers of television news often shape the content and form of broadcast news in ways that can compete for higher ratings and higher revenue.In particular, television news stories are increasingly accompanied by graphic images and horrific descriptions of murders, acts of terrorism, and plane crashes.

36. In his discussion of the media's discovery of the mods and rockers, Cohen (1972) defines a moral panic as follows:

> Societies appear to be subject, every now and then, to periods of moral panic. A condition, episode, person, or group of persons emerges to become defined as a threat to societal values and interests; its nature is presented in a stylized and stereotypical fashion by the mass media . . . and other right-thinking people. . . . Socially accredited experts pronounce their diagnoses and solutions; ways of coping are evolved or (more often) resorted to; the condition . . . deteriorates and becomes more visible. Sometimes the object of the panic is quite novel and at other times it is something which has been in existence long enough, but suddenly appears in the limelight. Sometimes the panic is passed over and forgotten, except in folklore and collective memory; at other times it has more serious and long-lasting repercussions and might produce such changes as those in legal and social policy or even in the way society conceives itself. (P. 28)

37. For a more detailed analysis, see Campbell and Reeves (1994).

38. Clandestine footage usually involves a TV camera crew's following a drug bust, or drug raid, into someone's place of residence.

39. Reeves and Campbell (1994) argue that the (re)writing of the cocaine narrative follows a journalistic rite of inclusion/exclusion. The authors write: "[R]ites of inclusion are not centrally about Us versus a marginal Them, but, instead, are devoted generally to the edification and internal discipline of those who are within the fold. Rites of inclusion are, in other words, stories about Us: about what it means to be Us; about what it means to stray away from Us . . . about what it means to be welcomed back to Us" (p. 39). Alternatively, rites of exclusion "are preoccupied with sustaining the central tenets of the existing moral order against threats from the margins. News reports that operate in this domain emphasize the reporter's role of maintaining the horizons of common sense by distinguishing between the threatened realm of Us and the threatening realm of Them" (pp. 41–42).

40. See Gordon (1994).

41. Various local ordinances in cities like Los Angeles; Dallas and Austin, Texas; Minneapolis; and New Orleans have been established to exercise greater control over youth. The enforcement of dress codes is a direct attempt to discipline the body. For example, in Irving, Texas, a suburb of Dallas, a large mall recently prohibited the wearing of baseball caps backward, baggy pants, or other "gang" paraphernalia. Many cities have also turned to nightly curfews that generally target black and Latino youth. See M. Davis (1992) for a discussion of how curfews are arbitrarily enforced in Los Angeles.

42. I use the term *symbolic capital* in this instance similarly to Bourdieu (1990), who refers to the capacity of cultural creators to enforce meaning, label, and define our world. I should also note that the symbolic capital gained by a rapper like Ice Cube in the commercial culture arena works differently, for instance, than the symbolic capital gained by a political figure like Newt Gingrich in the arena of legislative politics. Both are cultural producers. Both also attempt to pattern discourses about urban ghetto life. However, their efforts to shape the symbolic landscape take place on different terrain. More important, there is a differential in the kind and extent of power each terrain provides.

43. Rose (1994, 60).

44. Fischer contends that the study of technology and society can be broadly divided into two areas: technological determinism and symptomatic approaches. For a complete discussion of these two approaches, see Fischer (1992, 8–21).

45. Ibid., 17.

46. Ibid.

47. Indeed, the persistent call for regulating control over media content is driven by the belief that youth are especially impressionable and therefore vulnerable to media messages. Thus, the introduction of the V-chip is a more recent illustration of how prevalent technological determinism is in the larger public imagination.

48. Nightingale's (1993) study examines the experiences of black youth in Philadelphia.

49. For a more detailed discussion of the various alienation theories on black urban poverty, see Nightingale (1993).

50. Social movements come in different forms. Immediate examples of social movements include the civil rights movement, New Right conservatism, and feminism. Some representative work on social movements and social theory can be found in Morris's (1984) analysis of the civil rights movement and its relationship to the black church and political networks or the classic theoretical statement on the contexts and content of movements by Piven and Cloward (1979).

51. While hip hop is commonly associated with black American youth, the imprint, for example, of Caribbean musical forms on hip hop is clearly evident. Elsewhere, U.S. cultural critic Tricia Rose (1994b) and British cultural critics Isaac Julien and Paul Gilroy map out the African diasporic elements embedded in rap. See, for example, Gilroy (1993) and Julien's independent film feature *The Darker Side of Black* (1994). Julien discusses, for example, the similarities between gangsta rap in the United States and dance hall reggae in Jamaica (Grundmann 1995).

52. See Toop (1984), Guevara (1987), and Rose (1994b) for discussions of the formation of hip hop culture.

53. See Boyd (1997) for a more elaborate analysis of the class and generational dimensions of black popular culture forms.

54. See Guevara (1987) and Rose (1994b) for examples of this genre of scholarship. Also, Carby (1986) discusses the sexual politics of black women and the production of blues music.

55. For an interesting journalistic history of hip hop culture, see Owen (1994–95).

56. For discussions of the relationship between the transformation of urban life and the formation of hip hop culture, see, for example, Rose (1994b), Kelley (1994b), Cross (1994), and Boyd (1997). For an excellent discussion of the social and political retreat from racial equality, see Steinberg (1995).

57. The pessimistic viewpoints regarding the influence of electronically produced popular media cultures over capitalist societies were vehemently expressed by members of the Frankfurt school. For an example of this view, see Adorno and Horkheimer (1989). Also, for a history of the theories, ideas, and significance of the Frankfurt school approach, see Wiggershaus (1994). For an example of how the Frankfurt school influenced media studies, see Rosenberg and White (1957).

58. See, for example, Gendron (1987) and Kealy (1982).

59. See Rose (1992) for an informative discussion of the relationship between new music-recording technologies and rap music production.

60. Schudson (1994) considers how communications media technology establishes a context for societal integration and nation building.

61. See Meyrowitz (1985) for an intriguing analysis of how electronic forms of media transform social behavior and relations.

62. Anderson (1983) examines some of the factors crucial to how members imagine themselves to be part of a national culture.

63. Schudson (1994, 24).

64. I do not want to suggest that hip hop is expressed in a uniform fashion. For instance, rap varies sharply across regions, styles, subgenres, and gender. Nor do I want to suggest that there is a monolithic constituency operating within the hip hop community. Indeed, different subjective positions, ideas, and experiences are communicated through hip hop, thus creating a vastly diverse body of discourses and cultural practices. See Cross (1994) for a discussion of how hip develops locally specific features.

65. Rose (1994b, 40).

66. Ibid.

67. For example, the Internet, the Olympic Games, collegiate athletics, and national political party conventions have all been uniquely transformed as a result of their relationship to the corporate sphere. For a more complete discussion of the corporatization of culture, see Schiller (1989).

68. Williams (1977) discusses the relationship between what he calls hegemonic, residual, and emergent cultures. Williams argues that dominant, or hegemonic, cultures must always contend with emergent cultures that are constantly struggling to destabilize the hegemonic center.

69. Hebdige (1979, 94–95).

70. Kelley (1994a).

71. Basu's analysis (1997) is based on observational studies of how the rap music recording industry has created niches of entrepreneurship for black youth in Los Angeles.

72. Basu (1997). Greg Tate, a longtime observer and analyst of hip hop, contends that rap music is arguably the first black American expressive culture that African Americans have commercially exploited as much as, if not more than, whites.

73. For a candid discussion of white (and black) employer perceptions of black youth, see, for example, Kirschenman and Neckerman (1991).

74. See Anderson (1980) for an analysis of the disdain black youth developed toward menial labor.

75. McRobbie (1994, 161–62).

76. Powell (1996, 46) discusses hip hop culture as an avenue of social mobility for some black youth in the context of Death Row Record label, a successful producer of gangsta rap in particular.

77. For a discussion of the rise, vitality, and contradictions of message rap, see Allen (1996).

78. Dyson (1996, 77).

79. Take, for example, the rap entrepreneur Russell Simmons. Simmons started out as a rap performer but soon realized that his talents were best put to use on the business side of the hip hop industry. Using rap music as his core product, Simmons has created a multimillion-dollar entertainment company that features television sitcoms, cable television specials, and clothing merchandise (Hicks 1992). Simmons talks openly about the commercial viability of rap and the drive by many African Americans to exploit its commercial success (Marriott 1992).

80. Withers (1983, 8).

81. African American filmmakers who have achieved a notable degree of commercial success tend to be male graduates from prestigious film programs and business schools. For example, Spike Lee attended New York University film school, and John Singleton received several awards for writing while attending the University of Southern California filmic writing program. Reginald and Warrington Hudlin received their training from Harvard and Yale Universities, respectively. George Jackson, a successful producer of black films, graduated from Harvard Business School.

82. Lipsitz (1994) considers how changes in technology and the globalization of popular media cultures generate the possibility for aggrieved populations to engage in new forms of cultural production and resistance.

Chapter Three

1. Public Enemy (1989).

2. DiMaggio (1977) discusses the relationship between organizations, the creative process, and market structures.

3. Indeed, under the guise of global competition, massive media mergers have emerged to create unprecedented levels of concentrated ownership across many different media and entertainment technologies. For example, Disney's purchase of the American Broadcasting Companies (ABC) creates an entertainment conglomerate that has a controlling interest in numerous areas: theme amusement parks, network and cable television, book publishing, and film production. Also, Time Warner's merger with Turner Broadcasting has created the largest media entertainment conglomerate in the world. This merger gives Time Warner–Turner a significant advantage in cable television especially and movie production in both the first- and second-tier movie studio level. And finally, the joint effort of Bill Gates's Microsoft computer software giant and NBC News has

created MSNBC, an outfit that has now entered the twenty-four-hour cable television news business. More important, Gates is utilizing his dominance in computer software to make a serious bid to dominate Internet computing. Journalist Ken Auletta (1997) discusses some of the major players vying for dominance of the new information economy.

4. Bates (1991), for example, examined some of the factors that led to the increased interest in black filmmakers by movie studios.

5. See Crane (1992).

6. Featherstone (1991) considers some of the most prominent shifts in postwar consumer culture.

7. See West (1990) for a more elaborate discussion of what he calls the "cultural politics of difference."

8. Jowett and Linton (1989, 26).

9. For an excellent presentation of various academic approaches—historical, anthropological, sociological, and cultural—to the study of popular culture, see Mukerji and Schudson (1991).

10. For a history of the studio era of filmmaking, see Gomery (1986) and Schatz (1988).

11. For example, MGM became associated with the musical, Warner Brothers with the gangster film, and Universal with the horror film. See Balio (1976).

12. For an excellent historical treatment of the classical Hollywood style, see Bordwell, Staiger, and Thompson (1985).

13. See Strick (1978).

14. Balio (1990) and Nasaw (1993) discuss some of the numerous factors that contributed to the decline in movie attendance.

15. For a discussion of the relationship between "taste cultures" and popular culture, see Gans (1974).

16. For a discussion of the policing of moral and gender boundaries, see, for example, Staiger's (1995) discussion of "bad" women in American popular culture.

17. Bagdikian (1986) explains some of the merger trends of the 1970s and 1980s. Ken Auletta (1997) addresses some of the megamedia trends of the 1990s.

18. The typical deal involves assembling a production team that makes a prospective movie project attractive to studio executives. This includes, for example, assembling a team composed of celebrity figures, a director, writers, and other personnel that enhances the likelihood of obtaining studio financing.

19. Litwak (1986) considers how changes in the film industry necessitate changes in the roles directors play in the production of film.

20. Hirsch (1972) outlines how culture industries process fads and popular trends.

21. For a discussion of the role of marketing in popular film production, see Litwak (1986).

22. See, for example, Gans (1964) and Hirsch (1972).

23. The industry has employed numerous tactics to invigorate theatrical film attendance. For a discussion of the development and use of the "star system" in film production, see Gledhill (1991). Technological innovations also play a prominent role in stimulating movie attendance. The shifts from silent to talking

pictures, and from black-and-white to color movies, were two innovations that allowed the industry to reinvent itself. For a discussion of merchandise promotions, see Drabnisky (1976). Lees and Berkowitz (1981) discuss promotional tie-in strategies. The film industry has also learned to take advantage of other media to promote film-going. For a discussion of the use of press kits and television, see Ross (1976); for newspaper advertising, see Donahue (1987). Denisoff and Romanowski (1991) discuss the use of popular music trends to promote movies. Carefully calibrated release patterns are routinely practiced to generate interest in a film and attract moviegoers (Murphy 1983). The approach to marketing movies underwent a decisive shift in the mid-1970s with blockbuster movies like *Jaws* (1975) and *Star Wars* (1977). Many industry insiders believe that *Star Wars* set a precedent for movie merchandising with its extensive product licensing program, which generated additional revenue and "free" publicity. During the 1990s, the film industry has again turned to new developments in sound technology, especially stereo and Dolby sound systems, to invigorate the moviegoing experience. Moreover, computerization is creating even greater possibilities for film product and innovation. The success of Disney films like *The Lion King* is due, in part, to the new technologies that greatly enhance the quality of film animation. Computerized image scanning also generated great interest in viewing blockbusters like *Jurassic Park* and *The Lost World* (1993 and 1997), *Twister* (1996), and *Independence Day* (1996).

24. There is, however, some debate regarding whether or not the increase in screens translates into greater differentiation in movies exhibited by the commercial theater chains.

25. For additional evaluation of the multiplex phenomenon, see Gomery (1992) and Paul (1994).

26. In addition to screening movies, multiplex theaters are also equipped with video games and concession stands that sell movie merchandise linked to promotional tie-ins. The multiplex theater is moving toward becoming an entertainment complex, thus further differentiating film from both network and cable television, its most immediate competitors. See also Guback (1987).

27. This strategy was a direct attempt to win back the white, suburban, middle-class market the industry lost between 1965 and 1974 by making moviegoing more accessible and convenient. It was during this time that population shifts motivated by racial and class dynamics altered the general makeup of major metropolitan areas, where most of the major movie houses were built. See Paul (1994). Film was not the only entertainment industry that began cultivating new marketing strategies in the face of a rapidly changing racial geography that was in full motion by the mid–twentieth century. The business of sports has also adopted new strategies in order to appeal to white, middle-class, suburban communities. One direct change in professional sports is team expansion and the building of new sports stadiums and arenas. By the 1960s, the trend of relocating sports franchises and building new sports facilities in areas that appealed to suburbanites was firmly established. See, for example, Ken Burns's episodic documentary *Baseball* (1994). Burns discusses how the movement of teams from New York in the 1950s—both the New York Giants and the Brooklyn Dodgers—was inspired, in part, by the changing racial demographics of the communities where

the teams' baseball parks were located. This trend of moving away from central-city areas to suburban areas is also evident in professional football and basketball. There is, however, a reverse trend developing as many professional sports organizations are building new stadiums near downtown areas. Some examples in baseball include Jacobs Field (Cleveland Indians), Camden Yards (Baltimore Orioles), and Turner Field (Atlanta Braves).

28. For a recent discussion of the megaplex, see Hornaday (1996).

29. Wasko (1994) considers how the rapidly evolving information technology landscape is transforming the film industry.

30. See Pierson (1995) for a personal account of one man's involvement in the independent film industry.

31. Austin (1989).

32. Take, for example, the independent film company Orion Pictures. Despite the critical and commercial success of films like *Dances with Wolves* and *Silence of the Lambs,* the company experienced serious financial problems and ultimately had to suspend future projects. Brennan and Eller (1991) assert that a shifting marketplace, shortage of capital, and heavy reliance on the ancillary markets combined to topple the company.

33. The cable television empire Turner Broadcast purchased New Line Cinema and Castle Rock Entertainment, two small but successful independent distributors. Turner's merger with the already massive Time Warner conglomerate means that these former independents are now part of the same parent corporation as the major film distributor Warner Brothers.

34. The blockbuster film emerged in the mid- to late seventies with the success of movies like *The Godfather, Jaws,* and *Star Wars.* The majors rely on this type of film to generate tremendous amounts of revenue. The reliance on blockbusters to generate huge box-office revenue causes production and promotional costs to spiral out of control, due mainly to elaborate production budgets, celebrities who demand huge salaries, celebrity directors, saturation advertisement, and wide theatrical release. The main features of the specialty film are the exact opposite: small capital investment (that is, low budget), few if any celebrities, and a very modest promotional effort; targeting of a smaller, more specialized audience; and limited theatrical distribution.

35. A pickup occurs when a studio decides to distribute a film, usually low-budget, that originated outside its domain.

36. Quoted in Bates (1991, 18).

37. Wilson and Gutiérrez (1985, 153) contend that groups traditionally excluded from participation in communications media may: (1) seek access to the dominant media through employment; (2) develop and maintain their own, alternative communications media; or (3) apply pressure techniques of various forms to effect changes in media content as it relates to them.

38. I am referring here to the early pioneering days of the electronic communications media apparatus. During the zenith of radio as the principal form of electronic media popular culture, African Americans had little access as creators and producers of radio content and product. In later years, however, African Americans did begin to use radio as a source of both entrepreneurial activity and cultural pride. See Newman (1987) for a historical portrait of the pioneering efforts

of what he calls "black appeal" radio. During the years immediately following the post–World War II era, television emerged as the primary source of popular media entertainment. During this time, African American access to the medium was basically nonexistent. By the late 1960s, however, black household ownership of televisions began to increase. By the 1970s, television ownership by blacks and whites was essentially equal. The formation of the Public Broadcasting System in the 1960s and the cable television industry in the 1980s began to create alternative spaces for African Americans to emerge as suppliers of television content and product (Dates and Barrow 1990). Black Entertainment Television (BET) specifically targets middle-class African Americans in its cable television programming. For a more elaborate discussion of how the origins of the film industry produced spaces for African American innovation, see, for example, Cripps (1993a and 1993b).

39. For example, there was a rapid response by African Americans to D. W. Griffith's film *The Birth of a Nation*. A number of black entrepreneurs began the drive to create small black-owned film companies as a way of countering what they viewed as racist imagery. Cripps (1993b) discusses the origins of the early twentieth-century black film industry. Also, both W. E. B. Du Bois and Booker T. Washington believed that film necessitated greater involvement by blacks in media production. For a description of Washington's response, see Harlan (1983).

40. See, for example, Cripps (1993b) and Nesteby (1982). The documentary film *Midnight Ramble* (1994) also discusses the relationship between the urbanization of blacks and the production of race movies.

41. The emergence of black filmmakers was not a uniquely northern phenomenon either. For example, a collection of race movies was recently discovered in Waco, Texas (Jones 1991).

42. The career of Micheaux is discussed by Bogle (1989), hooks (1991), and Heller (1995). Also, for a series of critical essays, see Diawara (1993).

43. For an interesting history of the formation of black entrepreneurship, see Butler (1991).

44. See Gomery (1992).

45. See Cripps (1993b).

46. Cripps's (1993a) follow-up study to *Slow Fade to Black*, titled *Making Movies Black*, explores black film imagery during the 1940s and 1950s.

47. As a vehicle for attracting both a black and white audience, many of these films used black entertainers—musical personalities like Louis Armstrong, Fats Waller, and Cab Calloway; singers, who often included Lena Horne and Ethel Waters; and dancing sensations like the Nicholas Brothers or Bill "Bojangles" Robinson. The film *Stormy Weather* (1948) is an excellent example of a movie plot built largely on the desire to showcase black entertainers.

48. James (1987, 134).

49. Historian Clayborne Carson (1981) explores the rise of 1960s black political militancy.

50. The NAACP and the Southern Christian Leadership Conference were two of the dominant organizations in the civil rights movement. The leadership of many civil rights organizations was sharpened by middle-class experiences, motivations, and aspirations. See Morris (1984).

51. For a more elaborate discussion of how the black power movement in the United States influenced the contours of black popular expressive culture, see Van Deburg (1992).

52. For an excellent discussion of the rise and fall of the blaxploitation moviemaking cycle, see Guerrero (1993).

53. For a critique of the gender politics of the civil rights struggle, see Wallace (1990a) and Davis (1992).

54. See Leab (1975).

55. The losses included $52 million for Warner Brothers in 1969 and $77.4 million for 20th Century Fox and $45 million for United Artists in 1970.

56. For a discussion of the changing social and cultural landscape of the sixties and the culture industry's response, see, for example, Gitlin (1982 and 1983), Bodroghkozy (1991), and Martin Rubin (1994).

57. Ward (1976) and Gomery (1992).

58. For examples of the kinds of pressure applied by African Americans against blaxploitation, see Miller (1987).

59. Rhines (1995, 38). See Rhines (1995 and 1996) for an analysis of the political economy of black cinema.

60. During the mid-1960s, constant political pressure succeeded in creating the first national affairs documentary series—Black Journal—for the Public Broadcasting System (PBS). Independent black filmmakers and video specialists used this series to focus dialogue on issues directly related to the African American community. For a more detailed discussion of the relationship between black filmmakers, PBS, and documentary as a mode of cultural production, see Dates and Barrow (1990, 303–40) and Bourne (1990).

61. For a discussion of the 1970s L.A. school of black filmmakers, see Taylor (1986) and Miller (1987).

62. See Reid (1993, 109–24).

63. Henry Hampton, the founder of Blackside, an independent media production outfit out of Boston, has produced several successful documentaries, including *Eyes on the Prize, The War on Poverty,* and *Malcolm X: Make It Plain.*

64. This is especially the case in *Black Is . . . Black Ain't.* While making the film, Riggs was also battling AIDS-related illness, which inspired him to interweave his own personal struggles into the finished product.

65. The Black Filmmaker Foundation was created by Warrington Hudlin, a filmmaker; Alric Nembhard, a management consultant; and George Cunningham, a historian and an educator.

66. Many of the original BFF members received their film training and education from elite institutions like Harvard, Yale, and New York University.

67. My argument, in part, is based on an internship I performed with the Black Filmmaker Foundation in New York City. I was able to attend several BFF events and seminars that were designed to create a more empowering and supportive environment for black independent filmmakers.

68. African Americans have established several independent film companies that operate both inside and outside dominant culture industries. Some of these film companies include: Spike Lee's Forty Acres and a Mule Filmworks, John Singleton's New Deal Productions, Matty Rich's Blacks 'N Progress, and Julie

Dash's Geechi Girls. Media entrepreneurship is practiced by African Americans in other areas of production. For example, in video/documentary and television production, there is Henry Hampton's Blackside; Oprah Winfrey's Harpo Productions; and the first black-owned cable network, Black Entertainment Television (BET), created by Robert Johnson in 1980. BET is an example of the niche marketing that characterizes the production of most media products today. Interestingly enough, *Newsweek* magazine also recognized the growth of cultural entrepreneurship in the African American community. In a cover story discussing the "Cultural Elite"—important players in the shaping of the U.S. cultural landscape—filmmaker Spike Lee; television producers Oprah Winfrey and Arsenio Hall; and hip hop's Ice-T, Russell Simmons, and Public Enemy were all listed as part of this group. See Alter (1992).

69. Gates (1991a, 202).

70. For a discussion of the relationship between advertisers and black consumers, see Dates and Barrow (1990).

71. See Graham and Hamdan (1987).

72. Many of the African American–directed films associated with the revitalization of black commercial cinema were releases by independent distribution companies. *She's Gotta Have It* (Island Pictures), *Hollywood Shuffle* (Samuel Goldwyn), and *House Party* (New Line Cinema).

73. The influence of hip hop culture has not only benefited black filmmakers. White filmmaker Ted Demme, who has directed feature films like *Who's the Man?* (1993) and *The Ref* (1994), cultivated his skills producing and directing MTV's hit program *Yo, MTV Raps!*

Chapter Four

1. George (1994, 168). Lee begins each of his feature films with the signature label "A Spike Lee Joint." In the black vernacular, as McMillan (1991) points out, *joint* has a number of associative meanings: (1) a prison; (2) a place—any place, primarily, as in your home; (3) a cool or happening place to be; (4) a party. McMillan concludes that, in the case of Spike Lee's movies, *joint* is a combination of 2, 3, and 4. McMillan's point is instructive because it suggests that, for many black moviegoers, viewing a Spike Lee Joint is an important site of politics and pleasure.

2. Lee (1987, 181, 173).

3. The prospects of receiving sponsorship for independent film projects are small due to intense competition for diminishing resources. Moreover, most grants stipulate what types of films are eligible for support. In some instances, for example, there may be specifications regarding film structure—that is, a film may be required to be nonconventional. In the journal he kept while shooting the film, Lee expressed concern that the subject matter of *SGHI*—the exploration of black female sexuality—also reduced his chances of obtaining financial support from arts foundations.

4. After photography for a film is complete, money is then required for editing, sound mixing, and producing a print copy for duplication. In addition, for an independent project like *SGHI*, Lee needed money to pay debtors for equipment rental, crew, and cast members.

5. Hirsch (1973, 649) discusses how culture industries process and merchandise popular cultural products.

6. Local newspapers in Chicago, Los Angeles, Dallas, Atlanta, and New York, for example, each ran features on the film that generated additional publicity.

7. Lee, for example, openly criticized the crossover appeal of black performers like Eddie Murphy, Whoopi Goldberg, and Michael Jackson. Moreover, Lee expressed contempt for the film industry's treatment/neglect of black subject matter by denouncing films like *Soul Man* and *The Color Purple.* Lee's evolving public persona and the press coverage that it generated also created the most effective form of advertising—word of mouth.

8. The Paramount Pictures release *The Golden Child,* starring Eddie Murphy, opened later that year in 1,667 theaters nationwide.

9. The per-screen average refers to the weekly gross of a film divided by the number of screens exhibiting the film. So, for example, *Variety* listed the weekly gross of *SGHI* at $50,000. The film was exhibited on one screen; hence, its per-screen average was $50,000. Hollywood judges the financial success of a movie based on its per-screen average.

10. Litwak (1986, 9).

11. A copy of the questionnaire appears in Lee (1988, 169–71).

12. Ibid., 171–72.

13. *School Daze* was also screened in Washington, D.C., for a mostly black collegiate audience and in San Francisco for a more ethnically mixed audience.

14. Lee (1988, 175–78).

15. In his journal notes, Lee compares the screenings to workshops. Rather than rely on industry experts to determine which filmmaking strategies—editing, pacing, length—were most successful, Lee asserts that gauging the audience responses directly is invaluable. Lee also met and spoke with focus groups to further assess their response to *School Daze.*

16. Todd Gitlin (1983) describes the process as a form of self-censorship.

17. In his journal notes, Lee admits that during the filming of *School Daze,* he and his coproducer were unaware of many of the contractual specifications that dictate the production of Hollywood films. Lee eventually learned, however, that creative independence could be achieved contractually.

18. Morehouse is a prestigious all-male African American collegiate institution. Lee also wanted to shoot on other campuses affiliated with the Atlanta University Center: Spelman College (an all-female institution), Morris Brown College, and Atlanta's Clark College.

19. Lee (1988, 60) writes, "historically black colleges view themselves as the guardian of the race and often adhere to conservative political views." In addition to fearing that *SD* would project negative images of African Americans, the Atlanta University Center administrators believed rumors that *SGHI* was a pornographic film and did not want their college community associated with Lee's production company.

20. For a more complete discussion of this argument, see Mercer (1990).

21. Lee (1992, 22).

22. In addition, Columbia executives wanted to delay the opening of *SD* by two weeks because the film *Action Jackson,* starring the black actor Carl Weathers,

was opening on the same date. The promotional budget was much larger for *Action Jackson,* and executives feared *School Daze* would not be able to compete. Lee, however, berated the executives, charging that the black moviegoing audience was much more diverse than Columbia gave it credit for. The plan to delay the film suggests that the studio was indeed misinformed about black moviegoers and the unique audience profile of Lee's first feature, *SGHI.* The studio simply attempted to attract young black teens as the primary audience for *SD.*

23. *Parenthood,* another Universal product, was released five weeks after *Do the Right Thing* on 1,262 screens.

24. By this time, Lee was establishing himself in arenas of U.S. popular culture outside the film industry—most notably, TV endorsements and music videos. His most popular advertising campaign was with the shoe company Nike. It was a series of ads with Michael Jordan for Nike that began to gain Lee both "popular prestige" and the commercial currency that would elevate his status as a prominent player on the field of commercial culture.

25. Lee (1992, 28).

26. Ibid., 11.

27. For a thought-provoking account of why the studio had difficulty finding the "right" script for the film biography, see Bradley (1992).

28. Discussing preparation for the production phase, the film's line producer, Jon Kilik, states that, for *Do the Right Thing,* only two sets were created. See Lee (1992a, 68–73).

29. Lee (1992, 29).

30. Lee had to confront serious charges that his association with the athletic-shoe company Nike was encouraging poor and working-class black youth to covet high-priced shoes they could not afford. After a series of violent incidents in which black youth were killed for sports apparel, Lee and his popular television ads with Nike were heavily criticized. For a description of this particular form of criticism, see Katz (1994).

31. Amiri Baraka (1993) was a very vocal and visible critic of Lee's role as the director of *Malcolm X.*

32. Pressure from within the African American community was indeed immense. See, for example, Lee (1992).

33. The list of entertainers who donated money toward the completion of the project included television celebrities Bill Cosby and Oprah Winfrey, basketball players Earvin "Magic" Johnson and Michael Jordan, and popular music performers Janet Jackson and Tracy Chapman.

34. Quoted in Simpson (1992b, 66).

35. Gitlin (1983, 175).

36. For a discussion of the history and structure of Hollywood biopics, see Custen (1992).

37. See Gans (1957).

38. George (1992, 111).

39. Turner (1988, 1).

40. Bourdieu (1990) defines *symbolic capital* as the power granted to those who have amassed enough recognition to be in a position to broadly circulate their view of the world. This may also include positioning oneself to be able to

command resources from the culture industries that package and distribute cultural products.

41. Lee (1992, 23).

42. West (1990) posits that there are four basic options for people of color interested in representation. He asserts that the most desirable option for people of color who promote the new cultural politics of difference is to be a critical organic catalyst. West writes: "By this I mean a person who stays attuned to the best of what the mainstream has to offer . . . yet maintains a grounding in affirming and enabling subcultures of criticism. Prophetic critics and artists of color should be exemplars of what it means to be intellectual freedom-fighters, that is, cultural workers who simultaneously position themselves within (or alongside) the mainstream while clearly aligned with groups who vow to keep alive potent traditions of critique and resistance. . . . Openness to others—including the mainstream—does not entail wholesale co-optation, and group autonomy is not group insularity" (p. 33). Is Lee a contemporary example of a critical organic catalyst? He is strategically positioned in the corridors of official cultural production but also struggles to maintain a certain degree of autonomy and distance that works to continually refuel the contradictory, yet resistive, thrust of his cultural production. West points out that the new cultural politics of difference can thrive only if there are organizations and institutions that cultivate critical sensibilities without inhibiting the creative energies of expressive culture. The creation of Forty Acres and a Mule Filmworks is such an organizational context that allows Lee to establish a technical and creative subculture that facilitates the implementation of his cultural and economic agendas.

Chapter Five

1. Lee (1992, xiii). The title of this chapter, "Spike's Joint," is borrowed from the franchise chain of apparel shops Lee has created to merchandise memorabilia from his movies. The first shop was opened in Lee's home community of Fort Greene, Brooklyn, but he has expanded to Los Angeles, Tokyo, and London.

2. Ryan and Kellner (1988, 274) analyze the political dimensions of popular film culture, entertainment, and representation.

3. This quote is from the Marlon Riggs film *Color Adjustment* (1991).

4. Lubiano (1991) provides an excellent critique of what she calls the "Spike Lee Discourse." In short, she contends that Lee's emergence as an icon of black popular culture generated a broad range of discourses that circulated beyond Lee and films.

5. See Shohat (1991) for a discussion of the representation of ethnicity in American cinema.

6. LeRoi Jones (now Amiri Baraka) argues that Negro spirituals were a transitional cultural practice. More specifically, the songs indicate a shift from an African-based culture to an African American–based culture that demarcates a specific creative moment in the history of African diasporic culture more generally. The church was/is an important site of political and cultural activity for African Americans because it was one of the few spheres that was separate from whites. For a discussion, see Jones (1963).

7. In his analysis of the modern novel, Mikhail Bakhtin (1981) argues that

each character represents a highly particularized image of some specific social-ideological discourse within the narrative operations of the novel. According to Bakhtin: "A character in a novel always has a zone of his own, his own sphere of influence on the authorial context surrounding him, a sphere that extends—and often quite far—beyond the boundaries of the direct discourse allotted to him. The area occupied by an important character voice must in any event be broader than his direct and 'actual' words" (p. 320). I am indebted to Jimmie Reeves for introducing me to the Bakhtin (1981) notion of dialogic criticism.

8. For a further discussion of how character and dialogic analysis can be employed to study visual cultures like film and television, see Newcombe (1984).

9. For a discussion of the changing roles of manhood and fraternal life, see Rotundo (1993).

10. Frazier (1957) posits that black Greek-letter organizations arose as the result of the refusal of white Greek-letter societies to admit blacks. In his scathing critique of the "black bourgeoisie," Frazier claims, "[A]lthough the original aim was to bring together the 'aristocracy of black talent' it has become one of the main expressions of social snobbishness on the part of the black bourgeoisie" (p. 83). The first African American college fraternity—Alpha Phi Alpha—was founded in 1909 at Cornell University. In 1911, Kappa Alpha Psi was founded at Indiana University. The first two African American sororities were founded at Howard University. For an excellent historical account of the Delta Sigma Theta sorority, see Giddings (1984).

11. For more elaborate critiques of the film's gender and sexual politics, see Bambara (1991) and Lubiano (1991).

12. The role skin color plays in creating internal divisions within the African American community has been analyzed by Russell, Wilson, and Hall (1992).

13. For an interesting critique of black style politics and racial identity, see, for example, Mercer's (1990) critique of the Afro, a hairstyle popularized in the late 1960s and early 1970s.

14. My use of the term *essentialism* is informed by Omi and Winant (1994). The authors assert that racial essentialism can be described as "belief in real, true human essences, existing outside or impervious to social and historical context" (p. 181). The authors draw their definition of the term with small modification from Fuss (1989).

15. Guerrero (1993).

16. For example, Lee has become quite popular among college students; thus, he has been invited to speak at numerous universities. In the process, the filmmaker has been directly confronted with inquiries that call into question his gender and sexual representations in film. In addition, the filmmaker was invited to teach a course on black cinema at Harvard University, thus further immersing him in the world of academic and scholarly criticism. In truth, very few celebrities have this kind of direct contact with the academic world; hence, they seldom, if ever, are so directly engaged by the critiques and ideas that circulate in the academic arena.

17. Hall (1988, 443).

18. Ibid.

19. For an interesting discussion of the positive-image debate, see, for ex-

ample, Marlon Riggs's *Color Adjustment* (1991). The problem with the call for "positive images" is that it often implies projecting images of black middle-class respectability that privilege bourgeois norms and values.

20. Hall (1992, 30–31).

21. Gates (1991) also views the main character, Flipper Purify, as a discourse on the precarious experiences of middle-class blacks.

22. See, for example, MacDonald (1983), Gray (1986), Montgomery (1989), Dates and Barrow (1990), and Ely (1991).

23. See Gitlin (1983).

24. Neale and Krutnik (1990, 243).

25. After studying a sample of TV representations of African Americans, Jhally and Lewis (1992) conclude that the majority of these images since 1974 are middle-class–oriented.

26. Gates (1989, 1).

27. Studies of *The Cosby Show,* however, have produced intense debates on the social significance of the sitcom. On one hand, the sitcom is applauded because it is viewed as a well-crafted representation of African Americans that departs from traditional racial stereotypes (Dyson 1993) and dignifies black culture by recoding how TV constructs blackness (Dates and Barrow 1990 and Real 1990). On the other hand, the sitcom is criticized because it evades explicit racial themes that deal with the African American experience (Downing 1988 and Boyd 1997), it is an unrealistic representation of the contemporary African American experience (Gates 1989), and it reinforces the myth that American society no longer restricts upward mobility for African Americans (Gray 1989).

28. Also, Jhally and Lewis (1992) provide interesting insight into how TV audiences generate meaning from the show and how this meaning informs their formulation and understanding of race in contemporary society. According to the authors, the show appears to be popular among black and white audiences for different reasons shaped by specific social and cultural contexts. For instance, blacks tend to favor the show because of the portrayal of black men and women as responsible parents and professionals, and its departure from demeaning images that privilege put-downs and slapstick comedy. For whites, the show is appealing because it deviates from traditional black sitcoms by de-emphasizing "black culture" and focusing much of its narrative humor away from racial themes. White audiences tend to like the show because the fictional family is "average," "normal," and "just like any other family," which, according to the authors, implies that the family is unlike most black families. The authors conclude that the popularity of the show among white audiences tends to militate toward a complex and insidious form of "modern racism" that rejects the majority of blacks who are not like the Huxtables and, by implication, are not "normal."

29. For a recent exploration of the plight of black middle-class persons and families, see, for example, Feagin and Sikes (1994), Cose (1993), and Collins (1997).

30. See Gray (1989).

31. Ibid., 384.

32. Kellner (1982) contends that the comedy genre occasionally stretches

its conventions and develops programs that challenge hegemonic representations. He discusses some of the sitcoms developed by Norman Lear and also the comedy variety show *The Smothers Brothers*. For a discussion of how the culture industry sought to control the rebellious energies of 1960s youth culture by developing a number of youth-appeal comedy and variety shows, see Bodroghkozy (1991).

33. For a more elaborate discussion of narrative and comedy, see Neale and Krutnik (1990).

34. Gitlin (1983, 93).

35. Giannetti (1990, 447) defines the sequence shot as "a single lengthy shot, usually involving complex staging and camera movements."

36. Cose (1993) addresses the discomfort and instability experienced by many blacks working in predominantly white corporate settings.

37. hooks (1990, 54).

38. Mulvey (1975) outlines a more elaborate consideration of the way classical cinema produces a gendered — or more specifically, male — gaze.

39. See Carby (1992) for a provocative critique of the multicultural wars and the "people of color" discourse.

40. Lott's (1993) discussion of blackface minstrelsy in American culture is one such example. Also, historian Michael Rogin (1996) has discussed the role of the blackface aesthetic during the rise of popular film entertainment.

41. There is an expanding literature on the social construction, representation, and performative aspects of whiteness. See, for example, Frankenberg (1993), hooks (1990), Lipsitz (1995), Roediger (1991 and 1994), Saxton (1990), Wray and Newitz (1997), and Dyer (1997).

42. Of course, some critics disagree with this contention, arguing instead that Lee's portrayal of whites is racist and unsympathetic. For example, the filmmaker was heavily criticized for his portrayal of two Jewish nightclub owners in his film *Mo' Better Blues*. Some critics argue that the portrayal was stereotypical and depicted the nightclub owners as exploitative and money-grabbing.

43. In particular, the bat was a reference to the Howard Beach incident, which inflamed local racial tensions in New York City.

44. Many critics read *Do the Right Thing* too literally rather than as an allegorical or a highly symbolic narrative. One such example is Crouch (1990).

45. See Chrisman (1990, 54).

46. This dates back as far as the early decades of the twentieth century, when blacks derived immense racial pride from the accomplishments of a pantheon of early sports heroes like Jack Johnson, Joe Louis, Jackie Robinson, and Wilma Rudolph. For a good historical treatment of black icons, see Levine (1977).

47. Fiske (1986) considers the polysemic nature of popular television programs and how different cultural groups can derive pleasure from the same sources of popular culture but for different reasons.

48. This quote is from a popular rap album produced and performed by Eric B and Rakim (1989).

49. Bordwell, Staiger, and Thompson (1985) examine the evolution and transformations of the classical style of Hollywood filmmaking. The classical

Hollywood cinema has become the dominant model throughout the entire film-making world.

50. For a description of countercinema, see Wollen (1986).

51. Giannetti (1990, 3).

52. Ibid., 6.

53. Bordwell (1986, 21).

54. For a discussion of how television in particular has employed this technique with a high degree of frequency, see Gitlin (1982).

55. Lee (1988, 178).

56. For a more complete treatment of how the newly introduced filmmaking technologies and techniques have been incorporated into the classical Hollywood cinema, see the final two chapters in Bordwell, Staiger, and Thompson (1985, 365–85).

57. For a discussion of their respective contributions to film, see, for example, Lourdeaux (1990), Stern (1995), Lewis (1995), and Keyssar (1991).

58. For a discussion of Lee's neo–black nationalist politics, see Dyson (1993). Elsewhere, Todd Boyd (1997) argues that Lee's politics are grounded in a new black aesthetic that is inflected by bourgeois sensibilities and intentions.

Chapter Six

1. Willis (1990).

2. Reed (1989, 597).

3. In Lee's early film work, some of the symbolic elements that shaped the ghetto action film cycle are visible. Lee's early work, however, was substantially different from the ghetto film cycle in terms of both content and target audience. However, by 1995, Lee moved closer to the genre with his film adaptation of Richard Price's novel *Clockers.*

4. Quoted in Gates (1994, 176–77).

5. The films also reflected the gendered and generational dimensions of this awakening. As young African American male leadership began to question the efficacy of traditional civil rights leadership, it proposed in its place a hypermasculinist form that privileged male leaders over female leaders. See, for example, Wallace (1990) and A. Y. Davis (1992).

6. Cohn (1991, 6).

7. For a history of the exploitation film in American culture, see a special issue of the journal *Film History* (1994).

8. Doherty (1988, 8).

9. In the late 1960s, films like *Bonnie and Clyde* and *The Graduate* reflected this trend toward genre hybridity. For a discussion of genre realignment during the turbulent decades of the 1960s, see Rubin (1994).

10. Singleton was the first African American and youngest person nominated for "Best Director." He was also nominated for "Best Original Screenplay."

11. For a discussion of how the television industry negotiates market uncertainty, see Gitlin (1983) and Gray (1995).

12. Two of the most successful forms of commercial culture since the mid-eighties are both associated with the urban ghetto: basketball and hip hop cul-

ture. See Boyd (1997) for a consideration of the influence of both rap music and basketball on American culture. In fact, both have developed wide global appeal. See, for example, Lipsitz (1994) and Cornyetz (1994) for a discussion of the global appeal of rap music. The popularity of basketball is also global. Indeed, the collection of professional basketball players to represent the United States in Olympic competition was, in part, a strategy to combat the fact that basketball in the United States had become so popular worldwide that many European countries are developing styles, skills, and teams that mimic those of the United States, thus making them more competitive.

13. Rubin (1994) maps how the turbulent social context of the 1960s and a series of crimes by motorcycle gangs led to the creation of the biker film cycle.

14. Jones (1992, 270).

15. This particular framing device reached its zenith during the release of *Boyz*. Both ABC and CBS network news chose random incidents of violence at the film's opening as the lead story for their respective broadcasts.

16. Rose (1994a).

17. Quoted in Marriot (1992, sec. 9, p. V1).

18. Farai Chideya (1997, 47).

19. For a discussion of the impact of youth and youth culture on the production of Hollywood film, see Doherty (1988).

20. Spigel (1992) examines the role television has played in reorganizing American domestic life.

21. Discussing the racial contours of the fifties popular cultural landscape, historian David Halberstam (1993) argues that electronic media enabled white youth to enjoy greater access to the expressive cultures created by black youth.

22. For a discussion of how popular culture trends travel from local subcultures to national media organizations, see Crane (1992).

23. I note Run DMC because they were the first rap group to attract a large crossover audience. Run DMC was the first rap group to release a multiplatinum album, appear on the cover of *Rolling Stone* magazine, and break into the MTV music video rotation schedule. Public Enemy was one of the first rap groups projecting a more explicitly politicized message that developed a large following.

24. See Gray (1995) for an elaborate discussion of the competing discourses and claims on blackness throughout the 1980s.

25. Several authors have examined the origins and transformations of MTV. See, for example, Denisoff (1988), Kaplan (1987), and McGrath (1996).

26. Denisoff (1988) examines the commercial crisis of the music industry after the era of disco and the role MTV played in revitalizing the popular music industry.

27. In his discussion of prime-time television programming, Todd Gitlin (1983) makes the point that the exclusion of blacks from the world of network television during the first full decade of the medium's history was governed by a crude racial logic. However, he suggests that by the 1960s and 1970s, network exclusion of blacks was based mainly on market-based factors rather than overt racial hostility.

28. In 1988, the network initiated one of its most popular and profitable

programs "Yo, MTV Raps!" (Malanowski 1989). In 1991, MTV developed "Fade to Black," a program that featured black music acts not necessarily included in its main rotation of music videoclips (Newman 1991, 5).

29. One of the most visible and successful examples of this was the shoe company Nike. Before its rise to prominence in the 1980s, Nike was a small company that specialized mainly in running shoes for professional runners and recreational joggers. It was not until Nike began to aggressively associate its products with popular athletes that it began to emerge as a significant player in the sports shoe and apparel industry. The shoe market had long been dominated by Adidas in Europe and Converse in the United States. However, by the 1980s, Nike was well on its way to establishing itself as a global corporate powerhouse in the world of sports marketing and product retail. The company revolutionized sports merchandising, collegiate athletics, and athletic endorsements by aligning itself with some of the more popular rhythms and styles of black youth expressive culture. The most obvious example is, of course, Nike's successful marketing strategy in the area of professional basketball and its marketing muscle behind popular black athletes like Michael Jordan. The company also used filmmaker Spike Lee as a product spokesperson. Katz (1994) reports that Nike brings in more than $800 million a year in basketball shoe sales alone. That is around the same amount as the professional basketball league's total revenues.

30. Indeed, while MTV executives at the time refute the claim, some argue that Columbia's Epic Records threatened to cut the flow of other music videoclips to the network if MTV refused to include Michael Jackson in its rotation.

31. Neely (1992) and Lorch (1996).

32. Carter (1996).

33. During its beginning, the network was charged with deliberately excluding black recording artists from its video rotation. Rap signaled the beginning of MTV's incursion into black (music) culture. The network regularly includes black popular culture in its programming. The development of the Black Entertainment Network (BET), which targets middle-class African Americans, has also established outlets for broadening rap music's appeal for blacks. Rap, then, is not confined to any particular group. The creation of music video programs, radio airplay, and word of mouth continue to create a diverse group of consumers.

34. Quoted in Hirschberg (1996, 57).

35. For an excellent discussion of the history and evolution of the hard-core style in hip hop, see Kelley (1994b). Kelley maintains that the gangsta style was part of the general hip hop scene from its origins in the South Bronx during the mid-1970s. In fact, two of the earliest gangsta-style recordings were by Schooly D ("Smoke Some Kill"), a Philadelphia rapper, and the Bronx-based rapper KRS-1 and producer Scott La Rock ("Criminal Minded").

36. Rap music is a multilayered expressive culture that combines a broad range of discourses. Nationalist rap groups like Public Enemy tended to develop a performance aesthetic that focused much of its symbolic energies on reappropriating, for example, black nationalist traditions like "black power"; see Decker (1994). Dyson (1993, 8) defines "pop" rap as "exploration of common territory

between races and classes, usually devoid of social messages." Conversely, he defines hard-core rap as social consciousness and racial pride that contains social messages.

37. While his analysis of black youth culture is xenophobic and woefully inadequate, Farr (1994) does discuss the controversial relationship between Wright and Heller, and their collaborative efforts to build an independent-label powerhouse—Ruthless Records—en route to successfully marketing gangsta rap to a specifically youth market.

38. See Cross's (1994) interview with Eazy-E.

39. Hirschberg (1996, 26).

40. Shortly after the addition of Tupac to the Death Row roster, internal conflicts, power struggles, creative differences, and legal troubles began to erode the once mighty independent rap label's dominance of the hard-core rap market. Consequently, Dr. Dre's departure and the legal troubles of Knight and Snoop Doggy Dogg weakened it further. The most devastating blow, however, was the tragic murder of Tupac. His death heightened the growing tide of public outrage and discontent with hard-core and those associated with its production. In addition, it symbolized the demise of the gangsta genre and the waning popularity of Death Row.

41. One of the most vehement charges made against gangsta rap producers is that the lyrical content is excessively vulgar. But the use of material defined as vulgar by the dominant society has a long presence in black expressive culture. For example, the bad nigger image of Stagger Lee (Levine 1977), the chitlin comic circuit featuring black star comedians like Red Foxx and later Richard Pryor (Watkins 1994), and the blaxploitation films of the 1970s suggest that this particular trend in rap music culture is not exceptionally unique, although it does articulate with historically specific experiences.

42. Journalist Amy Linden (1994) discusses how record labels issue press releases that highlight the social problems that allegedly afflict the lives of their performers. One young gangsta rap group was introduced to the press as coming from a family of drug-addicted parents. In addition, the record label also indicated that some of the group's members had criminal records. According to Linden, these and other problems are emphasized to indicate a group's authenticity.

43. Rose (1992) argues that this is symptomatic of the production of popular culture in general. She argues that there are almost no black women rap producers and that spaces like the recording studio are overwhelmingly dominated by men.

44. Moreover, hard-core rap was a direct response by a community of rap producers to the brief dominance of pop rap, a subgenre whose following was substantially white and middle-class. Three of the biggest-selling rap albums include pop albums—*Hammer Don't Hurt 'em,* by Hammer (1990); *To the Extreme,* by Vanilla Ice (1990); and *Licensed to Ill,* by the Beastie Boys (1988). Each album appealed to white and black middle-class youth. Ironically, the marketplace for gangsta rap eventually broadened to include this same segment of the music-buying population.

45. Russell (1991) and McAdams (1991).

46. The creation of *Vibe* magazine is an example of a tie-in rap commodity.

The creators of *Vibe* acknowledge that rap has given rise to the same kind of pervasive culture that rock-and-roll music did a generation ago (Carmody 1992). The magazine is packaged similarly to *Rolling Stone* and targets 18- to 34-year-old individuals. Two hundred thousand copies of the introductory issue were distributed in major metropolitan areas. The editor in chief admits that the creators of *Vibe,* which was initially bankrolled by the Time Warner media conglomerate, also anticipate a multiethnic readership. As of 1996, the magazine had not yet turned into a profitable venture but was estimated to be worth $10–$15 million. Time Warner sold its rights back to the creators of the magazine. Baseball is also beginning to incorporate rap music into its promotional campaigns as the sport struggles to increase its favorability rating (Elliot 1994 and Sandomir 1996a, 1996b). Baseball officials attribute some of the sport's diminishing popularity to the fact that it does not appeal to youth. The inability to attract this audience has two disadvantages: first, it drives down television ratings—a major source of sports revenue—because it is unable to deliver a major market of potential consumers to companies that rely heavily on youth consumer behavior; and second, the sport is unable to employ promotional tie-in strategies that take advantage of popular trends in youth culture. Indeed, one of the primary reasons that basketball is so commercially successful is its ability to attract young consumers. Many of the promotional campaigns for professional basketball incorporate elements from hip hop culture. The National Basketball Association's "Stay in School" campaign targets youth and also sponsors pop music concerts that typically feature popular rap performers. In addition, the marketing of basketball sports apparel (e.g., shoes, caps, jackets) by Nike and Reebok draws much of its appeal from trends in youth subculture, which are heavily influenced by hip hop.

47. Quoted in Bates (1991, 18).

48. Critics consider *Flashdance* a mediocre film at best, but the circulation of music videoclips from the sound track on MTV helped to build and sustain an audience for the film (Gold 1984).

49. The commercial success of the film *House Party* (1990) helped to establish precedent for this strategy. The film starred two pop rap performers, Kid n' Play. Released by New Line Cinema, for a reported $ 2.5 million, the movie was not expected to generate a significant amount of revenue but eventually grossed over $28 million in domestic box-office receipts. See, for example, Bernard (1991).

50. *New Jack City* was produced for $6 million, *Boyz N the Hood* for $6 million, and *Menace II Society* for $3 million.

51. Ward (1976), Guerrero (1993), and Rhines (1996).

52. Price (1991, A14).

53. Denisoff and Romanowski (1991) discuss the relationship between popular music and film production trends.

54. DiMauro (1985) discusses the production of *Krush Groove.* Two rap-influenced feature-length films that preceded *Krush Groove* included *Beat Street* (1984) and *Breakin'* (1984).

55. Indeed, the most prominent spheres of popular culture in the 1990s rely substantially on the appeal of black expressive culture. Take, for example, the

representation of African Americans on television. Successful television sitcoms like *The Fresh Prince of Bel Air* (NBC) and *Martin* (FOX) draw much of their material from the popularization of black urban culture. The proliferation of television advertisements featuring black youth culture is a direct response by the culture industry to seize a competitive edge in the constantly evolving youth marketplace.

Chapter Seven

1. Guerrero (1993, 189).

2. Discussing the term, Williams (1977) writes, "[W]hat we are defining is a particular quality of social experience and relationship, historically distinct from other particular qualities, which gives the sense of a generation or of a period" (p. 131). Further, he adds, "the term is difficult, but 'feeling' is chosen to emphasize a distinction from more formal concepts of 'world-view' or 'ideology.' . . . [W]e are concerned with meanings and values as they are actively lived and felt, and the relations between these and formal or systematic beliefs are in practice variable (including historically variable), over a range from formal assent with private dissent to the more nuanced interaction between selected and interpreted beliefs and acted and justified experiences" (p. 132).

3. Gates (1991) points out, for instance, that the bulk of black cultural producers in commercial cinema come from privileged, middle-class institutions (i.e., film schools, business schools). These institutions, moreover, afford black cultural producers access to the technology, information networks, and resources specific to the productive sites in commodity culture. According to Gates, these privileged cultural producers seldom create characters as complex, contradictory, and multifarious as themselves.

4. More recently, the elaboration of ghettocentric narratives has moved beyond the sphere of popular music and film to the field of literature, too. See, for example, Shakur (1993), Ice-T (1994), and McCall (1994). While McCall's book is based on his experiences growing up in the 1960s and 1970s, much of the book's symbolic power resonates with current narratives about black urban ghetto life and, in particular, the urban cultures of young black males.

5. Shadoian (1977, 1).

6. See Kelley (1994b) for a historical critique of the relationship between the postindustrialization of Los Angeles and the production of gangsta rap.

7. One of the main difficulties in making sense of popular culture formations is the fact that they are constantly in process—that is to say, continually undergoing subtle and not-so-subtle shifts at the very moment cultural critics attempt to make sense of them. Since Kelley's (1994b) critique of gangsta rap, for example, the popularization of this subgenre has created a proliferation of "studio gangsters," who tend to celebrate male-on-male and male-on-female violence.

8. According to West (1992), the liberal structuralist analysis of urban poverty emphasizes the role of social structures in reproducing urban blight. West asserts that this perspective omits serious consideration of the role of values and culture in the reproduction of the urban poor. The conservative behaviorist perspective emphasizes the role of culture and behavior in the intergenerational

transmission of urban poverty. This perspective, according to West, fails to account for the role that social and economic institutions play in the reproduction of the urban poor.

9. Nightingale (1993).

10. Historically, the genre has exploited the growing ethnic diversity of America's cities. The genre has shifted much of its concern toward growing racial diversity and perceived chaos in America's most heavily populated cities. Todd Boyd (1997) contends that films like *Colors* (1987), *Warriors* (1986), *New Jack City* (1991), and *American Me* (1991) address the gangster in specifically racialized terms.

11. For further discussions of the gangster film genre, see, for example, Tudor (1974), Schatz (1981), Shadoian (1977), Nightingale (1993), and Boyd (1997).

12. Shadoian (1977, 3).

13. In several interviews, the Hughes brothers discussed their affinity for films like Brian DePalma's *Scarface* and *The Untouchables* and Martin Scorsese's *Goodfellas*.

14. West (1992, 40).

15. Steinberg (1995), Lott (1994).

16. My use of the term *master-status-determining characteristic* is informed by Anderson (1990). Discussing Becker's application of the term from Hughes (1945), Anderson quotes, "some statuses, in our society as in others, override all other statuses and have a certain priority. Race is one of these. Membership in the Negro race, as socially defined, will override most other status considerations in most situations; the fact that one is a physician or middle-class or female will not protect one from being treated as a Negro first and any of these other things second" (p. 165). According to Anderson, the master status of the young black male is determined by his youth, his blackness, his maleness, and what these attributes have come to stand for in the shadow of the ghetto.

17. For example, most public opinion polls that identify crime as a major concern generally focus on these types of crimes, which are predominantly associated with ghetto youth. Politicians and legislators, too, have responded to the crimes that are typically associated with youth. New crime laws and legislation have increased prison sentences for drug offenders, placed more police officers on the streets, and developed tougher laws directed against the trafficking of crack cocaine. All of these prescriptions for addressing crime are, of course, reactive and punitive rather than proactive and rehabilitative. See, for example, Donziger (1996).

18. Chatman (1978, 133).

19. My use of the terms *round* and *flat* is informed by Chatman's (1978) discussion of the narrative traits of film characters.

20. Chatman (1978, 132–33).

21. The voice-over in cinema can be defined as nonsynchronous spoken commentary in a movie, often used to convey a character's thoughts or memories (Giannetti 1990).

22. See Doane (1986).

23. The portrayal of the Korean vendors as greedy, rude, and disrespectful

endorses what Kim (1993b) describes as the new Korean stereotype in popular film. She notes that films like *Do the Right Thing* (1989) and *Falling Down* (1993) also employ this image. For a more elaborate discussion of media misrepresentations of Korean Americans, also see Kim (1993a).

24. Giannetti (1990, 319).

25. Ibid., 317.

26. This specific form of conflict is a subtle, yet crucial element of change that sociologist Elijah Anderson (1990) attempts to describe in his ethnographic study of black urban communities.

27. Ibid., 69.

28. Ibid., 72.

29. Anderson (1980).

30. This is not to suggest that the period following the urban unrest of the 1960s is the only time when black youth have struggled to construct oppositional identities. For example, see Robin D. G. Kelley's (1994b) discussion of black youth culture and identity politics during the 1940s.

31. Anderson (1980, 65–66). There is some disagreement among scholars of urban poverty regarding the willingness of blacks to work in menial forms of employment. For example, discussing the work of Katherine Newman, sociologist William Wilson (1996) argues that poor and working-class African Americans are more than willing to work in low-wage, low-prestige jobs. In one fast-food operation in Harlem, Newman concluded that for every job available, there were fourteen applicants.

32. Anderson (1980, 81) writes that "the underground economy consists of a network of informal connections and established means by which people gain money illegally. There forms a social and entrepreneurial network that spreads as a result of the participants' inability or unwillingness to participate in the regular economy. "The inability to thrive in the regular economy creates the motivation for a serious consideration of entering the underground economy despite the risks associated with this social network. Moreover, in his autobiography, writer Nathan McCall (1994) argues that he and several of his friends began to develop a more hostile demeanor toward the larger white society and mainstream values, which inevitably included participation in various street crimes.

33. In his study, Jankowski (1991) contends that participation in such organizations is generally based on the belief that gang life will lead to improved economic status.

34. See Bordwell (1985) for a more explicit film-based criticism of how the various elements of filmic discourse operate narratively.

35. Bourgois (1995, 8). The author's analysis of a Puerto Rican barrio community is marked with contradictions. While his definition of street culture is perceptive, more generally, his analysis of poor Latino/a youth is informed by a culture-of-poverty perspective. This is especially ironic because, at the beginning of his study, the author recognizes that overly moralizing critiques of urban dislocation fail to adequately comprehend the role that structural transformations play in the lived experiences of poor youth.

36. Indeed, one of the major overhauls of the criminal justice system has been the erosion of the long-standing practice of maintaining separate systems

for juveniles and adults. As a result, the criminal cases of youth are being handled like those of adults. In addition, this new ethos has ignited a move to place youth in adult prisons with hardened criminals rather than in separate facilities designed specifically for the rehabilitation of juveniles.

37. Gilroy (1990, 274). Gilroy (1990, 1991, and 1993) has written extensively on black diasporic music cultures.

38. Gilroy (1990, 274).

39. This quote is taken from Malcolm X's speech "Ballot or the Bullet." The speech appears in Breitman (1965, 23–44). However, only part of the quote appears in the printed text. In the recorded version of the speech, the quote as well as the majority of the speech are clearly audible.

40. Massey and Denton (1993) use the term *hypersegregation* to explain the varying and extreme forms of social dislocation that characterize black ghetto residential arrangements.

41. Bordwell (1985, 113).

42. See Bordwell (1986) for a more complete discussion of the dominant characteristics of the classical style.

43. See Wilson (1987, 46–62) for a more detailed discussion of ghetto life and social isolation.

44. Classical cutting is a style of editing in which a sequence of shots is determined by a scene's dramatic and emotional emphases rather than by physical action alone. The sequence of shots represents the breakdown of the event into its psychological and logical components; Giannetti (1990, 442).

45. In his autobiography, sports sociologist Harry Edwards (1980) discusses how the pressures on poor black youth to pursue sports as vehicle for escaping urban poverty are a phenomenon that dates back to the 1950s.

46. The relationship between poor young black males and athletics was candidly addressed in the independent and critically acclaimed film *Hoop Dreams*. The movie, in several instances, illuminates how the pursuit of black athletic talent has developed a rather sophisticated and elaborate system that begins recruiting young boys as early as the grade school and junior high school level. Because the rewards and prestige are often immediate, many young boys devote their entire lives to pursuing a dream that all too many, unfortunately, never realize. The underlying motivation for many of the young men is to escape the profound humiliation and stigma of poverty; thus, so few come to understand the exploitative dimensions of college athletics. For a further discussion, see, for example, Joravsky (1995) and Frey (1994).

47. Giannetti (1990, 119).

48. Despite their underdeveloped scholastic skills, black athletes from poor urban school districts are extravagantly wooed to attend predominantly white collegiate institutions as scholarship athletes. This development is, however, rooted in a system of economic exploitation: black athletes are overrepresented in the two sports—football and basketball—that generate millions of dollars to fund entire athletic departments, state-of-the-art sports complexes, new stadiums, and exorbitant salaries for coaches and administrators. According to Richard Lapchick at Northeastern University's Center for the Study of Sports in Society, 80–85 percent of black football and basketball players fail to graduate

from college. Sperber (1990) discusses how collegiate athletics has been transformed into a minicorporate outfit that operates relatively independently of the wider university system and rules.

49. See M. Davis (1992, 270) for a critique of how racial and class tensions in Los Angeles led to greater policing of black and Latino youth.

50. Anderson (1990, 190).

51. Mike Davis (1992) asserts that black middle-class anxiety over youth criminality often complies with many of the containment and policing strategies designed to exercise greater control over youth.

52. Bordwell (1985).

53. Gilroy (1990).

54. Gilroy (1991, 199).

55. For examples of the long academic debate on black familial life, see, for example, Billingsley (1992), Wilson (1987 and 1996), Stern (1993), and Coontz (1992).

56. While the nuclear family is often cited as the most stable and natural form of kinship, the model and its corresponding gender strategies are historically specific formations (Davis 1983; Coontz 1992).

57. The Moynihan Report is reprinted in Rainwater and Yancey (1967, 39–125).

58. In Donald Bogle's (1989) encyclopedic examination of the history of black Americans in film and television, more than half of the sitcoms featuring African Americans employ the matriarchal model as the basic organizing principle. It is also interesting to note that Norman Lear's sitcom *Good Times* was originally conceived as a fatherless household until the female actress Esther Rolle demanded that a father be included. Lear, generally applauded for his groundbreaking TV projects, also made the assumption that, in order for the show to deal with a "real" African American family, the father must be absent (see Riggs 1991). Of course, this trend was temporarily disrupted with the introduction of *The Cosby Show* and the imitative cycle that soon followed its lead.

59. A complex matrix of factors, for example, works to explain the increasing trend of younger female-headed households. Some scholars maintain that, as the educational and economic status of black women has improved, they have become less reliant upon men as breadwinners. For a review of this argument, see Testa et al. (1993). Anderson (1990) argues that changing sex codes and behaviors among youth account for the increase. Others have argued that the rise in female-headed households is due to a shrinking marriageable pool of black males as a result of three trends: high rates of black male homicide; high rates of unemployment, which provide less of a financial incentive for marriage; and finally, the increasing rate of black male incarceration (Wilson 1987). Others argue that welfare has created less of an incentive to get married, thus causing changes in the values and moral codes of the poor that fail to reinforce a commitment to ideal of marriage (Murray 1984). Luker (1996) contends that concerns about teenage unwed motherhood reflect a more conservative public mood rather than a demographic trend. She argues that the teenage birthrate has not increased much since the 1950s. Instead, she argues that the rate of single parenting is what is on the rise.

60. Brittan (1989, 183).

61. See Collins (1991, 67–90).

62. While *Boyz N the Hood* was widely praised, the film was also the focus of sharp criticism, especially its gender themes and politics. See, for example, Jones (1991) and hooks (1992).

63. Collins (1991, 76–77).

64. Eyer (1996) describes this phenomenon more broadly as "motherguilt."

65. Take, for example, the CBS television documentary "The Vanishing Black Family" (1987), hosted by Bill Moyers. This particular documentary represented black men as irresponsible and unwilling to assist in the rearing of children they eagerly help to reproduce.

66. In a short but informative book based on 1990 census data, Sam Roberts (1993, 189–212) discusses some of the population trends and demographic profiles that continue to remake the United States in ways that are both fascinating and alarming. Roberts, for example, discusses the changing contours of poverty, particularly as it relates to race, regional specificities, age, and gender. Also, he devotes a separate chapter (pp. 91–112) to what the data reveal specifically about African Americans.

67. Will (1993).

68. Allen and Gomery (1985, 154).

69. In his discussion of authorship, Foucault (1977, 124) writes that "the function of an author is to characterize the existence, circulation, and operation of certain discourses within a society."

70. See Foucault (1977).

71. See the introduction to Mukerji and Schudson (1991).

72. For example, the prominence of commercial film production tends to gloss over the rich terrain of black independent cinema. In fact, it is the independent circuit of black American filmmaking that often deals with the intricacies of black American life beyond the constraining formulaic conventions of commercial film production (Reid 1993).

73. *CBS Evening News,* July 19, 1991. The story was reported by Richard Roth.

74. In fact, Singleton was selected as ABC News's "Person of the Week" after being nominated for two Academy Awards for his film *Boyz N the Hood.* The network also did a feature on Matty Rich (May 22, 1991) after the release of his film *Straight out of Brooklyn.*

75. hooks (1994, 152).

Epilogue

1. Bates (1991, 5).

2. See note 100 to chapter 1.

Bibliography

Abercrombie, Nicholas, et al. 1980. *The Dominant Ideology Thesis*. London: G. Allen & Unwin.

Adorno, Theodor W., and Max Horkheimer. 1989. *Dialectic of Enlightenment*. New York: Continuum.

Allen, Ernest. 1996. "Making the Strong Survive: The Contours and Contradictions of Message Rap." In *Droppin' Science: Critical Essays on Rap Music and Hip Hop Culture*, edited by Eric Perkins. Philadelphia: Temple University Press.

Allen, Robert C., and Douglas Gomery. 1985. *Film History: Theory and Practice*. New York: Knopf.

Alter, Jonathan. 1992. "The Newsweek 100: The Cultural Elite." *Newsweek*, October 5, 36–39.

Althusser, Louis. 1971. "Ideology and the Ideological State Apparatuses." In *Lenin and Philosophy and Other Essays*. London: New Left Books.

Anderson, Benedict. 1983. *Imagined Communities: The Origins and Spread of Nationalism*. London: Verso.

Anderson, Elijah. 1980. "Some Observations of Black Youth Employment." In *Youth Employment and Public Policy*, edited by Bernard E. Anderson and Isabel V. Sawhill, 64–87. Englewood Cliffs, N.J.: Prentice Hall.

———. 1990. *Streetwise: Race, Class, and Change in an Urban Community*. Chicago: University of Chicago Press.

Applebome, Peter. 1996. *Dixie Rising: How the South Is Shaping American Values, Politics, and Culture*. New York: Times Books.

Auletta, Ken. 1997. *The Highwaymen: Warriors of the Information Superhighway*. New York: Random House.

Austin, Bruce A. 1989. *Immediate Seating: A Look at Movie Audiences*. Belmont, Calif.: Wadsworth.

Bagdikian, Ben. 1986. *The Media Monopoly*. Boston: Beacon Press.

Bakhtin, Mikhail. 1981. *The Dialogic Imagination: Four Essays*, edited by Michael Holquist, translated by Caryl Emerson and Michael Holquist. Austin: University of Texas Press.

Balio, Tino. 1990. *Hollywood in the Age of Television*. Boston: Unwin and Hyman.

Balz, Dan, and Ronald Brownstein. 1996. *Storming the Gates: Protest Politics and the Republican Revival*. Boston: Little, Brown.

Bambara, Toni Cade. 1991. "Programming with *School Daze*." In *Five for Five: The Films of Spike Lee*, edited by Spike Lee. New York: Stewart, Tabori & Chang.

Baraka, Amiri. 1993. "Spike Lee at the Movies." In *Black American Cinema,* edited by Manthia Diawara. New York: Routledge.

Barron, Harold M. 1971. "The Demand for Black Labor: Historical Notes on the Political Economy of Racism." *Radical America* 5, no. 2 (March–April): 1–46.

Basu, Dipannita. 1997. "The Economics of Rap Music: An Examination of the Opportunities and Resources of African Americans in the Business of Rap Music." Paper presented at the American Sociological Association Annual Meeting, Toronto, Ontario.

Bates, Karen Grigsby. 1991. "'They've Gotta Have Us': Hollywood's Black Directors." *New York Times Magazine,* July 14, 15–19, 38, 40, 44.

Becker, Howard. 1963. *Outsiders: Studies in the Sociology of Deviance.* New York: Free Press.

Bernard, James. 1991. "Rap Knocks. Hollywood Opens the Door." *New York Times,* October 20, sec. 2, pp. 7, 21.

Billingsley, Andrew. 1992. *Climbing Jacob's Ladder: The Enduring Legacy of African American Families.* New York: Simon and Schuster.

Bluestone, Barry, and Bennett Harrison. 1982. *The Deindustrialization of America: Plant Closings, Community Abandonment, and the Dismantling of Basic Industry.* New York: Basic Books.

Bodroghkozy, Aniko. 1991. "'We're the Young Generation and We've Got Something to Say'": A Gramscian Analysis of Entertainment Television and the Youth Rebellion of the 1960s." *Critical Studies in Mass Communication* 8, no. 2:217–30.

Bogle, Donald. 1989. *Blacks in American Films and Television: An Illustrated Encyclopedia.* New York: Fireside.

Bonacich, Edna. 1972. "A Theory of Ethnic Antagonism: The Split Labor Market." *American Sociological Review* 37 (October): 547–59.

Bordwell, David. 1985. *Narration in Fiction Film.* Madison: University of Wisconsin Press.

———. 1986. "Classical Hollywood Cinema: Narrational Principles and Procedures." In *Narrative, Apparatus, Ideology: A Film Theory Reader,* edited by Philip Rosen. New York: Columbia University Press.

Bordwell, David, Janet Staiger, and Kristin Thompson. 1985. *The Classical Hollywood Cinema: Film Style and Mode of Production to 1960.* New York: Columbia University Press.

Bourdieu, Pierre. 1990. *In Other Words: Essays towards a Reflexive Sociology.* Stanford, Calif.: Stanford University Press.

Bourgois, Philippe. 1995. *In Search of Respect: Selling Crack in el Barrio.* New York: Cambridge University Press.

Bourne, St. Clair. 1990. "The African American Image in American Cinema." *Black Scholar* 21, no. 2 (March–April–May): 12–19.

Boyd, Todd. 1997. *Am I Black Enough for You?: Popular Culture from the 'Hood and Beyond.* Bloomington: Indiana University Press.

Bradley, D. 1992. "Malcolm's Mythmaking." *Transition* 56:20–48.

Brain, D. 1994. "Cultural Production as 'Society in the Making': Architecture as an Exemplar of the Social Construction of Cultural Artifacts." In *The Soci-*

ology of Culture: Emerging Theoretical Perspectives, edited by Diana Crane. Cambridge, Mass.: Blackwell.

Breitman, George. 1965. *Malcolm X Speaks: Selected Speeches and Statements.* New York: Merit Publishers.

Brittan, Arthur. 1989. *Masculinity and Power.* New York: Blackwell.

Butler, John S. 1991. *Entrepreneurship and Self-Help among African Americans: A Reconsideration of Race and Economics.* Albany: State University of New York Press.

Campbell, Richard. 1991. *60 Minutes and the News: A Mythology for Middle America.* Urbana: University of Illinois Press.

Carby, Hazel. 1986. "It Jus Be's Dat Way Sometime: The Sexual Politics of Women's Blues." *Radical America* 20, no. 4:9–22.

———. 1987. *Reconstructing Womanhood: The Emergence of the Afro-American Woman Novelist.* New York: Oxford University Press.

———. 1992. "The Multicultural Wars." In *Black Popular Culture,* edited by Gina Dent. Seattle: Bay Press.

Carmody, Deidre. 1992. "Hip-Hop Dances to the Newsstands." *New York Times,* September 14, C6, D8.

Carson, Clayborne. 1981. *In Struggle: SNCC and the Black Awakening of the 1960s.* Cambridge, Mass.: Harvard University Press.

Carter, Bill. 1996. "Losing Their Way on the Trail of the Peacock." *New York Times,* January 28, sec. 2, pp. 1, 26.

Carter, Dan. 1995. *The Politics of Rage: George Wallace, the Origins of the New Conservatism, and the Transformation of American Politics.* New York: Simon and Schuster.

Center for the Study of Social Policy. 1992. *Kids Count: Data Book: State Profiles of Child Well-Being.* Washington, D.C.: Center for the Study of Social Policy.

Cham, Mbye B., and Claire Andrade-Watkins. 1988. *Blackframes: Critical Perspectives on Black Independent Cinema.* Cambridge, Mass.: MIT Press.

Chatman, Seymour. 1978. *Story and Discourse: Narrative Structure in Fiction and Film.* Ithaca, N.Y.: Cornell University Press.

Chideya, Farai. 1997. "All Eyez on Us." *Time,* March 24, 47.

Chrisman, Robert. 1990. "What Is the Right Thing? Notes on the Deconstruction of Black Ideology." *Black Scholar* 21, no. 2 (March–April–May): 53–57.

Cohen, Stanley. 1972. *Folk Devils and Moral Panics: The Creation of the Mods and Rockers.* London: MacGibbon & Kee.

Cohn, Lawrence. 1991. "National Box Office," *Variety,* May 27, 6.

Collins, Patricia Hill. 1991. *Black Feminist Thought: Knowledge, Consciousness, and the Politics of Empowerment.* New York: Routledge.

Collins, Sharon M. 1997. *Black Corporate Executives: The Making and Breaking of a Black Middle Class.* Philadelphia: Temple University Press.

Coontz, Stephanie. 1992. *The Way We Never Were: American Families and the Nostalgia Trap.* New York: Basic Books.

Cornyetz, Nina. 1994. "Fetishized Blackness: Hip Hop and Racial Desire in Contemporary Japan." *Social Text* 41 (winter): 113–39.

Cose, Ellis. 1993. *The Rage of a Privileged Class.* New York: HaperCollins.

Cox, Oliver C. 1970. *Caste, Class, and Race: A Study in Social Dynamics.* New York: Monthly Review Press.

Crane, Diana. 1992. *The Production of Culture: Media and the Urban Arts.* Newbury Park, Calif.: Sage Publications.

———, ed. 1994. *The Sociology of Culture.* Cambridge, Mass.: Blackwell.

Cripps, Thomas. 1979. "'Race Movies' as Voice of the Black Bourgeoisie: *The Scar of Shame* (1927)." In *American History/American Film: Interpreting the Hollywood Image,* edited by J. E. O'Connor and M. A. Jackson. New York: Urger Publishing Co.

———. 1993a. *Making Movies Black: The Hollywood Message Movie from World War II to the Civil Rights Era.* New York: Oxford University Press.

———. 1993b. *Slow Fade to Black: The Negro in American Film, 1900–1942.* New York: Oxford University Press.

Cross, Brian. 1994. *It's Not about a Salary: Rap, Race, and Resistance in Los Angeles.* London: Verso.

Crouch, Stanley. 1990. *Notes of a Hanging Judge: Essays and Reviews, 1979–1989.* New York: Oxford University Press.

Cusic, Don. 1995. "Country Green: The Money in Country Music." *Southern Atlantic Quarterly* 94 (winter): 231–41.

Custen, George F. 1992. *Bio/Pics: How Hollywood Constructed Public History.* New Brunswick, N.J.: Rutgers University Press.

Dallek, Robert. 1984. *Ronald Reagan: The Politics of Symbolism.* Cambridge, Mass.: Harvard University Press.

Dates, Jannette, and William Barrow. 1990. *Split Image: The Image of African Americans in the Mass Media.* Washington, D.C.: Howard University Press.

Davis, Angela Y. 1983. *Women, Race, and Class.* New York: Vintage Books.

———. 1992. "Black Nationalism: The Sixties and the Nineties." In *Black Popular Culture,* edited by Gina Dent. Seattle: Bay Press.

———. 1997. "Race and Criminalization: Black Americans and the Punishment Industry." In *The House That Race Built: Black Americans, U.S. Terrain,* edited by Wahneema Lubiano. New York: Pantheon.

Davis, Mike. 1988. "Urban Renaissance and the Spirit of Postmodernism." In *Postmodernism and Its Discontents: Theories, Practices,* edited by E. Ann Kaplan. New York: Vintage Books.

———. 1992. *City of Quartz: Excavating the Future in Los Angeles.* New York: Vintage.

Decker, Jeffrey. 1994. "The State of Rap." In *Microphone Fiends,* edited by Andrew Ross and Tricia Rose. New York: Routledge.

Demeter, John. 1986. "Winter in America: Notes on the Media and Race." *Radical America* 20, no. 5: 63–71.

Denisoff, R. Serge. 1988. *Inside MTV.* New Brunswick, N.J.: Transaction Books.

Denisoff, R. Serge, and William D. Romanowski. 1991. *Risky Business: Rock in Film.* New Brunswick, N.J.: Transaction Publishers.

Denzin, Norman K. 1991. *Images of Postmodern Society: Social Theory and Contemporary Cinema.* London: Sage Publications.

Diamond, Edwin, and Stephen Bates. 1992. *The Spot: The Rise of Political Advertising on Television.* Cambridge, Mass.: MIT Press.

Diawara, Manthia. 1993. *Black American Cinema.* New York: Routledge.

Dijk, Teun A. Van. 1987. *Communicating Racism.* Newbury Park, Calif.: Sage.

DiMaggio, Paul. 1977. "Market Structure, the Creative Process, and Popular Culture: Toward an Organizational Reinterpretation of Mass Culture Theory." *Journal of Popular Culture* 11:436–52.

DiMauro, Phil. 1985. "Schultz Lensed 'Groove' in 26 Days for $3,000,000." *Variety,* November 6, 7, 38.

Doane, Mary Ann. 1986. "The Voice in the Cinema: The Articulation of Body and Space." In *Narrative, Apparatus, Ideology: A Film Theory Reader,* edited by Philip Rosen. New York: Columbia University Press.

Doherty, Thomas P. 1988. *Teenagers and Teenpics: The Juvenilization of American Movies in the 1950s.* Boston: Unwin and Hyman.

Donahue, Suzanne Mary. 1987. *American Film Distribution: The Changing Marketplace.* Ann Arbor, Mich.: UMI Research Press.

Donziger, Steven A. 1996. *The Real War on Crime: The Report of the National Criminal Justice Commission.* New York: Harper Perennial.

Downing, John. 1988. "'The Cosby Show' and American Racial Discourse." In *Discourse and Discrimination,* edited by Geneva Smitherman Donaldson and Teun A. Van Dijk. Detroit: Wayne State University Press.

Drabnisky, Garth H. 1976. *Motion Pictures and the Arts in Canada: The Business and the Law.* Toronto: McGraw-Hill Ryerson.

Durwood, Stanley H., and Joel H. Resnick. 1983. "The Theater Chain: American Multi-Cinema." In *The Movie Business Book,* edited by Jason E. Squire. Englewood Cliffs, N.J.: Prentice Hall.

Dyer, Richard. 1997. *White.* New York: Routledge.

Dyson, Michael Eric. 1993. *Reflecting Black: African American Cultural Criticism.* Minneapolis: University of Minnesota Press.

———. 1996. *Between God and Gangsta Rap: Bearing Witness to Black Culture.* New York: Oxford University Press.

Eagleton, Terry. 1991. *Ideology.* London: Verso.

Edsall, Thomas, with Mary Edsall. 1992. *Chain Reaction: The Impact of Race, Rights, and Taxes on American Politics.* New York: Norton.

Edwards, Harry. 1980. *The Struggle That Must Be: An Autobiography.* New York: Macmillan.

Egerton, John. 1974. *The Americanization of Dixie: The Southernization of America.* New York: Harper's Magazine Press.

Eisenstein, Zillah R. 1982. "The Sexual Politics of the New Right: Understanding the 'Crisis of Liberalism' for the 1980's." *Signs* 7, no. 3 (spring): 567–88.

Eller, Claudia, and Judy Brennan. 1991. "Orion Dances with a Deal to Keep the Wolves at Bay." *Variety,* October 14, 5–6.

Elliot, Stuart. 1994. "Agency Sought for Baseball's Image." *New York Times,* May 3, C16, D22.

Ellwood, David T. 1986. "The Spatial Mismatch Hypothesis: Are There Teenage Jobs Missing in the Ghetto?" In *The Black Youth Employment Crisis,* edited by Richard B. Freeman and Harry J. Holzer. Chicago: University of Chicago Press.

Ely, Melvin Patrick. 1991. *The Adventures of Amos 'N' Andy: A Social History of an American Phenomenon.* New York: Free Press.

Entman, Robert. 1990. "Modern Racism and the Image of Blacks in Local Television News." *Critical Studies in Mass Communication* 7, no. 4 (December): 332–45.

———. 1994. "Representation and Reality in the Portrayal of Blacks on Network Television News." *Journalism Quarterly* 71, no. 3 (autumn): 509–20.

Eric B. & Rakim. 1987. *Paid in Full.* New York: 4th & Broadway.

Ericson, Richard V., Patricia M. Baranek, and Janet B. L. Chan. 1987. *Visualizing Deviance: A Study of News Organization.* Toronto: Toronto University Press.

Eyer, Diane. 1996. *Motherguilt: How Our Culture Blames Mothers for What's Wrong with Society.* New York: Times Books.

Fair, Jo Ellen. 1992. "Black-on-Black: Race, Space, and News of Africans and African Americans." Conference paper presented at SSRC workshop, The World the Diaspora Makes: Social Science and the Reinvention of Africa, Ann Arbor, Mich.

Faludi, Susan. 1991. *Backlash: The Undeclared War against American Women.* New York: Crown Publisher.

Farley, Reynolds, and Walter Allen. 1987. *The Color Line and the Quality of American Life.* New York: Russell Sage Foundation.

Farr, Jory. 1994. *Moguls and Madmen: The Pursuit of Power in Popular Music.* New York: Simon and Schuster.

Fass, Paula S. 1977. *The Damned and the Beautiful: American Youth in the 1920's.* New York: Oxford University Press.

Faulkner, Robert R., and Andy B. Anderson. 1987. "Short Term Projects and Emergent Careers: Evidence from Hollywood." *American Journal of Sociology* 92:879–909.

Feagin, Joe, and Melvin Sikes. 1994. *Living with Racism: The Black Middle-Class Experience.* Boston: Beacon Press.

Featherstone, Mike. 1991. *Consumer Culture and Postmodernism.* London: Sage Publications.

Feiler, Bruce. 1996. "Gone Country: The Voice of Suburban America." *New Republic,* February 5, 19–23.

Ferre, John P. 1990. *Channels of Belief: Religion and American Commercial Television.* Ames: Iowa State University Press.

Film History. 1994. Vol. 6, no. 4 (winter).

Fischer, Claude. 1992. *America Calling: A Social History of the Telephone to 1940.* Berkeley: University of California Press.

Fiske, John. 1986. "Television: Polysemy and Popularity." *Critical Studies in Mass Communication* 3:391–408.

———. 1987. *Television Culture.* London: Methuen.

Fiske, John, and John Hartley. 1978. *Reading Television.* London: Methuen.

Flemming, Michael, and Jim Robbins. 1991. " H'Wood Hanging with the 'Boyz.'" *Variety,* July 22, 1, 13.

Foucault, Michel. 1972. *The Archaeology of Knowledge.* New York: Harper.

———. 1977. "What Is an Author?" In *Language, Counter-Memory, Practice: Selected Essays and Interviews by Michel Foucault,* edited by Donald F. Bouchard. Ithaca, N.Y.: Cornell University Press.

Frankenberg, Ruth. 1993. *White Women, Race Matters: The Social Construction of Whiteness.* Minneapolis: University of Minnesota Press.

Franklin, Raymond S. 1991. *Shadows of Race and Class.* Minneapolis: University of Minnesota Press.

Frantz, Douglas. 1996. "Influential Group Brought into Campaign by Kemp." *New York Times,* September 1, sec. 1, p. 15.

Fraser, Steven, and Gary Gerstle. 1989. *The Rise and Fall of the New Deal Order, 1930–1980.* Princeton, N.J.: Princeton University Press.

Frazier, E. Franklin. 1957. *Black Bourgeoisie: The Rise of a New Black Middle Class in the United States.* New York: Macmillan.

Frey, Darcy. 1994. *The Last Shot: City Streets, Basketball Dreams.* Boston: Houghton Mifflin.

Frith, Simon. 1981. *Sound Effects: Youth, Leisure, and the Politics of Rock 'n' Roll.* New York: Pantheon Books.

Fuss, Diana. 1989. *Essentially Speaking: Feminism, Nature, and Difference.* New York: Routledge.

Gains, Jane. 1993. "Fire and Desire: Race, Melodrama, and Oscar Micheaux." In *Black American Cinema,* edited by Manthia Diawara. New York: Routledge.

Gans, Herbert J. 1957. "The Creator-Audience Relationship in the Mass Media: An Analysis of Movie Making." In *Mass Culture: The Popular Arts in America,* edited by Bernard Rosenberg and David M. White. New York: Free Press.

———. 1964. "The Rise of the Problem Film." *Social Problems* 11 (spring): 327–36.

———. 1974. *Popular Culture and High Culture: An Analysis and Evolution of Tastes.* New York: Basic Books.

———. 1979. *Deciding What's News: A Study of CBS Evening News, NBC Nightly News, Newsweek, and Time.* New York: Pantheon Books.

———. 1995. *The War against the Poor: The Underclass and Antipoverty Policy.* New York: Basic Books.

Gates, Henry Louis, Jr. 1989. "TV's Black World Turns—But Stays Unreal." *New York Times,* November 12, sec. 2, pp. 1, 40.

———. 1991a. "Final Cut." *Transition* 52:177–204.

———. 1991b. "Guess Who's Not Coming to Dinner?" In *Five for Five: The Films of Spike Lee,* edited by S. Lee. New York: Stewart, Tabori, and Chang.

———. 1992. "Generation X." *Transition* 56:176–90.

———. 1994. "Blood Brothers." *Transition* 63:164–77.

Gendron, B. 1987. "Theodor Adorno Meets the Cadillacs." In *Studies in Entertainment,* edited by T. Modleski. Bloomington: University of Indiana Press.

George, Nelson. 1988. *The Death of Rhythm and Blues.* New York: Pantheon Books.

———. 1992. *Buppies, B-Boys, Baps & Bohos: Notes on Post-Soul Black Culture.* New York: HarperCollins.

———. 1994. *Blackface: Reflections on African Americans and the Movies.* New York: HarperCollins.

Giannetti, L. 1990. *Understanding Movies.* Englewood Cliffs, New Jersey: Prentice Hall.

Giddens, Anthony. 1986. *Central Problems in Social Theory: Action, Structure, and Contradictions in Social Analysis.* Berkeley: University of California Press.

Giddings, Paula. 1984. *When and Where I Enter: The Impact of Black Women on Race and Sex in America.* New York: Morrow.

———. 1988. *In Search of Sisterhood: Delta Sigma Theta and the Challenge of the Black Sorority Movement.* New York: Morrow.

Gilroy, Paul. 1990. "One Nation under a Groove: The Cultural Politics of 'Race' and Racism in Britain." In *Anatomy of Racism,* edited by David T. Goldberg. Minneapolis: University of Minnesota Press.

———. 1991. *There Ain't No Black in the Union Jack: The Cultural Politics of Race and Nation.* Chicago: University of Chicago Press.

———. 1993. *The Black Atlantic: Modernity and Double Consciousness.* Cambridge, Mass.: Harvard University Press.

Gitlin, Todd. 1980. *The Whole World Is Watching: Mass Media in the Making and Unmaking of the New Left.* Berkeley: University of California Press.

———. 1982. "Prime-Time Ideology: The Hegemonic Process in Television Entertainment." In *Television: The Critical Review,* edited by Horace Newcomb, 426–54. 3d ed. New York: Oxford University Press.

———. 1983. *Inside Prime-Time.* New York: Pantheon Books.

Glasgow University Media Group. 1980. *More Bad News.* London: Routledge.

Gledhill, Christine. 1991. *Stardom: Industry of Desire.* New York: Routledge.

Gold, Richard. 1984. "Hollywood Majors Spinoff Videos from Youth Pix." *Variety,* February 22, 1, 108.

Goldberg, David T. 1990. *Anatomy of Racism.* Minneapolis: University of Minnesota Press.

Gomery, Douglas. 1986. *The Hollywood Studio System.* New York: St. Martin's Press.

———. 1992. *Shared Pleasures: A History of Movie Presentation in the United States.* Madison: University of Wisconsin Press.

Goodie Mob. 1995. *Soul Food.* New York: LaFace Records/Arista.

Goodman, Lizbeth. 1993. "Race and the Cinema: An Interview with Stuart Hall and Paul Gilroy." Taped on March 5, 1993, and broadcast on BBC Radio as part of its Open University–BBC *Art Works* series.

Gordon, Diana R. 1991. *The Justice Juggernaut: Fighting Street Crime, Controlling Citizens.* New Brunswick, N.J.: Rutgers University Press.

———. 1994. *The Return of the Dangerous Classes: Drug Prohibition and Policy Politics.* New York: Norton.

Gordy, Barry. 1994. *To Be Loved: The Music, the Magic, the Memories of Motown: An Autobiography.* New York: Warner Books.

Graham, Lawrence, and Lawrence Hamdan. 1987. *Youthtrends: Capturing the $200 Billion Youth Market.* New York: St. Martin's Press.

Gramsci, Antonio. 1971. *Selections from the Prison Notebooks.* London: Lawrence and Wishart.

Gray, Herman. 1986. "Television and the New Black Man: Black Male Images in the Prime-Time Situational Comedy." *Media, Culture, and Society* 8:223–42.

———. 1989. "Television, Blacks, and the American Dream." *Critical Studies in Mass Communication* 6 (December): 376–86.

———. 1995. *Watching Race: Television and the Struggle for "Blackness."* Minneapolis: University of Minnesota Press.

Green, J. Ronald. 1993. "'Twoness' in the Style of Oscar Micheaux." In *Black American Cinema,* edited by Manthia Diawara. New York: Routledge.

Griswold, Wendy. 1994. *Cultures and Societies in a Changing World.* Thousand Oaks, Calif.: Pine Forge Press.

Grossberg, Lawrence. 1992. *We Gotta Get Out of This Place: Popular Conservatism and Postmodern Culture.* New York: Routledge.

Grossberg, Lawrence, et al. 1992. *Cultural Studies.* New York: Routledge.

Grundmann, Roy. 1995. "Black Nationhood and the Rest of the West: An Interview with Isaac Julien." *Cineaste* 21, no. 1–2 (winter–spring): 28–30.

Guback, Thomas H. 1987. "The Evolution of the Motion Picture Theater Business in the 1980s." *Journal of Communication* 37, no. 2 (spring): 60–67.

Guerrero, Ed. 1993. *Framing Blackness: The African American Image in Film.* Philadelphia: Temple University Press.

Guevara, Nancy. 1987. "Women Writin' Rappin' Breakin'." In *The Year Left 2: Essays on Race, Ethnicity, Class, and Gender,* edited by Mike Davis et al. New York: Verso.

Halberstam, David. 1993. *The Fifties.* New York: Villard Books.

Hall, Stuart. 1977. "Culture, the Media, and the 'Ideological Effect.'" In *Mass Communication and Society,* edited by James Curran et al. Beverly Hills, Calif.: Sage Publications.

———. 1980a. "Cultural Studies and the Centre: Some Problematics and Problems." In *Culture, Media, Language,* edited by Stuart Hall et al. London: Hutchinson.

———. 1980b. "Introduction to Media Studies at the Centre." In *Culture, Media, Language,* edited by Stuart Hall et al. London: Hutchinson.

———. 1981a. "The Determinations of News Photographs." In *The Manufacture of News: Social Problems, Deviance, and the Mass Media,* edited by Stanley Cohen and Jack Young. London: Constable.

———. 1981b. "Notes on Deconstructing the Popular." In *People's History and Socialist Theory,* edited by Raphael Samuel. London: Routledge.

———. 1985. "Signification, Representation, Ideology: Althusser and the Post-Structuralist Debates." *Critical Studies in Mass Communication* 2:91–114.

———. 1987. *Hard Road to Renewal.* London: Verso.

———. 1988. "New Ethnicities." In *Black Film, British Cinema,* edited by Kobena Mercer. London: British Film Institute.

———. 1992. "What Is This 'Black' in Black Popular Culture?" In *Black Popular Culture,* edited by Gina Dent. Seattle: Bay Press.

Hall, Stuart, and Martin Jacques, eds. 1990. *New Times: The Changing Face of Politics in the 1990s.* London: Verso.

Harlan, Louis R. 1983. *Booker T. Washington: The Wizard of Tuskegee, 1901–1915.* New York: Oxford University Press.

Harmetz, Aljean. 1983. *Rolling Breaks and Other Movie Business.* New York: Knopf.

———. 1988. "Now Playing: The New Hollywood." *New York Times,* January 10, sec. 2, pp. 1, 26.

Hartley, John. 1982. *Understanding News.* London: Methuen.

Hartman, Paul, and Charles Husband. 1981. "The Mass Media and Racial Conflict." In *The Manufacture of News,* edited by Stanley Cohen and Jack Young. London: Constable.

Harvey, David. 1989. *The Condition of Postmodernity: An Enquiry into the Origins of Cultural Change.* Oxford: Blackwell.

Hebdige, Dick. 1979. *Subculture: The Meaning of Style.* London: Methuen.

———. 1990. "After the Masses." In *New Times: The Changing Face of Politics in the 1990s,* edited by Stuart Hall and Martin Jacques. London: Verso.

Heller, Scott. 1995. "A Pioneering Black Film Maker." *Chronicle of Higher Education* 41, no. 25 (March 3): A6–A7, A12–A13.

Hicks, Jonathan. 1992. "A Big Bet on the Godfather of Rap." *New York Times,* June 14, sec. 3, pp. 1, 6.

Hilgartner, Stephen, and Charles L. Bosk. 1988. "The Rise and Fall of Social Problems: A Public Arenas Model." *American Journal of Sociology* 94, no. 1:53–78.

Hirsch, Paul M. 1972. "Processing Fads and Fashions: An Organization-Set Analysis of Culture Industry Systems." *American Journal of Sociology* 77:639–59.

Hirschberg, Lynn. 1996. "Does a Sugar Bear Bite?" *New York Times Magazine,* January 14, 24–31, 39–40, 50, 57.

hooks, bell. 1988. *Talking Back: Thinking Feminist, Thinking Black.* Boston: South End Press.

———. 1990. *Yearning: Race, Gender, and Cultural Politics.* Boston: South End Press.

———. 1991. "Micheaux: Celebrating Blackness." *Black American Literature Forum* 25, no. 2 (summer): 351–60.

———. 1992. "Dialectically Down with the Critical Program." In *Black Popular Culture,* edited by Gina Dent. Seattle: Bay Press.

———. 1994. *Outlaw Culture: Resisting Representations.* New York: Routledge.

Hornaday, Ann. 1996. "At Many a Multiplex, Lots of Screens but Little Choice." *New York Times,* August 4, sec. 2, p. 18.

Hughes, Everett C. 1945. "Dilemmas and Contradictions of Status." *American Journal of Sociology* 50:353–59.

Ice-T. 1994. *The Ice Opinion: Ice-T as Told to Heidi Siegmund.* New York: St. Martin's Press.

Jacobs, Ronald N. 1996. "Civil Society and Crisis: Culture, Discourse, and the Rodney King Beating." *American Journal of Sociology* 101, no. 5:1238–72.

James, David E. 1987. "Chained to Devil Pictures: Cinema and Black Liberation in the Sixties." In *The Year Left 2: Essays on Race, Ethnicity, Class, and Gender,* edited by M. Davis et al. New York: Verso.

Jameson, Fredric. 1991. *Postmodernism, or the Cultural Logic of Late Capitalism.* Durham, N.C.: Duke University Press.

Jamieson, Kathleen Hall. 1992a. *Dirty Politics: Deception, Distraction, and Democracy.* New York: Oxford University Press.

———. 1992b. *History and Criticism of Presidential Campaign Advertising.* New York: Oxford University Press.

Jankowski, Martin Sanchez. 1991. *Islands in the Streets: Gangs and American Urban Society.* Berkeley: University of California Press.

Jeffords, Susan. 1994. *Hard Bodies: Hollywood Masculinity in the Reagan Era.* New Brunswick, N.J.: Rutgers University Press.

Jenkcs, Christopher, and Paul E. Peterson, eds. 1991. *The Urban Underclass.* Washington, D.C.: Brookings Institution.

Jhally, Sut, and Justin Lewis. 1992. *Enlightened Racism: The Cosby Show, Audiences, and the Myth of the American Dream.* Boulder, Colo.: Westview Press.

Jones, G. William. 1991. *Black Cinema Treasures: Lost and Found.* Denton: University of North Texas Press.

Jones, Jacqueline. 1992. *The Dispossessed: America's Underclasses from the Civil War to the Present.* New York: Basic Books.

Jones, Jacquie. 1991. "The New Ghetto Aesthetic." *Wide Angle* 13, nos. 3, 4 (July – October): 32 – 43.

Jones, Leroi. 1963. *Blues People: Negro Music in White America.* New York: William Morrow.

Joravsky, Ben. 1995. *Hoop Dreams: A True Story of Hardship and Triumph.* Atlanta: Turner Publishing.

Jowetti, Garth, and James M. Linton. 1989. *Movies as Mass Communication.* Newbury Park, Calif.: Sage Publications.

Julien, Isaac. 1992. "Black Is, Black Ain't: Notes on De-Essentializing Black Identities." In *Black Popular Culture,* edited by Gina Dent. Seattle: Bay Press.

Kaplan, E. Ann. 1987. *Rocking around the Clock: Music Television, Postmodernism, and Consumer Culture.* New York: Methuen.

Katz, Donald R. 1994. *Just Do It: The Nike Spirit in the Corporate World.* New York: Random House.

Katz, Michael B. 1989. *The Undeserving Poor: From the War on Poverty to the War on Welfare.* New York: Pantheon Books.

———. 1991. *The "Underclass" Debate: Views from History.* Princeton, N.J.: Princeton University Press.

Kazin, Michael. 1995. *The Populist Persuasion: An American History.* New York: Basic Books.

Kealy, Edward R. 1982. "Conventions and the Production of the Popular Music Aesthetic." *Journal of Popular Culture* 16, no. 2 (fall): 100 –15.

Kelley, Robin D. G. 1994. *Race Rebels: Culture, Politics, and the Black Working Class.* New York: Free Press.

———. 1997. "Playing for Keeps: Pleasure and Profit on the Postindustrial Playground." In *The House That Race Built: Black Americans, U.S. Terrain,* edited by Wahneema Lubiano. New York: Pantheon.

Kellner, Douglas. 1982. "TV Ideology and Emancipatory Popular Culture." In *Television: The Critical View,* edited by H. Newcomb. 4th ed. New York: Oxford University Press.

———. 1990. *Television and the Crisis of Democracy.* Boulder, Colo.: Westview Press.

Keyssar, Helene. 1991. *Robert Altman's America.* New York: Oxford University Press.

Kim, Elaine H. 1993a. "Home Is Where the 'Han' Is: A Korean American Perspective on the Los Angeles Upheavals." *Social Justice* 20: 1–21.

———. 1993b. "Open Season on Koreans?" *New York Newsday,* June 3.

Kirschenman, Joleen, and Kathryn M. Neckerman. 1991. "'We'd Love to Hire Them, but . . . ': The Meaning of Race for Employers." In *The Urban Under-*

class, edited by Christopher Jencks and Paul E. Peterson. Washington, D.C.: Brookings Institution.

Kozol, Jonathan. 1991. *Savage Inequalities: Children in America's Schools.* New York: Crown.

Lamont, Michéle. 1992. *Money, Morals, and Manners: The Culture of the French and American Upper-Middle Class.* Chicago: University of Chicago Press.

Lamont, Michéle, and Marcel Fournier. 1992. *Cultivating Differences: Symbolic Boundaries and the Making of Inequality.* Chicago: University of Chicago Press.

Lash, Scott, and John Urry. 1987. *The End of Organized Capitalism.* Madison: University of Wisconsin Press.

Lawrence, Errol. 1983. "Just Plain Common Sense: The 'Roots' of Racism." In *The Empire Strikes Back,* edited by P. Gilroy. London: Hutchinson.

Leab, Daniel J. 1975. *From Sambo to Superspade: The Black Experience in Motion Pictures.* Boston: Houghton Mifflin.

Lee, Spike. 1987. *Spike Lee's Gotta Have It: Inside Guerrilla Filmmaking.* New York: Simon and Schuster.

———. 1988. *Uplift the Race: The Construction of* School Daze. New York: Simon and Schuster.

———. 1989. *Do the Right Thing: A Spike Lee Joint.* New York: Fireside Press.

———. 1992. *By Any Means Necessary: The Trials and Tribulations of the Making of* Malcolm X. New York: Hyperion.

Lees, David, and Stan Berkowitz. 1981. *The Movie Business.* New York: Vintage Books.

Lemann, Nicholas. 1991. *The Promised Land: The Great Black Migration and How It Changed America.* New York: Knopf.

Lemert, Edwin M. 1972. *Human Deviance, Social Problems, and Social Control.* Englewood Cliffs, N.J.: Prentice Hall.

Lerner, Richard M. 1995. *American Youth in Crisis: Challenges and Options for Programs and Policies.* Thousand Oaks, Calif.: Sage.

Levine, Lawrence W. 1977. *Black Culture and Black Consciousness: Afro-American Folk Thought from Slavery to Freedom.* New York: Oxford University Press.

Lewis, Jon. 1995. *Whom God Wishes to Destroy: Francis Coppola and the New Hollywood.* Durham, N.C.: Duke University Press.

Lewis, Oscar. 1968. "The Culture of Poverty." In *On Understanding Poverty: Perspectives from the Social Sciences,* edited by D. P. Moynihan. New York: Basic Books.

Lind, Michael. 1996. *Up from Conservatism: Why the Right Is Wrong for America.* New York: Free Press.

Linden, Amy. 1994. "Niggas with Beatitude." *Transition* 62:176–87.

Lipsitz, George. 1990. *Time Passages: Collective Memory and American Popular Culture.* Minneapolis: University of Minnesota Press.

———. 1994. *Dangerous Crossroads: Popular Music, Postmodernism, and the Poetics of Place.* London: Verso.

———. 1995. "The Possessive Investment in Whiteness: Racialized Social Democracy and the 'White' Problem in American Studies." *American Quarterly* 47 (September): 369–87.

Litwak, Mark. 1986. *Reel Power: The Struggle for Influence and Success in the New Hollywood.* New York: Morrow.

Lorch, Donatella. 1996. "Young Voters, Diverse and Disillusioned, Are Unpredictable in '96 Race." *New York Times,* March 30, 7.

Lott, Eric. 1993. *Love and Theft: Blackface Minstrelsy and the American Working Class.* New York: Oxford University Press.

———. 1994. "Cornel West in the Hour of Chaos: Culture and Politics in Race Matters." *Social Text* (fall): 39–50.

Lourdeaux, Lee. 1990. *Italian and Irish Filmmakers in America: Ford, Capra, Coppola, and Scorsese.* Philadelphia: Temple University Press.

Lubiano, Wahneema. 1991. "But Compared to What? Reading Realism, Representation, and Essentialism in *School Daze, Do the Right Thing,* and the Spike Lee Discourse." *Black American Literature Forum* 25, no. 2 (summer): 253–82.

Luker, Kristin. 1996. *Dubious Conceptions: The Politics of Teenage Pregnancy.* Cambridge, Mass.: Harvard University Press.

Lusane, Clarence. 1991. *Pipe Dream Blues: Racism and the War on Drugs.* Boston: South End Press.

MacDonald, J. Fred. 1983. *Black and White TV: Afro-Americans in Television since 1948.* Chicago: Nelson-Hall.

Malanowski, Jamie. 1989. "Top Hip Hop." *Rolling Stone,* July 13, 77–78.

Malcolm X. 1989. "The Ballot or the Bullet." In *Malcolm X Speaks: Selected Speeches and Statements,* edited by George Breitman. New York: Pathfinder.

Mandel, Ernest. 1975. *Late Capitalism.* London: NLB.

Marchetti, Gina. 1989. "Action Adventure Films as Ideology." In *Cultural Politics in the Contemporary America,* edited by Ian Angus and Sut Jhally. New York: Routledge.

———. 1991. "Ethnicity, the Cinema, and Cultural Studies." In *Unspeakable Images: Ethnicity and the American Cinema,* edited by Lester D. Friedman. Urbana: University of Illinois Press.

Marriott, Michael. 1992. "Hip-Hop's Hostile Takeover: Rap Joins the Mainstream." *New York Times,* September 22, sec. 9, p. vi.

Marx, Karl, and Frederick Engels. 1972. *The German Ideology,* edited by C. J. Arthur. New York: International Publishers.

Massey, Douglas, and Nancy Denton. 1993. *American Apartheid: Segregation and the Making of the Underclass.* Cambridge, Mass.: Harvard University Press.

McAdams, Janice. 1991. "Low 'Priority': N.W.A.'s Chart Topping Album—Violence, Misogyny Mar Un-Eazy-E 'Efil4zaggin.'" *Billboard,* July 6, 23.

McCall, Nathan. 1994. *Makes Me Want to Holler: A Young Black Man in America.* New York: Random House.

McGrath, Tom. 1996. *MTV: The Making of a Revolution.* Philadelphia: Running Press.

McMillan, Terry. 1991. "Thoughts on *She's Gotta Have It.*" In *Five for Five: The Films of Spike Lee,* edited by Spike Lee. New York: Stewart, Tabori, and Chang.

McRobbie, Angela. 1991. *Feminism and Youth Culture: From "Jackie" to "Just Seventeen."* Boston: Unwin Hyman.

———. 1994. *Postmodernism and Popular Culture.* New York: Routledge.

Meier, August, and Elliot Rudwick. 1979. *Black Detroit and the Rise of the UAW.* New York: Oxford University Press.

Mercer, Kobena. 1989. "General Introduction." In *The Colour Black—Black Images in British Television,* edited by Theresa Daniels and Jane Gerson. London: British Film Institute.

———. 1990. "Black Hair/Style Politics." In *Out There: Marginalization and Contemporary Cultures,* edited by Russell Ferguson et al. Cambridge, Mass.: MIT Press.

———. 1991. "'1968': Periodizing Politics and Identity." In *Cultural Studies,* edited by Lawrence Grossberg et al. New York: Routledge.

Meyrowitz, Joshua. 1985. *No Sense of Place: The Impact of Electronic Media on Social Behavior.* New York: Oxford University Press.

Miller, Andrew T. 1993. "Social Science, Social Policy, and the Heritage of African American Families." In *The "Underclass" Debate: Views from History,* edited by Michael B. Katz. Princeton, N.J.: Princeton University Press.

Miller, James A. 1987. "From Sweetback to Celie: Blacks in Film into the 1980s." In *The Year Left 2: Essays on Race, Ethnicity, Class, and Gender,* edited by Mike Davis et al. New York: Verso.

Mills, C. Wright. 1956. *The Power Elite.* New York: Oxford University Press.

Montgomery, Kathryn C. 1989. *Target: Primetime: Advocacy Groups and the Struggle over Entertainment Television.* New York: Oxford University Press.

Morreale, Joanne. 1991. *A New Beginning: A Textual Frame Analysis of the Political Campaign Film.* Albany: State University of New York.

Morris, Aldon. 1984. *The Origins of the Civil Rights Movement: Black Communities Organizing for Change.* New York: Free Press.

Morris, Edward. 1992. "Country's Fan Base Is Wider Than Ever." *Billboard,* December 26, 5–6.

Mouffe, Chantel, ed. 1979. *Gramsci and Marxist Theory.* London: Routledge and Kegan Paul.

Moynihan, Daniel Patrick. 1965. *The Negro Family: The Case for National Action.* Washington, D.C.: Office of Policy Planning and Research, U.S. Department of Labor.

Mukerji, Chandra, and Michael Schudson. 1991. *Rethinking Popular Culture: Contemporary Perspectives in Cultural Studies.* Berkeley: University of California Press.

Mulvey, Laura. 1975. "Visual Pleasures and Narrative Cinema." *Screen* 16, no. 3 (autumn): 6–18.

Munch, Richard, and Neil Smelser. 1992. *Theory of Culture.* Berkeley: University of California Press.

Muñoz, Carlos. 1989. *Youth, Identity, Power: The Chicano Generation.* London: Verso.

Murphy, A. D. 1983. "Distribution and Exhibition: An Overview." In *The Movie Business Book,* edited by Jason E. Squire. Englewood Cliffs, N.J.: Prentice Hall.

Murray, Charles. 1984. *Losing Ground: American Social Policy, 1950–1980.* New York: Basic Books.

Murray, James P. 1973. *To Find an Image: Black Films from Uncle Tom to Superfly.* Indianapolis: Bobbs-Merrill.

Murray, Robin. 1990. "Fordism and Post-Fordism." In *New Times: The Changing Face of Politics in the 1990s,* edited by Stuart Hall and Martin Jacques. London: Verso.

Myers, Peter S. 1983. "The Studio as Distributor." In *The Movie Business Book,* edited by J. E. Squire. Englewood Cliffs, N.J.: Prentice Hall.

Nasaw, David. 1985. *Children of the City: At Work and at Play.* Garden City, N.J.: Anchor Press/Doubleday.

———. 1993. *Going Out: The Rise and Fall of Public Amusements.* New York: Basic Books.

Neale, Steve, and Frank Krutnik. 1990. *Popular Film and Television Comedy.* London: Routledge.

Neely, Kim. 1992. "Clinton: I Want My MTV Vote." *Rolling Stone,* August 6, 22.

Nesteby, James R. 1982. *Black Images in American Film, 1896–1954: The Interplay between Civil Rights and Film Culture.* Washington, D.C.: University Press of America.

Newcombe, Horace. 1984. "The Dialogic Aspects of Mass Communications." *Critical Studies in Mass Communication* 1:34–50.

Newman, Katherine. 1988. *Falling from Grace: The Experience of Downward Mobility in the American Middle Class.* New York: Free Press.

Newman, Mark. 1987. *Entrepreneurs of Profit and Pride: From Black Appeal to Radio Soul.* New York: Praeger.

Newman, Melinda. 1991. "MTV Puts R&B in Spotlight with Weekly Video Show." *Billboard,* October 26, 5–6.

New York Times. 1996. *The Downsizing of America.* New York: Times Books.

Nightingale, Carl Husemoller. 1993. *On the Edge: A History of Poor Black Children and Their American Dreams.* New York: Basic Books.

Omi, Michael, and Howard Winant. 1986. *Racial Formation in the United States: From the 1960s to the 1980s.* 2d ed. New York: Routledge.

———. 1994. *Racial Formation in the United States: From the 1960s to the 1990s.* 2d ed. New York: Routledge.

O'Reiley, Kenneth. 1989. *Racial Matters: The FBI's Secret File on Black America, 1960–1972.* New York: Free Press.

Owen, Frank. 1994–95. "Back in the Days." *Vibe* (December–January): 66–68.

Painton, Priscilla. 1992. "Country Rocks the Boomers." *Time,* March 30, 62–66.

Paul, William. 1994. "The K-Mart Audience at the Mall Movies." *Film History* 6, no. 4 (winter): 487–501.

Peele, Gillian. 1984. *Revival and Reaction: The Right in Contemporary America.* New York: Oxford University Press.

Perkins, Eric. 1990. "Renewing the African American Cinema: The Films of Spike Lee." *Cineaste* 17, no. 4:4–8.

Peterson, Richard. 1978. "The Production of Cultural Change: The Case of Contemporary Country Music." *Social Research* 45:292–314.

Pfeil, Fred. 1995. *White Guys: Studies in Postmodern Domination and Difference.* London: Verso.

Pierson, John. 1995. *Spike, Mike, Slackers, and Dykes: A Guided Tour across a Decade of American Independent Cinema.* New York: Hyperion.

Pinkney, Alphonso. 1984. *The Myth of Black Progress.* New York: Cambridge University Press.

Piven, Frances Fox, and Richard A. Cloward. 1979. *Poor People's Movements: Why They Succeed, How They Fail.* New York: Pantheon Books.

Powell, Kevin. 1994. "Enemy Territory." *Vibe* 2, no. 7 (September): 58–64.

———. 1996. "Live from Death Row." *Vibe* (February): 44–50.

Press, Andrea. 1991. *Women Watching Television: Gender, Class, and Generation in the American Television Experience.* Philadelphia: University of Pennsylvania Press.

Price, Frank. 1991. "Black Film's Ads Also Targeted Whites." *New York Times,* August 2, A14.

Public Enemy. 1989. *It Takes a Nation of Millions to Hold Us Back.* New York: Def Jam/Columbia Records.

Quadagno, Jill S. 1994. *The Color of Welfare: How Racism Undermined the War on Poverty.* New York: Oxford University Press.

Quinney, Richard. 1974. *Critique of Legal Order: Crime Control in Capitalist Society.* Boston: Little, Brown.

Radway, Janice. 1984. *Reading the Romance: Women, Patriarchy, and Popular Literature.* Chapel Hill: University of North Carolina Press.

Rainwater, Lee, and William L. Yancey. 1967. *The Moynihan Report and the Politics of Controversy.* Cambridge, Mass.: MIT Press.

Real, Michael R. 1991. "Bill Cosby and Recoding Ethnicity." In *Television Criticism: Approaches and Applications,* edited by Leah R. Vandenberg and Lawrence A. Wenner. New York: Longman.

Reed, Ishmael. 1989. "Crime, Drugs, and the Media: The Black Pathology Biz." *Nation,* November 20, 597–98.

Reed, Ralph. 1996. *Active Faith: How Christianity Is Changing the Soul of American Politics.* New York: Free Press.

Reeves, Jimmie, and Richard Campbell. 1994. *Cracked Coverage: Television News, Reaganism, and the Journalistic Crusade against Cocaine Use.* Durham, N.C.: Duke University Press.

Reid, Mark. 1993. *Redefining Black Film.* Berkeley: University of California Press.

Reider, Jonathan. 1989. "The Rise of the Silent Majority." In *The Rise and Fall of the New Deal Order, 1930–1980,* edited by Steve Fraser and Gary Gerstle. Princeton, N.J.: Princeton University Press.

Reiman, Jeffrey H. 1996. *. . . And the Poor Get Prison: Economic Bias in American Criminal Justice.* Boston: Allyn and Bacon.

Rhines, Jesse. 1995. "The Political Economy of Black Film." *Cineaste* 21, no. 3 (summer): 38–39.

———. 1996. *Black Film/White Money.* New Brunswick, N.J.: Rutgers University Press.

Riggs, Marlon. 1991. *Color Adjustment* (film). San Francisco: California Newsreel.

Roberts, Sam. 1993. *Who We Are: A Portrait of America Based on the Latest U.S. Census.* New York: Times Books.

Roediger, David R. 1991. *The Wages of Whiteness: Race and the Making of the American Working Class.* London: Verso.

————. 1994. *Toward the Abolition of Whiteness: Essays on Race, Politics, and Working Class History.* New York: Verso.

Rogin, Michael. 1987. *"Ronald Reagan," the Movie, and Other Episodes in Political Demonology.* Berkeley: University of California Press.

————. 1996. *Blackface, White Noise: Jewish Immigrants in the Hollywood Melting Pot.* Berkeley: University of California Press.

Rose, Tricia. 1989. "Orality and Technology: Rap Music and Afro-American Cultural Resistance." *Journal of Popular Music and Society* 13, no. 4 (winter): 35–44.

————. 1992. "Black Texts/Black Contexts." In *Black Popular Culture,* edited by Gina Dent. Seattle: Bay Press.

————. 1994a. "Black Males and the Demonization of Rap Music." In *Black Male: Representations of Masculinity in Contemporary American Art,* edited by Thelma Golden. New York: Whitney Museum of American Art. Distributed by N. H. Abrams.

————. 1994b. *Black Noise: Rap Music and Black Culture in Contemporary America.* Hanover, N.H.: Wesleyan University Press.

Rosen, Philip. 1986. *Narrative, Apparatus, Ideology: A Film Theory Reader.* New York: Columbia University Press.

Rosenberg, Bernard, and David Manning White, eds. 1957. *Mass Culture: The Popular Arts in America.* Glencoe, Ill.: Free Press.

Ross, Steven J. 1976. "The Symposium on Movie Business and Finance." *Journal of the University Film Association* 28, no. 1 (winter): 36–43.

Rotundo, E. Anthony. 1993. *American Manhood: Transformations in Masculinity from the Revolution to the Modern Era.* New York: Basic Books.

Rubin, Lillian B. 1994. *Families on the Fault Line: America's Working Class Speaks about the Family, the Economy, Race, and Ethnicity.* New York: Basic Books.

Rubin, Martin. 1994. "Make Love Make War: Cultural Confusion and the Biker Film Cycle." *Film History* 6, no. 4 (winter): 335–81.

Rusher, William. 1984. *The Rise of the Right.* New York: Morrow.

Russell, Deborah. 1991. "N.W.A. Displays a Winning Attitude: Stickered Album Is Nation's Top Seller." *Billboard,* June 22, 7–8.

Russell, Kathy, Midge Wilson, and Ronald Hall. 1992. *The Color Complex: The Politics of Skin Color among African Americans.* New York: Harcourt Brace Jovanovich.

Ryan, Michael, and Douglas Kellner. 1988. *Camera Politica: The Politics of Ideology in Contemporary Hollywood Film.* Bloomington: Indiana University Press.

Sandomir, Richard. 1996a. "Baseball's Marketing Plan: Take an Old Familiar Score and Energize It with Some Cool and Soul." *New York Times,* May 2, C4.

————. 1996b. "Fox Baseball: Alive and Aiming for the Youth." *New York Times,* June 2, sec. 8, p. S5.

Saxton, Alexander. 1990. *The Rise and Fall of the White Republic: Class Politics and Mass Culture in Nineteenth-Century America.* New York: Verso.

Schatz, Thomas. 1981. *Hollywood Genres.* New York: Random House.

————. 1988. *The Genius of the System: Hollywood Filmmaking in the Studio Era.* New York: Pantheon Books.

————. 1993. "The New Hollywood." In *Film Theory Goes to the Movies,* edited by Jim Collins et al. New York: Routledge.

Scheingold, Stuart A. 1984. *The Politics of Law and Order: Street Crime and Public Policy.* New York: Longman.

Scherman, Tony. 1994. "Country." *American Heritage,* November, 38–53.

Schiller, Herbert I. 1989. *Culture Inc.: The Corporate Takeover of Public Expression.* New York: Oxford University Press.

Schone, Mark. 1991. "Country Comes of Age." *Mediaweek,* September 9, 16–17.

Schor, Juliet B. 1991. *The Overworked American: The Unexpected Decline of Leisure.* New York: Basic Books.

Schudson, Michael. 1994. "Culture and the Integration of National Societies." In *The Sociology of Culture: Emergent Theoretical Perspectives,* edited by Diana Crane. Cambridge, Mass.: Blackwell.

Schur, Edwin M. 1971. *Labeling Deviant Behavior: Its Sociological Implications.* New York: Harper & Row.

Scott, James C. 1990. *Domination and the Arts of Resistance: Hidden Transcripts.* New Haven, Conn.: Yale University Press.

Shadoian, Jack. 1977. *Dreams and Dead Ends: The American Gangster/Crime Film.* Cambridge, Mass.: MIT Press.

Shakur, Sanyika (a.k.a. Kody Scott). 1993. *Monster: The Autobiography of an L.A. Gang Member.* Toronto: Penguin Books.

Shohat, Ella. 1991. "Ethnicities-in-Relation: Towards a Multicultural Reading of American Cinema." In *Unspeakable Images: Ethnicity and the American Cinema,* edited by Lester D. Friedman. Urbana: University of Illinois Press.

Simpson, Janice. 1992a. "Rock the Vote." *Time,* June 15, 66–67.

———. 1992b. "Words with Spike." *Time,* November 23, 66.

Sklar, Robert. 1994. *Movie-Made America: A Cultural History of American Movies.* New York: Vintage.

Smith, James P., and Finis R. Welch. 1986. *Closing the Gap: Forty Years of Economic Progress for Blacks.* Santa Monica, Calif.: Rand Corporation.

Sperber, Murray. 1990. *College Sports Inc.: The Athletic Department vs. the University.* New York: H. Holt.

Spigel, Lynn. 1992. *Make Room for TV: Television and the Family Ideal in Postwar America.* Chicago: University of Chicago Press.

Staiger, Janet. 1995. *Bad Women: Regulating Sexuality in Early American Cinema.* Minneapolis: University of Minnesota Press.

Stam, Robert. 1989. *Subversive Pleasures: Bakhtin, Cultural Criticism, and Film.* Baltimore: Johns Hopkins University Press.

Stam, Robert, and Louise Spence. 1985. "Colonialism, Racism, and Representation: An Introduction." In *Movies and Methods.* Vol. 2, *An Anthology,* edited by Bill Nichols. Berkeley: University of California Press.

Stark, Phyllis. 1994. "Interep Studies Country Listeners." *Billboard,* April 2, 69.

Steinberg, Cobbett. 1978. *Reel Facts: The Movie Book of Records.* New York: Vintage.

Steinberg, Stephen. 1982. *The Ethnic Myth: Race, Ethnicity, and Class in America.* Boston: Beacon Press.

———. 1995. *Turning Back: The Retreat from Racial Justice in American Thought and Policy.* Boston: Beacon Press.

Stern, Lesley. 1995. *The Scorsese Connection.* Bloomington: Indiana University Press.

Stern, Mark J. 1993. "Poverty and Family Composition since 1940." In *The "Underclass" Debate: Views from History*, edited by Michael B. Katz. Princeton, N.J.: Princeton University Press.

Strick, John. 1978. "The Economics of the Motion Picture Industry: A Survey." *Philosophy of Social Sciences* 8, no. 4 (December): 406–17.

Stuckey, Mary E. 1990. *Playing the Game: The Presidential Rhetoric of Ronald Reagan.* New York: Praeger.

Sugrue, Thomas. 1996. *The Origins of the Urban Crisis: Race and Inequality in Postwar Detroit.* Princeton, N.J.: Princeton University Press.

Swidler, Ann. 1986. "Culture in Action: Symbols and Strategies." *American Sociological Review* 51: 273–86.

Taylor, Clyde. 1986. "The LA Rebellion: New Spirit in American Film." *Black Film Review* 2: 2.

Testa, Mark, et al. 1993. "Employment and Marriage among Inner-City Families." In *The Ghetto Underclass: Social Science Perspectives*, edited by William J. Wilson. Newbury Park, Calif.: Sage.

Therborn, Göran. 1990. "The Two-Thirds, One-Third Society." In *New Times: The Changing Face of Politics in the 1990s*, edited by Stuart Hall and Martin Jacques. London: Verso.

Thomas, Rebecca. 1996. "There's a Whole Lot 'O Color in the White Man's Blues: Country Music's Selective Memory and the Challenge of Identity." *Midwest Quarterly* 38, no. 1 (autumn): 73–89.

Thompson, John B. 1990. *Ideology and Modern Culture: Critical Social Theory in the Era of Mass Communications.* Cambridge, Mass.: Polity.

Toop, David. 1984. *The Rap Attack: African Hand Jive to New York Hip Hop.* Boston: South End Press.

Tuchman, Gaye. 1978. *Making News: A Study in the Construction of Reality.* New York: Free Press.

Tudor, Andrew. 1974. *Image and Influence: Studies in the Sociology of Film.* London: Allen and Unwin.

Turner, Graeme. 1988. *Film as Social Practice.* New York: Routledge.

"TV's Black Viewers Make a Difference." 1996. *Mediaweek,* April 22, 30.

Van Deburg, William L. 1992. *New Day in Babylon: The Black Power Movement and American Culture, 1965–1975.* Chicago: University of Chicago Press.

Vedlitz, Arnold. 1988. *Conservative Mythology and Public Policy in America.* New York: Praeger.

Viguerie, Richard. 1980. *The New Right: We're Ready to Lead.* Falls Church, Va.: Viguerie Co.

Wallace, Michele. 1990a. *Black Macho and the Myth of the Superwoman.* New York: Verso.

———. 1990b. *Invisibility Blues: From Pop to Theory.* New York: Verso.

Walters, Ronald. 1991. "White Racial Nationalism in the United States." In *Prescriptions and Policies: The Social Well-Being of African Americans in the 1990s*, edited by Dionne J. Jones. New Brunswick, N.J.: Transaction Publishers.

Ward, Reneé. 1976. "Black Films, White Profits." *Black Scholar* 7, no. 8 (May): 13–24.

Wasko, Janet. 1994. *Hollywood in the Information Age: Beyond the Silver Screen.* Austin: University of Texas Press.

Watkins, Mel. 1994. *On the Real Side: Laughing, Lying, Signifying: The Underground Tradition of African American Humor That Transformed American Culture, from Slavery to Richard Pryor.* New York: Simon and Schuster.

Wattenberg, Ben. 1995. *Values Matter Most: How Republicans or Democrats or a Third Party Can Win and Renew the American Way of Life.* New York: Free Press.

Weber, Max. 1985. *The Protestant Ethic and the Spirit of Capitalism.* London: Unwin.

West, C. 1990. "The New Cultural Politics of Difference." In *Out There: Marginalization and Contemporary Cultures,* edited by Russell Ferguson et al. Cambridge, Mass.: MIT Press.

———. 1991. "The Postmodern Crisis of Black Intellectuals." In *Cultural Studies,* edited by Lawrence Grossberg. New York: Routledge.

———. 1992. "Nihilism in Black America." In *Black Popular Culture,* edited by Gina Dent. Seattle: Bay Press.

Wiegman, Robyn. 1990. "Black Bodies/American Commodities: Gender, Race, and the Bourgeois Ideal in Contemporary Film." In *Unspeakable Images: Ethnicity and the American Cinema,* edited by Lester D. Friedman. Urbana: University of Illinois Press.

Wiggershaus, Rolf. 1994. *The Frankfurt School: Its History, Theories, and Political Significance,* translated by Michael Robertson. Cambridge, England: Polity Press.

Will, George. 1990. *Suddenly: The American Idea Abroad and at Home, 1986–1990.* New York: Free Press.

———. 1993. "'Menace' Takes Romance out of Violence." *Detroit News,* June 20.

Williams, Raymond. 1977. *Marxism and Literature.* New York: Oxford University Press.

Willis, Paul. 1977. *Learning to Labor: How Working Class Youth Get Working Class Jobs.* New York: Columbia University Press.

———. 1990. *Common Culture: Symbolic Work at Play in the Everyday Culture of the Young.* Boulder, Colo.: Westview Press.

Wills, Garry. 1996. "It's His Party." *New York Times Magazine,* August 11, 30–37, 52, 55, 57–59.

Wilson, Clint, and Félix Gutiérrez. 1985. *Minorities and Media: Diversity and the End of Mass Communication.* Newbury Park, Calif.: Sage Publications.

Wilson, William Julius. 1979. *The Declining Significance of Race: Blacks and Changing American Institutions.* Chicago: University of Chicago Press.

———. 1987. *The Truly Disadvantaged: The Inner City, the Underclass, and Social Policy.* Chicago: University of Chicago Press.

———. 1996. *When Work Disappears: The World of the New Urban Poor.* New York: Knopf.

Winant, Howard. 1997. "Racial Dualism at Century's End." In *The House That Race Built: Black Americans, U.S. Terrain,* edited by Wahneema Lubiano. New York: Pantheon.

Winokur, Mark. 1990. "Black Is White/White Is Black: 'Passing' as a Strategy of Racial Compatibility in Contemporary Hollywood Comedy." In *Unspeakable*

Images: Ethnicity and the American Cinema, edited by Lester D. Freidman. Urbana: University of Illinois Press.

Withers, Robert S. 1983. *Introduction to Film.* New York: Barnes and Noble Books.

Wollen, Peter. 1986. "Godard and Counter-Cinema: *Vent d' Est.*" In *Narrative, Apparatus, Ideology: A Film Theory Reader,* edited by Philip Rosen. New York: Columbia University Press.

Wolsey, Roland Edgar. 1990. *The Black Press, U.S.A.* Ames: Iowa State University Press.

Wood, Joe. 1993. "John Singleton and the Impossible Greenback Bind of the Assimilated Black Artist." *Esquire,* August, 59 ff.

Wray, Matt, and Annalee Newitz. 1997. *White Trash: Race and Class in America.* New York: Routledge.

Index

Rolling Stone (magazine), 130
Rose, Tricia, 63, 67, 69, 176, 252n95, 256n51
Rubin, Lillian, 18
Rubin, Martin, 173, 174
Run DMC, 177, 272n23
Ruthless Records, 185, 274n37
Ryan, Michael, 138

Samuel Goldwyn, 102, 191
San Francisco Film Festival, 110
Schatz, Thomas, 89
School Daze: depiction of black diversity in, 139–46; gender politics of, 142–43; narrative structure of, 163; production of, 113–16; racial essentialism in, 143; test screening of, 265n13
Schor, Juliet, 55
Schudson, Michael, 68, 69
Scorsese, Martin, 164, 201
Shadoian, Jack, 199, 200
Shaffer, Paul, 45
Shakur, Tupac, 185, 239, 274n40
She's Gotta Have It, 79, 98, 102, 108–12
Shoat, Ella, 139
Simmons, Russell, 177, 183, 258n79, 264n68
Singleton, John, 6, 174, 222–24, 263n68
Sista Souljah, 239
60 Minutes, 130, 235, 252n100
Smothers Brothers, The, 270n32
Snoop Doggy Dogg, 185, 274n40
social problems, the construction of, 57–58
Soul Man, 111
Soul Train, 2, 245n3
SoundScan, 45, 186, 252n95
Spelman College, 265n18
Spielberg, Steven, 226
Stagger Lee, 274n41
Staiger, Janet, 164, 165
Stallone, Sylvester, 156
Star Wars, 260n23, 261n34

Steinberg, Stephen, 201
Stern, Mark, 22
Straight Out of Brooklyn, 174; coding of ghetto in, 215; gender representation in, 220–21; theatrical distribution of, 191
structure of feeling, 198; definition of, 276n2
suburbanization: and country music, 47–48; film industry response to, 83, 86; popular culture and, 260n27
Sugrue, Thomas, 22
Sundance Film Festival, 87, 174, 191
Stone, Oliver, 128, 131
Strick, Robert, 82
Sweet Sweetback's Baadasss Song, 93
Swidler, Ann, 54
symbolic capital, 256n42; definition of, 266–67n40; Spike Lee and, 133–35

Tate, Greg, 257n72
Taylor, Clyde, 97
technological determinism, 63–65
technology: hip hop culture and, 68–69; influence of, on media production, 68; use of to enhance film attendance, 259–60n23
teenpics, 173
television: African American access to, 262n38; decline of black programming in, 235–36, 272n27; depiction of African Americans in, 148–49, 280n58; influence of cable, on country music, 47; reception of, 269n28; religious right use of, 28, 248n35. See also BET; CMT; MTV; PBS; TNN
Terminator 2: Judgment Day, 172, 189
Thompson, Kristin, 164, 165
Three Men and a Baby, 119
Time (magazine), 48, 110, 131, 253n25
Time Warner, 192, 258n3, 261n33
TNN, 45

The Cover Design

Because of the peculiar history of race in the United States, the image on the cover may strike some as especially provocative. Because the black body is both desired and despised, its commodification is, inevitably, marked by tension and contradiction. It is this tension that resides at the heart of both the book and the cover design.

In truth, the commodification of blackness is increasingly influenced by the inventive ways black youth appropriate the symbolic power and allure of black bodies. The way black youth occupy public space, fashion new identities, and maneuver to participate in the world of popular media culture illuminates the creative confidence they exude in today's world. And while they use their bodies in ways that some believe problematic, their practices perform a pivotal role in shaping commercial culture.

However, representations of the black body are always mediated by the unanticipated currents of social change. Take as an example the popular ascendancy of supermodels Tyson Beckford and Alek Wek. Unlike previous "black" (not necessarily American) models their physical appearance is markedly African rather than European. Their popular status and prestige suggest that the culture industry's ideas about blackness, glamour, and consumer desire have been revised. But what accounts for this revised notion of blackness as a symbol of commercial vitality?

The ascendancy of Beckford and Wek illustrates how our market-driven culture not only tolerates racial difference but devours it. Still, it must be acknowledged that representations of the black body intersect with a volatile and complex history. And yet, it is precisely because black youth are so actively involved in the making of history that representations of the black body develop many different nuances. But while many of us pontificate on the greater circulation of black bodies throughout the public sphere, black youth are busy redefining the very ways in which blackness works as a marker of empowerment, symbolic capital, pleasure, and political struggle.